Treasure of Ambedkar Series 04

WHAT CONGRESS AND M. K. GANDHI HAVE DONE TO THE UNTOUCHABLES

Treasure of Ambedkar Series 04

WHAT CONGRESS AND M. K. GANDHI HAVE DONE TO THE UNTOUCHABLES

Dr B.R. Ambedkar

KALPAZ

Treasure of Ambedkar Series 04

WHAT CONGRESS AND M. K. GANDHI HAVE DONE TO THE UNTOUCHABLES

ISBN: 978-93-8639-7454

First Published 1945
Reprint **2017**, in India by
Kalpaz Publications
C-30, Satyawati Nagar,
Delhi – 110052
E-mail: kalpaz@hotmail.com
Ph.: 9212142040

Printed at: G. Print Process, Delhi

TABLE OF CONTENTS

Appendices

PREFACE

"In 1892, there took place in England a new election to Parliament, in which the Conservatives headed by Lord Salisbury lost and the Liberals headed by Mr. Gladstone won. The remarkable thing about this election was that notwithstanding the defeat of his party at the polls, Lord Salisbury—contrary to Parliamentary convention—refused to surrender his office to the leader of the Liberal Party. When Parliament assembled, the Queen delivered the usual gracious speech from the throne, containing the legislative programme of Lord Salisbury's Government and the usual Address to Her Majesty was moved from the Government side. Lord Salisbury's Government was an illegitimate Government. It was a challenge to the fundamental principle of the British Constitution, which recognised Parliamentary Majority as the only title deed for a Party's right to form a Government. The Liberals took up the challenge and tabled an amendment to the Address. The amendment sought to condemn Lord Salisbury's Government for its insistence on continuing in office, notwithstanding the fact that it had no majority behind it. The task of moving the amendment was entrusted to the late Lord (then Mr.) Asquith. In his speech in support of the amendment, Mr. Asquith used the now famous phrase—"*Causa finita est: Roma locuta est*" (Rome has spoken and the dispute must end). The phrase was originally used by St. Augustine, but in a different context. It was used in the course of a religious controversy and had come to be used as a foundation for Papal Sovereignty. Mr. Asquith used it as a political maxim, embodying the basic principle of Parliamentary Democracy. Today it is accepted as the fundamental principle on which Popular Government rests, namely, the Right of a Political Majority to Rule. It told instantaneously against Salisbury's Government and must tell against all parties who fail at the polls, wherever Parliamentary Democracy is in operation.

I was reminded of this maxim when the results of the Elections to the Provincial Legislatures in India, which took place in February 1937 under the Government of India Act, 1935, were announced. Congressmen did not actually say "*Causa finita est: India locuta est.*" But so far as the parties, which had opposed the Congress in the Elections, were concerned, that is what the results of the Elections seemed to proclaim. Having led the Untouchables against the Congress for full five years in the Round Table Conference and in the Joint Parliamentary Committee, I could not pretend to be unaffected by the results of the Elections. To me the question was: Had the Untouchables gone over to the Congress? Such a thing was to me unimaginable. For, I could not believe that the Untouchables—apart from a few agents of the Congress who are always tempted by the Congress gold to play the part of the traitor—could think of going over to the Congress *en masse* forgetting how Mr. Gandhi and the Congress opposed. inch by inch up to the very last moment, every one of their demands for political safeguards. I had therefore decided to study the Returns of the Elections that took place in 1937.

While I was convinced that such a study was of great necessity from the point of view of the Untouchables, the work proceeded at a snail's pace. This was due to three causes. The work had to be kept aside for some time to give precedence to other literary projects, the urgency of which demanded a degree of priority which it was not possible to refuse. Secondly, the Blue Book on the Election Results of 1937, which was submitted to Parliament soon after the elections had taken place and which is the primary source for figures regarding the elections, proved inadequate and insufficient for my purpose. It does not give separately figures showing how the Scheduled Castes electors voted and how many votes the Scheduled Caste candidates got. It gives figures showing how electors in different constituencies voted, without making any distinction between Hindu voters and the Scheduled Castes voters. Circular letters had therefore to be issued to the various Provincial Governments requesting them to send me the figures showing distribution of voting by Scheduled Caste electors and the number of votes secured by each Scheduled Caste candidate. This inevitably delayed the work. Thirdly, the examination of these election returns proved a very laborious task as the statistical tables given in the Appendices to this book will show.

The work thus lingered on. I regret very much this delay. For I know how much mischief has been done by the Congress during the interval. The Congress has advertised the election results to bolster up its claim to represent the Untouchables. The main point in the advertisement is that out of 151 seats assigned to the Scheduled Castes, the Independent Labour Party which was organized by me got only 12 seats and the rest of the seats were captured by the Congress. This mess is served out from the Congress kitchen as conclusive proof to show that the Congress represents the Untouchables. This false propaganda seems to have gone home in some quarters. Even a man like Mr. H. N. Brailsford has reproduced in his 'Subject India' this absurd Congress version, without any attempt at verification and with apparent acceptance of its truth. I am sure that the results of the Elections as set out in this book will hit the nail squarely on the head of this false propaganda. For, the Congress version of the results of the election is an utter perversion. As a matter of fact the results of 1937 Election conclusively disprove the Congress claim to represent the Untouchables. Far from supporting the Congress version, the results of the Election show : (1) that out of 151, the Congress got only 78 seats ; (2) that the Untouchables in almost every constituency fought against the Congress by putting up their own candidates ; (3) that the majority of 78 seats won by the Congress were won with the help of Hindu votes and they do not therefore in any way represent the Scheduled Castes ; and (4) that of 151 seats, those won by the Congress in the real sense, i.e., with the majority of votes of the Scheduled Castes, were only 88. As to the Independent Labour Party it was started in 1937 just a few months before the Elections. It functioned only in the Province of Bombay. There was no time to organize branches in other Provinces. Elections on the ticket of the Independent Labour Party were fought only in the Province of Bombay and there the Independent Labour Party far from being a failure obtained an astonishing degree of success. Out of the 15 seats assigned to the Scheduled Castes in Bombay Presidency, it captured 13 and in addition it won 2 general seats. I am therefore glad that at long last I have succeeded in completing the work, which proves beyond the shadow of doubt that the story that the Congress captured all the seats reserved for the Scheduled Castes and that the Independent Labour Party was a failure, is a wicked lie. I trust that the book will prove interesting and instructive for all those who are interested in the subject and who desire to know the truth.

Before closing this preface, I wish to express my gratitude to those from whom I have received assistance in one form or another. I am grateful to the Provincial Governments for the troubles they have taken in responding to my circular and sending me additional facts and figures which I had called for. My thanks are also due to Mr. Karan Singh Kane, B.A., M.L.A., at one time, Parliamentary Secretary in the U. P. Congress Government, for the help he has rendered in the most laborious task of preparing the tables."

The reader who reads the above preface and compares it with the table of contents will at once find that the book deals with topics which lie far outside its boundary. The curious may like to know how the foregoing part of the preface is related to the Table of Contents. The explanation lies in the fact that the book in its present final form is quite different from what it was in its original form. In its original form it covered in very brief compass matter now dealt with on a vastly bigger scale in Chapters IV, V, VI, VII and IX and the statistical appendices. The foregoing part of the preface belonged to the book in its original form. That is why I have put it in inverted commas. The curious may also like to know why the final form of the book came to be so different from the original. The explanation is quite simple. The proofs of the book in its original form were seen by a friend and co-worker. He was dissatisfied with the scope of the book and insisted that it is not enough to deal with Election results to expose the Congress claim to represent the Untouchables. I must do more. I must expose the efforts of the Congress and Mr. Gandhi to improve the lot of the Untouchables for the information of the Untouchables and also of the foreigners, whom the Congress had deluded into accepting its side by misrepresentation of facts. Besides the difficulties arising out of the fact that the book was already in proof form, this was a tall order and appeared to be beyond me having regard to other claims on my time. He would not, however, give way and I had therefore to accept his plan. The original work, which would have been about 75 pages in print, had to be completely recast and enlarged. The book in the present form is a complete transformation. It records the deeds of th Congress and Mr. Gandhi from 1917 to date in so far as they touch the problem of the Untouchables. Much is written about the Congress, far more about Mr. Gandhi. But no one has so far told the story of what they have done about the Untouchables. Everyone knows that Mr. Gandhi values more is reputation as the saviour of the Untouchables than his reputation as the champion of Swaraj or as the protagonist of *Ahimsa*. At the Round Table Conference he claimed to be the sole champion of the Untouchables and was not even prepared to share the honour with anyone else. I remember what a scene he created when his claim was contested. Mr. Gandhi does not merely claim for himself the championship of the Untouchables. He claims similar championship for the Congress. The Congress, he says, is fully pledged to redress the wrongs done to the Untouchables and argues that any attempt to give political safeguards to the Untouchables is unnecessary and harmful. It is therefore a great pity that no detailed study of these claims by Mr. Gandhi and the Congress has been undertaken so far.

With the Hindus who have been blind devotees of Mr. Gandhi, this study, although it is the first of its kind, will not find favour. Indeed it is sure to provoke their wrath. How can it be otherwise when the conclusion arrived at is : " Beware of Mr. Gandhi " ? Looking at it from a wider point of view, there is no reason for the Hindus to be enraged about it. The Untouchables are not the only community in India which thinks of Mr. Gandhi in these terms. The same view of Mr. Gandhi is entertained by the Muslims, the Sikhs and the Indian Christians. As a matter of fact, the Hindus should cogitate over the question and ask : why no community trusts Mr. Gandhi although he has been saying that he is the friend of the Muslims, Sikhs and the Scheduled Castes and what is the reason for this distrust ? In my judgment, there cannot be a greater tragedy for a leader to be distrusted by everybody as Mr. Gandhi is today. I am however certain that this is not how the Hindus will react. As usual, they will denounce the book and call me names. But as the proverb says : " The caravan must pass on, though the dogs bark." In the same way, I must do my duty, no matter what my adversaries may have to say. For, as Voltaire observed : "Who writes the history of his own time must expect to be attacked for everything he has said, and for everything he has not said : but these little drawbacks should not discourage a man who loves truth and liberty, expects nothing, fears nothing, asks nothing and limits his ambition to the cultivation of letters."

The book has become bulky. It may be said that it suffers by reason of over-elaboration and even by repetition. I am aware of this. But I have written the book especially for the Untouchables and for the foreigners. On behalf of neither could I presume knowledge of the relevant facts. For the particular audience I have in view, it is necessary for me to state both facts as well as arguments and pay no regard to the artistic sense or the fastidious taste of a cultivated and informed class of readers.

As it is my intention to make the book a complete compendium of information regarding the movement of the Untouchables for political safeguards, I have added several appendices other than those of statistical character. They contain relevant documents both official and non-official which have a bearing upon the movement. Those who are interested in the problem of the Untouchables will, I believe, be glad to have this information ready at hand. The general reader may complain that the material in the Appendices is much too much. Here again, I must state that the Untouchables are not likely to get the information which to the general reader may be easily accessible. The test adopted is the need of the Untouchables and not of the general reader.

One last word. The reader will find that I have used quite promiscuously in the course of this book a variety of nomenclature, such as Depressed Classes, Scheduled Castes, Harijans and Servile Classes, to designate the Untouchables. I am aware that this is likely to cause confusion especially for those who are not familiar with conditions in India. Nothing could have pleased me better than to have used one uniform nomenclature. The fault is not altogether mine. All these names have been used officially and unofficially at one time or other for the Untouchables. The term under the Government of India Act is 'Scheduled Castes.' But that came into use after 1935. Before that they were called 'Harijans' by Mr. Gandhi and 'Depressed Classes' by Government. In a flowing situation like that it is not possible to fix upon one name, which may be correct designation at one stage and incorrect at another. The reader will overcome all difficulties if he will remember that these terms are synonyms and represent the same class.

I am grateful to Professor Manohar Chitnis for the preparation of the Index and to Mr. S. C. Joshi for help in correcting the proofs.

B. R. AMBEDKAR.

24th June 1945.
22, Prithviraj Road,
New Delhi.

CHAPTER I

A STRANGE EVENT

Congress Takes Cognizance of the Untouchables

I

In the annual session of the Indian National Congress held at Calcutta in the year 1917 a strange event took place. In that session the Congress passed the following resolution :—

> "This Congress urges upon the people of India the necessity, justice and righteousness of removing all disabilities imposed by custom upon the Depressed Classes, the disabilities being of a most vexatious and oppressive character, subjecting those classes to considerable hardship and inconvenience."

The President of the session was Mrs. Annie Besant. The resolution was moved by Mr. G. A. Natesan of Madras and was supported by Mr. Bhulabhai Desai from Bombay, by Mr. Rama Iyer from Malabar and by Mr. Asaf Ali from Delhi. In moving the resolution, Mr. Natesan said :—

> "Ladies and Gentlemen,—This question has been receiving great attention for years in other platforms ; but in view of the unique character of this Congress, the Subjects Committee thought it necessary, after having framed a scheme of self-government for India, that we should complete that by asking us to prepare ourselves for the task of self-government. The first great duty is to see that all inequalities and injustices are removed. You will see that this resolution specially asks you to remove disabilities of a most vexatious and oppressive character. Without injuring your religious feelings, without giving up all that is best in your religious tradition, I think the Congress has a right to ask of you and of me and of others elsewhere that such absurd restrictions as the non-admission of these people to schools should be removed. The Congress has also a claim upon all human beings to see that in some portions of the country where these people are refused even the use of common well, these restrictions should disappear...In attempting to elevate ourselves and in trying to remove these galling restrictions we are but elevating Indian manhood ; and when Responsible Self-Government is to be given to us we shall be in a position to say that Indians of all classes, of all creeds, have the fullest rights, the commonest social rights, have free access to all schools, to all institutions so that Indian manhood may develop in all its truest, best and noblest traditions."

Mr. Bhulabhai Desai in supporting the resolution pointed out :—

"The disabilities under which some of our brethren suffer are a great blow to the equality and brotherhood of man that we preach. From the great height of the resolution that you have passed this morning, with what face will we approach the British Democracy or any other power if we are unable to uplift our own brethren? They will say 'What lies in your own power, the obliteration of the social degradation of a section of your own people, you have been unable to do!' We can do it by self-help and by self-help alone and in this matter we need not approach any other power but ourselves. That proves the necessity of the great forward step that this Congress has taken in allowing this resolution to be moved before you...The existence of this great bane is an insult to the name of Hinduism. Therefore, both on the ground of necessity and on the ground of justice, as well as on the ground of righteousness, for the truth that you cherish, how can you deny them what this resolution demands, when the justice lies in your own hands? And if you fail to do that, with what justice, with what face, will you demand Self-Government?"

Mr. Rama Iyer said :—

"This. . . resolution calls for social freedom by which we shall shatter the shackles that bind the lower classes. They are the foot of the nation and if you and I would climb the hill of Home Rule, we must first shatter the shackles on our feet and then and then only will Home Rule come to us . . . You cannot be political democrats and at the same time social autocrats. Remember that a man, a social slave, cannot be politically a free man. We all have come here to see the vision of United India, not only politically united but united all along the line...Therefore, let those of us, who are Brahmins, who belong to the higher castes, go to our villages and shatter the shackles of the low castes, people who are struggling against our own men—the social bureaucrats of our own land."

Mr. Asaf Ali observed :—

"The problem of the Depressed Classes was one of the most difficult of all. They had been crying shame upon the arbitrary and autocratic action of the bureaucratic bunglers, but now it was the turn of the Depressed Classes—the Untouchables—to cover them, Indians, with shame. There were many millions of these victims of misfortune who had been plying their degraded trades in utter muteness for thousands of years, never emerging from the abyss of degradation into which the cruel and utterly unjustified customs of the country had hurled them. Whether it was the spring-time of hope, or the summer of realisation to others, to these unfortunate creatures it was always the winter of black despair. It seemed a cruel irony of fate that those who were vociferously clamouring for the attainment or preservation of human rights themselves were so little mindful of the legitimate rights of others under them. Was it just or fair that a mute section of humanity should be left to suffer the very wrongs for whose redress others were shedding their blood in the battlefield? Why, even the 'untouchables,' in spite of all that cruel custom had subjected them to, were human beings and children of the soil, in whose veins coursed the self-same 'red-blood' as in the veins of those who arrogated superiority to themselves. The Depressed Classes were entitled to the same privileges as their betters in worldly circumstances and could not be debarred from the birthright of man. It was a standing reproach to the Indians that they had any Depressed Classes at all, and it was for the extinction of this reproach that they prayed."

Many people would wonder why I describe the passing of the Resolution by the Congress moved and supported in such eloquent terms, as a strange event. But those who know the antecedents will admit that it is not an improper description. It was strange for many reasons.

In the first place, the President of the Session was the late Mrs. Annie Besant. She was a well-known public figure and had many things for which she will be remembered by the future historian of India. She was the founder of the Theosophical Society which has its Home at Adyar. Mrs. Annie Besant was well known for rearing up Mr. Krishnamurti, the son of a retired Brahmin Registrar, for a future Massiah. Mrs. Annie Besant was known as the founder of the Home Rule League. There may be other things for which friends of Mrs. Annie Besant may claim for her a place of honour. But I don't know that she was ever a friend of the Untouchables. So far as I know she felt great antipathy towards the Untouchables. Expressing her opinion on the question whether the children of the Untouchables should or should not be admitted to the common school, Mrs. Annie Besant in an article headed 'The Uplift of the Depressed Classes' which appeared in the *Indian Review* for February 1909 said :—

" In every nation we find, as the basis of the social Pyramid, a large class of people, ignorant, degraded, unclean in language and habits, people who perform many tasks which are necessary for Society, but who are despised and neglected by the very Society to whose needs they minister. In England, this class is called the 'submerged tenth,' forming, as it does, one-tenth of the total population. It is ever on the verge of starvation, and the least extra pressure sends it over the edge. It suffers chronically from under-nutrition, and is a prey to the diseases which spring therefrom. It is prolific, like all creatures in whom the nervous system is of a low type, but its children die off rapidly, ill-nourished, rickety, often malformed. Its better type consists of unskilled labourers, who perform the roughest work, scavengers, sweepers, navvies, casual dock-labourers, costermongers; and into it, forming its worse type, drift all the wastrels of Society, the drunkards, the loafers, the coarsely dissolute, the tramps, the vagabonds, the clumsily criminal, the ruffians. The first type is, as a rule, honest and industrious; the second ought to be under continued control, and forced to labour sufficiently to earn its bread. In India, this class forms one-sixth of the total population, and goes by the generic name of the 'Depressed Classes.' It springs from the aboriginal inhabitants of the country, conquered and enslaved by the Aryan invaders,...It is drunken and utterly indifferent to cleanliness, whether of food, person or dwelling; but marriage is accompanied with some slight formality, children are kindly treated, and there is very little brutality, violence or criminality. Criminal communities, such as hereditary thieves, live apart, and do not mingle with the scavengers, sweepers, husbandmen and the followers of other simple crafts who make up the huge bulk of the depressed. They are gentle, docile, as a rule industrious, pathetically submissive, merry enough when not in actual want, with a bright though generally very limited intelligence; of truth and the civic virtues they are for the most part utterly devoid—how should they be anything else?—but they are affectionate, grateful for the slightest kindness, and with much 'natural religion.' In fact, they offer good material for simple and useful though humble civic life, . . .

"What can be done for them by those who feel the barbarity of the treatment meted out to them, by those who feel that the Indians who demand freedoms should show respect to others, and give to others a share of the consideration they claim for themselves?

"Here, as everywhere, education is the lever by which we may hope to raise them, but a difficulty arises at the outset, for one class of the community, moved by a noble feeling of compassion and benevolence, but not adding thereto a careful and detailed consideration of the conditions, demands, for the children of the pariah community admission to the schools frequented by the sons of the higher classes, and charges with lack of brotherhood those who are not in favour of this policy. It becomes, therefore, necessary to ask whether brotherhood is to mean levelling down, and whether it is usual in family to treat the elder children and the babies in exactly the same way. It is a zeal not according to knowledge—and not according to nature—which would substitute equality for brotherhood, and demand from the cultured and refined that they should forfeit the hardly won fruits of the education of generations, in order to create an artificial equality, as disastrous to the progress of the future as it would be useless for the improvement of the present. The children of the depressed classes need, first of all, to be taught cleanliness, outside decency of behaviour, and the earliest rudiments of education, religion and morality. Their bodies, at present, are ill-odorous and foul with the liquor and strong-smelling food out of which for generations they have been built up; it will need some generations of purer food and living to make their bodies fit to sit in the close neighbourhood of a school-room with children who have received bodies from an ancestry trained in habits of exquisite personal cleanliness, and fed on pure food-stuffs. We have to raise the Depressed Classes to a similar level of physical purity, not to drag down the clean to the level of the dirty, and until this is done, close association is undesirable. We are not blaming these children, nor their parents, for being what they are; we are stating a mere palpable fact. The first daily lesson in a school for these children should be a bath, and the putting on of a clean cloth; and the second should be a meal of clean wholesome food; those primary needs cannot be supplied in a school intended for children who take their daily bath in the early morning and who come to school well-fed.

"Another difficulty that faces teachers of these children are the contagious diseases that are bred from first; to take one example, eye-disease, wholly due to neglect, is one of the most common and 'catching' complaints among them. In our Panchama schools in Madras, the teachers are ever on the alert to detect and check this, and the children's eyes are daily washed and disease is thus prevented. But is it to be expected that fathers and mothers, whose daily care protects their children from such dirty diseases should deliberately expose them at school to this infection?

"Nor are the manner and habits of these forlorn little ones desirable things to be imitated by gently-nurtured children. Good manners, for instance, are the result of continual and rigid self-control, and of consideration for the comfort and convenience of others; children learn manners chiefly by imitation from well-bred parents and teachers and, secondarily, by suitable precept and reproof. If, at the school, they are to be made to associate with children not thus trained, they will quickly fall into the ways which they see around them. For, until good habits are rendered fixed by long practice, it is far easier to be slipshod than accurate, to be careless than careful. Ought the children of families in which good manners and courtesy are hereditary, to be robbed of their heritage, a robbery that enriches no one, but drags the whole nation down? Gentle speech, well-modulated voice, pleasant ways, these are the valuable results of long culture, and to let them be swamped out is no true brotherhood . . .

"In England, it has never been regarded as desirable to educate boys or girls of all classes side by side, and such grotesque equalising of the unequal would be scouted. Eton and Harrow are admittedly the schools for the higher classes; Rugby and Winchester are also schools for gentlemen's sons, though somewhat less aristocratic. Then come a number of schools, frequented chiefly by sons of the provincial middle class. Then the Board Schools, where the sons of artisans and the general manual labour classes are taught; and below all these, for the waifs and strays, are the 'ragged schools,' the name of which indicates the type of their scholars, and the numerous charitable institutions. A man in England who proposed that ragged school-children should be admitted to Eton and Harrow would not be argued with, but laughed at. Here, when a similar proposition is made in the name of brotherhood, people seem ashamed to point out frankly its absurdity, and they do not realise that the proposal is merely a violent reaction against the cruel wrongs which have been inflicted on the Depressed Classes, the outcry of an awakened conscience, which has not yet had time to call right reason to guide its emotions. It is sometimes said that Government schools pay no attention to social differences; therein they show that they are essentially 'foreign' in their spirit. They would not deal so with the sons of their own people, though they may be careless of the sons of Indians, and lump them all together, clean and dirty alike. It is very easy to see the differences of 'tone' in the youths when only the sons of the cultured classes are admitted to a school, and it is to the interest of the Indians that they should send their sons where they are guarded from coarse influences as Englishmen guard their own sons in England."

* * *

The second reason why one is justified in describing the passing of this resolution as a strange event lies in the fact that it was entirely opposed to the declared policy of the Congress. In these days when the "Constructive Programme" of the Congress is hawked from every street and at all times and when the Congress is resting after an active campaign of non-co-operation and civil disobedience, this statement may well cause surprise to present day Congressmen and their friends. The following extracts from the addresses of the Presidents who presided at the Annual Sessions of the Congress will suffice to bring home the fact that the Congress policy was to give no place to questions of Social Reform in the aims and objects of the Congress.

To begin with Mr. Dadabhai Naoroji who presided at the Second Session of the Indian National Congress held in Calcutta in the year 1886. In his presidential address he referred to the Congress attitude towards Social Reform and said:—

"It has been asserted that this Congress ought to take up questions of social reform (Cheers and cries of 'Yes, Yes') and our failure to do this has been urged as a reproach against us. Certainly no member of this National Congress is more alive to the necessity of social reform than I am; but, Gentlemen, for everything there are proper times, proper circumstances, proper parties and proper places (Cheers); we are met together as a political body to represent to our rulers our political aspirations, not to discuss social reforms, and if you blame us for ignoring these, you should equally blame the House of Commons for not discussing the abstruser problems of mathematics or metaphysics. But, besides this, there are here Hindus of every caste, amongst whom, even in the same province, customs and social arrangements differ widely—there are Mahomedans and Christians of various denominations, Parsis, Sikhs, Brahmos and what not—men indeed of each and of all those numerous classes which constitute in the aggregate the people of India. (Loud Cheers). How can this gathering of *all* classes discuss the social reforms needed in each individual class? . . . Only the members of that class can effectively deal with the reforms therein needed. A National Congress must confine itself to questions in which the entire nation has a direct participation, and it must leave the adjustment of social reforms and other class questions to Class Congresses . . ."

The subject was again referred to by the Hon. Mr. Budruddin Tyabji who presided over the Third Annual Session of the Congress held in 1887. Mr. Tyabji observed :—

" . . . It has been urged—solemnly urged—as an objection against our proceedings—that this Congress does not discuss the question of Social Reforms . . . I must confess that the objection seems to me strange, seeing that this Congress is composed of the representatives, not of any one class or community, not of one part of India, but of all the different parts, and of all the different classes, and of all the different communities of India. Whereas any question of Social Reform must of necessity affect some particular part or some particular community of India only and, therefore, Gentlemen, it seems to me, that although we, Mussalmans, have our own social problems to solve, just as our Hindu and Parsi friends have theirs, yet these questions can be best dealt with by the leaders of the particular communities to which they relate (Applause). I, therefore, think, Gentlemen, that the only wise and, indeed, the only possible course we can adopt is to confine our discussions to such questions as affect the whole of India at large, and to abstain from the discussion of questions that affect a particular part or a particular community only."

The third occasion the subject was referred to was in 1892, when Mr. W. C. Bonnerjee in his Presidential address to the Eighth Session of the Congress gave expression to the following sentiments :—

" Some of our critics have been busy in telling us, thinking they knew our affairs better than we know them ourselves, that we ought not to meddle with political matters, but leaving politics aside devote ourselves to social subjects and so improve the social system of our country ; I am one of those who have very little faith in the public discussion of social matters ; those are things which I think, ought to be left to the individuals of a community who belong to the same social organisation to do what they can for its improvement. We know how excited people become when social subjects are discussed in public. Not long ago we had an instance of this when what was called the Age of Consent Bill was introduced into the Viceregal Legislative Council. I do not propose to say one word as to the merits of the controversy that arose over that measure, but I allude to it to illustrate how apt the public mind is to get agitated over these social matters if they are discussed in a hostile and unfriendly spirit in public . . . I may point out that we do not all understand in the same sense what is meant by social reform. Some of us are anxious that our daughters should have the same education as our sons, that they should go to Universities, that they should adopt learned professions; others who are more timid would be content with seeing that their children are not given in marriage when very young, and that child widows should not remain widows all the days of their lives. Others more timid still would allow social problems to solve themselves . . . the Congress commenced and has since remained, and will, I sincerely trust, always remain as a purely political organization devoting its energies to political matters and political matters only. I am afraid that those whether belonging to our own country or to any other country, who find fault with us for not making social subjects a part of our work, cherish a secret wish that we might all be set by the ears, as we are all set by the ears by the Age of Consent Bill, and that thus we might come to an ignominious end. They mean us no good, and when we find critics of that description talking of the Congress as only fit to discuss social problems, I think the wider the berth we give them, the better . . ."

"I, for one, have no patience with those who say we shall not be fit for political reform until we reform our social system. I fail to see any connection between the two. Let me take, for instance, one of the political reforms which we have been suggesting year after year, viz., the separation of judicial from executive functions in the same officer. What possible connection can there be between this, which is a purely political reform and social reform? In the same way, take the Permanent Settlement which we have been advocating, the amendment of the law relating to forests and other such measures;—and I ask again, what have these to do with social reform? Are we not fit for them because our widows remain unmarried and our girls are given in marriage earlier than in other countries? because our wives and daughters do not drive about with us visiting our friends? because we do not send our daughters to Oxford or Cambridge? (Cheers.)"

The last occasion the Congress President is found to refer to this subject was in 1895 when the Congress Session was held in Poona and was presided over by Mr. Surendranath Bannerjee. Touching upon the subject, in his Presidential address, Mr. Bannerjee said :—

"We cannot afford to have a schism in our camp. Already

they tell us that it is a Hindu Congress, although the presence of our Mahomedan friends completely contradicts the statement. Let it not be said that this is the Congress of one social party rather than that of another. It is the Congress of United India, of Hindus and Mahomedans, of Christians, of Parsis and of Sikhs, of those who would reform their social customs and those who would not. Here we stand upon a common platform—here we have all agreed to bury our social and religious differences and recognise the one common fact that being subjects of the same Sovereign and living under the same Government and the same political institutions, we have common rights and common grievances. And we have called forth this Congress into existence with a view to safeguard and extend our rights and redress our grievances. What should we say of a Faculty of Doctors who fell out, because though in perfect accord as to the principles of their science, they could not agree as to the age at which they should marry their daughters, or whether they should remarry their widowed daughters or not . . . Ours is a political and not a social movement; and it cannot be made a matter of complaint against us that we are not a social organization any more than it can be urged against any of my lawyer friends that they are not doctors. Even in regard to political matters, such is our respect for the opinions of minorities, that so far back as 1887, I think it was at the instance of Mr. Budruddin Tyabji, who once was our President and whose elevation to the Bench of the Bombay High Court is a matter of national congratulation, a resolution was passed to the effect that where there is practical unanimity among a class, though in a minority in the Congress, that a question should not be discussed, it should forthwith be abandoned."

"There is special danger to which an organization such as ours is exposed and which must be guarded against, . . . the danger of there being developed from within the seeds of dissension and dispute."

II

There are two questions about these statements which need explanation. First is to know what the Social Reform Party was to which the Presidents refer. The second is why Mr. Surendranath Bannerjee's address to the Congress in 1895 was the last occasion when a Congress President found it necessary to refer to the relation of the Congress to the problem of Social Reform and why no president after 1895 thought it necessary to dwell on it.

To understand the first question it is necessary to note that when the Indian National Congress was founded at Bombay in 1885, it was felt by the leaders of the movement that the National movement should not be exclusively political but that side by side with the consideration of political questions, questions affecting Indian social economy should also be discussed and that the best endeavours of all should be put forth for vitalizing Hindu Society by removing all social evils and social wrongs. With this view, Dewan Bahadur R. Raghunath Rao and Mr. Justice (then Rao Bahadur) M. G. Ranade delivered addresses on Social Reform on the occasion of the meeting of the First Congress at Bombay. In 1886, at Calcutta, nothing further was done. Discussion, however, was going on among the leaders of the Congress movement and other leaders of educated Indian thought whether the Congress as such should concern itself with social questions or whether a separate body should be set up for the discussion of social questions. It was at last resolved after mature deliberation by, among others, Dewan Bahadur R. Raghunath Rao, Mr. Mahadeo Govind Ranade, Mr. Narendra Nath Sen and Mr. Janakinath Ghosal, that a separate organization, called the Indian National Social Conference, should be started for the consideration of subjects relating to Indian social economy. Madras had the honour of being the birth-place of the Conference, for, the First Indian National Social Conference was held at Madras in December 1887, with no less a man than the late Rajah Sir T. Madhavrao, K.C.S.I., the premier Indian statesman of his time, as the President. The work done at this First Conference, however, was not much. Among other important matters, the members then present recognized the necessity of holding annual National Conferences in different parts of India for considering and adopting measures necessary for the improvement of the status of our society, and of our social usages; and taking steps to organize and establish Provincial Sub-Committees of the Conferences. It was agreed that among social subjects which the Conference might take up, those relating to the disabilities attendant on distant sea-voyages, the ruinous expenses of marriage, the limitations of age below which marriages should not take place, the remarriages of youthful widows, the evils of the re-marriages of old men with young girls, the forms and evidences of marriages and inter-marriages between sub-divisions of the same caste should form the subjects for discussion and determination.

As to sanctions it was thought there should be different Sub-Committees appointed for dealing with different social questions. The Sub-Committees were to be left to evolve certain fundamental principles and penalties for breach of these principles, to be carried out and enforced as regards the members of Social Reform Party, who might agree to be bound by such penalties, (1) by the Sub-Committees themselves, or (2) through their spiritual heads, whenever it was possible to do so, or (3) through Civil Courts, or failing all (4) by application to Government for enabling the Committees to enforce the rules in respect of their own pledged members.

While the Social Reform Party had formed a separate organization of its own to discuss the many social evils which festered Hindu Society, they were not satisfied with the Congress attitude of completely dissociating itself from questions of social reform. Some of them were anxious to make it an issue whether Social Reform should not precede Political Reform and press for a decision. In this they had many friends to support them. Among them was to be found the Government of India. Sir Aukland Colvin, a member of the Viceroy's Executive Council, very clearly and very emphatically stated that Indians ought to turn their attention to Social Reform in preference to endeavours they were making "to teach the British what their duties were in regard to the Government of India."

The reference to Social Reform in the addresses of the Congress Presidents referred to above can now be easily understood. They are a reply to the criticism by the Social Reform Party against the Congress dissociating itself from the problem of removing social evils.

Turning to the second question as to why no Congress President has referred to the question of Social Reform in his Presidential address after 1895, the answer is that before 1895 there were two schools among Congressmen on the issue of social reform *versus* political reform. The viewpoint of the first school was that expressed by Mr. Dadabhoy Naoroji, Mr. Budruddin Tyabji and Mr. Surendranath Bannerjee. The viewpoint of the other school was that expressed by Mr. W. C.

Bonnerjee. The former did recognize the need of social reform but thought that the Congress Session was not the proper platform for it. The latter denied that there was need for social reform and challenged the view that there cannot be political reform without social reform. Though the two schools within the Congress were fundamentally opposed to each other, they had not upto 1895 developed a spirit of antagonism and intolerance towards each other and functioned as two parallel organizations each devoting itself to its own particular aims and objects. So great was the spirit of co-operation and good will between the two that the annual sessions of the National Congress and Social Conference were held in immediate succession in the same pandal and a large majority of those who came to attend the Congress Session also attended the Social Conference. The Social Conference was, however, an eyesore to the Congressmen who belonged to the Anti-Social Reform section. This section was evidently getting restive at the kindly disposition and the accommodating spirit which the dominant section in the Congress was showing to the Social Conference, particularly in the matter of allowing it to use the Congress pandal for holding its session. In 1895, when the Congress met in Poona, this Anti-Social Reform section rebelled and threatened to burn the Congress pandal if the Congress allowed it to be used by the Social Conference. This opposition to the Social Conference was headed by no other person than the late Mr. Tilak, who was one of those social tories and political radicals with whom India abounds, and who was the father of the slogan "Swaraj is my birthright" which is now seen blazoned on Congress banner. The rebellion succeeded largely because the Pro-Social Reform Party in the Congress was not prepared to fight its opponents.[1] This rebellion had one effect. It settled that the Congress was not to entertain any question of social reform,

[1] That the Pro-Social Reform Party in the Congress did not like to take up the challenge is evident from the letter which Mr. Surendranath Bannerjee wrote to Mr. Ranade over the question raised by Mr. Tilak's Party regarding the use of the Congress pandal by the Social Conference in which he said: "The *raison d'etre* for excluding social questions from our deliberations is that were we to take up such questions it might lead to serious differences ultimately culminating in a schism, and it is a matter of the first importance that we should prevent a split. The request of the other side is very unreasonable; but we have sometimes to submit to unreasonable demands to avert greater evils."

no matter how urgent.[1] This is the explanation why no Congress President after 1895 has referred to the question of social reform in his presidential address. The Congress by its action in 1895 had become a purely political body with no interest and no concern in the removal or mitigation of social wrongs.

III

Against this background the resolution passed by the Congress about the Depressed Classes in 1917 is obviously a strange event. The Congress had never done such a thing before although it had functioned for thirty-two years. It was even contrary to its declared policy.

Why did the Congress think it necessary to pass such a resolution in the year 1917 ? What made it take cognizance of the Untouchables ? What did it want to gain ? Whom did it want to deceive ? Was it because of a change in its angle of vision or was it because of some ulterior motive ? For an answer to these questions one must turn to the following resolutions passed by the Depressed Classes in the year 1917 at two separate meetings held in the City of Bombay under two different Presidents. The first of these meetings was held on the 11th November 1917 under the Chairmanship of the late Sir Narayan Chandavarkar. In that meeting the following resolutions[2] were passed :—

> " *First Resolution.*—Loyalty to British Government and prayer for victory to the Allies."
>
> " *Second Resolution* carried at the meeting by an overwhelming majority, the dissentients being about a dozen, *expressed approval of the scheme of reform in the administration of India recommended by the Indian National Congress and the All-India Muslim League.*"
>
> " *Third Resolution* carried unanimously was : ' As the population of the Depressed Classes in India, considered Untouchable and treated as such, is very large, as their condition is very

---

[1] Some of the leading Social Reformers welcomed this rebellion by the Anti-Social Reform Party in the Congress against the Conference. Dewan Bahadur R. Raghunath Rao wrote to Mr. Ranade that he " was glad that the pandal was not allowed to be used by the Social Conference, for the deception that used to be practised by the Congress upon the English people that it worked in conjunction with the Social Conference was unveiled, and the English people would now clearly understand that the Congress really did not mean to work with the Social Conference."

[2] Addresses presented to the Viceroy in India and the Right Hon'ble the Secretary of State for India (1918). Parliamentary Paper Cd. 9178, pages 74-75.

degraded owing to that treatment and as they are behind the rest of the people in point of education, being unable to secure fair opportunities for their improvement, this public meeting of the Depressed Classes strongly feels that in the scheme of reform and reconstitution of the Legislative Councils which Government may be pleased to adopt, due regard be paid to the interests of the said classes. This meeting therefore prays the British Government to be so gracious as to protect those interests by granting to those classes the right to elect their own representatives to the said Councils in proportion to their numbers."

" *Fouth Resolution* unanimously carried at the meeting was : 'That the Government be prayed for the adoption, with all convenient speed, of a compulsory and free system of education rendered necessary by the fact that the social elevation of any community depends upon the universal spread of education among its members and that degradation of the Depressed Classes is due to their illiteracy and ignorance.' "

" *Fifth Resolution* carried unanimously was as follows :— 'That the Chairman of this public meeting be authorised to *request the Indian National Congress to pass at its forthcoming session a distinct and independent resolution declaring to the people of India at large the necessity, justice, and righteousness of removing all the disabilities imposed by religion and custom upon the Depressed Classes*, those disabilities being of a most vexatious and oppressive character, subjecting those classes to considerable hardship and inconvenience by prohibiting them from admission into public schools, hospitals, courts of justice and public offices, and the use of public wells, etc. These disabilities, social in origin, amount in law and practice to political disabilities and as such fall legitimately within the political mission and propaganda of the Indian National Congress.' "

" *Sixth Resolution* prays all Hindus of the castes other than the Untouchables and Depressed, especially those of the higher castes, who claim political rights, to take steps for the purpose of removing the blot of degradation from the Depressed Classes, which has subjected those classes to the worst of treatment in their own country."

The second meeting was also held in November 1917, a week or so after the first meeting. The Chairman was one Bapuji Namdeo Bagade, a leader of the Non-Brahmin Party. At this meeting the following resolutions[1] were unanimously adopted :—

" (1) Resolution of loyalty to the British throne."

---

[1] *Ibid.*, p. 75.

"(2) That this meeting cannot give its support to the Congress-League Scheme in spite of its having been declared to have been passed at the meeting of 11th November 1917 by an overwhelming majority."

"(3) That it is the sense of this meeting that the administration of India should be largely under the control of the British till all classes and specially the Depressed Classes, rise up to a condition to effectually participate in the administration of the country."

"(4) That if the British Government have decided to give political concession to the Indian Public, this meeting prays that Government should grant the Untouchables their own representatives in the various legislative bodies to ensure to them their civil and political rights."

"(5) That this meeting approves of the objects of the Bahiskrit Bharat Samaj (Depressed India Association) and supports the deputation to be sent on its behalf to Mr. Montagu."

"(6) That this meeting prays that Government, looking to the special needs of the Depressed Classes, should make primary education both free and compulsory. That the meeting also requests the Government to give special facilities by way of scholarships to the students of the Depressed Classes."

"(7) That the meeting authorises the President to forward the above resolutions to the Viceroy and the Government of Bombay."

It is obvious that there is a close inter-connection between the resolution passed by the Depressed Classes at their meeting in Bombay under the chairmanship of Sir Narayan Chandavarkar and the Congress resolution of 1917 on the elevation of the Depressed Classes. This inter-connection will be easily understood by adverting to the political events of the year 1917. It will be recalled that it was in 1917 or to be precise, on the 20th August 1917 the late Mr. Montagu, the then Secretary of State for India, announced in the House of Commons the new policy of His Majesty's Government towards India, namely, the policy of "gradual development of self-governing institutions with a view to progressive realization of responsible government in India as an integral part of the British Empire." Leading Indian politicians were expecting some such declaration of policy on the part of His Majesty's Government and were preparing schemes for changes in the constitutional structure of India in anticipation of such a policy. Of the many schemes that were formulated, there were two around which public attention was centred. One was called "the Scheme of the Nineteen." The second was called "the Congress-League Scheme." The first was put forth by the 19 elected additional Members of the then Imperial Legislative Council. The second was an agreed scheme of political reforms supported by the Congress and the League otherwise known as the Lucknow Pact. Both these schemes had come into existence in 1916, a year before the announcement made by Mr. Montagu.

Of the two schemes, the Congress was interested in seeing that its own scheme was accepted by His Majesty's Government. The Congress with that purpose in view was keen on giving the Congress-League Scheme the status and character of a National Demand. This could happen only if the scheme had the backing of all communities in India. In as much as the Muslim League had accepted the scheme, the problem of securing the backing of the Muslim Community did not arise. Next in numbers came the Depressed Classes. Though not as well organized as the Muslims, they were politically very conscious as their Resolutions show. Not only were they politically conscious but they were all along anti-Congress. Indeed in 1895 when Mr. Tilak's followers threatened to burn the Congress pandal if its use was allowed to the Social Conference for ventilating social wrongs, the Untouchables organized a demonstration against the Congress and actually burned its effigy. This antipathy to the Congress has continued ever since. The resolutions passed by both the meetings of the Depressed Classes held in Bombay in 1917 give ample testimony to the existence of this antipathy in the minds of the Depressed Classes towards the Congress. The Congress, while anxious to get the support of the Depressed Classes to the Congress-League Scheme of Reforms, knew very well that it had no chance of getting it. As the Congress did not then practise—it had not learned it then—the art of corrupting people as it does now, it enlisted the services of the late Sir Narayan Chandavarkar, an Ex-President of the Congress. As the President of the Depressed Classes Mission Society he exercised considerable influence over the Depressed Classes. It was as a result of his influence and out of respect for him that a section of the Depressed Classes agreed to give support to the Congress-League Scheme.

The resolution as its text shows did not give unconditional support to the Congress-League Scheme. It agreed to give support on the condition that the Congress passed a resolution for the removal of the social disabilities of the Untouchables. The Congress resolution was a fulfilment of its part of the contract with the Depressed Classes which was negotiated through Sir Narayan Chandavarkar.

This explains the genesis of the Congress Resolution of 1917 on the Depressed Classes and its inter-connection with the Resolutions of the Depressed Classes passed under the Chairmanship of Sir Narayan Chandavarkar. This explanation proves that there was an ulterior motive behind the Congress Resolution. That motive was not a spiritual motive. It was a political motive.

What happened to the Congress Resolution ? The Depressed Classes in their Resolution had called upon the " higher castes, who claim political rights, to take steps for the purpose of removing the blot of degradation from the Depressed Classes, which has subjected these classes to the worst of treatment in their own country." What did the Congress do to give effect to this demand of the Depressed Classes ? In return for the support it got, the Congress was bound to organize a drive against untouchability to give effect to the sentiments expressed in its Resolution. The Congress did nothing. The passing of the Resolution was a heartless transaction. It was a formal fulfilment of a condition which the Depressed Classes had made for giving their support to the Congress-League Scheme. Congressmen did not appear to be charged with any qualms of conscience or with any sense of righteous indignation against man's inhumanity to man which is what untouchability is. They forgot the Resolution the very day on which it was passed. The Resolution was a dead letter. Nothing came out of it.

Thus ended the first chapter in the history of what the Congress has done to the Untouchables.

CHAPTER II

A SHABBY SHOW

Congress Abandons its Plan

I

MR. GANDHI entered Indian politics in 1919. Very soon thereafter, he captured the Congress. He not only captured it but overhauled it completely and changed it out of recognition. He introduced three main changes. The old Congress had no sanctions. It only passed a resolution and left it there, hoping that the British Government would take some action on it. If the British Government did not, it merely repeated the resolution next year and year after it. The old Congress was purely a gathering of intellectuals. It did not go down to the masses to secure their active participation in the political movement, as it did not believe in mass action. The old Congress had no machinery and no funds to carry on mass agitation. It did not believe in spectacular political demonstration to impress the British Government of the magnitude of its strength or to attract and interest the masses. The new Congress changed all this. It made the Congress a mass organization by opening its membership to all and sundry. Any one paying four annas a year could be a member of the Congress. It forged sanctions behind its resolutions by adopting the policy of non-co-operation and civil disobedience. It made it a policy to stage demonstration of non-co-operation and civil disobedience and to court gaol. It launched a country-wide organization and propaganda in favour of the Congress. It put out what is called a Constructive Programme of social amelioration. To finance these activities it started a fund of one crore of rupees. It was called the Tilak Swaraj Fund. Thus by 1922, the Congress was completely transformed by Mr. Gandhi. The new Congress was entirely different from the old, except in name.

The Constructive Programme of social amelioration was an important feature of the Congress. It was outlined by the Working Committee of the Congress at its meeting in Bardoli, held in February 1922. It was also known as the Bardoli

Programme. The resolution setting out the details of the programme ran as follows :—

" The Working Committee advises all Congress Organisations to be engaged in the following activities :—

(1) To enlist at least one crore members of the Congress.

* * *

(2) To popularize the spinning wheel and to organize the manufacture of hand-spun and handwoven khaddar.

* * *

(3) To organize national schools.

* * *

(4) To organize the Depressed Classes for a better life, to improve their social, mental and moral condition, to induce them to send their children to national schools and to provide for them the ordinary facilities which the other citizens enjoy.

* * *

(5) To organize the temperance campaign amongst the people addicted to the drink habit by house to house visits and to rely more upon appeal to the drinker in his home than upon picketting.

(6) To organize village and town Panchayats for the private settlement of all disputes, reliance being placed solely upon force of public opinion and the truthfulness of Panchayat decisions to ensure obedience to them.

(7) In order to promote and emphasise unity among all classes and races and mutual goodwill, the establishment of which is the aim of the movement of non-co-operation, to organize a social service department that will render help to all, irrespectives of differences, in times of illness or accident.

* * *

(8) To continue the Tilak Memorial Swaraj Fund collections and call upon every Congress man or Congress sympathiser to pay at least one-hundredth part of his annual income for 1921. Every province to send every month twenty-five per cent. of its income from the Tilak Memorial Swaraj Fund to the All-India Congress Committee."

The resolution was placed before the All-India Congress Committee at its meeting held in Delhi on 20th February 1922 for confirmation, which it did. I am not concerned to set out what happened to the different items in this Programme of constructive work. I am concerned with only one item namely that which relates to the Depressed Classes and it is that part fo ti which I propose to deal with.

I shall relate the story of the fate, which overtook this part of the Bardoli resolution relating to the Untouchables, stage by stage. After the Bardoli resolution was confirmed by the All-India Congress Committee, the matter was remitted to the Working Committee for action. The Working Committee took up the matter at its meeting held in Lucknow in June 1922. On that part of the Bardoli problem which related to the uplift of the Untouchables, the Working Committee passed the following resolution :—

> "This Committee hereby appoints a Committee consisting of Swami Shradhanandji, Mrs. Sarojini Naidu and Messrs. I. K. Yajnik and G. B. Deshpande to formulate a scheme embodying practical measures to be adopted for bettering the condition of the so-called Untouchables throughout the country and to place it for consideration before the next meeting of this Committee, the amount to be raised for the scheme to be Rs. 2 lakhs for the present."

This resolution of the Working Committee was placed before the All-India Congress Committee at its meeting held in Lucknow in June 1922. It accepted the resolution of the Working Committee after making an amendment to it saying that "the amount to be raised for the scheme should be 5 lakhs for the present" instead of 2 lakhs as put forth in the resolution of the Working Committee.

It seems that before the resolution appointing the Committee was adopted by the Working Committee, one of its members, Swami Shradhanand, tendered his resignation of the membership of the Committee. At the very sitting at which the Working Committee passed the resolution appointing a Committee, another resolution on the same subject and to the following effect was passed by it :—

> "Read letter from Swami Shradhanandji, dated 8th June 1922 for an advance for drawing up a scheme for Depressed Classes work. Resolved that Mr. Gangadhar Rao B. Deshpande be appointed convener of the Sub-Committee appointed for the purpose and he be requested to convene a meeting at an early date, and that Swami Shradhananda's letter be referred to the Sub-Committee."

The formation of a Committee marks the second stage in the history of this interesting resolution.

The next reference to the resolution appointing the Committee is found in the proceedings of the Congress Working Committee held in Bombay in July 1922. At that meeting the Committee passed the following resolution :—

> "That the General Secretary be asked to request Swami Shradhanand to reconsider his resignation and withdraw it and a sum of Rs. 500 be remitted to the Convener, Syt. G. B. Deshpande, for the contingent expenses of the Depressed Classes Sub-Committee."

Thus the matter stood, so far as the year 1922 was concerned. Nothing further seems to have been done. The year 1923 came on. Seeing that nothing was done to set going the Scheme for ameliorating the condition of the Untouchables, the Working Committee which met also at Gaya in January 1923 took up the matter and passed the following resolution :—

> "With reference to Swami Shradhanand's resignation, resolved that the remaining members of the Depressed Classes Sub-Committee do form the Committee and Mr. Yajnik be the convener."

Thereafter the All-India Congress Committee which met in Bombay in May 1923 passed the following resolution :—

> "Resolved that the question of the condition of the Untouchables be referred to the Working Committee for necessary action."

Here ends the second stage in the history of the resolution, remitting the question of the Untouchables to a special Committee. The third stage in its history is marked by the resolution of the Working Committee passed in May 1923 at its meeting held in Bombay. This resolution ran as follows :—

> "Resolved that while some improvement has been effected in the treatment of the so-called Untouchables in response of the policy of the Congress, this Committee is conscious that much work remained yet to be done in this respect and in as much as this question of untouchability concerns the Hindu community particularly, it requests the All-India Hindu Mahasabha also to take up this matter and to make strenuous efforts to remove this evil from amidst the Hindu Community."

This is the sad tale of the resolution, how it began and how it ended. What shameful close to a blazing start !

It will be seen how the Congress washed its hands of the problem of the Untouchables. It need not have added insult to injury by relegating it to the Hindu Mahasabha. There could not be a body more unsuited to take up the work of the uplift of the Untouchables than the Hindu Mahasabha. If there is any body which is quite unfit for addressing itself to the problem of the Untouchables, it is the Hindu Mahasabha. It is a militant Hindu organization. Its aim and object is to conserve in every way everything that is Hindu, religious and cultural. It is not a social reform association. It is a purely political organization, whose main object and aim are to combat the influence of the Muslims in Indian politics. Just to preserve its political strength, it wants to maintain its social solidarity, and its way to maintain social solidarity is not to talk about caste or untouchability. How could such a body have been selected by the Congress for carrying on the work of the Untouchables passes my comprehension. This shows that the Congress wanted somehow to get rid of an inconvenient problem and wash its hands of it. The Hindu Mahasabha of course did not come forth to undertake the work for it had no urge for it and also because the Congress had merely passed a pious resolution recommending the work to them without making any promise for financial provision. So the project came to an inglorious and ignominious end.

Before closing this chapter, it would not be unprofitable to ascertain why the Congress abandoned the work of social amelioration of the Untouchables of which it had made so much show. Was it because the Congress intended that the scheme should be a modest one not costing more than two to five lakhs of rupees but felt that from that point of view they had made a mistake in including Swami Shradhanand in the Committee and rather than allow the Swami to confront them with a huge scheme which the Congress could neither accept nor reject? The Congress thought it better in the first instance to refuse to make him the convener[1] and subsequently to dissolve the Committee and hand over the work to the Hindu Mahasabha. Circumstances are not quite against such a conclusion. The Swami was the greatest and the most sincere champion of the Untouchables. There is not the slightest

[1] The fact that the Congress was keen on having Mr. Deshpande as the convener shows that they did not like to leave matters in the hands of Swami Shradhanand. The choice of Mr. Deshpande also indicates that they did not want anything to be done for the simple reason that Mr. Deshpande was an Orthodox Brahmin who had taken no interest in the welfare of the Untouchables.

doubt that if he had worked on the Committee he would have produced a very big scheme. That the Congress did not want him in the Committee and was afraid that he would make a big demand on Congress funds for the cause of the Untouchables, is clear from the correspondence[1] between him and Pandit Motilal Nehru, the then General Secretary of the Congress, and which is printed in the Appendix I. If this conclusion is right, then it shows how empty of sincerity were the words of the Congress which passed that resolution.

Did the Congress abandon the programme because it was revolutionary ? The resolution was in no sense a revolutionary one. This will be clear from the note which the Working Committee had appended to the resolution and which the All-India Congress Committee had approved. The note said :—

> "Whilst therefore in places where the prejudice against the Untouchables is still strong separate schools and separate wells must be maintained out of Congress funds, every effort should be made to draw such children to national schools and to persuade the people to allow the Untouchables to use the common wells."

Obviously, the Congress was not out for the abolition of Untouchability. It had accepted the policy of separate schools and separate wells. The resolution did no more than to undertake amelioration of the condition of the Untouchables. And even such a timid and mild programme the Congress was unable to carry through and which the Congress gave up without remorse or shame.

II

Did the Congress abandon the programme because it had no funds ? Quite the contrary. The Congress had started the Tilak Swaraj Fund in 1921. How much money did the Congress collect ? The table on the next page will give some idea. Rupees one crore and thirty lakhs were contributed by the public to the fund. The fund was collected to carry out Congress propaganda and to finance the constructive programme of the Congress as drafted by the Working Committee at Bardoli. How was this huge amount spent by the Congress ? Some idea as to the purposes on which the money out of this fund was spent can be gathered from the list of grants voted by the Working Committee during the years 1921, 1922 and 1923.

---

[1] Appendix I.

Table 1

TILAK SWARAJ FUND*

RECEIPTS

—	1921			1922			1923			Total		
	Rs.	a.	p.	Rs.	a.	p.	Rs.	a.	p.	Rs.	a.	p.
General Collections Annexure No. I ...	64,31,779	15	1	3,92,430	2	6½	2,64,288	9	1	70,88,498	11	5½
Specific (ear-marked) Donations or Grants Annexure No. II	37,32,230	2	10½	9,45,552	1	4½	7,10,801	10	3	53,88,583	14	6
	1,01,64,010	2	8½	13,37,982	3	11	9,75,090	3	4	1,24,77,082	9	11½
Add—Miscellaneous Receipts, Interest, Other Funds, Famine, Flood, Provincial Membership, Delegation, Affiliation, etc., for 1921-23	—			—			—			5,42,332	5	7½
										1,30,19,415	15	7

* The Indian Annual Register—1923, p. 112.

A. *Grants Voted in 1921*[1]

I. Grants voted by the Working Committee at its meeting held in Calcutta on 31st January and 1st, 2nd and 3rd February 1921 :—

1. Rs. 1,00,000 to remain at the disposal of Mahatma Gandhi for the support of lawyers who give up their practice and stand in need of support (*iv*).

2. Read the following telegram dated the 31st January 1921 from Syt. C. Rajagopalachariar :—

> " Regret unable to attend meeting. Selected full time public workers for Tamil, Kerala part Karnatak about hundred, of whom about forty lawyers suspending practice. Pending collection Tilak Fund sanction drawing Rs. 5,600 per month. Students' movement progressing rapidly though newspapers do not show up news. Must carry on against parental opposition, least two months. Must draw three thousand per month for this. Committee must immediately wire authority issuing Swarajya Fund receipts in name of Congress for convenient denominations like Khilafat receipts. Confident to make up all advances in three months. Do not hope large sums Madras."

Resolved that a sum of Rs. 8,600 be advanced to Tamil, Kerala and the Karnatak parts of the Madras Presidency for one month for the present, and for future advances the matter be placed before the next meeting of the Working Committee (*xx*).

II. Grants voted by the Working Committee at its meeting held at Bezwada on the 31st March and 1st April 1921 :—

3. A lump sum of Rs. 6,000 be advanced to Pandit Mohanlal Nehru, Secretary, U.P. Provincial Congress Committee, for carrying on propaganda and collecting funds (*v*).

" 4. Rs. 17,000 be sanctioned for the remainder of the current year for the expenses of the office of the President, the Secretaries, the Cashier, and that out of the above a sum of Rs. 300 per mensem be assigned to Mr. C. Rajagopalachariar for the expenses of his secretary and the President's steno-typist (*vii*).

5. A sum of 1,000 dollars remitted by cable to Mr. D. V. S. Rao of the India Home Rule League of America, 1,400 Broadway, New York (*viii*)."

III. The Working Committee at its resolution No. 18 dated 31st July 1921 appointed a Grants Sub-Committee to

[1] Roman figures in the brackets after each grant refer to the resolution of the Working Committee by which the grant was made.

dispose of all applications for grants. The Sub-Committee consisted of Mr. Gandhi, Pandit Motilal Nehru and Seth Jamnalal Bajaj. The following grants were voted by the Grants Sub-Committee in the course of several meetings :—

"6. A sum of Rs. 1 lakh be voted as a grant for Swadeshi work in Bihar and a loan of Rs. 4 lakhs recommended for the same purpose (*i*).

7. A loan of Rs. 35,000 to the C. P. (Hindustani) Provincial Congress Committee for Swadeshi (*ii*).

8. Rs. 25,000 for famine relief in the U.P. (*iii*).

9. Rs. 25,000 to the Punjab Provincial Congress Committee for famine relief, and the Jagraon School (*iv*).

10. Rs. 50,000 on the telegraphic application for the relief of the distressed in Malabar (*v*).

11. Rs. 15,000 to the Gandhi Ashram, Benares City (*vi*).

12. Rs. 10,000 to the Pallipadu Ashram (*vii*).

13. Rs. 15,000 to the Andhra Jatheeya Kalashala, Masulipatam (*viii*).

14. Rs. 10,000 to the Secretary, Taluka Congress Committee, Karjat (Maharashtra) (*xx*).

15. Rs. 10,000 to the Anatha Vidyarthi Griha, Chinchwad (Maharashtra) (*x*).

16. The applications of (1) Mr. K. G. Patade, Assistant General Secretary of the Depressed Classes Mission Society of. India, (2) of the Kulladaikurichi National School, Vidyasangam and (3) of the Rajahmundry Depressed Classes Mission were rejected as unbacked and not in accordance with the instructions issued by the Sub-Committee (xiii).

17. Rs. 10,000 to the Kerala Provincial Congress Committee to be principally spent on Swadeshi and the popularising of the hand-spinning and hand-weaving (*xx*).

18. Rs. 60,000 to the Madras Provincial Congress Committee (*xxii*).

19. Rs. 1,50,000 set apart for the U. P. Provincial Congress Committee (*xxiii*).

20. Rs. 63,000 to the Sind Provincial Congress Committee (*xxiv*).

21. Rs. 25,000 for famine relief in the Ceded Districts in Andhra (*xxv*).

22. Rs. 20,000 to the Maharashtra Provincial Congress Committee (*xxvi*).

23. Rs. 20,000 be granted to the Ganjam District Congress Committee for Swadeshi and for popularising hand-spinning and hand-weaving (*xvii*)."

The Working Committee dissolved the Sub-Committee by resolution No. 8 dated the 6th November 1921 and took the question of voting grants in its own hands.

IV. Grants voted by the Working Committee at its meeting held at Delhi on the 3rd, 5th and 6th November 1921 :—

"24. Rs. 25,000 to Mr. Phukan of Assam for the purchase of cotton to be used in the manufacture of hand-spun yarn and khaddar (*ix*).

25. Rs. 5,000 to the Krishnapuram, Guntur, District Andhra (*x*).

26. Rs. 10,000 as an additional grant to the Andhra Jateeya Kalashala (*xi*).

27. Rs. 1,000 to the Rajahmundry Depressed Classes Mission (xii).

28. Rs. 5,000 to the Angalur Jateeya Parishramalayam (*xiii*).

29. Rs. 3,000 to Kautaram, Andhra (*xiv*).

30. Rs. 15,000 to the Andhra Provincial Congress Committee for general Swadeshi work (*xv*).

31. Rs. 3,000 to the Masulipatam District Congress Committee (*xvi*).

32. Rs. 30,000 to the Utkal Provincial Congress Committee earmarked for the manufacture of handspun yarn and khaddar (*xvii*).

33. Rs. 3,000 to help the toddy tappers of the Thana District who wanted to give up their profession (*xviii*).

34. Rs. 5,000 to the Nagpur Tilak Vidyalaya (*xix*).

35. Rs. 5,000 to the Nagpur Asahyogashram (*xx*).

36. Rs. 25,000 to the Ajmere Provincial Congress Committee for the purpose of increasing the production of khaddar and charkha yarn (*xxi*).

37. Rs. 18,00,000 if possible, and in any case, at least Rs. 10,00,000 for Gujarat (*xxii*).

38. Rs. 40,000 to be immediately remitted to Sjt. C. Rajagopalachariar for the relief of the distressed in Malabar (*xxiii*)."

V. Grants voted by the Working Committee at its meeting held in Bombay on the 22nd and 23rd November 1921 :—

"39. Rs. 10,000 to the Jat Anglo-Sanskrit High School, Rohtak, Punjab (*iii*).

40. Rs. 25,000 to the Bijapur District Congress Committee for famine relief and Swadeshi work (*iii*).

41. Rs. 30,000 to help the dismissed mill-labourers of Madras by giving them Swadeshi work (*iii*)."

B. Grants Voted in 1922

I. Grants voted by the Working Committee at its meeting held in Bombay on 17th January 1922 :—

" 42. Application by the U. P. Provincial Congress Committee for Rs. 50,000 already sanctioned and for a further grant of one lakh of rupees for Swadeshi work, be referred to Mahatma Gandhi for final disposal (*ii*).

43. The application of the Assam Provincial Congress Committee for a remittance of Rs. 25,000, the balance out of the sanctioned grant of Rs. 50,000 be referred to Mahatma Gandhi for final disposal (*vi*)."

II. Grants voted by the Working Committee at its meeting held in Delhi on 26th February 1922 :—

" 44. Rs. 10,000 for initial expenditure on foreign scheme prepared by Mahatma Gandhi (*i*).

45. Rs. 14,000 for the office expenditure for the current year (*iv*)."

III. Grants voted by the Working Committee at its meeting held in Ahmedabad on 17th and 18th March 1922 :—

" 46. Rs. 3,00,000 for organizing a larger production and marketing of khaddar (*i*).

47. Rs. 10,000 out of Rs. 50,000 already sanctioned for the U. P. Provincial Congress Committee (*ix*).

48. Rs. 5,000 to the Kerala Provincial Congress Committee for general Congress work ; amount to be deducted from the sum of Rs. 84,000 sanctioned for relief in Malabar and further Rs. 20,000 out of the above amount of Rs. 84,000 be remitted for relief work (*x*).

49. Rs. 10,000 to the Rohtak Anglo-Vernacular School (*xi*).

50. Rs. 15,000 out of the amount of Rs. 25,000 sanctioned for famine relief in the Ceded Districts be paid to Sjt. T. Prakasam representing the Andhra Provincial Congress Committee (*xii*)."

IV. Grants voted by the Working Committee at its meeting held at Calcutta on the 20th, 21st and 22nd April 1922 :—

" 51. Rs. 5,000 to the Antyaja Karyalaya, Ahmedabad, for organizing education amongst Depressed Classes in Gujarat (v).

52. Rs. 40,000 as loan to Moulvi Badrul Hasan of Hyderabad Deccan to be exclusively devoted to the Khaddar work (*vi*).

53. Rs. 25,000 to the Nationalist Journals Ltd., to enable them to re-start the *Independent* and run it on Congress lines, providing for a lien on properties of the Company for the amount advanced (*xix*)."

V. Grants voted by the Working Committee at its meeting held in Bombay on the 12th, 13th, 14th and 15th May 1922 :—

"54. Rs. 17,381 to the Antyaja Karyalaya, Ahmedabad, in addition to Rs. 5,000 already granted (x).

55. Resolved that the Punjab Provincial Congress Committee's application for Rs. 1,25,000 for Shahadara Depressed Classes settlement cannot be considered unless the Working Committee is satisfied that sufficient funds are raised locally to start the scheme and the scheme so started is in working order (xi).

56. Resolved that Rs. 5,000 be earmarked for Ahmednagar Depressed Classes home and that the amount be recommended to be paid when the Working Committee is satisfied that the home is started by local efforts and is in working order (xii).

57. Rs. 10,000 be earmarked for Depressed Classes work in Madras, as applied for by Mr. S. Srinivas Iyengar, to be paid when the application is sent to this Committee through the Provincial Congress Committee and on this Committee being satisfied that at least an equal amount is raised by local effort (xiii).

58. Rs. 7,000 to Mr. T. Prakasam for Depressed Classes work in Andhra (xxiv)."

VI. Grants voted by the Working Committee at its meeting held in Lucknow on 6th, 7th and 10th June 1922 :—

"59. Rs. 50,000 for khaddar work in Sind Province (*vii*).

60. Rs. 1,000 be advanced to Sjt. C. Rajagopalachariar for contingent expenses (*viii*)."

VII. Grants voted by the Working Committee at its meeting held in Delhi on 30th June 1922 :—

"61. Rs. 180 per mensem for the next three months be sanctioned for the expenses of six workers from Bengal to serve in Assam (*vi*)."

VIII. Grants voted by the Working Committee at its meeting held in Bombay on 18th and 19th July 1922 :—

"62. Rs. 5,000 to Assam (*i*).

63. Rs. 1,50,000 each as loan for Khaddar work in Andhra and Utkal (*x*)."

IX. Grants voted by the Working Committee at its meeting held in Calcutta on 18th, 19th and 25th November 1922 :—

" 64. Rs. 3,00,000 to Gujarat as grant (*xii*).

65. Rs. 16,000 for the expenses for the Civil Disobedience Enquiry Committee (*xxi*)."

C. *Grants Voted in 1923*

I. Grants voted by the Working Committee at its meeting held in Gaya on the 1st and 2nd of January 1923 :—

" 66. Rs. 3,000 to the General Secretary, Indian National Social Conference, for the removal of untouchability and the promotion of temperance and inter-communal unity (xxii).

67. Rs. 1,200 as aid to the *Navayuga*, a Hindi daily paper of Allahabad, on condition that it would carry on propaganda in pursuance of the resolutions of the Congress held at Gaya (*xxxi*).

68. Rs. 10,000 for the Congress Publicity Bureau (*xxxii*)."

II. Grants voted by the Working Committee at its meeting held in Allahabad on 26th and 28th February 1923 :—

" 69. Rs. 10,000 for the Depressed Classes work by the Tamil Desh Provincial Congress Committee (vi).

70. Loan of Rs. 15,000 be advanced to the U. P. Provincial Congress Committee on the application of Pandit Jawaharlal Nehru (*x*).

71. A loan of Rs. 15,000 be advanced to Tamil Desh Provincial Congress Committee on the application of Mr. C. Rajagopalachariar (*x*).

72. Rs. 5,000 granted to the U. P. Provincial Congress Committee for Gandhi Ashram, Benares (*xi*)."

III. Grants voted by the Working Committee at its meeting held in Bombay on 23rd, 24th, 25th, 26th, 27th and 28th May 1923 :—

" 73. Loan of Rs. 5 lakhs to the Gujarat Provincial Congress Committee to relieve the surplus stock of khadi in various provinces in the country (*v*).

74. Loan of Rs. 50,000 be advanced to Bengal Provincial Congress Committee for Khadi work (*viii*).

75. Rs. 15,000 to the Bihar Rashtriya Vidyalaya (*xii*).

76. Rs. 10,000 for the Satyavadi Vidyalaya.

77. Rs. 5,000 Swavalamban Rashtriya Pathshala (*xiv*).

78. Rs. 5,000 to Dr. Sathaye for carrying on such work as the Congress Labour Committee decides (*xxxiv*)."

IV. Grants voted by the Working Committee at its meeting held in Nagpur on 7th, 8th, 11th and 12th July 1923 :—

" 79. Rs. 20,000 to Sjt. Brajaraj, Secretary, Hindi Sahitya Sammelan for the work of teaching Hindustani in the Madras Presidency (*ix*).

80. Rs. 2,000 to the C. P. Hindustani Provincial Congress Committee to be utilized for general Congress purposes with special regard to rendering help to Satyagraha in Nagpur (*xi*)."

The reader may not get a precise idea of the management or mismanagement of public funds by the Congress from this itemized account of expenditure. Was this expenditure regulated by any principle ? Was it distributed according to the needs of the Provinces ? Consider the following table :—

Table 2

Provinces	*Amount Granted*	*Population*†	*Percentage Grant due on the basis of Population ratio to total Population*	*Percentage of Grant actually paid*
	Rs.			
General—All India* ...	4,94,000	227,238,000	—	10
Bombay	26,90,381	16,012,623	8	54.3
Madras	5,05,000	42,319,000	18	10.1
Bihar and Orissa	5,65,000	33,820,000	15	11.3
U. P.	3,11,200	45,376,000	20	6.26
Sind	1,13,000	3,279,377	—	2.2
Assam	51,080	6,735,000	3	1.1
Bengal	50,000	46,241,000	20	1.0
C. P.	47,000	12,780,000	5	.95
Punjab	45,000	20,675,000	9	.9
Hyderabad	40,000	—	—	.81
Ajmer	25,000	—	—	.5
Foreign	14,000	—	—	.28
Total ...	49,50,661			

* Excluding Burma and Native States.

† These figures are taken from the Simon Commission Report, Vol. I, and refer to the year 1921.

Was it distributed on the basis of cultural units and their relative size? Compare the following figures :—

Table 3

Linguistic Areas	*Total Grant*	*Amount of Grant*	*Percentage of the Total Grant to the Province*	*Percentage of Population of the Area to the Population of the Province*
	Rs.	Rs.		
Bombay Presidency	26,90,381	—	—	100
Gujarat	—	26,22,381	97.4	18
Maharashtra	—	43,000	1.6	69
Karnatak	—	25,000	0.93	13
Central Provinces	47,000	—	—	100
Marathi Districts ...	—	10,000	21.2	45
Hindustani Districts ...	—	37,000	78.7	55
Madras Presidency	5,05,000	—	—	100
Tamil Nad	—	1,03,000	20.4	38
Andhra	—	3,02,000	60.0	52
Kerala	—	1,00,000	19.6	10
Bihar and Orissa	5,65,000	—	—	100
Bihar	—	5,15,000	91.0	73
Orissa	—	50,000	0.9	27

From these figures it is clear that the distribution of these sums was not made on the basis of any intelligible principle. There is no relation between the grants and the population, nor between the grants and the claims of the cultural units. A province like Bombay with a population of one and a half crores gets as much as 27 lakhs while U. P. and Madras with a population of about 4 crores each get no more than about 5 lakhs severally. Consider the grants in relation to cultural units. Take Bombay Presidency. It includes 3 cultural units, Maharashtra, Gujarat and Karnatak. Out of the 26 lakhs and 90 thousand given to the Bombay Presidency Gujarat with only 18 per cent. of the population of the Province got as much as 26 lakhs and 22 thousand i.e., 97.4 per cent. and Maharashtra with a population of 69 per cent got only Rs. 43,000 or 1.6 per cent and Karnatak with a population of 13 per cent got Rs. 25,000 or .9 per cent of the grant. In C. P. out of a total grant of Rs. 47,000 the Hindustani districts having 55 per cent of the population got Rs. 37,000 or 78.7 per cent while the Marathi speaking districts having 45 per cent of the population got only Rs. 10,000 i.e., 21.2 per cent. In

Bihar and Orissa out of the total grant of 5 lakhs and 65 thousand Bihar got 5 lakhs and 15 thousand or 91 per cent with a population of 73 per cent, and Orissa got only 50 thousand or 9 per cent while its population was as much as 27 per cent. The same inequity is noticeable in the distribution of grants in the three areas of the Madras Presidency.

There was not only no principle, there was shameful favouritism in the distribution of the fund. Out of the total of 49½ lakhs which was distributed in the three years Gujarat—Mr. Gandhi's province—got 26¼ lakhs while the rest of India got 23 lakhs. This means that a population numbering 29½ lakhs got 26¼ lakhs while the rest of India numbering about 23 crores got 23 lakhs !

There was no check, no control, no knowing for what purpose money was voted and to whom it was granted. Note the following cases :—

Table 4

Moneys allotted but kept at the disposal of individuals without appropriating them to any specified purpose	Rs.	*Moneys allotted without appropriation to any purpose and without naming the grantee*	Rs.
Moulvi Badrul Hasan ...	40,000	To Gujarat	3,00,000
T. Prakasam	7,000	To Gujarat	18,00,000
C. Rajagopalachariar ...	1,000	To Gujarat	3,00,000
Brajraj	20,000		
Mr. Gandhi	1,00,000		

It is not known whether these huge sums kept at the disposal of the named payees were accounted for or who received the formidable amounts made payable to the nameless payees. Even if there were satisfactory answers to these questions, there can be no doubt that a worse case of frenzied finance of extravagance and waste, it would be very difficult to find. It is a sad episode marked by a reckless plunder, committed by the predatory leaders of the Congress, of the public money for nursing their own constituencies without any qualms of conscience.

It is unnecessary to pursue the story of the organized and systematic loot by Congressmen of the balance of 1 crore and

80 lakhs which was spent in subsequent years. It is enough to say that never was there such an organized loot of public money. The point of immediate interest however is that the scrutiny of this list of grants does not show that amelioration of the condition of the Untouchables, which was one of the purposes for which money had been advanced from the Swaraj Fund was at all present to the mind of the Congressmen. One would have expected the Congress to make the amelioration of the Untouchables as the first charge on the Swaraj Fund. It should have at least made it a charge, if not the first charge, especially when thousands of rupees were spent on feeding briefless lawyers who were alleged to have given up practice in the cause of the nation without even an inquiry whether they had any and toddy drawers who had given up their profession for living on alms from public fund and on many other wild cat schemes carrying the marks of dishonesty on their faces. But it did nothing of the kind. Instead, the Congress proposed that a separate fund should be started for the amelioration of the Untouchables. And what was to be the dimension of this separate Untouchable Fund? The All-India Congress Committee fixed it at five lakhs. The Working Committee felt it was too big an amount for so unimportant and so unprofitable a work as the amelioration of the Untouchables and reduced its total to Rs. 2 lakhs. Two lakhs for 60 millions Untouchables!

This was the grand sum that was fixed by the Congress for the salvage of the Untouchables. How much of this was actually appropriated? Here are the figures :—

Table 5

Purpose	*Amount sanctioned*
	Rs.
Rajahmundry Depressed Class Mission	1,000
Antyaj Karyalaya, Ahmedabad	5,000
Antyaj Karyalaya, Ahmedabad	17,381
Depressed Classes Work in Andhra	7,000
National Social Conference for Depressed Classes Work	3,000
Tamil District P.C.C. for Depressed Classes Work	10,000
Total Rs. ...	43,381

To sum up, the Congress could find only Rs. 43,381 out of Rs. 49½ lakhs which it spent for carrying out the Constructive otherwise known as the Bardoli Programme in which the uplift of the Untouchables was given so much prominence. Can there be a grosser instance of insincerity than this? Where is the love for the Untouchables which the Congress professed for the Untouchables? Where is the desire of the Congress to undertake the uplift of the Untouchables? Would it be wrong to say that the Bardoli resolution was a fraud in so far as it related to the Untouchables?

One is however bound to ask one question. Where was Mr. Gandhi when all this was happening to the cause of the Untouchables in the Congress Camp? The question is very relevant because it was Mr. Gandhi who had laid stress, ever since he entered the Congress, upon the intimate relation between the winning of Swaraj and the abolition of Untouchability. In the *Young India*, which was Mr. Gandhi's organ, of 3rd November 1921, Mr. Gandhi wrote :—

> "Untouchability cannot be given a secondary place on the programme. Without the removal of the taint Swaraj is a meaningless term. Workers should welcome social boycott and even public execration in the prosecution of their work. I consider the removal of untouchability as a most powerful factor in the process of attainment of Swaraj."

Accordingly, he had been exhorting the Untouchables not to join hands with the British against Swaraj but to make common cause with the Hindus and help to win Swaraj. In an article in *Young India* dated 20th October 1920, Mr. Gandhi addressed the Untouchables in the following terms :—

> "There are three courses open to these down-trodden members of the nation. For their impatience they may call in the assistance of the slave-owning Government. They will get it, but they will fall from the frying pan into the fire. To-day they are slaves of slaves. By seeking Government aid, they will be used for suppressing their kith and kin. Instead of being sinned against, they will themselves be the sinners. The Musalmans tried it and failed. They found that they were worse than before. The Sikhs did it unwittingly and failed. To-day there is no more discontented community in India than the Sikhs. Government aid is, therefore, no solution.
>
> The second is rejection of Hinduism and wholesale conversion to Islam or Christianity. And if a change of religion

could be justified for worldly betterment I would advise it without hesitation. But religion is a matter of the heart. No physical inconvenience can warrant abandonment of one's own religion. If the inhuman treatment of the Panchamas were a part of Hinduism, its rejection would be a paramount duty both for them and for those like me who would not make a fetish even of religion and condone every evil in its sacred name. But I believe that untouchability is no part of Hinduism. It is rather its excrescence to be removed by every effort. And there is quite an army of Hindu reformers who have set their heart upon ridding Hinduism of this blot. Conversion therefore, I hold, is no remedy whatsoever.

Then, there remains, finally, self-help and self-dependence, with such aid as the non-Panchama Hindus will render of their own motion, not as a matter of duty. And herein comes the use of Non-co-operation . . . Therefore, by way of protest against Hinduism, the Panchamas can certainly stop all contact and connection with the other Hindus so long as the special grievances are maintained. But this means organised intelligent effort. And so far as I can see, there is no leader among the Panchamas who can lead them to victory through Non-co-operation.

The better way therefore, perhaps, is for the Panchamas heartily to join the great national movement that is now going on for throwing off the slavery of the present Government. It is easy enough for the Panchama friends to see that Non-co-operation against this evil Government pre-supposes co-operation between the different sections forming the Indian nation."

In the same article Mr. Gandhi told the Hindus :—

"The Hindus must realise that, if they wish to offer successful Non-co-operation against the Government they must make common cause with the Panchamas, even as they have made common cause with the Musalmans."

He repeated the warning in the *Young India* of 29th December 1920 in which he said :—

"Non-co-operation against the Government means co-operation among the governed, and if Hindus do not remove the sin of untouchability, there will be no Swaraj whether in one year or in one hundred years . . . Swaraj is as unattainable without the removal of the sins of untouchability as it is without Hindu-Muslim unity."

From all this, one would expect Mr. Gandhi to see that the Congress policy of ameliorating the condition of the Untouchables as set out in the Bardoli resolution was given effect to. The fact is that Mr. Gandhi, besides giving utterance to pious platitude, did not take the slightest interest in the programme of the amelioration. If he was so minded, he could have appointed another Committee. If he was so minded, he could have saved a large part of the Tilak Swaraj Fund from the organized loot that was being carried on by Congressmen and reserved it for the benefit of the Untouchables. Strange as it may appear, he sat silent and unconcerned. Instead of feeling any remorse, Mr. Gandhi justified his indifference to the cause of the Untouchables by arguments which are remarkable for their subtlety and sophistry if not for their casuistry and cunning. They are to be found in the *Young India* of 20th October 1920 :—

> "Should not we the Hindus wash our bloodstained hands before we ask the English to wash theirs? This is a proper question reasonably put. And if a member of a slave nation could deliver the suppressed classes from their slavery, without freeing myself from my own I would do so to-day. But it is an impossible task. A slave has not the freedom even to do the right thing."

Mr. Gandhi concluded by saying :—

> "That process has commenced and whether the Panchamas deliberately take part in it or not, the rest of the Hindus dare not neglect them without hampering their own progress. Hence though the Panchama problem is as dear to me as life itself, I rest satisfied with the exclusive attention to national non-co-operation. I feel sure that the greater includes the less."

Thus ended the second chapter of what the Congress has done to the Untouchables. The regrettable part of this tragedy is the realization of the fact how Mr. Gandhi has learned to find unction in illusions. Whether Mr. Gandhi likes to live in a world of illusions may be a matter of doubt. But there is no doubt he likes to create illusions in order to use them as arguments to support his cherished proposition. The reason he has given for not taking personal responsibility for the uplift of the Untouchables furnishes the best evidence of this habit of Mr. Gandhi. To tell the Untouchables that they must not act against the Hindus, because they will be acting against their kith and kin, may be understood. But to assume that the Hindus regard the Untouchables as their kith and kin is to set up an illusion. To ask the Hindus to undertake the removal of untouchability is good advice. But to go to the length of assuring oneself that the Hindus are so overwhelmed with a sense of shame for the inhuman treatment they have accorded to the Untouchables that they dare not fail to abolish untouchability and that there is a band of Hindu Reformers pledged to do nothing but remove untouchability is to conjure an illusion to fool the Untouchables and to fool the world at large. It may be sound logic to argue that what benefits the whole also benefits the part and that one need not confine oneself to looking after the part. But to assume that a piece, as separate as the Untouchables, is a part of the Hindu whole is to deceive oneself. Few know what tragedies the Untouchables as well as the country have had to go through on account of the illusions of Mr. Gandhi.

CHAPTER III

A MEAN DEAL

Congress Refuses to part with Power

I

In the Government of India Act of 1919, there was a provision which had imposed an obligation on His Majesty's Government to appoint at the end of ten years a Royal Commission to investigate into the working of the Constitution and report upon such changes as may be found necessary. Accordingly, in 1928 a Royal Commission was appointed under the Chairmanship of Sir John Simon. Indians expected that the Commission would be mixed in its personnel. But Lord Birkenhead who was then the Secretary of State for India was opposed to the inclusion of Indians and insisted on making it a purely Parliamentary Commission. At this, the Congress and the Liberals took great offence and treated it as an insult. They boycotted the Commission and carried on a great agitation against it. To assuage this feeling of opposition it was announced by His Majesty's Government that after the work of the Commission was completed representative Indians would be assembled for a discussion before the new Constitution for India was settled. In accordance with this announcement representative Indians were called to London at a Round Table Conference with the Representatives of Parliament and of His Majesty's Government.

On the 12th November 1930, His late Majesty King George V formally inaugurated the Indian Round Table Conference. From the point of view of Indians the Round Table Conference was an event of great significance. Its significance lay in the recognition by His Majesty's Government of the right of Indians to be consulted in the matter of framing a constitution for India. For the Untouchables it was a landmark in their history. For, the Untouchables were for the first time allowed to be represented separately by two delegates who happened to be myself and Dewan Bahadur R. Srinivasan. This meant that the Untouchables were regarded not merely as a separate element from the Hindus but also of such importance as to have the right to be consulted in the framing of a constitution for India.

The work of the Conference was distributed among nine committees. One of these committees was called the Minorities Committee to which was assigned the most difficult work of finding a solution of the Communal question. Anticipating that this Committee was the most important committee the Prime Minister, the late Mr. Ramsay MacDonald, himself assumed its chairmanship. The proceedings of the Minorities Committee are of the greatest importance to the Untouchables. For, much of what happened between the Congress and the Untouchables and which has led to bitterness between them will be found in the proceedings of that Committee.

When the Round Table Conference met the political demands of communities other than the Untouchables were quite well known. Indeed, the Constitution of 1919 had recognized them as statutory minorities and provisions relating to their safety and security were embodied in it. In their case the question was of expanding those provisions or altering their shape. With regard to the Depressed Classes the position was different. The Montagu-Chelmsford Report which preceded the Constitution of 1919 had said in quite unmistakable terms that provision must be made in the Constitution for their protection. But unfortunately when the details of the Constitution were framed, the Government of India found it difficult to devise any provisions for their protection except to give them token representation in the legislatures by nomination. The first thing that was required to be done was to formulate the safeguards deemed necessary by the Untouchables for their protection against the tyranny and oppression of the Hindus. This I did by submitting a Memorandum to the Minorities Committee of the Round Table Conference. To give an idea of the safeguards that were formulated by me, I reproduce below the text of the Memorandum :—

A Scheme of Political Safeguards for the Protection of the Depressed Classes in the Future Constitution of a self-governing India, submitted to the Indian Round Table Conference.

The following are the terms and conditions on which the Depressed Classes will consent to place themselves under a majority rule in a self-governing India.

Condition No. I :

EQUAL CITIZENSHIP

The Depressed Classes cannot consent to subject themselves to majority rule in their present state of hereditary bondsmen. Before majority rule is established their emancipation from the system of untouchability must be an accomplished fact. It must not be left to the will of the majority. The Depressed Classes must be made free citizens entitled to all the rights of citizenship in common with other citizens of the State.

(*A*) *To secure the abolition of untouchability and to create the equality of citizenship, it is proposed that the following fundamental right shall be made part of the constitution of India.*

FUNDAMENTAL RIGHT

U.S.A. Constitution Amendment XIV and Government of Ireland Act 1920, 10 & 11, Geo. V. Ch. 67, Sec. 5 (2).

" *All subjects of the State in India are equal before the law and possess equal civic rights. Any existing enactment, regulation, order, custom or interpretation of law by which any penalty, disadvantage, disability is imposed upon or any discrimination is made against any subject of the State on account of untouchability shall, as from the day on which this Constitution comes into operation, cease to have any effect in India.*"

This is so in all Constitutions. See Prof. Keith's remarks in Cmd. 207, p. 56.

(*B*) *To abolish the immunities and exemptions now enjoyed by executive officers by virtue of Sections 110 and 111 of the Government of India Act, 1919, and their liability for executive action be made co-extensive with what it is in the case of a European British Subject.*

Condition No. II :

FREE ENJOYMENT OF EQUAL RIGHTS

It is no use for the Depressed Classes to have a declaration of equal rights. There can be no doubt that the Depressed Classes will have to face the whole force of orthodox society if they try to exercise the equal rights of citizenship. The Depressed Classes therefore feel that if these declarations of rights are not to be mere pious pronouncements, but are to be realities of everyday life, then they should be protected by adequate pains and penalties from interference in the enjoyment of these declared rights.

(A) *The Depressed Classes therefore propose that the following section should be added to Part XI of the Government of India Act, 1919, dealing with Offences, Procedure and Penalties :—*

(i) *Offence of Infringement of Citizenship.*

U.S. Statutes at Large. Civil Rights Protection Acts of April 9, 1866, and of March 1, 1875—passed in the interest of the Negroes after their emancipation.

" *Whoever denies to any person except for reasons by law applicable to persons of all classes and regardless of any previous condition of untouchability the full enjoyment of any of the accommodations, advantages, facilities, privileges of inns, educational institutions, roads, paths, streets, tanks, wells and other watering places, public conveyances on land, air or water, theatres or other places of public amusement, resort or convenience whether they are dedicated to or maintained or licensed for the use of the public shall be punished with imprisonment of either description for a term which may extend to five years and shall also be liable to fine.*"

(B) Obstruction by orthodox individuals is not the only menace to the Depressed Classes in the way of peaceful enjoyment of their rights. The commonest form of obstruction is the social boycott. It is the most formidable weapon in the hands of the orthodox classes with which they beat down any attempt on the part of the Depressed Classes to undertake any activity if it happens to be unpalatable to them. The way it works and the occasions on which it is brought into operation are well described in the Report of the Committee appointed by the Government of Bombay in 1928 " to enquire into the educational, economic and social condition of the Depressed Classes (untouchables) and of the Aboriginal Tribes in the Presidency and to recommend measures for their uplift." The following is an extract from the same :—

Depressed Classes and Social Boycott

" 102. Although we have recommended various remedies to secure to the Depressed Classes their rights to all public utilities we fear that there will be difficulties in the way of their exercising them for a long time to come. The first difficulty is the fear of open violence against them by the orthodox classes. It must be noted that the Depressed Classes form a small minority in every village, opposed to which is a great majority of the orthodox who are bent on protecting their interests and dignity from any supposed invasion by the Depressed Classes at any cost. The danger of prosecution by the Police has put a limitation upon the use of violence by the orthodox classes and consequently such cases are rare.

" The second difficulty arises from the economic position in which the Depressed Classes are found to-day. The Depressed Classes have no economic independence in most parts of the Presidency. Some cultivate the lands of the orthodox classes as their tenants at will. Others live on their earnings as farm labourers employed by the orthodox classes and the rest subsist on the food or grain given to them by the orthodox classes in lieu of service rendered to them as village servants. We have heard of numerous instances where the orthodox classes have used their economic power as a weapon against those Depressed Classes in their villages, when the latter have dared to exercise their rights, and have evicted them from their land, and stopped their employment and discontinued their remuneration as village servants. This boycott is often planned on such an extensive scale as to include the prevention of the Depressed Classes from using the commonly used paths and the stoppage of sale of the necessaries of life by the village Bania. According to the evidence sometimes small causes suffice for the proclamation of a social boycott against the Depressed Classes. Frequently it follows on the exercise by the Depressed Classes of their right to the use of the common-well, but cases have been by no means rare where a stringent boycott has been proclaimed simply because a Depressed Class man has put on the sacred thread, has bought a piece of land, has put on good clothes or ornaments, or has carried a marriage procession with the bridegroom on the horse through the public street.

" We do not know of any weapon more effective than this social boycott which could have been invented for the suppression of the Depressed Classes. The method of open violence pales away before it, for it has the most far-reaching and deadening effects. It is the more dangerous because it passes as a lawful method consistent with the theory of freedom of contact. We agree that this tyranny of the majority must be put down with a firm hand, if we are to guarantee the Depressed Classes the freedom of speech and action necessary for their uplift."

In the opinion of the Depressed Classes the only way to overcome this kind of menace to their rights and liberties is to make social boycott an offence punishable by law. They are therefore bound to insist that the following sections should be added to those included in Part XI, of the Government of India Act 1919, dealing with Offences, Procedure and Penalties.

I. OFFENCE OF BOYCOTT DEFINED

(i) *A person shall be deemed to boycott another who—*

This and the following legal provisions are bodily taken from Burma Anti-Boycott Act, 1922, with a few changes to suit the necessities of the case.

(a) *refuses to let or use or occupy any house or land, or to deal with, work for hire, or do business with another person, or to render to him or receive from him any service, or refuses to do any of the said things on the terms on which such things should commonly be done in the ordinary course of business,* or

(b) *abstains from such social, professional or business relations as he would, having regard to such existing customs in the community which are not inconsistent with any fundamental right or other rights of citizenship declared in the Constitution ordinarily maintain with such person,* or

(c) *in any way injures, annoys or interferes with such other person in the exercise of his lawful rights.*

II. PUNISHMENT FOR BOYCOTTING

Whoever, in consequence of any person having done any act which he was legally entitled to do or of his having omitted to do any act which he was legally entitled to omit to do, or with intent to cause any person to do any act which he is not legally bound to do or to omit to do any act which he is legally entitled to do, or with intent to cause harm to such person in body, mind, reputation or property, or in his business or means of living, boycotts such person or any person in whom such person is interested, shall be punished with imprisonment of either description which may extend to seven years or with fine or with both.

Provided that no offence shall be deemed to have been committed under this Section, if the Court is satisfied that the accused person has not acted at the instigation of or in collusion with any other person or in pursuance of any conspiracy or of any agreement or combination to boycott.

III. PUNISHMENT FOR INSTIGATING OR PROMOTING A BOYCOTT

Whoever—

(a) *publicly makes or publishes or circulates a proposal for,* or

(b) *makes, publishes or circulates any statement, rumour or report with intent to, or which he has reason to believe to be likely to, cause* or

(c) *in any other way instigates or promotes the boycotting of any person or class of persons, shall be punished with imprisonment which may extend to five years, or with fine or with both.*

Explanation.—An offence under this section shall be deemed to have been committed although the person affected or likely to be affected by any action of the nature referred to herein is not designated by name or class but only by his acting or abstaining from acting in some specified manner.

IV. PUNISHMENT FOR THREATENING A BOYCOTT

Whoever, in consequence of any person having done any act which he was legally entitled to do or of his having omitted to do any act which he was legally entitled to omit to do, or with intent to cause any person to do any act which he is not legally bound to do, or to omit to do any act which he is legally entitled to do, threatens to cause such person or any person in whom such person is interested, to be boycotted shall be punished with imprisonment of either description for a term which may extend to five years or with fine or with both.

Exception :—It is not boycott

(i) *to do any act in furtherance of a* bona fide *labour dispute,*

(ii) *to do any act in the ordinary course of business competition.*

N.B.—*All these offences shall be deemed to be cognizable offences.*

Condition No. III.

PROTECTION AGAINST DISCRIMINATION

The Depressed Classes entertain grave fears of discrimination either by legislation or by executive order being made in the future. They cannot therefore consent to subject themselves to majority rule unless it is rendered impossible in law for the legislature or the executive to make any invidious discrimination against the Depressed Classes.

It is therefore proposed that the following Statutory provision be made in the constitutional law of India :—

" *It shall not be competent for any Legislature or executive in India to pass a law or issue an order, rule or regulation so as to violate the rights of the Subjects of the State, regardless of any previous condition of untouchability, in all territories subject to the jurisdiction of the dominion of India,*

(1) *to make and enforce contracts, to sue, be parties, and give evidence, to inherit, purchase, lease, sell, hold and convey real and personal property,*

(2) *to be eligible for entry into the civil and military employ and to all educational institutions except for such conditions and limitations as may be necessary to provide for the due and adequate representation of all classes of the subjects of the State,*

(3) *to be entitled to the full and equal enjoyment of the accommodations, advantages, facilities, educational institutions, privileges of inns, rivers, streams, wells, tanks, roads, paths, streets, public conveyances on land, air and water, theatres, and other places of public resort or amusement except for such conditions and limitations applicable alike to all subjects of every race, class, caste, colour or creed,*

(4) *to be deemed fit for and capable of sharing without distinction the benefits of any religious or charitable trust dedicated to or created, maintained or licensed for the general public or for persons of the same faith and religion,*

(5) *to claim full and equal benefit of all laws and proceedings for the security of person and property as is enjoyed by other subjects regardless of any previous condition of untouchability and be subject to like punishment pains and penalties and to none other.*

Condition No. IV

ADEQUATE REPRESENTATION IN THE LEGISLATURES

The Depressed Classes must be given sufficient political power to influence legislative and executive action for the purpose of securing their welfare. *In view of this they demand that the following provisions shall be made in the electoral law so as to give them—*

(1) *Right to adequate representation in the Legislatures of the Country, Provincial and Central.*

(2) *Right to elect their own men as their representatives,*

- (a) *by adult suffrage,* and
- (b) *by separate electorates for the first ten years and thereafter by joint electorates and reserved seats, it being understood that joint electorates shall not be forced upon the Depressed Classes against their will unless such joint electorates are accompanied by adult suffrage.*

N.B.—Adequate Representation for the Depressed Classes cannot be defined in quantitative terms until the extent of representation allowed to other communities is known. But it must be understood that the Depressed Classes will not consent to the representation of any other community being settled on better terms than those allowed to them. They will not agree to being placed at a disadvantage in this matter. In any case the Depressed Classes of Bombay and Madras must have weightage over their population ratio of representation, irrespective of the extent of representation allowed to other minorities in the Provinces.

Condition No. V

ADEQUATE REPRESENTATION IN THE SERVICES

The Depressed Classes have suffered enormously at the hands of the high caste officers who have monopolized the Public Services by abusing the law or by misusing the discretion vested in them in administering it to the prejudice of the Depressed Classes and to the advantage of the caste Hindus without any regard to justice, equity or good conscience. This mischief can only be avoided by destroying the monopoly of caste Hindus in the Public Services and by regulating the recruitment to them in such a manner that all communities including the Depressed will have an adequate share in them. For this purpose the Depressed Classes have to make the following proposals for statutory enactment as part of the constitutional law :—

(1) *There shall be established in India and in each Province in India a public Services Commission to undertake the recruitment and control of the Public Services.*

(2) *No member of the Public Service Commission shall be removed except by a resolution passed by the Legislature nor shall he be appointed to any office under the Crown after his retirement.*

(3) *It shall be the duty of the Public Service Commission, subject to the tests of efficiency as may be prescribed,*

- (a) *to recruit the Services in such a manner as will secure due and adequate representation of all communities*, and
- (b) *to regulate from time to time priority in employment in accordance with the existing extent of the representation of the various communities in any particular service concerned.*

Condition No. VI

REDRESS AGAINST PREJUDICIAL ACTION OR NEGLECT OF INTERESTS

In view of the fact that the Majority Rule of the future will be the rule of the orthodox, the Depressed Classes fear that such a Majority Rule will not be sympathetic to them and that the probability of prejudice to their interests and neglect of their vital needs cannot be overlooked. It must be provided against particularly because, however adequately represented the

Depressed Classes will be in a minority in all legislatures. The Depressed Classes think it very necessary that they should have the means of redress given to them in the constitution. *It is therefore proposed that the following provision should be made in the constitution of India :—*

British North America Act, 1867, Sec. 93

" In and for each Province and in and for India it shall be the duty and obligation of the Legislature and the Executive or any other Authority established by Law to make adequate provision for the education, sanitation, recruitment in Public Services and other matters of social and political advancement of the Depressed Classes and to do nothing that will prejudicially affect them.

" (2) *Where in any Province or in India the provisions of this section are violated an appeal shall lie to the Governor-General in Council from any act or decision of any Provincial Authority and to the Secretary of State from any act or decision of a Central Authority affecting the matter.*

" (3) *In every such case where it appears to the Governor-General in Council or to the Secretary of State that the Provincial Authority or Central Authority does not take steps requisite for the due execution of the provisions of this Section then and in every such case, and as far only as the circumstances of each case require the Governor-General in Council or the Secretary of State acting as an appellate authority may prescribe, for such period as they may deem fit, remedial measures for the due execution of the provisions of this Section and of any of its decisions under this Section and which shall be binding upon the authority appealed against.*

Condition No. VII

SPECIAL DEPARTMENTAL CARE

The helpless, hapless and sapless condition of the Depressed Classes must be entirely attributed to the dogged and determined opposition of the whole mass of the orthodox population which will not allow the Depressed Classes to have equality of status or equality of treatment. It is not enough to say of their economic condition that they are poverty-stricken or that they are a class of landless labourers, although both these statements are statements of fact. It has to be noted that the poverty of the Depressed Classes is due largely to the social prejudices in consequence of which many an occupation for earning a living is closed to them. This is a fact which differentiates the position of the Depressed Classes from that of the ordinary caste labourer and is often a source of trouble between the two. It has also to be borne in mind that the forms of tyranny and oppression practised against the Depressed Classes are very various and the capacity of the Depressed Classes to protect themselves is extremely limited. The facts, which obtain in this connection and which are of common occurrence throughout India, are well described in the Abstracts of Proceedings of the Board of Revenue of the Government of Madras dated 5th November, 1892, No. 723, from which the following is an extract :—

" 134. There are forms of oppression only hitherto hinted at which must be at least cursorily mentioned. To punish disobedience of Pariahs, their masters—

(*a*) Bring false cases in the village court or in the criminal courts.

(*b*) Obtain, on application, from Government waste lands lying all round the paracheri, so as to impound the Pariahs' cattle or obstruct the way to their temple.

(*c*) Have mirasi names fraudulently entered in the Government account against the paracheri.

(*d*) Pull down the huts and destroy the growth in the backyards.

(*e*) Deny occupancy right in immemorial sub-tenancies.

(*f*) Forcibly cut the Pariahs' crops, and on being resisted, charge them with theft and rioting.

(*g*) Under misrepresentations, get them to execute documents by which they are afterwards ruined.

(*h*) Cut off the flow of water from their fields.

(*i*) Without legal notice, have the property of sub-tenants attached for the land-lords' arrears of revenue.

" 135. It will be said there are civil and criminal courts for the redress of any of these injuries. There are the courts indeed; but India does not breed village Hampdens. One must have courage to go to the courts ; money to employ legal knowledge, and meet legal expenses ; and means to live during the case and the appeals. Further most cases depend upon the decision of the first court ; and these courts are presided over by officials who are sometimes corrupt and who generally, for other reasons, sympathize with the wealthy and landed classes to which they belong.

" 136. The influence of these classes with the official world can hardly be exaggerated. It is extreme with natives and great even with Europeans. Every office, from the highest to the lowest, is stocked with their representatives, and there is no proposal affecting their interests but they can bring a score of influence to bear upon it in its course from inception to execution."

There can be no doubt that in view of these circumstances the uplift of the Depressed Classes will remain a pious hope unless the task is placed in the forefront of all governmental activities and unless equalization of opportunities is realized in practice by a definite policy and determined effort on the part of Government. *To secure this end the proposal of the Depressed Classes is that the Constitutional Law should impose upon the Government of India a statutory obligation to maintain at all times a department to deal with their problems by the addition of a section in the Government of India Act to the following effect :—*

"*1. Simultaneously with the introduction of this Constitution and as part thereof, there shall be created in the Government of India a Department to be in charge of a Minister for the purpose of watching the interests of the Depressed Classes and promoting their welfare.*

"*2. The Minister shall hold office so long as he retains the confidence of the Central Legislature.*

"*3. It shall be the duty of the Minister in the exercise of any powers and duties conferred upon him or transferred to him by law, to take all such steps as may be desirable to secure the preparation, effective carrying out and co-ordination of measures preventative of acts of social injustice, tyranny or oppression against the Depressed Classes and conducive to their welfare throughout India.*

"*4. It shall be lawful for the Governor-General—*

(a) *to transfer to the Minister all or any powers or duties in respect of the welfare of the Depressed Classes arising from any enactment relating to education, sanitation, etc.*

(b) *to appoint Depressed Classes welfare bureaus in each province to work under the authority of and in co-operation with the Minister.*"

Condition No. VIII

DEPRESSED CLASSES AND THE CABINET

Just as it is necessary that the Depressed Classes should have the power to influence governmental action by seats in the Legislature so also it is desirable that the Depressed Classes should have the opportunity to frame the general policy of the Government. This they can do only if they can find a seat in the Cabinet. The Depressed Classes therefore claim that in common with other minorities, their moral rights to be represented in the Cabinet should be recognized. With this purpose in view *the Depressed Classes propose ;*

that in the Instrument of Instructions an obligation shall be placed upon the Governor and the Governor-General to endeavour to secure the representation of the Depressed Classes in his Cabinet.

II

What happened to these demands of the Untouchables and how the members of the Minorities Committee reacted to them can be well understood by a perusal of the Report made by the Minorities Committee to the Round Table Conference. I give below a few extracts from that Report :—

" 5. Claims were therefore advanced by various committees that arrangements should be made for communal representation and for fixed proportions of seats. It was also urged that the number of seats reserved for a minority community should in no case be less than its proportion in the population. The methods by which this could be secured were mainly three : (1) nomination, (2) electorates and (3) separate electorates.

" 6. Nomination was unanimously deprecated.

" 7. Joint electorates were proposed with the proviso that a propertion of seats should be reserved to the communities. Thus a more democratic form would be given to the elections whilst the purpose of the electorate system would be secured. Doubts were expressed that, whilst such a system of election might secure the representation of minorities, it provided no guarantee that the representation would be genuine, but that it might, in its working, mean the nomination or, in any event, the election of minority representatives by the majority communities.

It was pointed out that this was in fact only a form of community representation and had in practice all the objections to the more direct form of community electorates.

" 8. The discussion made it evident that the demand which remained as the only one which would be generally acceptable was separate eletorates. The general objection to this scheme has been subject to much previous discussion in India. It involves what is a very difficult problem for solution, viz., what should be the amount of communal representation in the various provinces and in the Centre ; that, if the whole, or practically the whole, of the seats in a legislature are to be assigned to communities, there will be no room for the growth of independent political opinion or of true political parties, and this problem received a serious complication by the demand of the representative of the Depressed Classes that they should be deducted from the Hindu population and be regarded, for electoral purposes, as a separate community.

" 9. It was suggested that, in order to meet the most obvious objection to the ear-marking of seats to communities, only a proportion should be so assigned—say 80 per cent. or 90 per cent.—and that the rest should be filled by open election. This, however, was not regarded by some of the communities as giving them the guarantees they required.

" 10. The scheme proposed by Maulana Muhammad Ali, a member of the Sub-Committee, whose death we deplore, that, as far as possible no communal candidate should be elected unless he secured at least 40 per cent. according to arrangement, of the votes of the other community, was also considered. It was, however, pointed out that such a scheme necessarily involved the maintenance of communal registers and so was open to objections similar to those urged against separate electorates.

" 11. No claim for separate electorate or for the reservation of seats in joint electorates was made on behalf of women who should continue to be eligible for election on the same footing as men. But, in order to familiarize the public mind with the idea of women taking an active part in political life and to secure their interim representation on the legislature, it was urged that 5 per cent. of the seats in the first three Councils should be reserved for women and it was suggested that they should be filled by co-option by the elected members voting by proportional representation.

" 12. There was general agreement with the recommendation of Sub-Committee No. II (Provincial Constitution) that the representation on the Provincial Executive of important minority communities was a matter of the greatest practical importance for the successful working of the new constitution, and it was also agreed that, on the same grounds, Muhammadans should be represented on the Federal Executive. On behalf of the smaller minorities a claim was put forward for their representation, either individually or collectively, on the Provincial and Federal Executives or that, if this should be found impossible, in each Cabinet there should be a Minister specially charged with the duty of protecting minority interests.

(Dr. Ambedkar and Sardar Ujjal Singh would add the words "and other important minorities" after the word Muhammadans in line 6).

The difficulty of working jointly responsible Executives under such a scheme as this was pointed out.

"13. As regards the administration, it was agreed that recruitment to both Provincial and Central Services should be entrusted to Public Service Commissions, with instructions to reconcile the claims of the various communities to fair and adequate representation in the Public Services, whilst providing for the maintenance of a proper standard of efficiency.

* * *

"16. It has also been made clear that the British Government cannot, with any chance of agreement, impose upon the communities an electoral principle which, in some feature or other, would be met by their opposition. It was therefore plain that, failing an agreement, separate electorates, with all their drawbacks and difficulties, would have to be retained as the basis of the electoral arrangements under the new constitution. From this the question of proportions would arise. Under these circumstances, the claims of the Depressed Classes will have to be considered adequately.

* * *

"18. The Minorities and Depressed Classes were definite in their assertion that they could not consent to any self-governing constitution for India unless their demands were met in a reasonable manner."

The Federal Structure Committee, another Committee appointed by the Round Table Conference to discuss the form and functions of the Central Government, had also to consider the question of the Untouchables in connection with the composition of the Federal Legislatures. In the report it made to the Conference it said :—

"Opinion was unanimous in the sub-committee that, subject to any report of the Minorities Sub-Committee, provision should be made for the representation, possibly in both Chambers and certainly in the Lower Chamber, of certain special interests, namely, the Depressed Classes, Indian Christians, Europeans, Anglo-Indians, Landlords, Commerce (European and Indian) and Labour."

III

Before the first session of the Round Table Conference was concluded the reports of both the Committees were placed before the Conference and were passed by the Conference. It will be noticed that although agreement on details was lacking it was unanimously accepted that the Untouchables were entitled to recognition as a separate entity for political and constitutional purposes.

The only party in the country whose attitude to this decision of the Round Table Conference was not known when the First Session of the Round Table Conference was closed, was the Congress. This was because the Congress had boycotted the Round Table Conference and was busy in carrying on civil disobedience against the Government. By the time the Second Session of the Round Table Conference became due, a compromise between His Majesty's Government and the Congress was reached as a result of which the Congress agreed to participate in it and make its contribution to the solution of the many problems confronting the Conference. Everybody, who had witnessed the good temper, happy relationship and the spirit of give and take shown by the delegates at the first session of the Round Table Conference, hoped that the progress made would be maintained from session to session. Indeed the rate of progress in forging an agreement was expected to be much more rapid as a result of the advent of the Congress. In fact, friends of Congress were alleging that if the session did not produce an agreement it was because of the absence of the Congress.

Everybody was therefore looking forward to the Congress to lead the Conference to success. Unfortunately, the Congress chose Mr. Gandhi as its representative. A worse person could not have been chosen to guide India's destiny. As a unifying force he was a failure. Mr. Gandhi presents himself as a man full of humility. But his behaviour at the Round Table Conference showed that in the flush of victory Mr. Gandhi can be very petty-minded. As a result of his successful compromise with the Government just before he came, Mr. Gandhi treated the whole Non-Congress delegation with contempt. He insulted them whenever an occasion furnished him with an excuse by openly telling them that they were nobodies and that he alone, as the delegate of the Congress, represented the country. Instead of unifying the Indian delegation, Mr. Gandhi widened the breach. From the point of view of knowledge, Mr. Gandhi proved himself to be a very ill-equipped person. On the many constitutional and communal questions with which the Conference was confronted, Mr. Gandhi had many platitudes to utter but no views or suggestions of a constructive character to offer. He presented a curious complex of a man who in some cases would threaten to resist in every possible way any compromise on what he regarded as a principle though others regarded it as a pure prejudice but in other cases would not mind making the worst compromises on issues which appeared to others as matters of fundamental principle on which no compromise should be made.

Mr. Gandhi's attitude to the demands of the Untouchables at the Second Session of the Round Table Conference furnishes the best illustration of this rather queer trait in his character. When the delegates assembled for the Second Session of the Round Table Conference the Federal Structure Committee met first. In the very first speech which he made in the Federal Structure Committee on 15th September 1931, Mr. Gandhi referred to the question of the Untouchables. Mr. Gandhi said :—

> "The Congress has, from its very commencement, taken up the cause of the so-called 'Untouchables.' There was a time when the Congress had at every annual session as its adjunct the Social Conference, to which the late Ranade dedicated his energies, among his many other activities. Headed by him you will find, in the programme of the Social Conference, reform in connection with the 'Untouchables' taking a prominent place. But, in 1920, the Congress took a large step and brought in the question of the removal of untouchability as a plank on the political platform, making it an important item of the political programme. Just as the Congress considered the Hindu-Muslim unity—thereby meaning unity amongst all the classes—to be indispensable for the attainment of Swaraj, so also did the Congress consider the removal of the curse of untouchability as an indispensable condition for the attainment of full freedom. The position the Congress took up in 1920 remains the same today; and so you will see the Congress has attempted from its very beginning to be what it described itself to be, namely, national in every sense of the term."

Anyone, who has perused how the Congress failed to carry out the 1922 programme for the uplift of the Untouchables which was included in the Bardoli programme and how it left it to the Hindu Mahasabha, could have no hesitation in saying that what Mr. Gandhi said was untrue. The speech however gave no indication as to what line Mr. Gandhi was going to take on the demands presented by the Untouchables, although I could see the drift of it.[1] But he did not leave people long

[1] Before going to the First Session of the Round Table Conference I had an interview with Mr. Gandhi in Bombay in which he had told me that he was not in favour of regarding the Untouchables as a separate entity for political purposes.

to imagine what his position was going to be. The meeting of the Federal Structure Committee held on the 17th of September 1931 provided him the necessary occasion. The agenda for the meeting included the question of election of members of the Federal Legislatures. Expressing his views on the subject, Mr. Gandhi made the following statement :—

> "I come to sub-head (*v*)—representation by special constituencies of special interests. I here speak for the Congress. The Congress has reconciled itself to special treatment of the Hindu-Muslim-Sikh tangle. There are sound historical reasons for it but the Congress will not extend that doctrine in any shape or form. I listened to the list of special interests. So far as the Untouchables are concerned, I have not yet quite grasped what Dr. Ambedkar has to say : but of course the Congress will share the honour with Dr. Ambedkar of representing the interests of the Untouchables. They are as clear to the Congress as the interests of any other body or of any other individual throughout the length and breadth of India. Therefore I would most strongly resist any further special representation."

This was nothing but a declaration of War by Mr. Gandhi and the Congress against the Untouchables. In any case, it resulted in a war between the two. After this declaration by Mr. Gandhi, I knew what he would do in the Minorities Committee which was the main forum for the discussion of this question.

Mr. Gandhi was making his plans to bypass the Untouchables and to close the communal problem by bringing about a settlement among the three parties, the Hindus, the Muslims and the Sikhs. He had been carrying on negotiations privately with the Muslims before the Minorities Committee met, but evidently they had not been concluded. Consequently, when the Minorities Committee met on 28th September 1931, Sir Ali Imam, representing the Nationalist Muslim point of view, started the debate. He began by saying :—

> "I am personally not aware if there are any negotiations going on so far as the Muslim Delegation is concerned. I have had no opportunity of knowing that there are any proposals at present that are under consideration. It may be, as I have heard generally, that some kind of understanding may be arrived at, I do not vouch for it ; I know nothing about it. If you desire, Sir, that I should put before you the Muslim Nationalists' point of view, I shall be ready to do so ; but, of course, I must have

your permission, because it may take a little time and economy of time in a meeting like this is one's principal aim.

"*Chairman :* The point is that this Committee's business is very strictly limited to a consolidation of the Minorities problem.

Sir Ali Imam : It is from that point of view that I shall approach the subject.

Chairman : If there is no other official intervention shall I call on Sir Ali Imam ?"

Then followed His Highness the Aga Khan who said :—

"I believe that Mahatma Gandhi is going to see the Muslim Delegation to-night. We hope to-night to have a friendly talk with our friend. That is all that I can tell you as far as any possible negotiation is concerned."

Pandit Madan Mohan Malaviya also suggested that a short adjournment may be fruitful of results. Knowing that this was a mischievous move I got up and spoke as follows :—

"I should like to say one word before we adjourn. As regards your suggestion—that while these negotiations are going on members of the other minority communities should prepare their case—I should like to say that so far as the Depressed Classes are concerned, we have already presented our case to the Minorities Sub-Committee last time.

"The only thing which remains for me to do is to put before this Committee a short statement[1] suggesting the quantum of representation which we want in the different Legislatures. Beyond that I do not think I am called upon to do anything ; but the point I am anxious to make at the very outset is this. I have heard with great pleasure that further negotiations are going to take place for the settlement of the communal issue, but I would like to make our position clear at the very start. I do not wish any doubt should be left on this question. Those who are negotiating ought to understand that they are not plenipotentiaries appointed by the Committee to negotiate a settlement ; that whatever may be the representative character of Mr. Gandhi or of the other parties with whom he wishes to negotiate, they certainly are not in a position to bind us—certainly not. I say that most emphatically in this meeting.

"Another thing I want to say is this—that the claims put forward by the various minorities are claims put forward by them irrespective of the consideration as to whether the claims that they have put forward are consistent with the claims of the other minorities. Consequently, any settlement which takes

[1] This I did by putting in another memorandum which is included as Appendix II.

place between one minority on the one hand and the Congress or any other party for the matter of that on the other hand, without taking into consideration the claims which have been put forward by other minorities, can have no binding force as far as I am concerned. I have no quarrel with the question whether any particular community should get weightage or not, but I do want to say most emphatically that whoever claims weightage and whoever is willing to give that weightage he must not give it—he cannot give it—out of my share. I want to make that absolutely plain."

What followed will be clear from the extract from the proceedings given below :—

"*Chairman :* Do not let there be any misunderstanding. This is the body before which the final settlement must come, and the suggestion is merely that if there are minorities or communities that hitherto have been in conflict with each other they should use a short time for the purpose of trying to overcome their difficulties. That will be a step and a very important and essential step, towards a general agreement, but the agreement is going to be a general one.

"*Dr. Ambedkar :* I have made my position absolutely clear.

"*Chairman :* Dr. Ambedkar's position has been made absolutely clear ; in his usual splendid way he has left no doubt at all about it, and that will come up when this body resumes its discussion. What I would like to do is to get you all to feel that we are co-operating together for a general settlement ; not for a settlement between any two or any three, but a complete settlement.

"*Chairman :* The position is this. We will adjourn now, I think, and later continue our meetings. Pending any negotiations that may be going on between any two or any three of you, we can take up the time in listening to a statement of the claims of the other minorities. I think that would be very useful. It would save time, and it would not mar the possibility of any harmony that may be reached between, say, our Sikh friends—who, we know, can look after themselves with a great deal of persistence—Mr. Gandhi and his friends and the Aga Khan and his.

"*Dr. Ambedkar :* I should like to suggest whether it would not be possible for you to appoint a small Committee consisting of members drawn from the various minority communities, along with the Congress representatives, to sit in an informal manner and discuss this problem during the period of the adjournment.

"*Chairman* : I was going to make this suggestion. Do not ask me to appoint that Committee ; do it yourselves. I have invited you to get together. Could not you manage to hold an informal meeting amongst yourselves and talk the matter over, and then when you speak here you will speak with some sort of knowledge of the effect of what you are saying on others ? Could we leave it in that way ?

"*Dr. Ambedkar* : As you like.

"*Chairman* : That would be far better."

No settlement was evidently arrived at between the three parties during the adjournment. Consequently when the Minorities Committee met again on 1st October 1931, Mr. Gandhi said :—

"Prime Minister, after consultation with His Highness the Aga Khan and other Muslim friends last night, we came to the conclusion that the purpose for which we meet here would be better served if a week's adjournment was asked for. I have not had the opportunity of consulting my other colleagues, but I have no doubt that they will also agree in the proposal I am making."

The proposal was seconded by the Aga Khan. I got up to oppose the motion. What I said will be clear from the following extract from the proceedings :—

"*Dr. Ambedkar* : I do not wish to create any difficulty in our making every possible attempt to arrive at some solution of the problem with which this Committee has to deal, and if a solution can be arrived at by the means suggested by Mahatma Gandhi, I, for one, will have no objection to that proposal.

"But there is just this one difficulty with which I, as representing the Depressed Classes, am faced. I do not know what sort of committee Mahatma Gandhi proposes to appoint to consider this question during the period of adjournment, but I suppose that the Depressed Classes will be represented on this Committee.

"*Mr. Gandhi* : Without doubt.

"*Dr. Ambedkar* : Thank you. But I do not know whether in the position in which I am to-day it would be of any use for me to work on the proposed Committee. And for this reason. Mahatma Gandhi told us on the first day that he spoke in the Federal Structure Committee that as a representative of the Indian National Congress he was not prepared to give political recognition to any community other than the Muhammadans and the Sikhs. He was not prepared to recognize the Anglo-Indians, the Depressed Classes, and the Indian Christians.

I do not think that I am doing any violence to etiquette by stating in this Committee that when I had the pleasure of meeting Mahatma Gandhi a week ago and discussing the question of the Depressed Classes with him, and when we, as members of the other minorities, had the chance of talking with him yesterday in his office, he told us in quite plain terms that the attitude that he had taken in the Federal Structure Committee was a firm and well considered attitude. What I would like to say is that unless at the outset I know that the Depressed Classes are going to be recognised as a community entitled to political recognition in the future Constitution of India, I do not know whether it will serve any purpose for me to join the committee that is proposed by Mahatma Gandhi to be constituted to go into this matter. Unless, therefore, I have an assurance that this Committee will start with the assumption that all those communities which the Minorities Sub-Committee last year recommended as fit for recognition in the future constitution of India will be included, I do not know that I can whole-heartedly support the proposition for adjournment, or that I can whole-heartedly co-operate with the Committee that is going to be nominated. That is what I wish to be clear about.

* * *

" *Dr. Ambedkar* : I should like to make my position further clear. It seems that there has been a certain misunderstanding regarding what I said. It is not that I object to adjournment; it is not that I object to serving on any Committee that might be appointed to consider the question. What I would like to know before I enter upon this committee, if they give me the privilege of serving on it, is : What is the thing that this Committee is going to consider ? Is it only going to consider the question of the Muhammadans *vis-a-vis* the Hindus ? Is it going to consider the question of the Muhammadans *vis-a-vis* the Sikhs in the Punjab ? Or is it going to consider the question of the Christians, the Anglo-Indians and the Depressed Classes ?

" If we understand perfectly well before we start that this committee will not merely concern itself with the question of the Hindus and the Muhammadans, of the Hindus and the Sikhs, but will also take upon itself the responsibility of considering the case of the Depressed Classes, the Anglo-Indians and the Christians, I am perfectly willing to allow this adjournment resolution to be passed without any objection. But I do want to say this, that if I am to be left out in the cold and if this interval is going to be utilised for the purposes of solving the Hindu-Muslim question, I would press that the Minorities

Committee should itself grapple with the question and consider it, rather than allow the question to be dealt with by some other informal Committee for arriving at a solution of the communal question in respect of some minorities only.

" *Mr. Gandhi* : Prime Minister and friends, I see that there is some kind of misunderstanding with reference to the scope of the work that some of us have set before ourselves. I fear that Dr. Ambedkar, Colonel Gidney and other friends are unnecessarily nervous about what is going to happen. Who am I to deny political status to any single interest or class or even individual in India ? As a representative of the Congress I should be unworthy of the trust that has been reposed in me by the Congress if I were guilty of sacrificing a single national interest. I have undoubtedly given expression to my own views on these points. I must confess that I hold to those views also. But there are ways and ways of guaranteeing protection to every single interest. It will be for those of us who will be putting our heads together to try to evolve a scheme. Nobody would be hampered in pressing his own views on the members of this very informal conference or meeting.

" I do not think, therefore, that anybody need be afraid as to being able to express his opinion or carrying his opinion also. Mine will be there equal to that of every one of us ; it will carry no greater weight ; I have no authority behind me to carry my opinion against the opinion of anybody. I have simply given expression to my views in the national interest, and I shall give expression to these views whenever they are opportune. It will be for you, it is for you to reject or accept these opinions. Therefore please disabuse your minds, to everyone of us, of the idea that there is going to be any steam-rolling in the Conference and the informal meetings that I have adumbrated. But if you think that this is one way of coming closer together than by sitting stiffly at this table, you will not carry this adjournment motion but give your whole-hearted co-operation to the proposal that I have made in connection with these informal meetings.

* * *

" *Chairman* : Then I shall proceed to put it. I put it on the clear understanding, my friends, that the time is not going to be wasted and that these conferences—as Mr. Gandhi has said, informal conferences, but nevertheless I hope very valuable and fruitful conferences—will take place between now and our next meeting. I hope you will all pledge yourselves to use the time in that way."

It is unnecessary for me to recite what happened at the informal meeting held after the adjournment. It was a complete failure, if not a fiasco. The meeting was presided over by Mr. Gandhi. Mr. Gandhi began with the most difficult part of the Communal question namely the dispute between the Sikhs and the Muslims in the Punjab. This problem at one stage appeared to be nearer solution when the parties agreed to abide by the decision of an arbitrator. The Sikhs, however, refused to proceed further in the matter until they knew who the arbitrator was. As the Musalmans were not prepared to have the name of the arbitrator disclosed, the matter fell through. Mr. Gandhi was not interested in the problem of the other minorities, such as the Untouchables, although he enacted the farce of calling upon the representatives of the other minorities to present a catalogue of their demands. He heard them ; but took no notice of them. Did he place them before the meeting for its consideration ? As soon as the Sikh-Muslim settlement broke up, Mr. Gandhi dissolved the meeting. The Minorities Committee met on 8th October 1931. The Prime Minister having called upon Mr. Gandhi to speak first, the latter said :—

> " Prime Minister and friends, it is with deep sorrow and deeper humiliation that I have to announce utter failure on my part to secure an agreed solution of the communal question through informal conversations among and with the representatives of different groups. I apologise to you, Mr. Prime Minister, and the other colleagues for the waste of a precious week. My only consolation lies in the fact that when I accepted the burden of carrying on these talks I knew that there was much hope of success and still more in the fact that I am not aware of having spared any effort to reach a solution.
>
> " But to say that the conversations have to our utter shame failed is not to say the whole truth. Causes of failure were inherent in the composition of the Indian Delegation. We are almost all not elected representatives of the parties or groups whom we are presumed to represent ; we are here by nomination of the Government. Nor are those whose presence was absolutely necessary for an agreed solution to be found here. Further, you will allow me to say that this was hardly the time to summon the Minorities Committee. It lacks the sense of reality in that we do not know what it is that we are going to get. If we knew in a definite manner that we were going to get the thing we want, we should hesitate fifty times before we

threw it away in a sinful wrangle as it would be if we are told that the getting of it would depend upon the ability of the present Delegation to produce an agreed solution of the communal tangle. The solution can be the crown of the Swaraj constitution, not its foundation—if only because our differences have hardened, if they have not arisen, by reason of the foreign domination. I have not a shadow of a doubt that the icebag of communal differences will melt under the warmth of the sun of freedom.

"I, therefore, venture to suggest that the Minorities Committee be adjourned *sine die* and that the fundamentals of the constitution be hammered into shape as quickly as may be. Meanwhile, the informal work of discovering a true solution of the communal problem will and must continue; only it must not baulk or be allowed to block the progress of constitution-building. Attention must be diverted from it and concentrated on the main part of the structure.

"I hardly need point out to the Committee that my failure does not mean the end of all hope of arriving at an agreed solution. My failure does not even mean my utter defeat; there is no such word in the dictionary. My confession merely means failure of special effort for which I presumed to ask for a week's indulgence, which you so generously gave.

"I propose to use the failure as a stepping-stone to success, and I invite you all to do likewise; but, should all effort at agreement fail, even when the Round Table Conference reaches the end of its labours, I would suggest the addition of a clause to the expected constitution appointing a judicial tribunal that would examine all claims and give its final decision on all the points that may be left unsettled."

In the discussion that followed everybody refuted Mr. Gandhi's allegation that the delegates were nominated by Government and did not represent the people. Getting up to make my position clear, I said :—

"Mr. Prime Minister, last night when we parted at the conclusion of the meeting of the informal Committee, we parted, although with a sense of failure, at least with one common understanding, and that was that when we met here to-day none of us should make any speech or any comment that would cause exasperation. I am sorry to see that Mr. Gandhi should have been guilty of a breach of this understanding. Excuse me, I must have the opportunity to speak. He started by giving what were, according to him, the causes of the failure of the informal Committee. Now, I have my own view of the causes which I think were responsible for the failure of the informal Committee to reach an agreement, but I do not propose to discuss them now. What disturbs me after hearing Mr. Gandhi is that instead of confining himself to his proposition, namely, that the Minorities Committee should adjourn *sine die*, he started casting certain reflections upon the representatives of the different communities who are sitting round this table. He said that the Delegates were nominees of the Government, and that they did not represent the views of their respective communities for whom they stood. We cannot deny the allegation that we are nominees of the Government, but, speaking for myself, I have not the slightest doubt that even if the Depressed Classes of India were given the chance of electing their representatives to this Conference, I would, all the same, find a place here. I say therefore that whether I am a nominee or not, I fully represent the claims of my community. Let no man be under the mistaken impression as regards that.

" The Mahatma has been always claiming that the Congress stands for the Depressed Classes, and that the Congress represents the Depressed Classes more than I or my colleague can do. To that claim I can only say that it is one of the many false claims which irresponsible people keep on making, although the persons concerned with regard to those claims have been invariably denying them.

" I have here a telegram which I have just received from a place which I have never visited and from a man whom I have never seen—from the President the Depressed Classes Union, Kumaun, Almora, which I believe is in the United Provinces, and which contains the following resolution :

> " This Meeting declares its non-confidence in the Congress movement which has been carried on in and outside the country, and condemns the methods adopted by the Congress workers."

I do not care to read further, but I can say this (and I think if Mr. Gandhi will examine his position he will find out the truth), that although there may be people in the Congress who may be showing sympathy towards the Depressed Classes, the Depressed Classes are not in the Congress. That is a proposition which I propose to substantiate. I do not wish to enter into these points of controversy. They seem to be somewhat outside the main proposition. The main proposition which Mr. Gandhi has made is that this Committee should be adjourned *sine die*. With regard to that proposition, I entirely agree with the attitude taken up by Sir Muhammad Shafi. I, for one, cannot consent to this proposition. It seems to me that there are only two alternatives—either that this Minorities Committee should go on tackling the problem and trying to arrive at some satisfactory solution, if that is possible, and then, if that is not possible, the British Government should undertake the solution of that problem. We cannot consent to leave this to the arbitration of third parties whose sense of responsibility may not be the same as must be the sense of responsibility of the British Government.

"Prime Minister, permit me to make one thing clear. The Depressed Classes are not anxious, they are not clamorous, they have not started any movement for claiming that there shall be an immediate transfer of power from the British to the Indian people. They have their particular grievances against the British people and I think I have voiced them sufficiently to make it clear that we feel those grievances most acutely. But, to be true to facts, the position is that the Depressed Classes are not clamouring for transfer of political power. Their position, to put it plainly, is that we are not anxious for the transfer of power; but if the British Government is unable to resist the forces that have been set up in the country which do clamour for transference of political power—and we know the Depressed Classes in their present circumstances are not in a position to resist that—then our submission is that if you make that transfer, that transfer will be accompanied by such conditions and by such provisions that the power shall not fall into the hands of a clique, into the hands of an oligarchy, or into the hands of a group of people, whether Muhammadans or Hindus; but that that solution shall be such that the power shall be shared by all communities in their respective proportions. Taking that view, I do not see how I, for one, can take any serious part in the deliberation of the Federal Structure Committee unless I know where I and my community stand."

The Prime Minister in his concluding observations said :—

"Let us adjourn, and I will call you together again. In the meantime what I would like would be if those of you who are sitting opposite me, the representatives of the small minorities, would also try your hands.

"If there are any common agreements among yourselves, I would suggest that you circulate them . . . It is not the British Government that is going to stand in the way of any agreement . . . Therefore what I would like you to have in your minds after the rather depressing statements to which we have listened, is this: That the British Government wants to go on; the

British Government wants you to go on. The British Government will take its action if you cannot go on to an end, because we are determined to make such improvements in the Government of India as will make the Government of India consistent with our own ideas, as will make the Government of India something that is capable of greater and greater expansion towards liberty. That is what we want. I appeal to the Delegates here to-day—Delegates representing all communities —Do not stand in our way ; because that is what is happening."

IV

Acting on the suggestion of the Prime Minister the minorities met to consider if they could produce a settlement. They tried and produced a settlement which was submitted to the Prime Minister in the evening before the next meeting of the Minorities Committee which took place on 13th November 1931. In his opening remarks the Prime Minister said :—

"The work of this Committee, therefore, was from the very beginning of supreme importance, and I am sorry that you have been unable to present to us an agreed plan.

"Last night, however, I received a deputation representing the Muhammadans, the Depressed Classes, at any rate a section of the Indian Christians, the Anglo-Indians and the British Community. I think that is the complete range. They came and saw me in my room in the House of Commons last night with a document which embodied an agreement that they had come to amongst themselves. They informed me, in presenting the document to me, that it covered something in the region of 46 per cent. of the population of British India.

"I think the best thing would be, as we have had no time to consider this, to treat this document as a document which is official to the records of this Committee and in order that that may be done I shall ask His Highness The Aga Khan formally to present it here, so that it may be entered in our official record."

His Highness The Aga Khan then got up and said :—

"Mr. Prime Minister, on behalf of the Muhammadans, the Depressed Classes, the Anglo-Indians, the Europeans and a considerable section of the Indian Christian groups, I present the document embodying the agreement which has been arrived at between them with regard to the intercommunal problem with which the Round Table Conference in general and the Minorities Committee in particular are concerned. We desire to make it clear that this agreement has been arrived at after careful and anxious consideration of this difficult and complicated problem and must be taken as a whole. All parts of the agreement are interdependent and agreements stand or fall as a whole."

This document was known as the Minorities Pact.[1] In the general discussion that followed Mr. Gandhi's speech no doubt attracted the greatest attention. Mr. Gandhi was furious. He attacked everybody who had taken part in producing the Minorities Pact. He was particularly furious for the recognition given to the Untouchables as a separate political entity. This is what Mr. Gandhi said :—

"I would like to repeat what I have said before, that, while the Congress will always accept any solution that may be acceptable to the Hindus, the Muhammadans and the Sikhs, Congress will be no party to the special electorates for any other minorities . . . One word more as to the so-called Untouchables. I can understand the claims advanced by other minorities, but the claims advanced on behalf of the Untouchables, that time is the 'unkindest cut of all.' It means the perpetual bar-sinister. I would not sell the vital interests of the Untouchables even for the sake of winning the freedom of India. I claim myself in my own person to represent the vast mass of the Untouchables. Here I speak not merely on behalf of the Congress, but I speak on my own behalf, and I claim that I would get, if there was a referendum of the Untouchables, their vote, and that I would top the poll. And I would work from one end of India to the other to tell the Untouchables that separate electorates and separate reservation is not the way to remove this bar-sinister, which is the shame, not of them, but of orthodox Hinduism.

"Let this Committee and let the whole world know that to-day there is a body of Hindu reformers who are pledged to remove this blot of untouchability. We do not want on our register and on our census Untouchables classified as a separate class. Sikhs may remain as such in perpetuity, so may Muhammadans, so may Europeans. Will Untouchables remain Untouchables in perpetuity ? I would far rather that Hinduism died than that Untouchability lived. Therefore, with all my regard for Dr. Ambedkar, and for his desire to see the Untouchables uplifted, with all my regard for his ability, I must say in all

[1] It is reproduced as Appendix III.

humility that here the great wrong under which he has laboured and perhaps the bitter experiences that he has undergone have for the moment warped his judgment. It hurts me to have to say this, but I would be untrue to the cause of the Untouchables, which is as dear to me as life itself, if I did not say it. I will not bargain away their rights for the kingdom of the whole world. I am speaking with a due sense of responsibility, and I say that it is not a proper claim which is registered by Dr. Ambedkar when he seeks to speak for the whole of the Untouchables of India. It will create a division in Hinduism which I cannot possibly look forward to with any satisfaction whatsoever. I do not mind Untouchables, if they so desire, being converted to Islam or Christianity. I should tolerate that, but I cannot possibly tolerate what is in store for Hinduism if there are two divisions set forth in the villages. Those who speak of the political right of Untouchables do not know their India, do not know how Indian Society is to-day constructed, and therefore I want to say with all the emphasis that I can command that if I was the only person to resist this thing I would resist it with my life."

The Chairman knowing that there was no hope of getting an agreed solution before adjourning the Minorities Committee *sine die* made a suggestion to the delegates. He said :—

"Will you, each of you, every member of this Committee, sign a request to me to settle the community question and pledge yourselves to accept my decision ? That, I think, is a very fair offer . . . I do want any section, or any one man. Will the members of this Committee sign a declaration asking me to give a decision, even a temporary one, on the community question, and say that you will agree ? I do not want it now. I say, will you put your names to it and give that to me, with the assurance that the decision come to will be accepted by you and will be worked by you to the best of your ability in the course of the working of the new constitution ? I have asked several sections—at least, individuals—from time to time for that, and I have never got it. That would certainly straighten out the position, but apart from that, do, please, not forget what I said in opening this meeting—that the Government will not allow community differences to prevent it from carrying out its pledges and producing a constitution. Therefore do not make the community difference more important than it is."

V

Thus ended the efforts by the Minorities Committee to bring about a solution of the communal problem. The discussion in the Committee threw Mr. Gandhi's attitude to the Untouchables in relief. Everybody felt that Mr. Gandhi was the most determined enemy of the Untouchables. So much of his energy and attention did Mr. Gandhi concentrate on the question of the Untouchables that it would not be unfair if it was said that the main purpose for which Mr. Gandhi came to the Round Table Conference was to oppose the demands of the Untouchables.

Those, who were friends of Mr. Gandhi, could not understand Mr. Gandhi's attitude to the demands of the Untouchables. To give recognition to the Muslims and the Sikhs and to refuse it to the Untouchables came to them as a surprise and a puzzle. Whenever they asked for an explanation, Mr. Gandhi did nothing except to get angry. Mr. Gandhi himself could not give a logical and consistent defence of his opposition to the Untouchables. Inside the Round Table Conference his defence was that the Hindus had seriously taken up the cause of the Untouchables and that therefore there was no reason to give them political safeguards. Outside the Round Table Conference he gave totally different reasons. In a speech in defence of his position Mr. Gandhi said :—

> "Muslims and Sikhs are all well organized. The 'Untouchables' are not. There is very little political consciousness among them and they are so horribly treated that I want to save them against themselves. If they had separate electorates their lives would be miserable in villages which are the strongholds of Hindu orthodoxy. It is the superior class of Hindus who have to do penance for having neglected the 'Untouchables' for ages. That penance can be done by active social reform and by making the lot of the 'Untouchables' more bearable by acts of service, but not by asking for separate electorates for them. By giving them separate electorates you will throw the apple of discord between the 'Untouchables' and the orthodox. You must understand I can tolerate the proposal for special representation of the Musalmans and the Sikhs only as a necessary evil. It would be a positive danger for the 'Untouchables.' I am certain that the question of separate electorates for the 'Untouchables' is a modern manufacture of Government. The only thing needed is to put them on the

voters' list, and provide for fundamental rights for them in the constitution. In cases they are unjustly treated and their representative is deliberately excluded they would have the right to special election tribunal which would give them complete protection. It should be open to these tribunals to order the unseating of an elected candidate and the election of the excluded men.

"Separate electorates to the 'Untouchables' will ensure them bondage in perpetuity. The Musalmans will never cease to be Musalmans by having separate electorates. Do you want the 'Untouchables' to remain 'Untouchables' for ever? Well, the separate electorates would perpetuate the stigma. What is needed is destruction of untouchability, and when you have done it, the bar-sinister which has been imposed by an insolent 'superior' class upon an 'inferior' class will be destroyed. When you have destroyed the bar-sinister, to whom will you give the separate electorates? Look at the history of Europe. Have you got separate electorates for the working classes or women? With adult franchise, you give the 'Untouchables' complete security. Even the orthodox would have to approach them for votes.

"Now then you ask, does Dr. Ambedkar, their representative, insist on separate electorates for them? I have the highest regard for Dr. Ambedkar. He has every right to be bitter. That he does not break our heads is an act of self-restraint on his part. He is today so much saturated with suspicion that he cannot see anything else. He sees in every Hindu a determined opponent of the 'Untouchables' and it is quite natural. The same thing happened to me in my early days in South Africa, where I was hounded out by Europeans wherever I went. It is quite natural for him to vent his wrath. But the separate electorates that he seeks will not give him social reform. He may himself mount to power and position but nothing good will accrue to the 'Untouchables.' I can say all this with authority, having lived with the 'Untouchables' and having shared their joys and sorrows all these years."

Mr. Gandhi at the Round Table Conference was not satisfied with mere propaganda. When he found that the propaganda was not succeeding as well as he expected he resorted to intrigue. When Mr. Gandhi heard that at the suggestion of the Prime Minister the minorities were about to produce a settlement and that this settlement would have the effect of the Untouchables getting the support of the other minorities and particularly of the Muslims, Mr. Gandhi felt considerably disturbed. He devised a scheme to isolate the Untouchables. For this Mr. Gandhi planned to buy out the Musalmans by giving to the Musalmans their 14 demands, which Mr. Gandhi was not in the beginning prepared to agree. When Mr. Gandhi found the Musalmans were lending their support to the Untouchables he agreed to them their 14 points on condition that they withdrew their support from the Untouchables. The agreement was actually drafted. The text of it is given below :—

"DRAFT OF GANDHI-MUSLIM PACT[1]

MUSLIM DELEGATION TO THE ROUND TABLE CONFERENCE[2]

Tel. : VICTORIA 2360
Telegrams : "COURTLIKE" LONDON

QUEEN'S HOUSE,
57, ST. JAMES' COURT,
BUCKINGHAM GATE,
LONDON, S.W. 1.
6th October 1931.

The following proposals were discussed by Mr. Gandhi and the Muslim Delegation at 10 p.m. last night. They are divided into two parts—The proposals made by the Muslims for safeguarding their rights and the proposals made by Mr. Gandhi regarding the Congress policy. They are given herewith as approved by Mr. Gandhi, and placed for submission to the Muslim Delegation for their opinion.

MUSLIM PROPOSALS	MR. GANDHI'S PROPOSALS
1. In the Punjab and Bengal bare majority of one per cent. of Musalmans but the question of whether it should be by means of joint electorates and reservation of 51 per cent. of the whole house should be referred to the Musalman voters before the new constitution comes into force and their verdict should be accepted.	1. That the Franchise should be on the basis of adult suffrage. 2. *No special reservations to any other community save Sikhs and Hindu Minorities.* (*Italics are not in the original*) 3. The Congress demands : A. Complete Independence.

[1] This document was printed by me in 1939 in my *Thoughts on Pakistan* as an Appendix. It was the first time it saw the light of the day. Its genuineness has never been questioned. I was able to get a copy from a Hindu Delegate to the Round Table Conference who was privileged by the Muslim League to share the secret.

[2] This shows that the document was typed on the stationery of the Muslim League Delegation.

2. In other provinces where the Musalmans are in a minority the present weightage enjoyed by them to continue, but whether the seats should be reserved to a joint electorate, or whether they should have separate electorates should be determined by the Musalman voters by a referendum under the new constitution, and their verdict should be accepted.

3. That the Musalman representatives to the Central Legislature in both the houses should be 26 per cent. of the total number of the British India representatives, and 7 per cent. at least by convention should be Musalmans, out of the quota that may be assigned to Indian States, that is to say, one-third of the whole house when taken together.

4. That the residuary power should vest in the federating Provinces of British India.

5. That the other points as follows being agreed to :

1. Sindh.[1]
2. N.W.F.P.[2]
3. Services.[3]
4. Cabinet.[4]
5. Fundamental rights and safeguards for religion and culture.
6. Safeguards against legislation affecting any community.

B. Complete control over the defence immediately.

C. Complete control over external affairs.

D. Complete control over Finance.

E. Investigation of public debts and other obligations by an independent tribunal.

F. As in the case of a partnership, right of either party to terminate it.

---

[1] Stands for separation of Sindh.
[2] Stands for Provincial Autonomy and Responsible Government for the N. W. F. Province.
[3] Stands for Representation in Services.
[4] Stands for Representation in the Cabinet.

It is true that the Untouchables are not mentioned in this draft agreement. But that the Musalmans are bound not to support any other minority except the Sikhs makes it quite clear that they were not to support the Untouchables. In this intrigue, Mr. Gandhi failed as he was bound to. The Musalmans who were out to demand safeguards for themselves could not stand up and oppose the demands of the Untouchables. Mr. Gandhi in his passion for suppressing the Untouchables had lost his sense of discrimination to such an extent as not to be able to distinguish between means which are fair and means which are foul. Mr. Gandhi did not care to honour his word. In the Minorities Committee, Mr. Gandhi had said that if the Committee agreed to accept the claim of the Untouchables for separate recognition it was free to do so, which meant that he would abide by the decision of the majority. But when he came to know that the other minorities had agreed to support the Untouchables, he did not hesitate to approach the Musalmans and turn them against the Untouchables by accepting their 14 points which the Congress, the Hindu Mahasabha and even the Simon Commission had rejected. Even if Mr. Gandhi was prepared to flout public opinion and public morality this diabolical plot of Mr. Gandhi fell through because the Musalmans refused to disgrace themselves by joining in it. When the second session of the Round Table Conference was dissolved the delegates to the Minorities Committee accepted the proposal of the Prime Minister to put in a signed requisition authorizing him to arbitrate and give his decision on the communal issue. Many delegates did it including Mr. Gandhi.[1] There was nothing left for the delegates but to return to India and await the decision of the Prime Minister and having made him the sole arbitrator to accept it with good cheer.

VI

Before I resume the narrative and state what decision the Prime Minister gave, I must describe the strange phenomenon which I, as a member of the Franchise Committee, witnessed. After the close of the second session of the Round Table Conference, the Prime Minister thought it advisable to have

[1] I did not make any such requisition. I felt that the demands of the Untouchables were so reasonable that no arbitration was necessary.

the question of franchise for the new constitution examined by a Committee. Accordingly, in December 1931 he appointed a Committee with the late Lord Lothian as its Chairman. Its main term of reference was to devise a system of franchise whereby, to use the language of the Prime Minister's letter of instructions to the Chairman,

> "The legislatures to which responsibility is to be entrusted should be representative of the general mass of the population, and that no important section of the community may lack the means of expressing its needs and its opinions."

The Committee started its work early in January 1932. For doing its work the Committee took the help of the Provincial Governments and of the Provincial Franchise Committees consisting of non-officials specially constituted for that purpose. The Committee issued questionnaires. They were replied to by the Provincial Governments, by the Provincial Franchise Committees and by individuals. Witnesses were examined by the Committee sitting with each Provincial Franchise Committee. The Provincial Governments and the Provincial Committees submitted their reports separately to the Committee. They were discussed by the Committee with the Provincial Government and the Provincial Committee before it came to its own conclusion. Besides the general tasks assigned to the Lothian Committee, it had a special task with which it was charged by the Prime Minister. It had relation to the political demands of the Untouchables which the Prime Minister had referred to in the following terms in his letter of instructions to the Chairman :—

> "It is evident from the discussions which have occurred in various connections in the Conference that the new constitution must make adequate provision for the representation of the Depressed Classes, and that the method of representation by nomination is no longer regarded as appropriate. As you are aware, there is a difference of opinion whether the system of separate electorates should be instituted for the Depressed Classes and your committee's investigations should contribute towards the decision of this question by indicating the extent to which the Depressed Classes would be likely, through such general extension of the franchise as you may recommend, to secure the right to vote in ordinary electorates. On the other hand, should it be decided eventually to constitute separate electorates for the Depressed Classes, either generally or in those

provinces in which they form a distinct and separable element in the population, your Committee's inquiry into the general problem of extending the franchise should place you in possession of facts which would facilitate the devising of a method of separate representation for the Depressed Classes."

Following upon these instructions, it became the task of the Committee to come to some conclusion as to the total population of the Untouchables in British India.

To the question what is the population of the Untouchables, the replies received were enough to stagger anybody. Witness after witness came forward to say that the Untouchables in his Province were infinitesimally small. Witnesses were not wanting to say that there were no Untouchables at all! It was a most extraordinary sight to see Hindu witnesses perjuring themselves regardless of truth by denying the existence of the Untouchables or by reducing their number to a negligible figure. The members of the Provincial Franchise Committee were also a party to this plan. Strange to say that some of the Hindu members of the Lothian Committee were in the game. This move of denying the very existence of the Untouchables or reducing their number almost to nil was particularly rampant in certain Provinces. How the Hindus were prepared to economise truth, even to a vanishing point, will be evident from the following figures. In the United Provinces, the Census Commissioner in 1931 had estimated the total population of the Untouchables at 12.6 millions, the Provincial Government at 6.8 millions but the Provincial Franchise Committee at .6 millions only! In Bengal, the Census gave the figures of 10.3 millions, Provincial Government fixed it as 11.2 millions but the Provincial Franchise Committee at .07 millions only!

Previous to the Round Table Conference no Hindu bothered about the exact population of the Untouchables and were quite satisfied with the accuracy of the Census figures which gave the total of the Untouchables at about 70 to 80 millions. Why did then the Hindus start suddenly to challenge this figure when the question was taken up by the Lothian Committee? The answer is very clear. Before the time of the Lothian Committee the population of the Untouchables had no value. But after the Round Table Conference the Hindus had come to know that the Untouchables were demanding separate allotment of their share of representation, that such share must come out of the lump which the Hindus had been enjoying in the past and that the measure of the share must depend upon the population of the Untouchables. The Hindus had realized that to admit the existence of the Untouchables was detrimental to their interest. They did not mind sacrificing truth and decency and decided to adopt the safest course, namely, to deny that there are any Untouchables in India at all, and thereby knock out the bottom of the political demands of the Untouchables and leave no room for argument. This shows how the Hindus can conspire in a cold, calculated manner against the Untouchables out of pure selfishness and do indirectly what they cannot do directly.

VII

To resume the thread. Having been disgusted with the Round Table Conference where there were critics but no devotees, Mr. Gandhi was the first to return to India. On account of a statement which he is alleged to have made in an interview he gave to a newspaper correspondent in Rome wherein he threatened to revive his campaign of civil disobedience, Mr. Gandhi on his arrival was arrested and put in jail. Though in jail, not Swaraj but the Untouchables were on his brain. He feared that notwithstanding his threat to resist it with his life, the Prime Minister as a sole arbitrator might accept the claims made on behalf of the Untouchables at the Round Table Conference. Long before any decision was given by the Prime Minister, Mr. Gandhi on 11th March 1932 addressed from jail a letter to Sir Samuel Hoare, the then Secretary of State for India, reminding him of his opposition to the claim of the Untouchables. The following is the text of that letter :—

" Dear Sir Samuel,

You will perhaps recollect that at the end of my speech at the Round Table Conference when the Minorities' claim was presented, I had said that I should resist with my life the grant of separate electorates to the Depressed Classes. This was not said in the heat of the moment nor by way of rhetoric. It was meant to be a serious statement. In pursuance of that statement, I had hoped on my return to India to mobilize public opinion against separate electorates, at any rate, for the Depressed Classes. But it was not to be.

"From the newspapers I am permitted to read, I observe that any moment His Majesty's Government may declare their decision. At first I had thought, if the decision was found to create separate electorates for the Depressed Classes, I should take such steps as I might then consider necessary to give effect to my vow. But I feel it would be unfair to the British Government for me to act without giving previous notice. Naturally, they could not attach the significance I give to my statement.

"I need hardly reiterate all the objections I have to the creation of separate electorates for the Depressed Classes. I feel as if I was one of them. Their case stands on a wholly different footing from that of others. I am not against their representation in the legislatures. I should favour everyone of their adults, male and female, being registered as voters irrespective of education or property qualification, even though the franchise test may be stricter for others. But I hold that separate electorate is harmful for them and for Hinduism. whatever it may be from the purely political standpoint. To appreciate the harm that separate electorate would do them, one has to know how they are distributed amongst the so-called Caste Hindus and how dependent they are on the latter. So far as Hinduism is concerned, separate electorates would simply vivisect and disrupt it.

"For me the question of these classes is predominantly moral and religious. The political aspect, important though it is, dwindles into insignificance compared to the moral and religious issue.

"You will have to appreciate my feelings in this matter by remembering that I have been interested in the condition of these classes from my boyhood and have more than once staked my all for their sake. I say this not to pride myself in any way. For, I feel that no penance that the Hindus may do can in any way compensate for the calculated degradation to which they have consigned the Depressed Classes for centuries.

"But I know that separate electorate is neither a penance nor any remedy for the crushing degradation they have groaned under. I, therefore, respectfully inform His Majesty's Government that in the event of their decision creating separate electorate for the Depressed Classes, I must fast unto death.

"I am painfully conscious of the fact that such a step, whilst I am a prisoner, must cause grave embarrassment to His Majesty's Government, and that it will be regarded by many as highly improper on the part of one holding my position to introduce into the political field methods which they would describe as hysterical if not much worse. All I can urge in defence is that for me the contemplated step is not a method, it is part of my being. It is the call of conscience which I dare not disobey, even though it may cost whatever reputation for sanity I may possess. So far as I can see now my discharge from imprisonment would not make the duty of fasting any the less imperative. I am hoping, however, all my fears are wholly unjustified and the British Government have no intention whatever of creating separate electorate for the Depressed Classes."

The following reply was sent to Mr. Gandhi by the Secretary of State :—

INDIA OFFICE, WHITEHALL.
April 13, 1932.

"DEAR MR. GANDHI,

"I write this in answer to your letter of 11th March, and I say at once I realize fully the strength of your feeling upon the question of separate electorates for the Depressed Classes. I can only say that we intend to give any decision that may be necessary solely and only upon the merits of the case. As you are aware, Lord Lothian's Committee has not yet completed its tour and it must be some weeks before we can receive any conclusions at which it may have arrived. When we receive that report we shall have to give most careful consideration to its recommendations, and we shall not give a decision until we have taken into account, in addition to the view expressed by the Committee, the views that you and those who think with you have so forcibly expressed. I feel sure if you were in our position you would be taking exactly the same action we intend to take. You would admit the Committee's report, you would then give it your fullest consideration, and before arriving at a final decision you would take into account the views that have been expressed on both sides of the controversy. More than this I cannot say. Indeed I do not imagine you would expect me to say more."

After giving this warning, Mr. Gandhi slept over the matter thinking that a repetition of his threat to fast unto death was sufficient to paralyse the British Government and prevent them from accepting the claim of the Untouchables for special representation. On the 17th August 1932, the decision of the Prime Minister on the communal question was announced.

That part of the decision which relates to the Untouchables is produced below :—

"In the statement made by the Prime Minister on 1st December last on behalf of His Majesty's Government at the close of the second session of the Round Table Conference, which was immediately afterwards endorsed by both Houses of Parliament, it was made plain that if the communities in India were unable to reach a settlement acceptable to all parties on the communal questions which the Conference had failed to solve, His Majesty's Government were determined that India's constitutional advance should not on that account be frustrated, and that they would remove this obstacle by devising and applying themselves a provisional scheme.

2. On the 19th March last His Majesty's Government, having been informed that the continued failure of the communities to reach agreement was blocking the progress of the plans for the framing of a new Constitution, stated that they were engaged upon a careful re-examination of the difficult and controversial questions which arise. They are now satisfied that without a decision of at least some aspects of the problems connected with the position of minorities under the new Constitution, no further progress can be made with the framing of the Constitution.

3. His Majesty's Government have accordingly decided that they will include provisions to give effect to the scheme set out below in the proposals relating to the Indian Constitution to be laid in due course before Parliament. The scope of this scheme is purposely confined to the arrangements to be made for the representation of the British Indian communities in the Provincial Legislatures, consideration of representation in the Legislature at the Centre being deferred for the reason given in paragraph 20 below. The decision to limit the scope of the scheme implies no failure to realize that the framing of the Constitution will necessitate the decision of a number of other problems of great importance to minorities, but has been taken in the hope that once a pronouncement has been made upon the basic questions of method and proportions of representation the communities themselves may find it possible to arrive at *modus vivendi* on other communal problems, which have not received the examination they require.

4. His Majesty's Government wish it to be most clearly understood that they themselves can be no parties to any negotiations which may be initiated with a view to the revision of their decision, and will not be prepared to give consideration to any representation aimed at securing the modification of it

which is not supported by all the parties affected. But they are most desirous to close no door to an agreed settlement should such happily be forthcoming. If, therefore, before a new Government of India Act has passed into law, they are satisfied that the communities who are concerned are mutually agreed upon a practicable alternative scheme, either in respect of any one or more of the Governors' Provinces or in respect of the whole of the British India, they will be prepared to recommend to Parliament that that alternative should be substituted for the provisions now outlined.

5. * * * * *

6. * * * * *

7. * * * * *

8. * * * * *

9. Members of the " depressed classes " qualified to vote will vote in a general constituency. In view of the fact that for a considerable period these classes would be unlikely, by this means alone, to secure any adequate representation in the Legislature, a number of special seats will be assigned to them as shown in the table. These seats will be filled by election from special constituencies in which only members of the " depressed classes " electorally qualified will be entitled to vote. Any person voting in such a special constituency will, as stated above, be also entitled to vote in a general constituency. It is intended that these constituencies should be formed in selected areas where the depressed classes are most numerous, and that, except in Madras, they should not cover the whole area of the Province.

In Bengal it seems possible that in some general constituencies a majority of the voters will belong to the Depressed Classes. Accordingly, pending further investigation, no number has been fixed for the members to be returned from the special Depressed Class constituencies in that Province. It is intended to secure that the Depressed Classes should obtain not less than 10 seats in the Bengal Legislature.

The precise definition in each Province of those who (if electorally qualified) will be entitled to vote in the special Depressed Class constituencies has not yet been finally determined. It will be based as a rule on the general principles advocated in the Franchise Committee's Report. Modification may, however, be found necessary in some Provinces in Northern India where the application of the general criteria of untouchability might result in a definition unsuitable in some respects to the special conditions of the Province.

His Majesty's Government do not consider that these special Depressed Classes constituencies will be required for more than limited time. They intend that the Constitution shall provide that they shall come to an end after 20 years if they have not previously been abolished under the general powers of electoral revision referred to in paragraph 6."

VIII

Mr. Gandhi found that his threat had failed to have any effect. He did not care that he was a signatory to the requisition asking the Prime Minister to arbitrate. He forgot that as a signatory to the requisition he was bound to accept the award. He started to undo what the Prime Minister had done. He first tried to get the terms of the Communal Award revised. Accordingly, he addressed the following letter to the Prime Minister :—

" YERAVDA CENTRAL PRISON,
August 18, 1932.

DEAR FRIEND,

There can be no doubt that Sir Samuel Hoare has showed you and the Cabinet my letter to him of 11th March on the question of the representation of the Depressed Classes. That letter should be treated as part of this letter and be read together with this.

I have read the British Government's decision on the representation of minorities and have slept over it. In pursuance of my letter to Sir Samuel Hoare and my declaration at the meeting of the Minorities Committee of the Round Table Conference on 13th November, 1931, at St. James' Palace, I have to resist your decision with my life. The only way I can do so is by declaring a perpetual fast unto death from food of any kind save water with or without salt and soda. This fast will cease if during its progress the British Government, of its own motion or under pressure of public opinion, revise their decision and withdraw their scheme of communal electorates for the Depressed Classes, whose representatives should be elected by the general electorate under the common franchise, no matter how wide it is.

The proposed fast will come into operation in the ordinary course from the noon of 20th September next, unless the said decision is meanwhile revised in the manner suggested above,

I am asking the authorities here to cable the text of this letter to you so as to give you ample notice. But in any case, I am leaving sufficient time for this letter to reach you in time by the slowest route.

I also ask that this letter and my letter to Sir Samuel Hoare already referred to be published at the earliest possible moment. On my part, I have scrupulously observed the rule of the jail and have communicated my desire or the contents of the two letters to no one, save my two companions, Sardar Vallabhbhai Patel and Mr. Mahadev Desai. But I want, if you make it possible, public opinion to be affected by my letters. Hence my request for their early publication.

I regret the decision I have taken. But as a man of religion that I hold myself to be, I have no other course left open to me. As I have said in my letter to Sir Samuel Hoare, even if His Majesty's Government decided to release me in order to save themselves from embarrassment, my fast will have to continue. For, I cannot now hope to resist the decision by any other means; and I have no desire whatsoever to compass my release by any means other than honourable.

It may be that my judgment is warped and that I am wholly in error in regarding separate electorates for the Depressed Classes as harmful to them or to Hinduism. If so, I am not likely to be in the right with reference to other parts of my philosophy of life. In that case, my death by fasting will be at once a penance for my error and a lifting of a weight from off these numberless men and women who have childlike faith in my wisdom. Whereas if my judgment is right, as I have little doubt it is, the contemplated step is but due to the fulfilment of the scheme of life which I have tried for more than a quarter of a century, apparently not without considerable success.

I remain,
Your faithful friend,
M. K. Gandhi."

The Prime Minister replied as under :—

"10, Downing Street,
September 8th, 1932.

Dear Mr. Gandhi,

I have received your letter with much surprise and, let me add, with very sincere regret. Moreover, I cannot help thinking that you have written it under a misunderstanding as to what the decision of His Majesty's Government as regards the

Depressed Classes really implies. We have always understood you were irrevocably opposed to the permanent segregation of the Depressed Classes from the Hindu community. You made your position very clear on the Minorities Committee of the Round Table Conference and you expressed it again in the letter you wrote to Sir Samuel Hoare on 11th March. We also knew your view was shared by the great body of Hindu opinion, and we, therefore, took it into most careful account when we were considering the question of representation of the Depressed Classes.

Whilst, in view of the numerous appeals we have received from Depressed Class Organizations and the generally admitted social disabilities under which they labour and which you have often recognized, we felt it our duty to safeguard what we believe to be the right of the Depressed Classes to a fair proportion of representation in the legislatures, we were equally careful to do nothing that would split off their community from the Hindu world. You yourself stated in your letter of March 11, that you were not against their representation in the legislatures.

Under the Government scheme the Depressed Classes will remain part of the Hindu community and will vote with the Hindu electorate on an equal footing but for the first twenty years, while still remaining electorally part of the Hindu community, they will receive through a limited number of special constituencies, means of safeguarding their rights and interests that, we are convinced, is necessary under present conditions.

Where these constituencies are created, members of the Depressed Classes will not be deprived of their votes in the general Hindu constituencies, but will have two votes in order that their membership of the Hindu community should remain unimpaired.

We have deliberately decided against the creation of what you describe as a communal electorate for the Depressed Classes and included all Depressed Class voters in the general or Hindu constituencies so that the higher caste candidates should have to solicit their votes or Depressed Class candidates should have to solicit the votes of the higher castes at elections. Thus, in every way was the unity of Hindu society preserved.

We felt, however, that during the early period of responsible Government, when power in the Provinces would pass to whoever possessed a majority in the legislatures, it was essential that the Depressed Classes whom you have yourself described in your letter to Sir Samuel Hoare as having been consigned by Caste Hindus to calculated degradation for centuries, should return a certain number of members of their own choosing to legislatures of seven of the nine provinces to voice their grievances and their ideals and prevent decisions going against them without the legislature and the Government listening to their case—in a word, to place them in a position to speak for themselves, which every fair-minded person must agree to be necessary. We did not consider the method of electing special representatives by reservation of seats in the existing conditions, under any system of franchise which is practicable, members who could genuinely represent them and be responsible for them, because in practically all cases, such members would be elected by a majority consisting of higher caste Hindus.

The special advantage initially given under our scheme to the Depressed Classes by means of a limited number of special constituencies, in addition to their normal electoral rights in the general Hindu constituencies, is wholly different in conception and effect from the method of representation adopted for a minority such as the Moslems by means of separate communal electorates. For example, a Moslem cannot vote or be a candidate in a general constituency, whereas any electorally qualified member of the Depressed Classes can vote in and stand for the general constituency.

The number of territorial seats allotted to Moslems is naturally conditioned by the fact that it is impossible for them to gain any further territorial seats and in most provinces they enjoy weightage in excess of their population ratio ; the number of special seats to be filled from special Depressed Classes constituencies will be seen to be small and has been fixed not to provide a quota numerically appropriate for the total representation of the whole of the Depressed Class population, but solely to secure a minimum number of spokesmen for the Depressed Classes in the legislatures who are chosen exclusively by the Depressed Classes. The proportion of their special seats is everywhere much below the population percentage of the Depressed Classes.

As I understand your attitude, you propose to adopt the extreme course of starving yourself to death not in order to secure that the Depressed Classes should have joint electorate with other Hindus, because that is already provided, nor to maintain the unity of Hindus, which is also provided, but solely to prevent the Depressed Classes, who admittedly suffer from terrible disabilities to-day, from being able to secure a limited number of representatives of their own choosing to speak on their behalf in the legislatures which will have a dominating influence over their future.

In the light of these very fair and cautious proposals, I am quite unable to understand the reason of the decision you have taken and can only think you have made it under a misapprehension of the actual facts.

In response to a very general request from Indians after they had failed to produce a settlement themselves the Government much against its will, undertook to give a decision on the minorities question. They have now given it, and they cannot be expected to alter it except on the condition they have stated. I am afraid, therefore, that my answer to you must be that the Government's decision stands and that only agreement of the communities themselves can substitute other electoral arrangements for those that Government have devised in a sincere endeavour to weigh the conflicting claims on their just merits.

You ask that this correspondence, including your letter to Sir Samuel Hoare of March 11th, should be published. As it would seem to me unfair if your present internment were to deprive you of the opportunity of explaining to the public the reason why you intend to fast, I readily accede to the request, if on reconsideration you repeat it. Let me, however, once again urge you to consider the actual details of Government's decision and ask yourself seriously the question whether it really justifies you in taking the action you contemplate.

I am,
Yours very sincerely,
J. RAMSAY MACDONALD."

Finding that the Prime Minister would not yield he sent him the following letter informing him that he was determined to carry out his threat of fast unto death :—

" YERAVDA CENTRAL PRISON,
September 9th, 1932.

DEAR FRIEND,

I have to thank you for your frank and full letter telegraphed and received this day. I am sorry, however, that you put upon the contemplated step an interpretation that never crossed my mind. I have claimed to speak on behalf of the very class, to sacrifice whose interests you impute to me a desire to fast myself to death. I had hoped that the extreme step itself would effectively prevent any such selfish interpretation. Without arguing, I affirm that for me this matter is one of pure religion. The mere fact of the Depressed Classes having double votes does not protect them or Hindu society in general from being disrupted. In the establishment of separate electorate at all for the Depressed Classes I sense the injection of poison that is calculated to destroy Hinduism and do no good whatever to the Depressed Classes. You will please permit me to say that no matter how sympathetic you may be, you cannot come to a correct decision on a matter of such vital and religious importance to the parties concerned.

I should not be against even over-representation of the Depressed Classes. What I am against is their statutory separation even in a limited form, from the Hindu fold, so long as they choose to belong to it. Do you realize that if your decision stands and the constitution comes into being, you arrest the marvellous growth of the work of Hindu reformers, who have dedicated themselves to the uplift of their suppresssed brethren in every walk of life ?

I have, therefore, been compelled reluctantly to adhere to the decision conveyed to you.

As your letter may give rise to a misunderstanding, I wish to state that the fact of my having isolated for special treatment the Depressed Classes question from other parts of your decision does not in any way mean that I approve of or am reconciled to other parts of the decision. In my opinion, many other parts are open to very grave objection. Only, I do not consider them to be any warrant for calling from me such self immolation as my conscience has promoted me to in the matter of the Depressed Classes.

I remain,
Your faithful friend,
M. K. Gandhi."

Accordingly, on the 20th September 1932, Mr. Gandhi commenced his "fast unto death" as a protest against the grant of separate electorates to the Untouchables.

The story of this fact has been told by Mr. Pyarelal in a volume which bears the picturesque and flamboyant title of *The Epic Fast*. The curious may refer it. I must, however, warn him that it is written by a Boswell and has all the faults of a Boswelliana. There is another side to it, but there is neither time nor space to present it here. All I can do is to invite attention to the statement[1] I issued to the Press on the eve of Mr. Gandhi's fast exposing his tactics. Suffice it to say that although Mr. Gandhi declared a fast unto death, he did not want to die. He wanted very much to live.

[1] Appendix IV.

The fast nonetheless created a problem, and that prolem was how to save Mr. Gandhi's life. The only way to save his life was to alter the Communal Award which Mr. Gandhi said hurt his conscience so much. The Prime Minister had made it quite clear that the British Cabinet would not withdraw it or alter it of its own, but that they were ready to substitute for it a formula that may be agreed upon by the Caste Hindus and the Untouchables. As I had the privilege of representing the Untouchables at the Round Table Conference, it was assumed that the assent of the Untouchables would not be valid unless I was a party to it. The surprising fact is that my position as the leader of the Untouchables of India was not only not questioned by Congressmen but it was accepted as a fact. All eyes naturally turned to me as the man of the moment or rather as the villain of the piece.

As to myself, it is no exaggeration to say that no man was placed in a greater and graver dilemma than I was then. It was a baffling situation. I had to make a choice between two different alternatives. There was before me the duty, which I owed as a part of common humanity, to save Gandhi from sure death. There was before me the problem of saving for the Untouchables the political rights which the Prime Minister had given them. I responded to the call of humanity and saved the life of Mr. Gandhi by agreeing to alter the Communal Award in a manner satisfactory to Mr. Gandhi. This agreement is known as the Poona Pact. The following is the text of the agreement :—

Text of Poona Pact

(1) There shall be seats reserved for the Depressed Classes out of the general electorate seats in the Provincial Legislatures as follows :

Madras 30; Bombay with Sind 15; Punjab 8; Bihar and Orissa 18; Central Provinces 20; Assam 7; Bengal 30; United Provinces 20; Total 148.

These figures are based on the total strength of the Provincial Councils, announced in the Prime Minister's decision.

(2) Election to these seats shall be by joint electorates subject, however, to the following procedure :

All the members of the Depressed Classes, registered in the general electoral roll in a constituency, will form an electoral college, which will elect a panel of four candidates belonging to the Depressed Classes for each of such reserved seats, by the method of the single vote ; the four persons getting the highest number of votes in such primary election, shall be candidates for election by the general electorate.

(3) Representation of the Depressed Classes in the Central Legislature shall likewise be on the principle of joint electorates and reserved seats by the method of primary election in the manner provided for in Clause 2 above, for their representation in the Provincial Legislatures.

(4) In the Central Legislature, eighteen per cent. of the seats allotted to the general electorate for British India in the said legislature shall be reserved for the Depressed Classes.

(5) The system of primary election to a panel of candidates for election to the Central and Provincial Legislatures, as hereinbefore mentioned, shall come to an end after the first ten years, unless terminated sooner by mutual agreement under the provision of Clause 6 below.

(6) The system of representation of the Depressed Classes by reserved seats in the Provincial and Central Legislatures as provided for in Clauses 1 and 4 shall continue until determined by mutual agreement between the communities concerned in the settlement.

(7) Franchise for the Central and Provincial Legislatures for the Depressed Classes shall be as indicated in the Lothian Committee Report.

(8) There shall be no disabilities attaching to any one on the ground of his being a member of the Depressed Classes in regard to any elections to local bodies or appointment to the Public Services. Every endeavour shall be made to secure fair representation of the Depressed Classes in these respects, subject to such educational qualifications as may be laid down for appointment to the Public Services.

(9) In every province out of the educational grant, an adequate sum shall be earmarked for providing educational facilities to the Members of the Depressed Classes.

The terms of the Pact were accepted by Mr. Gandhi and given effect to by Government by embodying them in the Government of India Act. The Poona Pact had produced different reactions. The Untouchables were sad. They had every reason to be. There are, however, people who do not accept this. They never fail to point out that the Poona Pact gave the Untouchables larger number of seats than what was given to them by the Prime Minister in his Communal

Award. It is true that the Poona Pact gave the Untouchables 148 seats, while the Award had only given them 78. But to conclude from this that the Poona Pact gave them more than what was given by the Award is to ignore what the Award had in fact given to the Untouchables.

The Communal Award gave the Untouchables two benefits :—(i) a fixed quota of seats to be elected by separate electorate of Untouchables and to be filled by persons belonging to the Untouchables ; (ii) double vote, one to be used through separate electorates and the other to be used in the general electorates.

Now, if the Poona Pact increased the quota of seats for the Untouchables it took away the right to the double vote given to them by the Communal Award. This increase in seats can never be deemed to be a compensation for the loss of the double vote. The second vote given by the Communal Award was a priceless privilege. Its value as a political weapon was beyond reckoning. The voting strength of the Untouchables in each constituency is one to ten. With this voting strength free to be used in the election of caste Hindu candidates, the Untouchables would have been in a position to determine, if not to dictate, the issue of the General Election. No caste Hindu candidate could have dared to neglect the Untouchable in his constituency or be hostile to their interest, if he was made dependent upon the votes of the Untouchables. Today the Untouchables have a few more seats than were given to them by the Communal Award. But this is all that they have. Every other member is indifferent, if not hostile. If the Communal Award with its system of double voting had remained, the Untouchables would have had a few seats less but every other member would have been a member for the Untouchables. The increase in the number of seats for the Untouchables is no increase at all and was no recompense for the loss of separate electorate and the double vote. The Hindus, although they did not celebrate the Poona Pact, did not like it. Throughout their commotion to save Mr. Gandhi's life there was a definite current of conscious feeling that the cost of saving his life may be great. Therefore, when they saw the terms of the Pact they very definitely disliked it, although they had not the courage to reject it. Disliked by the Hindus and disfavoured by the Untouchables, the Poona Pact was given recognition by both parties and was embodied in the Government of India Act.

IX

The signing of the Poona Pact was followed by the appointment of the Hammond Committee to demarcate constituencies, to fix the number of seats for each constituency and settle the system of voting for the legislatures to be set up under the new constitution.

In carrying out its functions, the Hammond Committee had to take into account the terms of the Poona Pact and the special sort of electoral plan agreed upon to meet the needs of the Untouchables. Unfortunately, the Poona Pact having been concluded in a hurry had left many things undefined. Of the things that were left undefined the most important were two namely : (1) Does the 'panel of four' to be elected at the primary election imply four as a maximum or a minimum ? (2) What was intended to be the method of voting in the final election ? It was contended on behalf of the Hindus that the panel of four was intended to be a minimum. If four candidates are not forthcoming there could be no primary election and therefore there can be no election for the reserved seat, which they said must remain vacant and the Untouchables should go without representation. On behalf of the Untouchables, I was called to state my interpretation of the disputed points. I contended that four in the Poona Pact meant "not more than four." It did not mean "not less than four." On the question of voting, the Hindus contended that the compulsory distributive vote was the most appropriate method. On behalf of the Untouchables I contended that the cumulative system of voting was the proper system to be introduced. Fortunately for the Untouchables the Hammond Committee accepted the views propounded by me and rejected those put forth by the Hindus.

It is interesting to know why the caste Hindus put forth this proposal. There is no doubt that it was not a matter of honest feeling which led the Hindus to insist that the Poona Pact by its terms required a minimum of four candidates as a condition for a valid primary election and failure to comply with it meant a violation of the Poona Pact. It was undoubtedly a matter of strategy, the motive behind which was to prepare the ground so as to make it easy for the Hindus to get an Untouchable candidate who though a statutory representative of the Untouchables would be willing to be a nominee and a tool of the Hindus elected with the help of Hindu votes. The Hindus had, it seems, made it their objective to defeat the purpose of the Poona Pact by this means. But they also knew that such a consummation which they so devoutly wished for, cannot happen, if in the Primary election there is only one Untouchable candidate for the simple reason that when there is only one Untouchable candidate he is bound to be automatically elected in the final election leaving the Hindus with no chance for manipulation. If there were two Untouchable candidates in the primary election the situation from the point of view of the Hindus is better. For such a situation is bound to lead to a final election which would give a chance to the Hindus to manipulate by winning over one of the two candidates and then getting him elected with Hindu votes and then use him as the tool of the Hindus. Even with two, the Hindus can't be sure of having a hand in the election to the seat reserved for the Untouchables. For it may be quite possible for the Untouchables to persuade one of the two candidates to withdraw and thereby nullify the prospect of final election. With three in a primary election the Hindus have more certainty of taking matters to the stage of final election because if one is made to withdraw at least two would remain requiring a final election to settle their claim to represent the Untouchables. With four candidates in the primary election the chances of the Hindus for winning the seat for their nominee are much brighter than they are when there are three and so on. This is, I am sure, the motive which made the Hindus put forth such absurd proposal before the Hammond Committee. This throws a flood of light on the Hindu mentality of making by the right hand a concession which they cannot oppose and stealing it away by the left.

The object of insisting upon the system of compulsory distributive vote was the same namely to enable the Hindus to capture the seats reserved for the Untouchables. Under the cumulative vote the elector has as many votes as there are seats. He may give them all to one candidate or he may distribute them over two or more candidates as he may desire. Under the distributive system of voting the elector has also as many votes as there are seats, but he can give only one vote to any one candidate. Although the two look different yet in effect there may be no difference, because even under the cumulative vote a voter is not prevented from distributing his votes. He is free to give one vote to one candidate. But the Hindus did not want to take any chance. Their main object was to flood the election to the seat reserved for the Untouchables in the joint electorate by using the surplus votes of the Hindus in favour of the Untouchable candidate, who happens to be their nominee. The object was to outnumber the Untouchable voters and prevent them from electing their own nominee. This cannot be done unless the surplus votes of the Hindu voters were diverted from the Hindu candidate towards the Untouchable candidates. There is a greater chance of the diversion of these surplus votes under the distributive system than there is under the cumulative system. Under the former the Hindu voter can give only one vote to the Hindu candidate. The other vote not being of use to the Hindu candidate is usable only for an Untouchable candidate. The distributive system thus had the possibility of flooding the election to the seat reserved for the Untouchables and this is why the Hindus preferred it to the system of cumulative voting. But they did not want to leave it to chance. For, even the distributive system from their point of view was not fool-proof. Under the distributive system there was no compulsion upon the voter to use all his votes. He may use one vote for the caste Hindu candidate and may not at all use the balance of his votes. If this happened the purpose of getting in their Untouchable nominee would be defeated. Not to leave things to chance, the Hindus wanted that the distributive system of voting should be made compulsory so that a caste Hindu voter whether he wants it or not can have no option but to vote for the Untouchable candidate who may be the nominee of the Hindus, and thus make his election sure and certain.

In the light of these considerations, it cannot but appear that the Poona Pact was only the first blow inflicted upon the Untouchables and that the Hindus who disliked it were bent on inflicting on it other blows as and when circumstances gave them an occasion to do so. The two contentions, which the Hindus raised before the Hammond Committee, furnish the best evidence of the existence of a conspiracy by the Hindus the object of which was to make the Poona Pact, as it could not be repudiated, of no benefit to the Untouchables. The story of how the Congress dealt with the political demands of the Untouchables cannot be left here for the simple reason that it does not end here. The subsequent parts of it are more instructive than those that have gone before.

X

Continuing the story, the next part of it relates to the election that took place in February 1937 to the Provincial Legislatures, as reconstituted under the Government of India Act, 1935. This was the first occasion in its life-time that the Congress came down to fight an election. It was also the first time that the Untouchables got the privilege to elect their own representatives. Some leaders of the Untouchables, who were siding with the Congress when the Poona Pact was being forged—such as the late Dewan Bahadur M.C. Raja—cherished the fond hope that the Congress will not inter-meddle in the elections of the Untouchables to the seats reserved for them. But this hope was dashed to pieces. The Congress had a double purpose to play its part in the election to the reserved seats of the Untouchables. In the first place, it was out to capture in order to build up its majority which was essential for enabling it to form a Government. In the second place, it had to prove the statement of Mr. Gandhi that the Congress represented the Untouchables and that the Untouchables believed in the Congress. The Congress, therefore, did not hesitate to play a full, mighty and, I may say so, a malevolent part in the election of the Untouchables by putting up Untouchable candidates on Congress ticket pledged to Congress programme for seats reserved for the Untouchables. With the financial resources of the Congress it made a distinct gain.

The total number of seats allotted to the Untouchables under the Government of India Act, 1935 is 151.[1] The following table (see page 95) shows how many were captured by the Untouchable candidates who stood on the Congress Ticket.

This shows that the Congress got just about 51 per cent of the seats reserved for the Untouchables.

The Congress in capturing 78 seats left only 73 seats to be filled by true and independent representatives of the Untouchables. The Untouchables were worse off under the Poona Pact than they would have been under the Prime Minister's Award.

---

[1] This number of 148 seats was raised to 151 in making adjustments of seats for Bihar and Orissa.

In point of effective representation, the Untouchables got less than what the Prime Minister had given them. The Congress on the other hand gained by the Poona Pact. Although under the Poona Pact it gave 151 to the Untouchables it took back 78 and thereby made a handsome profit on its political transaction.[1]

Table 6

Province	*Total Seats Reserved for the Untouchables*	*Total Seats Captured by the Congress*
United Provinces	20	16
Madras	30	26
Bengal	30	6
Central Provinces	20	7
Bombay	15	4
Bihar	15	11
Punjab	8	*Nil.*
Assam	7	4
Orissa	6	4
Total ...	151	78

XI

This is by no means the sum total of the losses which the Congress inflicted on the Untouchables in the elections of 1937. There was another and a greater blow which the Congress inflicted on the Untouchables. It deprived them of any share in the Executive.

From the very beginning, I had been pressing in the discussions in the Round Table Conference that the Untouchables must not only have the right to be represented in the legislature, they must also have the right to be represented in the Cabinet. The woes of the Untouchables are not due so much to bad laws as to the hostility of the administration, which is controlled by the Hindus who import into administration their age-old prejudices against the Untouchables. The Untouchables can never hope to get protection from the police, justice from the judiciary or benefit of a statutory law from the administrators, so long as the Public Services continue to be manned by the Hindus. The only hope of making the Public Services

[1] For a detailed analysis of these 78 seats see Chapter VI.

less malevolent and more responsible to the needs of the Untouchables, is to have members of the Untouchables in the higher Executive. For these reasons, I had at the Round Table Conference pressed the claim of the Untouchables for the recognition of their right to representation in the Cabinet with the same emphasis as I had done for the recognition of their right to representation in the Legislature. The Round Table Conference accepted the validity of the claim and considered ways and means of giving effect to it. There were two ways of giving effect to this proposal. One was to have a statutory provision in the Government of India Act so as to make it a binding obligation which it would be impossible to evade or to escape ; the other way was not to have a statutory provision but to leave it to a gentleman's agreement—to a convention—as is the case in the English Constitution. I and the representatives of the other minorities although we did not insist upon the first in deference to the wishes of some leading Indians not to show such distrust in our own countrymen were not prepared to accept the second alternative as there was no enforceable sanction behind it. A *via media* was agreed upon. It was to introduce a clause in the Instrument of Instructions to the Governors imposing an obligation upon them to see that in the formation of the Cabinet representatives of the Minorities were included. The clause ran as follows :—

> " In making appointments to his Council of Ministers our Governor shall use his best endeavours to select his Ministers in the following manner, that is to say, to appoint in consultation with the person who in his judgment is most likely to command a stable majority in the Legislature those persons (including so far as practicable members of important minority communities) who will best be in a position collectively to command the confidence of the Legislature. In so acting, he shall bear constantly in mind the need for fostering a sense of joint responsibility among his Ministers."

What happened to this provision is an interesting story. The Congress declared that they were not prepared to accept the Government of India Act 1935 for various reasons which it is not necessary to reproduce. It was obvious to all and even to many Congressmen that there was no sincerity behind this declaration. Behind this show of non-acceptance there was no other motive but to enhance the prestige of the Congress in the eyes of the public by making it appear that the Congress was a radical and revolutionary body which was out to destroy and bury British Imperialism. It was a mere matter of tactics. The Congress wanted to take the powers which the Governors had been given under the Constitution to intervene whenever matters which were his special responsibilities were involved. The Congress did not mind making the declaration rejecting the Constitution because it thought that as it was the only body which could run the new Parliamentary system the British Government would be obliged to come to terms with it. The British Government threatened to bypass the Congress. It not only appointed 1st April 1937 as the date of the inauguration of the Provincial part of the Constitution but actually went to the length of appointing an interim Ministry of non-Congressmen. Congressmen, who were hungering for power and who constitute a most jealous crowd of politicians, were shaken and felt that they were going to be deprived of the fruits of their labours. Negotiations were started between His Majesty's Government and the Congress High Command. The Congress High Command demanded that if an undertaking was given by His Majesty's Government that the Governors will not use their powers given to them under the Special Responsibility Clauses in the Constitution by interfering in the day to day administration of the Provinces, the Government which was most anxious that the new Constitution should begin to operate with the goodwill of the majority, agreed to give the undertaking demanded. The surprising part of it is that the Congress High Command enlarged the scope of this undertaking so as to include in the undertaking the non-exercise, by the Governors of the Provinces, of the powers given to them under the Instruments of Instructions to see that the representatives of the minorities were included in the Provincial Ministries. The Governors who gave full accommodation to the Congress surrendered their authority and allowed the Congress to ride rough shod through a very important part of the Constitution with the result that the Untouchables and the other minorities were deprived of their right to representation in the Cabinet by the Congress with impunity and with alacrity.

The deprivation of the Untouchables by the Congress of their right to representation in the Cabinet has the appearance of malice aforethought. One of the grounds, urged by the Congress for the non-inclusion of representatives of the minorities in their Cabinets, was that a cabinet must be a party Cabinet if it is to take collective responsibility and that the Congress was quite ready to include members of the Minority communities in its Cabinet provided they were prepared to join the Congress and sign the Congress pledge. Whatever may be the value of such argument against other minorities, it had absolutely no value against the Untouchables. The Congress could not use it to defend its conduct in excluding the Untouchables from the Cabinet for two reasons. In the first place, the Congress was bound by the terms of the Poona Pact to give representation to the Untouchables in the Cabinet. In the second place, the Congress could not say that there were no Untouchables in the Legislatures who were not members of the Congress Party. On the contrary, there were as many as 78 Untouchables returned on the Congress ticket and pledged to the Congress policy. Why then did the Congress not include them in the Cabinet ? The only answer is that it was a part of the Congress policy not to admit the right of the Untouchables to be represented in the Cabinet and that this policy had the support of Mr. Gandhi. Those who may have any doubt as to the correctness of this statement may well consider the evidence set out below.

The first piece of evidence lies imbedded in the story of the expulsion of the Hon'ble Dr. Khare from the Congress. As is well-known, Dr. Khare was the Prime Minister in the Congress Ministry in the Central Provinces. To end the internal quarrels among the members of his Cabinet, and to get rid of those that were inconvenient to him, Dr. Khare adopted the perfectly normal course of tendering his own resignation and that of the other ministers to the Governor with a view to form a new Cabinet. Thereafter, the Governor in full conformity with constitutional practice recalled Dr. Khare and asked him to form another Cabinet with himself as the Premier. Dr. Khare accepted the invitation and formed a new Cabinet dropping old and inconvenient hands and taking in some new ones. Dr. Khare's new Cabinet was different from the old in one important respect namely, that it included Mr. Agnibhoj, an Untouchable, who was a member of the Legislative Assembly of the Central Provinces, who belonged to the Congress Party and who by his education was well qualified to be a minister. On the 26th July 1938, the Congress Working Committee met in Wardha and passed a resolution condemning Dr. Khare on the ground that in tendering the resignation of his colleagues in the old ministry he was guilty of a grave error of judgment and that in forming a new ministry he was guilty of indiscipline. In explaining what was behind this charge of indiscipline in forming a new ministry, Dr. Khare openly said that according to Mr. Gandhi the act of indiscipline consisted in the inclusion of an Untouchable in the Ministry. Dr. Khare also said that Mr. Gandhi told him that it was wrong on his part to have raised such aspirations and ambitions in the Untouchables and it was such an act of bad judgment that he would never forgive him. This statement was repeatedly made by Dr. Khare from platforms. Mr. Gandhi has never contradicted it.

There is, however, more direct evidence on this point. In 1942 there was held All-India Conference of the Untouchables. In that Conference resolutions setting out the political demands of the Untouchables were passed. An Untouchable of the Congress Party who attended the Conference went to Mr. Gandhi to ascertain what Mr. Gandhi had to say about these demands and put him the following five questions :—

> " 1. What will be the position of the Harijans in the future constitution to be framed ?
>
> " 2. Will you advise the Government and the Congress to agree to fix the five seats from a Panchayat Board upwards to the State Council on population basis ?
>
> " 3. Will you advise the Congress and the leaders of the various majority parties in the legislatures in the provinces to nominate the Cabinet members from among the Scheduled Caste legislators who enjoy the confidence of the majority of Scheduled Caste members ?
>
> " 4. In view of the backwardness of the Harijans, will you advise the Government to make a provision in the Act that *Executive posts* in the Local Boards and Municipal Councils be held on communal rotation, so as to enable the Harijans to become Presidents and Chairmen ?
>
> " 5. Why do you not fix some percentage of seats for Harijans from District Congress Committee upwards to the Working Committee of the Congress ?

Mr. Gandhi gave his answers in the issue of the *Harijan* dated 2nd August 1942. This is what Mr. Gandhi said :—

> " 1. The constitution, which I could influence, would contain a provision making the observance of untouchability in any shape or form an offence. The so-called ' untouchables '

would have seats reserved for them in all elected bodies according to their population within the elected area concerned.

"2. You will see that the answer is covered by the foregoing.

"3. I cannot. The principle is dangerous. Protection of its neglected classes should not be carried to an extent which will harm them and harm the country. A cabinet minister should be a topmost man commanding universal confidence. A person after he has secured a seat in an elected body should depend upon his intrinsic merit and popularity to secure coveted positions.

"4. In the first place, I am not interested in the present Act which is as good as dead. But I am opposed to your proposal on the ground already mentioned.

"5. I am opposed for the reasons mentioned. But I should like to compel large elective Congress organizations to ensure the election of Harijan members in proportion to their numbers on the Congress register. If Harijans are not interested enough in the Congress to become 4 anna members, they may not expect to find their names in elective bodies. But I would strongly advise Congress workers to see that they approach Harijans and induce them to become members of the Congress."

Is there any doubt that Mr. Gandhi and the Congress were determined on principle not to recognize the right of the Untouchables to be represented in the Cabinet? As to the question of qualifications, there would have been some sense if Mr. Gandhi had that limiting condition applicable to all minorities. Dare Mr. Gandhi say that about the Muslim demand? What is the use in strutting it out in the case of the Untouchables only! Nobody has claimed that an unqualified Untouchable should be made a Minister. It only confirms the inner feeling of opposition that lies locked in the heart of Mr. Gandhi.

XII

In the series of acts, which the Congress perpetrated in order to nullify the Poona Pact, there remain two more to mention. First relates to the policy adopted by the Congress Parliamentary Board in selecting candidates for election. Unfortunately, this question has not been studied as deeply as its importance demands. I have examined this question and I hope to publish the results along with the evidence in a separate treatise. Here, all I can do is to set out the general principles which seem to have been adopted by these Boards in selecting candidates for election. Communal principle played a very great part in it. In a constituency where there were two candidates to choose from, the Congress did not feel it necessary to choose the one more worthy. It chose him who belonged to a more populous caste. Considerations of wealth also played their part. A wealthier candidate was often preferred to a poor and a better qualified candidate. These considerations were unjustifiable. But they could be understood as the object was to adopt a safe candidate who will pull through.

But there were other principles followed which reveal a deep-seated plot. Different classes of qualifications were set down for different classes of candidates. From candidates who came from high caste Hindus as Brahmins and the allied communities those with the highest qualifications were selected. In the case of the Non-Brahmins those with low qualifications were preferred to those with higher qualifications. And in the case of the Untouchables those with little or no qualifications were selected in preference to those who had. I don't say that is true in every case. But the general result was that of the candidates selected by the Congress, the candidates from the Brahmin and allied communities were the most highly educated, candidates from the non-Brahmins were moderately educated and those from the Untouchables just about literates. This system of selection is very intriguing. There seems to be a deep laid game behind it. Any one who studies it carefully will find that it is designed to allow none but the Brahmins and the allied castes to form the main part of the ministry and to secure for them the support of a docile unintelligent crowd of non-Brahmins and Untouchables who by their intellectual attainments could never dream of becoming rivals of the minister-folk but would be content to follow the lead for no other consideration except that of having been raised to the status of members of the Legislatures.

Mr. Gandhi did not see this aspect of the case when he said that to be a minister the Untouchable aspiring for it must be a qualified person. Otherwise, he would have seen that if there were no qualified persons among the Untouchable Congressmen, it was because the Congress Parliamentary Board did not choose well-qualified candidates from the Untouchables.

If the present system of election continues the Congress can always prevent educated Indians from becoming members of the Legislature which is the stepping-stone for becoming a member of the Cabinet. It is a very grave prospect and some steps will have to be taken to retrieve the position. In the meantime, it is enough to say that the scheme of selecting candidates adopted by the Congress dealt the Untouchables a severe blow by depriving them of Executive power under the cover of there being no qualified men to hold it which it created for itself by such clandestine and subterranean means.

The second misdeed of the Congress was to subject the Untouchable Congressmen to the rigours of party discipline. They were completely under the control of the Congress Party Executive. They could not ask a question which it did not like. They could not move a resolution which it did not permit. They could not bring in legislation to which it objected. They could not vote as they chose and could not speak what they felt. They were there as dumb driven cattle. One of the objects of obtaining representation in the Legislature for the Untouchables is to enable them to ventilate their grievances and to obtain redress for their wrongs. The Congress successfully and effectively prevented this from happening.

To end this long and sad story, the Congress sucked the juice out of the Poona Pact and threw the rind in the face of the Untouchables.

CHAPTER IV

AN ABJECT SURRENDER

Congress Beats an Inglorious Retreat

I

THE Poona Pact was signed on the 24th September 1932. On 25th September 1932, a public meeting of the Hindus was held in Bombay to accord to it their support. At that meeting the following resolution was passed :—

> "This Conference confirms the Poona agreement arrived at between the leaders of the Caste Hindus and Depressed Classes on September 24, 1932, and trusts that the British Government will withdraw its decision creating separate electorates within the Hindu community and accept the agreement in full. The Conference urges that immediate action be taken by Government so as to enable Mahatma Gandhi to break his fast within the terms of his vow and before it is too late. The Conference appeals to the leaders of the communities concerned to realize the implications of the agreement and of this resolution and to make earnest endeavour to fulfil them.
>
> "This Conference resolves that henceforth, amongst Hindus, no one shall be regarded as an Untouchable by reason of his birth, and that those who have been so regarded hitherto will have the same right as other Hindus in regard to the use of public wells, public schools, public roads, and all other public institutions. This right shall have statutory recognition at the first opportunity and shall be one of the earliest Acts of the Swaraj Parliament, if it shall not have received such recognition before that time.
>
> "It is further agreed that it shall be the duty of all Hindu leaders to secure, by every legitimate and peaceful means, an early removal of all social disabilities now imposed by custom upon the so-called Untouchable Classes, including the bar in respect of admission to temples."

This resolution was followed by a feverish activity on the part of the Hindus to throw open temples to the Untouchables. No week passed in which the *Harijan*, a weekly paper started by Mr. Gandhi, did not publish a long list of temples thrown open, wells thrown open and schools thrown open to the

Untouchables set out under special column headed "Week to Week" on the first page. As samples I produce below these "Week to Week" columns from two issues from the *Harijan*.

'Harijan' of 18th February 1933

WEEK TO WEEK

(During the Week ending 7th February 1938)

TEMPLES THROWN OPEN

One temple recently built at a cost of a lakh and half rupees in North Calcutta.

One temple in village Bhapur, District Ganjam, Madras.

One Thakurdwar temple at Naurania, in Jullundar, Punjab.

WELLS OPENED

One Municipal well at Guriapur in Jaipur Town, District Cuttack, Orissa.

Two wells in Wazirpura and Nikigali, Agra, U.P.

In Trichinopoly (Madras) an orthodox Brahmin has offered expenses necessary for digging three wells for the common use of Harijans and caste Hindus.

SCHOOL STARTED

A free school in Bachrota, District Meerut, U.P.

One school at Metah District in Rajputana.

Three schools at Fatehpur, Chemun and Abhaypur in Jaipur State, Rajputana.

One school at Fatehghar, District Farukhabad, U.P.

Three night schools in Muttra, U.P.

Three night schools in Gorakhpur Town, U.P.

One night school in Hata Tehsil, District Gorakhpur, U.P.

One night school at Sakhonia.

INDIAN STATES

1. The Palitana State (Kathiawar) Assembly has passed by a large majority three resolutions relating to the facilities to be given to the Harijans.

2. A standing committee has been appointed by the Government of Sandhur State, Madras, to concert measures calculated to ameliorate the condition of the Harijans in the State.

GENERAL

1. The Harijans in various villages near Kashia in Gorakhpur District have given up carrion eating.

2. On the occasion of the 'Basantpanchami' festival 'Basantotsava' was celebrated at Muzaffarpur (Bihar) under the auspices of the Harijan Seva Sangh in the temple of Sri Chaturbhujnathji in which all castes of Hindus took part.

A. V. THAKKAR,
General Secretary.

Sjt. V. R. Shinde, President, All-India Anti-Untouchability League and Founder-Trustee of the Depressed Mission Society of India, Poona, has addressed an open letter to the members of the Legislative Assembly on Sjt. Ranga Iyer's Untouchability Bills, strongly urging them to support the two measures.

In Taikalwadi in 'G' Ward of Bombay, there was an outbreak of fire recently which caused very serious damage to the huts and belongings of 48 Mahar families. The President of the Bombay Provincial Board of the Servants of Untouchables Society sanctioned Rs. 500 for giving relief to these families, and the relief was organised by a sub-Committee of the 'G' Ward Committee of the Society. A sum of Rs. 402-8 was distributed as an urgent measure of help to the 48 families, containing in all 163 persons.

The Bombay Government has issued orders that requests from local bodies for assignment of Government lands for wells, tanks, dharamshalas, etc., should not be granted except on condition that all castes alike will have equal use of such wells, tanks, etc.

'Harijan' of July 15, 1933

WEEK TO WEEK

Educational Facilities

Three reading rooms for Harijans have been opened in the North Arcot District by the S.U.S.

In the Madura District S.U.S. workers got Harijan children admitted into the Viraganur taluq board school.

Banians, towels, slates, etc., were distributed free to the children of the Melacheri school established by the Madura S.U.S.

Two Harijan students of Ramjas College, Delhi, have been allowed free scholarship and free lodging and one a free scholarship by Principal Thadani of the College.

One night school for adult Harijans was opened under the auspices of the Lahore Harijan Seva Sangh in the Harijan quarters outside Mochi Gate. The opening ceremony was performed by Mrs. Brij Lal Nehru.

It has been decided to start one more hostel for Harijan students in Brahmana Kodur (Guntur).

The East Godavery District Harijan Seva Sangham has resolved to start a hostel for Harijan Girl Students studying in Coconada. A sum of Rs. 630, 20 bags of rice, fuel necessary for one year, have been already received as donations for the hostel, which will be started with 15 students.

The Anantapur District Harijan Seva Sangam has

decided to start a hostel for Harijan students in Uravakonda. Some provisions and money have already been collected and it is intended to start the hostel with 20 students.

Owing to the unremitting efforts of the District Harijan Seva Sangham, Guntur, Harijan boys have been allowed into the savarna schools in a manner of villages and towns.

WELLS

Three wells in Coimbatore District which were in a bad condition, were cleaned and made available for use.

The District Board President, South Arcot, has promised to dig four wells in *cheries* selected by the S.U.S.

During the fortnight ending 31-5-33, no less than 125 wells in all were opened to Harijans and 5 new ones constructed in Andhradesh.

GENERAL

A shop has been opened in a bustee near Hogg Market (Calcutta) where Doms live, for supplying them with articles of food at cheap rates.

Rs. 60 has been paid by the S.U.S. Bengal for paying up the debts of a Harijan family at Bibi Bagan bustee (Calcutta).

The Amrita Samaj (Calcutta) has given service to some Harijans.

450 Harijans of Bolpur (Birbhum) have given up drinking habits and 1,275 Muchis have taken a vow not to take beef.

Three new district centres of S.U.S. have been opened during the month in Bankura, Murshidabad, and 24 Parganas.

Trichinopoly, Tanjore, Tinnevelley, Salem, Dindigul, North Arcot and Madura have all taken up the idea of a Gandhi Harijan Service corps for direct and personal service in the cheris.

Alandural, a Harijan village 12 miles from Coimbatore was given Rs. 25 worth of grain, Rs. 100 worth of cloth and Rs. 5 worth of oil, as relief after a fire in the village.

A Harijan Youth League has been formed in Chidambaram.

A shop to supply provisions at cost price to the Harijans has been set up in Tenali and is being made use of by them.

A sum of Rs. 110 was spent in giving help for rebuilding houses of Harijans in Valanna Palem (East Kistna) recently destroyed by fire.

A sum of Rs. 100 was contributed by the Provincial Committee towards the relief of Harijans in Yellamanchili (Vizag) who lost their houses by a fire. The local Harijan Seva Sangham is endeavouring to erect new houses for the Harijans in a better locality and is collecting donations—in cash and building materials.

One Harijan has been employed as a servant by a savarna gentleman in Gollapalem.

When the owners or trustees of temples were not prepared to throw open their temples to the Untouchables, the Hindus actually started *satyagraha* against them to compel them to fall in line. The satyagraha by Mr. Kelappan for securing entry to the Untouchables in the temple at Guruvayur was a part of this agitation. To force the hands of the trustees of the temples who had the courage to stand against the current, many Hindu legislators came forward, tumbling over one another, with Bills requiring the trustees to throw open temples to the Untouchables if a referendum showed that the majority of the Hindu worshippers voted in favour. There was a spate of such Bills and a race among legislators to take the first place. There was a Temple Entry Bill by Dr. Subbaroyan of the Madras Legislative Council. There were four Bills introduced in the Central Assembly. One was by Mr. C. S. Ranga Iyer, another by Mr. Harabilas Sarda, and a third by Mr. Lalchand Navalrai.

In this agitation, Mr. Gandhi also joined. Before 1932, Mr. Gandhi was opposed to allow Untouchables to enter Hindu temples. To quote his own words Mr. Gandhi said[1] :—

> " How is it possible that the Antyajas (Untouchables) should have the right to enter all the existing temples ? As long as the law of caste and ashram has the chief place in Hindu Religion, to say that every Hindu can enter every temple is a thing that is not possible to-day."

His joining the movement for Temple Entry must therefore remain a matter of great surprise. Why Mr. Gandhi took this somersault it is difficult to imagine. Was it an honest act of change of heart, due to a conviction that he was in error in opposing the entry of the Untouchables in Hindu temples ? Was it due to a realization that the political separation between the Hindus and the Untouchables brought about by the Poona Pact might lead to a complete severance of the cultural and religious ties and that it was necessary to counteract the tendency by some such measure as Temple Entry as will bind the two together ? Or was his object in joining the Temple Entry movement to destroy the basis of the claim of the Untouchables for political rights by destroying the barrier between them and the Hindus which makes them separate from the Hindus ? Or was it because Mr. Gandhi saw before

---

[1] Gandhi Shikshan, Vol. II, p. 132.

him looming large a possibility of adding to his name and fame and rushed to make the most of it, as is his habit to do? The second or the third explanation may be nearer the truth.

II

What was the attitude of the Untouchables to this movement for Temple Entry? I was asked by Mr. Gandhi to lend my support to the movement for Temple Entry. I declined to do so and issued a statement on the subject to the Press. As it will help the reader to know the grounds for my attitude to this question, I have thought it well to set it in full. Here it is;

Statement on Temple Entry Bill
14th February, 1933

Although the controversy regarding the question of Temple Entry is confined to the Sanatanists and Mahatma Gandhi, the Depressed Classes have undoubtedly a very important part to play in it, in so far as their position is bound to weigh the scales one way or the other when the issue comes up for a final settlement. It is, therefore, necessary that their viewpoint should be defined and stated so as to leave no ambiguity about it.

To the Temple-Entry Bill of Mr. Ranga Iyer as now drafted, the Depressed Classes cannot possibly give their support. The principle of the Bill is that if a majority of Municipal and Local Board voters in the vicinity of any particular temple on a referendum decide by a majority that the Depressed Classes shall be allowed to enter the temple, the Trustees or the Manager of that temple shall give effect to that decision. The principle is an ordinary principle of Majority rule, and there is nothing radical or revolutionary about the Bill, and if the Sanatanists were a wise lot, they would accept it without demur.

The reasons why the Depressed Classes cannot support a Bill based upon this principle are two: One reason is that the Bill cannot hasten the day of temple-entry for the Depressed Classes any nearer than would otherwise be the case. It is true that under the Bill, the minority will not have the right to obtain an injunction against the Trustee, or the Manager who throws open the temple to the Depressed Classes in accordance with the decision of the majority. But before one can draw any satisfaction from this clause and congratulate the author of the Bill, one must first of all feel assured that when the question is put to the vote there will be a majority in favour of Temple Entry. If one is not suffering from illusions of any kind one must accept that the hope of a majority voting in favour of Temple-Entry will be very rarely realised, if at all. Without doubt, the majority is definitely opposed to-day—a fact which is conceded by the author of the Bill himself in his correspondence with the Shankaracharya.

What is there in the situation as created after the passing of the Bill, which can lead one to hope that the majority will act differently ? I find nothing. I shall, no doubt, be reminded of the results of the referendum with regard to the Guruvayur Temple. But I refuse to accept a referendum so overweighted as it was by the life of Mahatma Gandhi as the normal result. In any such calculations, the life of the Mahatma must necessarily be deducted.

Secondly, the Bill does not regard Untouchability in temples as a sinful custom. It regards Untouchability merely as a social evil not necessarily worse than social evils of other sorts. For, it does not declare Untouchability as such to be illegal. Its binding force is taken away, only, if a majority decides to do so. Sin and immorality cannot become tolerable because a majority is addicted to them or because the majority chooses to practise them. If Untouchability is a sinful and an immoral custom, then in the view of the Depressed Classes it must be destroyed without any hesitation even if it was acceptable to the majority. This is the way in which all customs are dealt with by Courts of Law, if they find them to be immoral and against public policy.

This is exactly what the Bill does not do. The author of the Bill takes no more serious view of the custom of Untouchability than does the temperance reformer of the habit of drinking. Indeed, so much is he impressed by the assumed similarity between the two that the method he has adopted is a method which is advocated by temperance reformers to eradicate the evil habit of drinking, namely, by local option. One cannot feel much grateful to a friend of the Depressed Classes, who holds Untouchability to be no worse than drinking. If Mr. Ranga Iyer had not forgotten that only a few months ago Mahatma Gandhi had prepared himself to fast unto death if Untouchability was not removed, he would have taken a more serious view of this curse and proposed a most thorough-going reform to ensure its removal lock, stock and barrel. Whatever its shortcomings may be from the standpoint of efficacy, the least that the Depressed Classes could expect is for the Bill to recognise the principle that Untouchability is a sin.

I really cannot understand how the Bill satisfies Mahatma Gandhi, who has been insisting that Untouchability is a sin! It certainly does not satisfy the Depressed Classes. The question whether this particular Bill is good or bad, sufficient or insufficient, is a subsidiary question.

The main question is : Do the Depressed Classes desire Temple Entry or do they not? This main question is being viewed by the Depressed Classes by two points of view. One is the materialistic point of view. Starting from it, the Depressed Classes think that the surest way for their elevation lies in higher education, higher employment and better ways of earning a living. Once they become well placed in the scale of social life, they would become respectable and once they become respectable the religious outlook of the orthodox towards them is sure to undergo change, and even if this did not happen, it can do no injury to their material interest. Proceeding on these lines the Depressed Classes say that they will not spend their resources on such an empty thing as Temple Entry. There is also another reason why they do not care to fight for it. That argument is the argument of self-respect.

Not very long ago there used to be boards on club doors and other social resorts maintained by Europeans in India, which said "Dogs and Indians" not allowed. The temples of Hindus carry similar boards to-day, the only difference is that the boards on the Hindu temples practically say : "All Hindus and all animals including dogs are admitted, only Untouchables not admitted." The situation in both cases is on a parity. But Hindus never begged for admission in those places from which the Europeans in their arrogance had excluded them. Why should an Untouchable beg for admission in a place from which he has been excluded by the arrogance of the Hindus? This is the reason of the Depressed Class man who is interested in his material welfare. He is prepared to say to the Hindus, "to open or not to open your temples is a question for you to consider and not for me to agitate. If you think, it is bad manners not to respect the sacredness of human personality, open your temples and be a gentleman. If you rather be a Hindu than be a gentleman, then shut the doors and damn yourself for I don't care to come."

I found it necessary to put the argument in this form, because I want to disabuse the minds of men like Pandit Madan Mohan Malaviya of their belief that the Depressed Classes are looking forward expectantly for their patronage.

The second point of view is the spiritual one. As religiously minded people, do the Depressed Classes desire temple entry or do they not? That is the question. From the spiritual point of view, they are not indifferent to temple entry as they would be, if the material point of view alone were to prevail. But their final answer must depend upon the reply which Mahatma Gandhi and the Hindus give to the question namely: What is the drive behind this offer of temple entry? Is temple entry to be the final goal of the advancement in the social status of the Depressed Classes in the Hindu fold? Or is it only the first step and if it is the first step, what is the ultimate goal? Temple Entry as a final goal, the Depressed Classes can never support. Indeed they will not only reject it, but they would then regard themselves as rejected by Hindu Society and free to find their own destiny elsewhere. On the other hand, if it is only to be a first step in the direction they may be inclined to support it. The position would then be analogous to what is happening in the politics of India to-day. All Indians have claimed Dominion Status for India. The actual constitution will fall short of Dominion Status and many Indians will accept it. Why? The answer is that as the goal is defined, it does not matter much if it is to be reached by steps and not in one jump. But if the British had not accepted the goal of Dominion Status, no one would have accepted the partial reforms which many are now prepared to accept. In the same way, if Mahatma Gandhi and the reformers were to proclaim what the goal which they have set before themselves is for the advancement of the Social Status of the Depressed Classes in the Hindu fold, it would be easier for the Depressed Classes to define their attitude towards Temple Entry. The goal of the Depressed Classes might as well be stated here for the information and consideration of all concerned. What the Depressed Classes want is a religion, which will give them equality of social status. To prevent any misunderstanding, I would like to elaborate the point by drawing a distinction between social evils which are the results of secular causes and social evils which are founded upon the doctrine of religion. Social evils can have no justification whatsoever in a civilised society. But nothing can be more odious and vile than that admitted social evils should be sought to be justified on the ground of religion. The Depressed Classes may not be able to overthrow inequities to which they are being subjected. But they have made up their mind not to tolerate a religion that will lend its support to the continuance of these inequities.

If the Hindu religion is to be their religion, then it must become a religion of Social Equality. The mere amendment of Hindu religious code by the mere inclusion in it of a provision to permit temple entry for all, cannot make it a religion of equality of social status. All that it can do is to recognize them as nationals and not aliens, if I may use in this connection terms which have become so familiar in politics. But that cannot mean that they would thereby reach a position where they would be free and equal, without being above or below any one else, for the simple reason that the Hindu religion does not recognize the principle of equality of social status; on the other hand it fosters inequality by insisting upon grading people as Brahmins, Kshatriyas, Vaishyas and Shudras, which now stand towards one another in an ascending scale of hatred and descending scale of contempt. If the Hindu religion is to be a religion of social equality then an amendment of its code to provide temple-entry is not enough. What is required is to purge it of the doctrine of Chaturvarna. That is the root cause of all in equality and also the parent of the caste system and Untouchability, which are merely forms of inequality. Unless it is done not only will the Depressed Classes reject Temple Entry, they will also reject the Hindu faith. Chaturvarna and the Caste System are incompatible with the self-respect of the Depressed Classes. So long as they stand to be its cardinal doctrine the Depressed Classes must continue to be looked upon as low. The Depressed Classes can say that they are Hindus only when the theory of Chaturvarna and Caste System is abandoned and expunged from the Hindu Shastras. Do the Mahatma and the Hindu reformers accept this as their goal and will they show the courage to work for it? I shall look forward to their pronouncements on this issue, before I decide upon my final attitude. But whether Mahatma Gandhi and the Hindus are prepared for this or not, let it be known once for all that nothing short of this will satisfy the Depressed Classes and make them accept Temple Entry. To accept temple entry and be content with it, is to temporise with evil and barter away the sacredness of human personality that dwells in them.

There is, however, one argument which Mahatma Gandhi and the reforming Hindus may advance against the position I have taken. They may say: "acceptance by the Depressed Classes of Temple Entry now, will not prevent them from agitating hereafter for the abolition of Chaturvarna and Caste." If that is their view, I like to meet the argument right at this stage so as to clinch the issue and clear the road for future developments. My reply is that it is true that my right to agitate for the abolition of Chaturvarna and Caste System will not be lost, if I accept Temple Entry now. But the question is on what side will Mahatma Gandhi be at the time when the question is put. If he will be in the camp of my opponents, I must tell him that I cannot be in his camp now. If he will be in my camp he ought to be in it now.

B. R. AMBEDKAR.

Dewan Bahadur R. Srinivasan who along with me represented the Untouchables at the Round Table Conference also did not support the movement for Temple Entry. In a statement to the Press, he said :—

"When a Depressed Classes member is permitted to enter into the caste Hindu temples he would not be taken into any one of the four castes, but treated as a man of fifth or the last or the lower caste, a stigma worse than the one to be called an Untouchable. At the same time he would be subjected to so many caste restrictions and humiliations. The Depressed Classes shun the one who enters like that and exclude him as casteman. The crores of Depressed Classes would not submit to caste restrictions. They will be divided into sections if they do. Temple entry cannot be forced by law. The village castemen openly or indirectly defy the law. To the village Depressed Class man it would be like a scrap of paper on which the "sugar" was written and placed in hands for him to taste. The above facts are placed before the public in time to save confusion and disturbance in the country."

To the question I put to Mr. Gandhi in my statement he gave a straight reply. He said that though he was against untouchability he was not against caste. If at all, he was in favour of it and that he would not therefore carry his social reform beyond removing untouchability. This was enough for me to settle my attitude. I decided to take no further part in it.

The only leading member from the Untouchable community was the late Dewan Bahadur Rajah. One cannot help saying that he played a very regrettable part in this business. The Dewan Bahadur was a nominated member of the Central Assembly from 1927. He had nothing to do with the Congress either inside or outside the Assembly. Neither by accident nor by mistake did he appear on the same side of the Congress. Indeed, he was not merely a critic of the Congress but its adversary. He was the staunchest friend of the Government and never hesitated to stand by the Government. He stood for separate electorates for the Untouchables to which the

Congress was bitterly opposed. In the crisis of 1932, the Dewan Bahadur suddenly decided to desert the Government and take sides with the Congress. He became the spearhead of the Congress movement for joint electorates and Temple Entry. It is impossible to discover a parallel in the conduct of any other public cause. The worst part of the business was that it had none but personal motive behind. The Dewan Bahadur was deeply cut because the Government did not nominate him as a delegate to the Round Table Conference to represent the Untouchables and in his stead nominated Dewan Bahadur R. Srinivasan. The Government of India had good ground for not nominating him. It was decided that neither the members of the Simon Commission nor the members of the Central Legislative Committee should have a place in the Round Table Conference. The Dewan Bahadur was a member of the Central Legislative Committee and had therefore to be dropped. This was quite a natural explanation. But the wounded pride of Dewan Bahadur Rajah could not let him see it. When the Congress Ministry took office in Madras, when he saw how the Poona Pact was being trampled upon, how his rival was made a Minister and how notwithstanding his services to the Congress he was left out, he bitterly regretted what he did! The fact, however, remains that in the critical year of 1932, Dewan Bahadur Rajah lent his full support to the Congress. He was not only running with the Congress crowd but he took care not to fall out in the race for legislation against untouchability. He too had sponsored two Bills. One of them was called the Removal of Untouchability Bill and the other was called the Criminal Procedure Amendment Bill.

III

Mr. Gandhi did not mind any opposition and was indifferent as to whether it came from the orthodox Hindus or from the Untouchables. He went on in mad pursuit of his object. It is interesting to ask, what happened to this movement? Within the short compass of this book it is not possible to spread out this inquiry and cover everything that was done and claimed as evidence of the success of the movement.

To put it briefly, after a short spurt of activity in the direction of removing untouchability by throwing open temples and wells the Hindu mind returned to its original state. The reports appearing in the "Week to Week" columns of the *Harijan* subsided, became few and far between and ultimately vanished. For myself, I was not surprised to find that the Hindu heart was so soon stricken with palsy. For I never believed that there was so much milk of human kindness locked up in the Hindu breast as the "Week to Week" column in the *Harijan* would have the world believe. As a matter of fact a large part of the news that appeared in the "Week to Week" was faked and was nothing but a lying propaganda engineered by Congressmen to deceive the world that the Hindus were determined to fight untouchability. Few temples if any were really opened and of those that were reported to have been opened most were dilapidated and deserted temples which were used by none but dogs and donkeys. One of the evil effects of the Congress agitation is that it has made the political minded Hindus a lying squad which will not hesitate to tell any lie if it can help the Congress. Thus ended the part which the Hindu public played or was made to appear to play in this Temple-Entry movement. The same fate overtook the Guruvayur Temple Satyagraha and the legislation for securing Temple-Entry for the Untouchables. As these are matters which were pursued by Mr. Gandhi and Congressmen their history might be told in some detail inasmuch as it reveals the true mentality of Mr. Gandhi and the Congress towards the Untouchables.

IV

To begin with the Guruvayur Temple Satyagraha. A temple of Krishna is situated at Guruvayur in the Ponnani taluk in Malabar. The Zamorin of Calicut is the trustee of the temple. One Mr. Kelappan, a Hindu working for the cause of the Untouchables of Malabar, began an agitation for securing the Untouchables entry into the temple. The Zamorin of Calicut as the trustee of the temple refused to throw open the temple to the Untouchables and in support of his action cited Section 40 of the Hindu Religious Endowments Act which said that no trustee could do anything against the custom and usage of the temples entrusted to him. On the 20th September 1932, Mr. Kelappan commenced a fast in protest lying in front of the temple in the sun till the Zamorin revised his views in favour of the Untouchables. To get rid of this annoyance and embarrassment the Zamorin appealed to Mr. Gandhi to request

Mr. Kelappan to suspend his fast for a time. After a fast for ten days Mr. Kelappan at the request of Mr. Gandhi suspended the fast on 1st October 1932 for three months. The Zamorin did nothing. Mr. Gandhi sent him a wire telling him that he must move in the matter and get over all difficulties legal or otherwise. Mr. Gandhi also told the Zamorin that as Mr. Kelappan had suspended his fast on his advice he had become responsible for securing to the Untouchables entry into the temple to the extent of sharing the fast with Mr. Kelappan. On 5th November 1932, Mr. Gandhi issued the following statement to the press :—

> "There is another fast which is a near possibility and that in connection with the opening of the Guruvayur temple in Kerala. It was at my urgent request that Mr. Kelappan suspended his fast for three months, a fast that had well nigh brought him to death's door. I would be in honour bound to fast with him if on or before *1st January 1933* that temple is not opened to the Untouchables precisely on the same terms as to the Touchables, and if it becomes necessary for Mr. Kelappan to resume his fast."

The Zamorin refused to yield and issued a counter-statement to the press in which he said :—

> "The various appeals that are being made for throwing open the temples to Avarnas proceed upon an inadequate appreciation of such difficulties. In these circumstances, there is hardly any justification for thinking that it is in my power to throw open the Guruvayur temple to the Avarnas as desired by the supporters of the temple-entry campaign."

In these circumstances a fast by Mr. Gandhi became inevitable, and obligatory. But Mr. Gandhi did not go on fast. He modified his position and said that he would refrain from fasting if a referendum was taken in Ponnani taluk in which the temple was situated and if the referendum showed that the majority was against the throwing open of the temple to the Untouchables. Accordingly, a referendum was taken. Voting was confined to those who were actual temple goers. Those who were not entitled to enter the temple and those who would not enter it were excluded from the voters' list. It was reported that 78 per cent. of eligible voters voted. The result of the poll was 56 per cent. were in favour of temple entry, 9 per cent. against, 8 per cent. were neutral and 27 per cent. abstained from recording their votes.

On this result of the referendum, Mr. Gandhi was bound to start the fast. But he did not. Instead, on the 29th of December 1932 Mr. Gandhi issued a statement to the press which he concluded by saying :—

> "In view of the official announcement that the Viceregal decision as to sanction for the introduction, in the Madras Legislative Council, of Dr. Subbaroyan's permissive Bill with reference to the temple-entry could not possibly be announced before the 15th January, the *fast* contemplated to take place on the second day of the New Year will be indefinitely postponed and in any case up to the date of the announcement of the Viceregal decision. Mr. Kelappan concurs in this postponement."

The Viceregal pronouncement mentioned by Mr. Gandhi had reference to the Viceroy's granting permission or refusing permission to the moving of the Temple Entry Bills in the Legislature. That permission was given by the Viceroy. Yet Mr. Gandhi did not fast. Not only did he not fast, he completely forgot the matter as though it was of no moment. Since then nothing has been heard about Guruvayur Temple Satyagraha though the Temple remains closed to the Untouchables even to-day.

V

Thus ended Guruvayur. Let me now turn to the other project namely legislation for Temple-Entry. Of the many bills the one in the name of Mr. Ranga Iyer in the Central Legislature was pursued. The rest were dropped. There was a storm at the very birth of the Bill. Under the Government of India Act as it then stood no legislative measure which affected religion and customs and usages based on religion could be introduced in the Assembly unless it had the previous sanction of the Governor-General. When the Bill was sent for such sanction another commotion was created by the reports that were circulated that the Governor-General was going to refuse his sanction. Mr. Gandhi was considerably excited over these reports. In a statement to the press issued on the 21st January 1933, Mr. Gandhi said :—

> "If the report is an intelligent anticipation of the forthcoming Viceregal decision, I can only say that it will be a tragedy . . . I emphatically repudiate the suggestion that there

is any political objective behind these measures. If court decisions had not hardened a doubtful custom into law, no legislation would be required. I would myself regard State interference in religious matters as an intolerable nuisance. But here legislation becomes an imperative necessity in order to remove the legal obstruction and based as it will be on popular will, as far as I can see, there can be no question of clash between parties representing rival opinions."

The decision of the Government was announced on the 23rd of January 1933. Lord Willingdon refused sanction to Dr. Subbaroyan's Temple-Entry Bill in the Madras Council, but His Excellency permitted the introduction, in the Legislative Assembly, of Mr. Ranga Iyer's Untouchability Abolition Bill. The Government emphasised the need of ascertainment of Hindu opinion before they (Government) could decide what attitude to adopt. The announcement further stated that the Governor-General and the Government of India desired to make it plain that it was essential that consideration of any such measure should not proceed unless the proposals were subjected to the fullest examination in all their aspects, not merely in the Legislature but also outside it, by all who would be affected by them. This condition can only be satisfied if the Bill is circulated in the widest manner for the purpose of eliciting public opinion. It must also be understood that the grant of sanction to the introduction, in the Central Legislature, of the Bills relating to temple entry does not commit the Government in any way to the acceptance or support of the principles contained therein. On the next day, Mr. Gandhi issued a statement in which he said :—

"I must try to trace the hand of God in it. He wants to try me through and through. The sanction given to the All-India Bill was an unintentional challenge to Hinduism and the reformer. Hinduism will take care of itself if the reformer will be true to himself. Thus considered the Government of India's decision must be regarded as God-send. It clears the issue. It makes it for India and the world to understand the tremendous importance of the moral struggle now going on in India. But whatever the Sanatanists may decide the movement for Temple-Entry now broadens from Guruvayur in the extreme south to Hardwar in the north and my fast, though it remains further postponed, depends not now upon Guruvayur only but extends automatically to temples in general."

One can well realize under what fanfare the Bill began its legislative career. On the 24th of March 1933, Mr. Ranga Iyer formally introduced the Bill in the Assembly. As it was a Bill for Mr. Gandhi the Congress members of the Assembly were of course ready to give it their support. Mr. Gandhi had appointed Mr. Rajagopalachari and Mr. G. D. Birla to canvass support for the Bill among the Non-Congress members with a view to ensure safe passage for the Bill. He said they were better lobbyists than he was. The motion for introduction was opposed by the Raja of Kollengode and Mr. Thampan raised a preliminary objection that the Bill was ultra vires of the legislature. The latter objection was overruled by the President and the House allowed the Bill to be introduced. Mr. Ranga Iyer next moved that the Temple-Entry Bill be circulated to elicit public opinion by the 30th July. Raja Bahadur Krishnamachari opposed the circulation motion and condemned the proposed legislation in strong terms. At last he urged that the date for circulation should be 31st December instead of 31st July. Mr. Gunjal opposed the circulation motion and asked the House not to support the Bill. As it was already 5 p.m. and as that was the last day of the session for non-official business, the President wanted to take the sense of the House for a late sitting. As there was no overwhelming majority for it, the President adjourned the House. So the Bill stood postponed to the Autumn session of the Assembly.

The discussion of the Bill was resumed on 24th August 1933 during the Autumn session of the Central Legislature. Sir Harry Haig on behalf of the Government explained that their support to the motion for circulation of the Bill should in no way be construed as implying support to its provisions. It was true that the Government sympathized for the Depressed Classes and were anxious to do what they could for their social and economic improvement. He quoted from the *communique* issued in January last, wherein the Government's view was fully explained. In his opinion, circulation by the end of June was a fair and reasonable time to secure the widest possible circulation. As regards the limit of circulation to temple going Hindus, Sir Harry Haig said from the practical viewpoint that it would really hardly be possible to impose the restriction as proposed. The Government wanted the matter to be fully discussed by all classes of Hindus and were therefore prepared to give their support to the amendment of Mr. Sharma. Closure was moved and the House accepted Mr. Sharma's motion for circulation of the Bill by the end of June 1934. Opinions were duly received. They fill a whole volume of over a thousand foolscap pages. The Bill was ready for the next stage namely to move for the appointment of a Select Committee. Mr. Ranga Iyer had even given notice for such a motion. A strange thing happened. The Government of India decided to dissolve the Assembly and order new election. The result of this announcement was a sudden change in the attitude of the Congress members in the Central Legislature towards Mr. Ranga's Bill. One and all stood out against it and refused to give any further support to the Bill. They were terrified of the electorates. Mr. Ranga Iyer's position was very pitiable. He described it in very biting language, the venom of which could hardly be improved upon. So well did he describe the situation that I make no apology for reproducing the following extract from his speech. Rising to move his motion, Mr. Ranga Iyer said :

> " Sir, I rise to move what is known as the Temple-Entry Bill, to remove the disabilities of the so-called Depressed Classes. Sir, I move :—
>
> ' That the Bill to remove the disabilities of the so-called Depressed Classes in regard to entry into Hindu temples be referred to a Select Committee consisting of the Honourable Sir Nripendra Sircar, the Honourable Sir Henry Craik, Bhai Parma Nand, Rao Bahadur M. C. Rajah, Mr. T. N. Ramakrishna Reddi, Rao Bahadur B. L. Patil and the Mover.'
>
> " I will delete with your permission, the words 'with instructions to report within a fortnight' and then I will continue the remaining portion of the motion :
>
> ' and that the number of members whose presence shall be necessary to constitute a meeting of the Committee shall be five.'
>
> " Sir, at the time I gave notice of this motion, I did not think that before a fortnight we would be going into the wilderness. Therefore, I recognise the limitations of this motion, for there will be no time even to go to a Select Committee. I recognise that it gives us an opportunity to express our opinion on the subject.
>
> " I have already stated that I owed an apology to Mr. Satyamurthi for while interrupting Mr. Mudaliar, I was not in a

position naturally as he was rushing along with his speech to explain myself fully and he would have been at a disadvantage if I had done so. I recognise that Mr. Satyamurthi, who was at no time in favour of the Temple Entry Bill, has succeeded in making the Congress drop it. I read the following written statement of Mr. C. Rajagopalachariar in the *Hindu* of Madras, dated the 16th August. The *Hindu* is a very responsible newspaper, and as it is not a mere telegraphic interview but a written statement, I believe Mr. Rajagopalachariar's statement can be taken as accurate. Mr. Rajagopalachariar is apologising to the public for his betrayal of the cause of the Untouchables. As the principal lieutenant of Mahatma Gandhi, his betrayal must be placed on record. He says:

> 'The question has been asked by some Sanatanists whether Congress candidates will give an undertaking that Congress will not support any legislative interference with religious observances. Similar questions may be asked on a variety of topics by persons and groups interested in each one of them. That such questions are asked only of the Congress candidates and similar elucidation is not attempted in respect of other parties and independent candidates is a very great compliment paid to the Congress.'

"So says, Sriman Rajagopalachariar. And, instead of following up the compliment and arousing public opinion on an unpopular measure, here is a great Congress leader who sat *dharna* at our house with his son-in-law, Devidas Gandhi, who repeatedly called on me at Delhi and said 'We seek joint support for this legislative measure,'—here is a man who goes back 'like a crab,' to borrow the language of Shakespeare. Political parties, explains this subtle brain from the South, have distinctive policies on various questions covering a wide field:

> 'Not all of them, however, are made into election issues at any one time.'

"Sir, this Congress leader is afraid of facing the public opinion which he has roused.

"Sir, are the Congress people slaves?

> 'They are slaves who fear to speak,
> For the fallen and the weak.'

"According to Milton, 'To say and straight unsay argues no liar but a coward traced.' . . . Mr. Rajagopalachariar unsays now what he had been saying long before the General Election from every platform in the following words:

> 'The Congress candidates go to the electorate in this election on well-defined political issues.'

"That is to say, they go to the electorate with a view to pandering to the prejudice of the masses whom they have misled, so much so, that they have got themselves into a bog. Lord Willingdon came to their rescue, to take them out of the bog by announcing the dissolution of this Assembly and giving them an opportunity, as a Constitutional Viceroy, to return to the sheltered paths of constitutionalism. Therefore, they have run away from their own convictions and are playing every trick to come back to the Legislature with as large a number as possible. Had they gone on with the Temple Entry Bill or the Untouchability question, they would have lost many votes, for it is not a popular issue. I said so, though Mahatma Gandhi contradicted me publicly at the time, I said so when Shankaracharya was staying in Malabar in my brother's house at Palghat. My brother came on a deputation to the Viceroy to oppose the Bill. I said : 'I know, the reformer is not in a majority in Malabar.' Nowhere else are the reformers in a majority but the reformers believe in persuading the majority to their way of thinking. Then, I said—whatever the result of a referendum, the Congress people might have taken in Guruvayur in Malabar, might be, I could not for a moment believe that the majority of the temple-going people in Malabar were in favour of admitting the Untouchables into the temples ; but I was prepared to fight them, also to argue with them and to persuade them and to make them take an interest in the cause and the case of the Untouchables, for, I feel, the Untouchables are a part of my community. Sir, if one-third of my community is to remain submerged in exclusion in the name of religion, I feel, as I have always felt and said, that that community has no right to existence. It is with a view to the unification of the Hindu community, it is with a view to building up the greatness of the future of that community on the past of that community, when Untouchability was quite unknown as in the Vedic ages, that I have taken up their cause. And now, I find Congressmen, so keen about Untouchability yesterday, explaining why they are not taking it up today. Mr. Rajagopalachariar has driven the last nail into the coffin of the Temple Entry Bill as Raja Bahadur Krishnamachariar, the Raja Saheb of Kollengode or Sir Satya Charan Mukherji would perhaps like to say, representing as they do the various Sanatanist groups of the country.

"Sir, Mr. Rajagopalachariar goes on to say that they asked to be returned 'on no other issue,' that is to say, not on Temple Entry issue, but merely on a political Anglo-phobia issue, an anti-British issue, because, having traded on public feeling, having tried to give it as much racial antipathy as possible in the name of non-violence, in the name of religion itself, because non-violence was sometimes given a religious bias, having created that atmosphere of distrust in the country, finding that that atmosphere might not help them in the election if they fought it on a bigger, a cleaner and higher issue, namely, the removal of Untouchability itself, they side-track the issue, they run away from their conviction :

> 'They are slaves who dare not be
> In the right with two or three.'

"Then he, a principal lieutenant of Gandhiji, goes on to say :

'If successful at the polls, they cannot believe they will receive the mandate of the electorate on any other questions.'

"That is to say, they are not receiving the mandate of the electorate on the Temple Entry Bill. This man, who came screaming at our doors, begging us for support—these beggars in the cause of the Congress—who just begged of us to proceed with this Temple Entry Bill, are not only betraying the cause of the Untouchables, but they are betraying the principles of the Mahatma himself, for, we know, that Mahatma's fast was directed toward the uplift of the Untouchables by giving them concession in regard to the Communal Award, which the Congress naturally has hesitated to repudiate, and we, therefore, know that that has a direct bearing on the Untouchability question to approach which, to solve which, the Mahatma, the great Mahatma, wanted to tour the country, but today the Congress, who betrayed him first in the betrayal of the Congress boycott of the Councils, have, by seeking to come to the Councils, further betrayed him with the assistance of his own *samandhi*, Rajagopalachariar, and they say that they are not going to proceed with the Untouchability question and the Temple Entry Bill without a mandate from the people !

"Sir, where is the difference, I ask, between Raja Bahadur Krishnamachariar and Sriman Rajagopalachariar ? Raja Bahadur Krishnamachariar has always conceded—'take a mandate from the people and then come and legislate.' Sir, he is not a coward ; a great Sanatanist himself, he is willing to face the music. On the contrary, these people who pillory the Sanatanists up and down the country, forgetting that Sanatan Dharma is eternal truth itself, are behaving in a manner which even the Sanatanists will not appreciate, for Sanatan Dharma is eternal truth and the betrayal of truth is worthy only of untruthful people ! Having betrayed many a principle which would lead us to our national goal, having taken up the case of the Untouchables only to save their faces, with no conviction behind them, as we now see, the great Congress leaders with the exception of Mahatma Gandhi, have said through Rajagopalachariar, the Organizer-in-chief of the coming elections on behalf of the Congress :

> 'It will be open to all Congressmen to have the matter duly considered before it is ever made into an official Congress Bill.'

"For this betrayal of the cause of the Untouchables, I hope constitutionalists will organize themselves, whether Hindus or Mussalmans. They can agree to differ later on on communal issues, but they will unite and offer a great battle to the Congress and bring that organ of masqueraders down on its knees. Sir, I think here is a betrayal of the cause of the Untouchables and the Depressed Classes; and, if I did not believe in this movement before Mahatma Gandhi could take it up or Mr. Rajagopalachariar went from door to door in Delhi, I should not have been here to move this Bill."

VI

Here is a case of retreat from glory! And what an ignominious retreat? How did Mr. Gandhi react to it? In a statement issued on 4th November 1932, Mr. Gandhi said :—

> "Untouchables in the villages should be made to feel that their shackles have been broken, that they are in no way inferior to their fellow villagers, that they are worshippers of the same God as the other villagers and entitled to the same rights and privileges that the latter enjoy.
>
> "But if these vital conditions of the Pact are not carried out by caste-Hindus, could I possibly live to face God and man? I ventured even to tell Dr. Ambedkar, Rao Bahadur M.C. Raja and other friends belonging to the suppressed group that they should regard me as a hostage for the due fulfilment by caste-Hindus of the conditions of the Pact. The fast, if it is to come, will not be for coercion of those who are opponents of reform, but it will be intended to sting into action those who have been my comrades or who have taken pledges for the removal of Untouchability. If they belie their pledges or if they never meant to abide by them and their Hinduism was a mere camouflage, I should have no interest left in life."

He was never tired of repeating this. Exclusion of the Untouchables from the Hindu Temples, he described, as the agony of his soul. What did Mr. Gandhi do in this connection? Did he resent this betrayal by Mr. Rajagopalachari of this project without which he said he had no interest left in life? One would naturally expect Mr. Gandhi to denounce this betrayal by the Congress Party to achieve success at the polls? Quite the contrary. Instead of blaming Mr. Rajagopalachari, he blamed Mr. Ranga Iyer for his violent denunciation of the Congress Party for withdrawing its support to the Bill. This is what Mr. Gandhi said in the issue of the *Harijan* dated August 31, 1934:—

> "The ill-fated Temple Entry Bill deserved a more decent burial, if it deserved it at all, than it received at the hands of the mover of the Bill. It was not a bill promoted by, and on behalf of, the reformers. The mover should, therefore, have consulted reformers and acted under instructions from them. So far as I am aware, there was hardly any occasion for the anger into which he allowed himself to be betrayed or the displeasure which he expressed towards Congressmen. On the face of it, it was, and was designed to be, a measure pertaining to religion, framed in pursuance of the solemn declaration publicly made in Bombay at a meeting of representative Hindus, who met under the chairmanship of Pandit Malaviyaji on 25th September, 1932. The curious may read the declaration printed almost every week on the front page of *Harijan*. Therefore, every Hindu, caste or Harijan, was interested in the measure. It was not a measure in which Congress Hindus were more interested than the other Hindus. To have, therefore, dragged the Congress name into the discussion was unfortunate. The Bill deserved a gentler handling."

The Temple Entry, what one is to say of it except to describe it a strange game of political acrobatics! Mr. Gandhi begins as an opponent of Temple Entry. When the Untouchables put forth a demand for political rights, he changes his position and becomes a supporter of Temple Entry. When the Hindus threaten to defeat the Congress in the election, if it pursues the matter to a conclusion, Mr. Gandhi, in order to preserve political power in the hands of the Congress, gives up Temple Entry! Is this sincerity? Does this show conviction? Was the "agony of soul," which Mr. Gandhi spoke of, more than a phrase?

CHAPTER V

A POLITICAL CHARITY

Congress Plan to Kill Untouchables by Kindness

I

On the 30th September 1932, a largely attended meeting of the Hindus of Bombay was held in the Cowasjee Jehangir Hall under the Presidentship of Pandit Malaviya. The object of the meeting was to form an All-India Anti-Untouchability League with branches in different provincial centres. The headquarters of the League were to be in Delhi. The aims of the organization were stated to be :—

> " Carrying propaganda against Untouchability and taking immediate steps to secure as early as practicable that all public wells, dharmasalas, roads, schools, crematoriums, burning ghats and all public temples be declared open to the Depressed Classes, provided that no compulsion or force shall be used and that only peaceful persuasion shall be adopted towards this end."

Mr. G. D. Birla was to be the President and Mr. Amritlal V. Thakkar, General Secretary. The All-India Anti-Untouchability League was Mr. Gandhi's project. It was inspired by him and was the direct outcome of the Poona Pact. At any rate, Mr. Gandhi adopted it as his baby, the moment it was born. The first thing Mr. Gandhi did was to change its name. In a press message issued on 9th December 1932, Mr. Gandhi told the public that the organisation would thenceforth be known as Servants of the Untouchables Society. This name also did not appear to Mr. Gandhi as the best. He was searching for another. Ultimately he decided to give it a new name. He called it the *Harijan Sevak Sangh*, which means a society of those engaged in Service to the Untouchables. This was a natural sequence of the name *Harijan* by which Mr. Gandhi used to call the Untouchables. This change did not pass off without a controversy between the Shaivas and Vaishnavas. *Hari* is one of the hundred names of Vishnu, while *Har* is one of the hundred names of Shiva. For choosing the name *Harijan*, Mr. Gandhi was accused of sectarian partiality by the Shaivas who pressed that the Untouchables should be called *Harijan*. Mr. Gandhi did not yield and as the first fruits of this new organisation the Untouchables got a new name.

On the 3rd November 1932, Mr. Birla and Mr. Thakkar issued a statement to the Press in which they set out the programme of this organization and the set-up of the machinery to carry out the programme.

As to the programme the statement said :—

"The League believes that reasonable persons among the Sanatanists are not much against the removal of Untouchability as such, as they are against inter-caste dinners and marriages. Since it is not the ambition of the League to undertake reforms beyond its own scope, it is desirable to make it clear that while the League will work by persuasion among the caste Hindus to remove every vestige of untouchability, the main line of work will be constructive, such as the uplift of Depressed Classes educationally, economically and socially, which itself will go a great way to remove Untouchability. With such a work, even a staunch Sanatanist can have nothing but sympathy. And it is for such work mainly that the League has been established. Social reforms like the abolition of the caste system and inter-dining are kept outside the scope of the League."

For the convenient prosecution of the programme, it was proposed that each Province should be divided into a number of units and each unit to be in charge of paid workers. A unit may or may not be coterminus with a district. It may be formed by grouping together two districts or two States.

The statement also set out a normal Budget for the year. It was to be of the following dimensions :—

"Not less than two-thirds of the expenditure should be devoted to actual welfare work, the remaining one-third to staff and their allowances. Two paid workers are considered the minimum staff and they should be moving about 15 to 29 days in a month in villages.

Maintenance allowance for two itinerant workers	30+20=50×12=	600
Travelling charges for two itinerant workers	2×10×12 =	240
Miscellaneous expenditure by and through the workers	2×10×12 =	240
Welfare work, i.e., cost of school books, scholarships, prizes, contributions for wells, if any, and formation of Harijan Panchayats..		2,000
	TOTAL ...	3,080

Budget for the Whole Country

We give below a rough idea of the minimum total amount which may have to be spent for the whole of India. The scheme is modest enough in view of the gigantic nature of the work and it should not be difficult for the public to raise the required fund. Every pie contributed to the fund will make a valuable contribution and therefore we appeal to the public to make some sacrifices for the cause. The number of units proposed for each province is only a tentative proposal. The final decision, of course, will have to be taken by the Provincial Boards themselves.

" It is calculated that at least the following number of units will be required to be worked in different provinces, the number of districts and states being shown against each province :—

Name of Province		*No. of Dists.*	*No. of Units*
Assam		11	6
Andhra		—	6
Bengal		26	15
Calcutta City		1	3
Bihar		16	16
Bombay, Bombay City and Suburban District ...		1	3
Maharashtra		10	8
Gujerat, Baroda, Kathiawar, Cutch and other States 5 and States 10			
Central Provinces and Berar (Marathi)		9	7
Central India States		11	8
Delhi Province		1	2
Kashmir		1	1
Malabar, Cochin and Travancore ... ..., ...		4	10
Mysore and Karnatak Districts of Bombay and Madras		8	10
Nizam's Dominion		14	10
Orissa Feudatory States	5×26=States		8
Punjab and N. W. F. Province and the Punjab States	32×7=	39	10
Rajputana States Ajmer-Merwar State ...	18		
British District	1	19	9
Sind		8	5
Tamil Nadu		13	8
United Provinces		48	24
Total		...	·184

The expenditure for 184 Units would be			
3,000×184	=	Rs.	5,52,000
CENTRAL AND PROVINCIAL OFFICES			
Central Office, 1,000×12	=	Rs.	12,000
Provincial Offices, 4,000×12	=	Rs.	48,000
Total	...	Rs.	60,000
GRAND TOTAL	...	Rs.	6,12,000
	or say,	Rs.	6,00,000

This amount will have to be made up both from the Central Fund as well as from funds raised by provinces and districts.

It can be seen that a sum of six lakhs of rupees is intended to be collected and spent per year in the whole country for the removal of Untouchability and ameliorative work of Harijans. This programme, particularly if the ameliorative work is to be effective, should continue at least for 5 years. When spread out over 22 provinces, including States and 4 crores or 400 lakhs of Harijans in the country, this is a small budget indeed."

To provide funds for the work of the Sangh Mr. Gandhi started an All-India tour which began on 7th November 1933 and ended on 29th July 1934. As the object of the tour was to arouse enthusiasm among the Hindus for the cause of the Untouchables as also to collect funds, Mr. Gandhi did most of the tour on foot. The total amount collected was Rs. 8 lakhs.[1] With this amount and the annual donation of Mr. Gandhi's monied friends the Sangh started its work.

The Harijan Sevak Sangh has been going on since September 1932. It has been held out as a glorious testimony to the agony of Mr. Gandhi's soul for the condition of the Untouchables and to the passion he feels for their elevation. The General Secretary of the Sangh has invited many Americans to the Home of the Sangh in Delhi and shown them round as an unrivalled piece of social work that is being done by Mr. Gandhi for the welfare of the Untouchables.

Any welfare work for a down-trodden people must be welcomed by all. But this does not mean that it must never be criticised. That can hardly be accepted. It would be legitimate to inquire what work the Sangh is doing since so much is made of it. Any one who has read the Annual Reports of the Sangh will see that it follows certain well defined and stereotyped lines. In the field of education, the Sangh has

[1] *Harijan*, August 3, 1934.

sought to encourage higher education among the Untouchables by instituting scholarships for the Arts, technical and professional courses. The Sangh also gives scholarships to High School students. The Sangh also maintains Hostels for Untouchable students attending colleges and high schools. The great part of the educational activities of the Sangh is taken up in maintaining separate schools for primary stage children, where there were no common schools in the vicinity or where common schools were closed to them.

Next come the welfare activities of the Sangh. The medical aid which the Sangh undertakes to render to the Untouchables falls under this head. This is done by itinerant workers of the Sangh who go in Harijan quarters to give medical aid to the sick and the ailing among the Untouchables. The Sangh also maintains a few dispensaries for the use of the Untouchables. This is a very small activity of the Sangh.

The more important part of the welfare activity of the Sangh relates to water supply. The Sangh does this by (1) sinking new wells or installing tube wells and pumps for the use of the Untouchables, (2) repairing old ones and (3) persuading Local Governments and Bodies to sink and repair wells for the Untouchables.

The third line of activity undertaken by the Sangh is economic. The Sangh seems to run a few industrial schools and it is claimed that the industrial schools run by the Sangh produced a number of trained artisans who have taken to independent living. But according to the reports, more successful and substantial work was done by way of organizing and supervising co-operative societies among the Untouchables.

From this summary of its activities an impression may be created that the Sangh must be spending quite a lot of money on the welfare of the Untouchables. What are the facts ? It will be recalled that the normal amount of money which the Sangh expected to be able to spend on the uplift work among the Untouchables was to be about Rs. 6,00,000 per year. How much has the Sangh been actually spending ? The Secretary of the Sangh in his Report issued in May 1941 says[1] :—

"During the course of the last 8 years the various branches and the central office of the Sangh have spent approximately

[1] Report, p. 58.

> Rs. 24,25,700 and Rs. 3,41,607 respectively, on the Harijan work. Looking to the needs of the problem, this sum of Rs. 27,67,307 is too insignificant an amount."

On this basis, the Sangh's expenditure comes to about Rs. 3,45,888 per year, which is 50 per cent. less than what the Sangh hoped to collect. It will be seen that the Sangh is not as big as it is made out to be by its friends. The Sangh has been carrying on a very poor existence. A Budget of three lakhs per year for a population of 50 millions of Untouchables is not a matter on which the Untouchables need be very jubilant. Even this much show, the Sangh would not have been able to put up if during the two years that they were in office the Congress Governments in different Provinces had not given large grants to the Sangh.

The Sangh cannot be blamed for its poor finances. The blame lies with the Hindus. The stagnant, if not the deteriorating, condition of the Sangh shows how little the Hindus care for the welfare of the Untouchables. For political purposes they contributed one crore of Rupees which went to make up the Tilak Swaraj Fund. For General Welfare work they have very recently contributed one crore and 15 lakhs which will make up the Kasturba Memorial Fund. Compared with these the contributions made by the Hindus to the Harijan Sevak Sangh are paltry.

There is however one thing about the Sangh which is not easily accountable. It relates to the nature of the welfare work it does. Much of the work the Sangh does is obviously the work which any civilized Government is bound to undertake out of public revenues. It is difficult to understand why the Sangh should not ask Government to undertake the work and use its funds on projects which Government does not do and yet are urgently required to be done. Evidently, the Sangh wants to do many numerous and petty things as would make it popular and not those which are necessary and fundamental for the uplift of the Untouchables.

II

These are matters which are the private concern of the Sangh. But there is another matter which is of public importance and of which separate mention must be done. It is the feeling of hostility which the Untouchables entertain towards the Sangh. This circumstance and its causes were referred[1] to by a writer in the *Indian Social Reformer* of 14th October 1944. He said :—

> " A deputation of Harijans waited on Gandhiji at Sevagram with the request that members of the castes grouped under the head of 'Scheduled Castes' should be allowed representation on the governing body of the Harijan Sevak Sangh. Gandhiji is reported to have replied that the Sangh is meant to help Harijans and was not a Harijan organization and, therefore, their request was inadmissible. At the Round Table Conference Gandhiji opposed reservation of seats for Harijans on the ground that they were Hindus and should not be separated from the general body. Subsequently in the Yeravda Pact he was obliged to consent to an allocation of seats for them specially, from the Hindu quota. When the draft formula conceding this came up for ratification before a general meeting in Bombay, over which Pandit Madan Mohan Malaviya presided, one of those present pointed out to an impatient audience that it was not necessary to collect a large fund (as Panditjee suggested) to remove from Hindu society the blot of Untouchability and that if each one of those present resolved that he or she (a large number of women were present) would receive Harijans in their homes just like other Hindus, the problem would at once cease to exist. A Bombay business magnate turned to the intruder and remarked quietly : 'You have told them a home truth. None of them is prepared to follow it.' From the first it has struck me that this has been the fundamental weakness of the Harijan Sevak Sangh. What is the result ? Nearly every beneficiary of the Sangh is an ardent follower of Dr. Ambedkar, which is nothing, but for the fact that they share to the full the fanatical and bitter hatred of Dr. Ambedkar to the Hindus. I can give several instances to illustrate this statement. But that would only make matters worse. I think that this may be avoided by associating Harijan gentlemen and women with other Hindus in all important bodies, local and central, thus giving them the decisive voice in moulding policy. The idea of helping Harijans without associating with them, is contrary to the spirit of social reform. I was associated with the earlier movements for the uplift of Harijans and I never found this spirit of antagonism aroused among the men and women with whom one came in

[1] The occasion for his comments was furnished by the report in the newspapers that on September 26, 1944, some Untouchables waited on Mr. Gandhi and urged upon him to appoint representatives of the Untouchables on the Governing Body of the Harijan Sevak Sangh and Mr. Gandhi refused. The writer is believed to be no other than Mr. K. Natarajan.

contact. This was because the promoters of the movement—I have the Depressed Classes Mission prominently in view—were by religious faith and social conviction pledged to avoid all discrimination in their behaviour to members of the Depressed Classes. I think that Gandhiji was not quite right when he said that the Harijan Sangh could not admit members of the Scheduled Castes. Dr. Ambedkar, a friend reminds me, was a member of the Sangh when it was formed."

I quote this because it gives me the occasion to explain the causes of the hostility and expose the true character of the Sangh.

III

The writer in the *Indian Social Reformer* pleads that Untouchables should be associated with the management of the Sangh. His statement might lead people to believe that Untouchables were never represented on the Central Board of the Sangh. That would be a mistake. The correct position is that when the Sangh was started prominent Untouchables in substantial numbers were on the Central Board of the Sangh. The statement issued by Mr. Birla and Mr. Thakkar on 3rd November 1932 gives the names of those who were constituting the Central Board. It was announced that :—

> "The Central Board has been constituted with the following organising members :—
>
> Sjt. G. D. Birla, Delhi and Calcutta ; Sir Purshotamdas Thakurdas, Bombay ; Sir Lallubhai Samaldas, Bombay ; Dr. B. R. Ambedkar, Bombay ; Sheth Ambalal Sarabhai, Ahmedabad ; Dr. B. C. Roy, Calcutta ; Lala Shri Ram, Delhi ; Rao Bahadur M. C. Raja, Madras ; Dr. T. S. S. Rajan, Trichinopoly ; Rao Bahadur Srinivasan, Madras ; Mr. A. V. Thakkar, General Secretary, Delhi."

It will be seen that out of 8 members 3 were drawn from the Untouchables. After my retirement from the Board, the other two namely Rao Bahadur M. C. Rajah and Rao Bahadur Srinivasan also retired. I do not know the reasons why they dissociated themselves from the Sangh.

It is right and proper that I should state the reasons why I severed my connection with the Sangh. After the Poona Pact I proceeded in a spirit of forget and forgive. I accepted the *bona fides* of Mr. Gandhi as I was asked to do by many of his friends. It was in that spirit that I accepted a place on the Central Board of the Sangh and was looking forward to play my part in its activities. In fact, I wanted to discuss with Mr. Gandhi the programme of work which I felt the Sangh should undertake, Before I could do that, I was called to go to London to attend the third Round Table Conference. The next best thing I could do was to communicate my views to Mr. A. V. Thakkar, the Secretary of the Sangh. Accordingly I wrote the following letter from the steamer :—

M/N "VICTORIA,"
PORT SAID,
November 14, 1932.

DEAR MR. THAKKAR,

I received your wire previous to my departure to London, informing me of the acceptance of my suggestion regarding the nomination of Rao Bahadur Shrinivasan to the Central Board and Mr. D. V. Naik to the Bombay Provincial Board, I am glad that this question has been amicably settled and that we can now conjointly work out the programme of the Anti-Untouchability League.[1] I wish I had an opportunity to meet the members of the Central Board to discuss with them the principles which the League should follow in framing its programme of work, but unfortunately owing to my having to leave for London at a very short notice, I have had to forego that opportunity. I am however doing the second best namely to convey to you my views in writing for placing them before the Board for their consideration.

In my opinion there can be two distinct methods of approaching the task of uplifting the Depressed Classes. There is a school, which proceeds on the assumption that the fact of the individual belonging to the Depressed Classes is bound up with his personal conduct. If he is suffering from want and misery it is because he must be vicious and sinful. Starting from this hypothesis this School of social workers concentrates all its efforts and its resources on fostering personal virtue by adopting a programme which includes items such as temperance, gymnasium, co-operation, libraries, schools, etc., which are calculated to make the individual a better and virtuous individual. In my opinion, there is also another method of approach to this problem. It starts with the hypothesis that the fate of the individual is governed by his environment and the circumstances he is obliged to live under, and if an individual is suffering from want and misery it is because his

[1] Harijan Sevak Sangh was the name given to the League at a later stage.

environment is not propitious. I have no doubt that of the two views the latter is the more correct, the former may raise a few stray individuals above the level of the class to which they belong. It cannot lift the class as a whole. My view of the aim of the Anti-Untouchability League is that it has come into existence not for helping a few individuals at random or a few selected boys belonging to the Depressed Classes but for raising the whole class to a higher level. Consequently, I would not like the League to dissipate its energies on a programme calculated to foster private virtue. I would like the Board to concentrate all its energies on a programme that will effect a change in the social environment of the Depressed Classes. Having stated in general terms my views, I venture to place some concrete proposals for work to be undertaken by the League.

1. A Campaign to secure Civil Rights

I think the first thing that the League should undertake is a campaign all over India to secure to the Depressed Classes the enjoyment of their civic rights such as taking water from the village wells, entry in village schools, admission to village chawdi, use of public conveyance, etc. Such a programme if carried into villages will bring about the necessary social revolution in the Hindu Society, without which it will never be possible for the Depressed Classes to get equal social status. The Board must, however, know what difficulties it will have to face if this campaign of civic rights is to be carried through. Here I can speak from experience, because I, as President, know what happened when the Depressed Classes Institute and the Social Equality League launched such a plan in the Kolaba and the Nasik Districts of the Bombay Presidency. First of all, there will be riots between the Depressed Classes and the caste Hindus which will result in breaking heads and in criminal prosecutions of one side or the other. In this struggle, the Depressed Classes will suffer badly because the Police and the Magistracy will always be against them. There has not been a single case in the course of the social struggle carried on in these two districts, in which the Police and the Magistracy have come to the rescue of the Depressed Classes even when justice was on their side. The Police and the Magistracy are as corrupt as they could be, but what is worse is that they are definitely political in the sense that they are out not to see that justice is done but to see that the dignity and interests of the caste Hindus as against the Depressed Classes are upheld. Secondly the villages will proclaim a complete boycott of the Depressed

Classes, the moment they see the latter are trying to reach a status of equality along with them. You know what harrowing tales of harassment, unemployment and starvation, which the Depressed Classes repeated before the Starte Committee of which you were a member. I therefore do not think it necessary to say anything more about the severity of this weapon and of its dreadful power to bring all efforts of the Depressed Classes to rise above their degraded station to a standstill.

I have mentioned only two of the many obstacles which the League will have to overcome, if this campaign of civil rights is to be successful and the League will have to have an army of workers in the rural parts, who will encourage the Depressed Classes to fight for their rights and who will help them in any legal proceedings arising therefrom to a successful issue. I am so much convinced by the efficiency of this programme that I have not the slightest hesitation in saying that the League ought to look upon this as primary in comparison to everything else. It is true that this programme involves social disturbance and even bloodshed. But I do not think that it can be avoided. I know the alternative policy of adopting the line of least resistance. I am convinced that it will be ineffective in the matter of uprooting untouchability. The silent infiltration of rational ideas among the ignorant mass of caste Hindus cannot, I am sure, work for the elevation of the Depressed Classes. First of all, the caste Hindu like all human beings follows his customary conduct in observing untouchability towards the Depressed Classes. Ordinarily people do not give up their customary mode of behaviour because somebody is preaching against it. But when that customary mode of behaviour has or is believed to have behind it the sanction of religion mere preaching, if it is not resented and resisted, will be allowed to waft along the wind without creating any effect on the mind. The salvation of the Depressed Classes will come only when the Caste Hindu is made to think and is forced to feel that he must alter his ways. For that you must create a crisis by direct action against his customary code of conduct. The crisis will compel him to think and once he begins to think he will be more ready to change than he is otherwise likely to be. The great defect in the policy of least resistance and silent infiltration of rational ideas lies in this that they do not *compel* thought, for they do not produce crisis. The direct action in respect of Chawdar Tank in Mahad, the Kalaram Temple in Nasik and the Guruvayur Temple in Malabar have done in a few days what million days of preaching by reformers would never have done. I therefore strongly recommend this campaign of direct action for securing civil rights of the Depressed Classes for adoption by the Anti-Untouchability League. I know the difficulties of this campaign, and from such experience as I have of it I am convinced that the forces in charge of Law and Order must be on our side, if it is to end in success. It is because of this that I have deliberately excluded temples from its scope and confined it only to public rights of a civic nature, the exercise of which I feel Government is bound to protect.

2. Equality of Opportunity

The second thing I would like the Anti-Untouchability League to work for, is to bring about equality of opportunity for the Depressed Classes. Much of the misery and poverty of the Depressed Classes is due to the absence of equality of opportunity which in its turn is due to untouchability. I am sure you are aware that the Depressed Classes in villages and even in towns cannot sell vegetables, milk or butter—ways of earning a living which are open to all and sundry. A caste Hindu will buy these things from a non-Hindu, but he will not buy them from the Depressed Classes. In the matter of enployment, his condition is the worst. In Government Departments the bar-sinister operates and he is denied the place of a constable or even a messenger. In industries he fares no better. Like the Negro in America he is the last to be employed in days of prosperity and the first to be fired in days of adversity. And even when he gets a foothold, what are his prospects ? In the Cotton Mills in Bombay and Ahmedabad he is confined to the lowest paid department where he can earn only Rs. 25 per month. More paying departments like the weaving department are permanently closed to him. Even in the low paid departments he cannot rise to the highest rung of the ladder. The place of the boss is reserved for the caste Hindu while the Depressed Class worker must slave as his underdog, no matter how senior or how efficient. In departments where the earning depends on piece work, he has failed to earn as well as Caste Hindu employees because of social discrimination. Depressed Classes women working in the Winding and Reeling Departments have come to me in hundreds complaining that the Naikins instead of distributing the raw material to all employees equally or in fair proportion, give all of it to the caste Hindu women and leave them in the cold. I have given only a few of the instances of the gross inequality of opportunity from which the Depressed Classes are suffering mainly at the hands of the Hindus. I think it would be fit and proper, if the Anti-Untouchability League were to take up this question by creating public opinion in condemnation of it and establishing bureaus to deal with urgent cases of inequality. I would particularly desire the League to tackle the problem of opening the Weaving department of the Cotton mills to the Depressed Classes as it is likely to make a very large opening for prosperous employment to members of the Depressed Classes. Much can be done by private firms and companies managed by Hindus by extending their patronage to the Depressed Classes and by employing them in their offices in various grades and occupations suited to the capacities of the applicants.

3. Social Intercourse

Lastly, I think the League should attempt to dissolve that nausea, which the touchables feel towards the Untouchables and which is the reason why the two sections have remained so much apart as to constitute separate and distinct entities. In my opinion the best way of achieving it is to establish closer contact between the two. Only a common cycle of participation can help people to overcome the strangeness of feeling which one has, when brought into contact with the other. Nothing can do this more effectively in my opinion than the admission of the Depressed Classes to the houses of the caste Hindus as guests or servants. The live contact thus established will familiarize both to a common and associated life and will pave the way for that unity which we are all striving after. I am sorry that many caste Hindus who have shown themselves responsive are not prepared for this. During those ten days of the Mahatma's fast that shook the Indian world, there were cases in Vile Parle and in Mahad where the caste Hindu servants had struck work because their masters had abrogated the rules of untouchability by fraternising with the Untouchables. I expected that they would end the strike and teach a lesson to the erring masses by filling the vacancies by employing Depressed Classes in their place. Instead of doing that they capitulated with the forces of orthodoxy and strengthened them. I do not know how far such fair-weather friends of the Depressed Classes would be of help to them. People in distress can have very little consolation from the fact that they have sympathisers, if those sympathisers will do nothing more than sympathise, and I may as well tell the League that the Depressed Classes will never be satisfied of the *bona fides* of these caste Hindu sympathisers until it is proved that they are prepared to go to the same length of fighting against their own kith and kin actual warfare if it came to that for the sake of the Depressed Classes as the Whites of the North did against their own kith and kin, namely, the Whites of the South for the sake of the emancipation of the Negro. But this thing apart, I think it is necessary that the League should endeavour to inculcate upon the mind of the Hindu public the necessity of establishing contact and social intercourse between the touchables and the Untouchables in the way I have mentioned.

4. Agency to be Employed

The League will have to employ a very large army of workers to carry out its programme. The appointment of social workers might perhaps be looked upon as a minor question. Speaking for myself, I attach very great importance to the selection of a proper agency to be employed in this behalf. There can always be found workers to do a particular piece of work or any other for the matter of that if they are paid for it. I am sure such mercenary workers will not serve the purpose of the League. As Tolstoy said : "Only those who love can serve." In my opinion that test is more likely to be fulfilled by workers drawn from the Depressed Classes. I should therefore like the League to bear this aspect of the question in mind in deciding upon whom to appoint and when not to appoint. I do not suggest that there are not scoundrels among the Depressed Classes who have not made social service their last refuge. But largely speaking you can be more sure that a worker drawn from the Depressed Classes will regard the work as love's labour—a thing which is so essential to the success of the League. Secondly, there are agencies which are already engaged in some sort of social service without any confines as to class or purpose —and may be prepared to supplement their activity by taking up the work of Anti-Untouchability League in consideration of a grant-in-aid. I am sure this hire-purchase system of work —if I may use that expression—can produce no lasting good. What is wanted in an agency is a single-minded devotion to one task and one task only. We want bodies and organisations which have deliberately chosen to be narrow-minded in order to be enthusiastic about their cause. The work it is to be assigned must be assigned to those who would undertake to devote themselves exclusively to the work of the Depressed Classes.

I am afraid I have already trespassed the limits of a letter and I do not think I can err further in that direction without being tediously long. I had many other things to say but I now propose to reserve them for another occasion. Before closing this I wish to say just this. It was Balfour I think who said that what could hold the British Empire together was love and not law. I think that observation applies equally to the Hindu Society. The touchables and the Untouchables cannot be held together by law—certainly not by any electoral law substituting joint electorates for separate electorates. The only thing that can hold them together is love. Outside the family justice alone in my opinion can open the possibility of love, and it should be the duty of the Anti-Untouchability League to see that the touchable does, or failing that is made to do, justice to the Untouchable. Nothing else in my opinion can justify the project or the existence of the League.

With best wishes and kind regards.

I am,
Yours sincerely,
(Sd.) B. R. AMBEDKAR.

P.S.

I am releasing this to the Press so that the general public may know my views and have an opportunity to consider them.

To·

A. V. THAKKAR, ESQ.,
General Secretary,
Anti-Untouchability League,
Birla House,
New Delhi.

IV

To my great surprise, I found that no attention was paid to my proposals. Indeed, my letter was not even acknowledged ! I felt that there was no use in my remaining in the Sangh. I dissociated myself from it. I found that in my absence the aims and objects of the Sangh had undergone a complete change.

In the statement issued by Mr. G. D. Birla and Mr. A. V. Thakkar on the 3rd November two months after its inauguration it was stated :—

"The League believes that reasonable persons among the Sanatanists are not much against the removal of Untouchability as such, as they are against inter-caste dinners and marriages. Since it is not the ambition of the League to undertake reforms beyond its own scope, it is desirable to make it clear that while the League will work by persuasion among the caste Hindus to remove every vestige of Untouchability, the main line of work will be constructive, such as the uplift of Depressed Classes educationally, economically and socially, which itself will go a great way to remove untouchability. With such a work even a staunch Sanatanist can have nothing but sympathy. And it is for such work mainly that the League has been established. Social reforms like the abolition of the caste system and inter-dining are kept outside the scope of the League."

Here there was a complete departure from the original aims of the organization as propounded[1] at the meeting held in the Cowasji Jehangir Hall in Bombay on the 30th September 1932. Removal of Untouchability had only a nominal place in the programme. Constructive work became the main part of the work of the Sangh. It is pertinent to ask why this change in the aims and objects was made. This change in the aims and objects could not have been brought about without the knowledge and consent of Mr. Gandhi. The only reason one can see is that the original programme was most inconvenient to Mr. Gandhi. Removal of Untouchability as a platform was very good, but as a programme of action it was bound to have made Mr. Gandhi very unpopular with the Hindus. He was not prepared to court such unpopularity. He therefore preferred the programme of constructive work which had all advantages and no disadvantages. The Hindus did not mind it. Mr. Gandhi could pursue it without incurring the displeasure of the Hindus. The programme of constructive work had no such disadvantage. On the other hand, it had a positive advantage to recommend it. It had the possibility of destroying the independent movement which the Untouchables had built up and which had forced Mr. Gandhi in 1932 to yield to its demands by agreeing to the Poona Pact by dangling well before them the benefits of the constructive work, a consummation which all Congressmen so devoutly wish. It could make Untouchables Congressmen and most gracefully too. The programme of constructive work had the possibility of being converted into a plan to kill Untouchables by kindness. This as a matter of fact has happened. The Harijan Sevak Sangh is intolerent of any movement on the part of the Untouchables which is independent

[1] See p. 126.

of and opposed to the Hindus and the Congress and is out to destroy it. Anticipating that such would be the consequences of the change in the aims and objects, I retired from the Sangh.

Since the first batch of the Untouchables left the Sangh no attempt was made by Mr. Gandhi to appoint other Untouchables in their places. Instead, the management of the Sangh has been allowed to pass entirely into the hands of the Hindus of the Congress persuasion. Indeed, it is now the policy of the Sangh to exclude Untouchables from the management and higher direction of the Sangh. As will be seen from the refusal of Mr. Gandhi to agree to the suggestion made by deputation of Untouchables[1] requesting him to appoint Untouchables to the managing body. Mr. Gandhi has propounded a new doctrine in defence of his position. He says : " the welfare work for the Untouchables is a penance which the Hindus have to do for the sin of Untouchability. The money that has been collected has been contributed by the Hindus. From both points of view the Hindus alone must run the Sangh. Neither ethics nor right would justify Untouchables in claiming a seat on the Board of the Sangh." Mr. Gandhi does not realize how greatly he has insulted the Untouchables by his doctrine, the ingenuity of which has not succeeded in concealing its gross and coarse character. If Mr. Gandhi's point is that the money is collected by the Hindus and the Untouchables have therefore no right to say how it shall be spent, no self respecting Untouchable will bother him and fortunately those Untouchables who have gone to him for such favour are just unemployed loafers who are seeking to make politics a source of their livelihood. But Mr. Gandhi must realize that what he says is only a justification for the change. It does not explain what has been the cause of this profound change in the original conception of the Sangh. It is pertinent to ask : why at one time he was anxious to have Untouchables on the Governing Body of the Sangh and why he is determined now to exclude them ?

V

The writer of the letter in the *Indian Social Reformer* is right when he says the Untouchables felt no hostility towards

[1] The deputation of the Untouchables that waited on Mr. Gandhi is not the first of its kind. Others have done so previously with the same result.

the Depressed Classes Mission Society which like the Harijan Sevak Sangh was also engaged in doing welfare work among the Untouchables. Hindus and Untouchables both worked together in perfect harmony towards furthering the work of the Mission. The writer is not quite correct when he says that this was due to the Depressed Classes Mission having always taken care to have on its Managing Committee a certain number of Untouchables. This is quite true. But the reason why there was no hostility between the Mission and the Untouchables and why there is between the Untouchables and the Sangh is quite different. It lies in the fact that the Mission had no political objective behind its work but the Sangh has.

It is true that the original intention was to keep the Sangh scrupulously aloof from politics. It was stated in the statement issued on 3rd November 1932 that :—

> " In order that the League may be able to carry on its work on a non-party basis, it has decided not to associate itself with politics or religious propaganda of any kind. The heads of Provincial as well as Central Executive will, therefore, have to be very careful in the selection of their active workers. With this object in view it is necessary that all whole-time paid workers of the League should not take part in politics or in any sectional or religious propaganda."

But this pronouncement was respected more in its breach than in the observance thereof. It may be that it was impossible to resist the temptation of using the Harijan Sevak Sangh for bringing the Untouchables into the Congress fold, make them accept Congress politics and impress upon them Congress ideologies, especially when the sense of gratitude for service rendered, no matter how petty, would naturally induce in them such a mentality. It may be that it was necessary to make the Harijan Sevak Sangh a political manufactory in addition to its being a service station for the Untouchables. To have equipped the Untouchables for their struggle in life and to have left them free to choose their politics would be charity pure and simple. But how long would the Hindus have supported such a charity ? Not very long. There being no sense of sin behind the treatment of Untouchables by the Hindus and no cause for repentance or expiation, the charity on which the Sangh lives would have dried out. To prevent this the Sangh may have felt that to get continued charity it must show results, i.e., to prove to the Hindus that the Untouchables are no longer independent of and opposed to the Hindus in the matter of religion and politics. My analysis of the causes may not be accurate. But there is no denying the fact that the Harijan Sevak Sangh is a political organization the aim and object of which are to draw the Untouchables into the Congress fold.

I can give only a few instances which strike me as important. The Harijan Sevak Sangh holds Conferences of its workers. These Conferences were ostensibly " organized for the purpose of examining the progress of work in different linguistic provinces and for exchanging ideas and experiences." One such conference was held in Poona in the first week of June 1939. It was found that this Conference had planned to pass a resolution asking Government to change the system of voting under the Poona Pact by substituting distributive system for cumulative voting. I have already pointed out how after its surrender marked by the Poona Pact, the Congress insisted upon the adoption of the distributive system of voting and how dangerous it was to the Untouchables and how it would have nullified the Poona Pact. The Congress failed. What the Congress failed to do the Sangh took upon itself to advocate knowing full well that it was opposed by the Untouchables. A strange resolution for a non-political body! It is like a drunkard with a red nose trying to convince his neighbours that he is a teetotaler. The Sangh was prevented from pursuing the course by a demonstration of the Untouchables.

I am in a position to state that the Bombay Branch of the Harijan Sevak Sangh had followed the policy of black listing some of the Untouchable communities residing in Bombay on account of its Anti-Congress attitude. Students from communities which were black listed were refused scholarships and other educational aids. The Mahar Community, which forms the spearhead of the political movement of the Untouchables and has all along fought with the Congress, was black listed and Mahar students were generally subjected to discrimination unless the student proved that he did not share the Anti-Congress sentiments of the Community.

The last instance I would refer to has reference to Mr. A. V. Thakkar, the General Secretary of the Harijan Sevak Sangh. Mr. Thakkar is also a member of the Backward Classes Board of the Bombay Government. It was established in 1929. It meets periodically and advises Government on matters affecting the Untouchables and other backward Classes.

Mr. Thakkar brought a resolution in the meeting of the Board recommending to Government that scholarships set apart by Government for Untouchable boys should not be given to the Mahar boys alleging that the Mahar Community had become very much advanced in education and was appropriating—or according to him misappropriating—the share of Government funds which ought to be reserved for other Untouchable Communities. The resolution was sent down for investigation of the facts on which it was founded. The inquiry showed that the facts were wrong and that the Mahars instead of being forward were really backward in education as compared with other Untouchable Communities. The resolution was nothing but a political manœuvre by no less a person than the General Secretary of the Harijan Sevak Sangh to punish the Mahars for their Anti-Congress politics.

What does all this show? Does it not show that the Harijan Sevak Sangh is a charitable organization only in name, and that its real aim is to ensnare the Untouchables, to make them the camp-followers of the Hindus and the Congress and to scotch any movement by them the aim and object of which are to free themselves from the social, religious, economic and political domination of the Hindus? Is there any wonder if the Untouchables look upon the Harijan Sevak Sangh as an abomination, the object of which is to kill them by kindness?

CHAPTER VI

A FALSE CLAIM

Does Congress Represent All?

I

The Congress has been loudly and insistently claiming that it is the only political organization in India which is representative of the people of India. At one time it used to claim that it represents the Musalmans also. This it does not now do, at any rate not so loudly and insistently. But so far as the Untouchables are concerned the Congress maintains most vehemently that it does represent them. On the other hand, the non-Congress political parties have always denied this claim. This is particularly true of the Untouchables who have never hesitated to repudiate the Congress claim to represent them.

In this rivalry, the Congress has been able to beat down the Untouchables and the other non-Congress Parties by the sheer strength of the resources in publicity and propaganda. The result has been that most foreigners interested in Indian affairs have become infected by this propaganda, and have come to believe in the validity of the Congress claim. So long as the world had to depend upon nothing but propaganda, the Congress could very easily fool the foreigner and there was no help for those who denied the Congress claim to represent all. They had no means of coping with the situation. But since the Election of 1937 to the Provincial Legislatures the situation has been altered. Instead of depending upon general statements backed by propaganda, one can now determine the issue in terms of seats and votes which is a more concrete measure of appraisement than mere propaganda.

What do the election returns show? What is the total number of seats captured by the Congress? What is the total number of votes secured by the Congress?

First, let us ascertain the number of seats captured by the Congress. Soon after the elections had taken place, the Congress held a Convention of all those who were elected to the Provincial Legislatures on the Congress ticket, which met in New Delhi on March 19, and 20, 1937. In that connection, the Congress issued a bulletin in which their names are given. Taking that information as accurate, the following appears to be the strength of the Congress in each Provincial Legislature :—

Table 7

Congress Strength in Provincial Assemblies

Province	*Total Strength of the Assembly*	*Congress Strength in the Assembly*
Assam	108	35
Bengal	250	60
Bihar	152	95
Bombay	175	85
C. P. and Berar	112	70
Madras	215	159
Orissa	60	36
Punjab	175	18
Sind	60	8
U. P.	228	134
N.W.F.P.	50	19
Total ...	1,585	719

Table 8

Congress Strength in Provincial Councils

Province	*Total Strength of the Council*	*Congress Strength in the Council*
Assam	18	*Nil.*
Bengal	57	10
Bihar	26	8
Bombay	26	14
Madras	46	26
U.P.	52	8
Total ...	225	66

These tables show that taking the two Houses together the Congress secured 777 seats out of a total of 1,758. The Congress obviously is not a majority party. It did not secure even half the number of seats.

This is the position of the Congress in terms of the number of seats. What is the position of the Congress in terms of voting strength ? The following figures will show that even in point of voting strength the Congress came out as a minority.

Table 9

Abstract of Votes cast in the Election distributed as between Congress and Non-Congress Parties

Province		Total Votes cast	Votes cast in favour of Congress	Votes cast in favour of Non-Congress
Madras ...	Assembly ...	4,327,734	2,658,966	1,668,768
	Council ...	33,511	16,907	16,604
Bombay ...	Assembly ...	3,408,308	1,568,093	1,840,215
	Council ...	23,730	9,420	14,310
Bengal ...	Assembly ...	3,475,730	1,055,900	2,419,830
	Council ...	5,593	1,489	4,104
U. P. ...	Assembly ...	3,362,736	1,899,325	1,463,411
	Council ...	9,795	1,580	8,215
Bihar ...	Assembly ...	1,477,668	992,642	485,026
	Council ...	4,318	96	4,222
Punjab ...	Assembly ...	1,710,934	181,265	1,529,669
C. P. ...	Assembly ...	1,317,461	678,265	639,196
Assam ...	Assembly ...	522,332	129,218	393,114
	Council ...	2,623	*Nil.*	2,623
N.W.F.P. ...	Assembly ...	179,529	43,845	135,684
Orissa ...	Assembly ...	304,749	198,680	106,069
Sind ...	Assembly ...	333,589	18,944	314,645
	Total ...	20,500,340	9,454,635	11,045,705

It is not enough to know these figures. They must be read in the light of other circumstances. The first such circumstance is the level of the franchise. The other is the relative position of the two parties in the election. Without taking these into account it would not be possible to understand the full significance of the election results. As to franchise, it is very high, and the electorate, compared with the total population, is indeed very small. How small a part of the total population it formed will be seen from the comparative figures given in the following table :—

Table 10

Province	Population (1931)	Electorate
Madras	47,193,602	6,145,450
Bombay and Sind	26,398,997	3,249,500
Bengal	51,087,338	6,695,483
U. P.	49,614,833	5,335,309
Punjab	24,018,639	2,686,094
Bihar and Orissa	42,329,583	2,932,454
C. P.	17,990,937	1,741,364
Assam	9,247,857	815,341
N.W.F.P.	4,684,364	246,609
Total ...	272,566,150	29,847,604

Only about ten per cent. of the population was given the right to vote. The high franchise made the electorate a hive of the middle and the intellectual classes, both of which were intensely pro-Congress. Coming to the relative position of the Congress and the Non-Congress Parties, the following points call for special notice. On the Congress side there were massed all the sinews of war, money and organization. The Non-Congress candidates were without a party chest and had no organization. The Congress candidates were the blue boys of the public. They were enemies of British Imperialism, out to achieve freedom and independence of the country. Gaol life had invested the Congress candidates with the halo of martyrdom. As a rule no one was selected as a Congress candidate who had not gone to gaol. The Non-Congress candidates were represented by the Congress Press—and as I have said there is no other press in India—as the showboys of the British, with no record of service to or sacrifice for the country, agents of British Imperialism, enemies of the country, job-hunters, fellows out to sell the interests of the country for a mess of pottage and so on. There was another factor which told in favour of the Congress candidates and against the Non-Congress candidates. The Congress had boycotted the Montagu-Chelmsford Reforms of 1920 and the Congress candidates had not to answer for any act of commission or omission in regard to the administration of the country. The Non-Congress candidates on the other hand were drawn from those who had worked the Reforms and had to answer for many acts of omission and commission, which is the lot of all those who have the courage to take upon their shoulders the responsibilities of administration. The Non-Congress candidates were accused of having made the places dirty and the Congress candidates were proclaimed as angels going to clean the augean stables. In a situation like this, any one, knowing how the dice was loaded in favour of the Congress, cannot but feel surprised at the sorry figure the Congress cut in the election. With all its resources, prestige and public sympathy the Congress should have swept the polls. But it did not even get fifty per cent. of the seats or the votes.

Is there any doubt that the Congress claim to represent all classes and communities is a hollow claim with no foundation in fact ?

II

Let me next proceed to examine the Congress claim to represent the Untouchables. This claim also can now be determined by reference to the results of the elections that took place in 1937. A correct understanding of the results of the electoral contests between Congress and the Untouchables, I fear, will not be possible to those who have no knowledge of the electoral plan devised to give representation to the Untouchables. I therefore feel it necessary to explain in the first instance the Indian Electoral system, particularly for the benefit of the foreigner. It may be described by reference to the four elements of an Electoral System, namely, (1) Electorates which is the Indian term for constituencies, (2) Right to vote, (3) Right to stand as a candidate for election and (4) Rules for determining who is a successful candidate.

1. There are two sorts of Electorates recognized by the Government of India Act, 1935 :—

(1) Non-Territorial.

(2) Territorial.

2. Non-Territorial Electorates are Electorates which are designed to give representation to special interests such as Landlords, Chambers of Commerce, Trade Unions, etc.

3. Territorial Electorates fall into three categories :—

(*i*) Separate Territorial Electorates known in their abbreviated form as Separate Electorates.

(*ii*) General Territorial Electorates.

(*iii*) Joint Territorial Electorates with Reserved Seats, commonly spoken of as Joint Electorates.

4. Separate Electorates are Communal Electorates. They are designed to give representation to specified Communities, namely, Muslims, Indian Christians, Europeans and Anglo-Indians. The voters of each of these Communities in a given area are grouped into one Electorate, separate from the rest. They elect a voter of their Community as their representative exclusively by their own votes. The governing feature of a separate electorate is that in an election through a separate electorate only voters of a Community can vote and stand for election. If it is a Muslim Electorate the voter and the

candidate must be a Musalman; if it is a Christian Electorate the voter and the candidate must be a Christian and so on. The election is decided by a majority of votes cast by voters of the particular community.

5. A General Electorate is the normal, usual form of the electorate and comprises of voters of all communities living in an area but which are outside the system of Separate Electorates. It is called a General Electorate because it is an electorate in which neither community nor religion finds any recognition. It is an electorate of the Rest, i.e., other than Muslims, Indian Christians, Europeans and Anglo-Indians. In a General Electorate—

(*i*) no voter who is in a Separate Electorate has a right to vote or stand for election,

(*ii*) every voter who is on its electoral roll has a right to vote and to stand for election without reference to his caste, creed or community, and

(*iii*) the result of the election is determined by a simple majority of votes cast.

6. A Joint Electorate is a cross between a Separate Electorate and a General Electorate. It has some things in common with Separate Electorate and General Electorate. But it also differs from both in other particulars. The points of agreement and of difference are set out below :—

(*i*) *Joint Electorate compared with Separate Electorate :—*

(1) Joint Electorate is akin to Separate Electorate in as much as both aim to earmark a seat for a particular community.

(2) Joint Electorate differs from Separate Electorate in two respects :—

(*a*) In Separate Electorate the right to vote in the election is confined to voters of the community for which the seat is earmarked, while in Joint Electorate, though the seat is earmarked for a particular community, in other words though the right to stand is confined to a member of a particular community, the right to vote in the election for that seat is open to other communities which make up General Electorate.

(*b*) In both cases the poll is declared on the basis of majority votes. But in the case of a Separate Electorate the majority is and must be of the voters belonging to the same community as that of the candidate, while in the case of a Joint Electorate majority need not be of the same community as that of the candidate.

(*ii*) *Joint Electorate compared with General Electorate* :—

(1) Joint Electorate is akin to General Electorate in as much as in both a voter is free to vote for any candidate standing for a general Constituency.

(2) Joint Electorate differs from Separate Electorate in two respects :—

(*a*) General Electorate may be a single member electorate. But Joint Electorate must at least be a two-member electorate, one general and one reserved.

(*b*) In General Electorate no seat is earmarked for any community. But in Joint Electorate one at least must be reserved.

7. *Special Features of Joint Electorate.*

Joint Electorate with Reserved Seat or Seats is essentially a General Electorate with the following distinguishing features :—

(1) General Electorate may be a single member electorate. But Joint Electorate must necessarily be a plural member Electorate.

(2) In General Electorate the seat or seats to be filled by Election are open to all, and all communities not enclosed in Separate Electorates are entitled to contest and the result of the election is determined by the majority of votes polled by the candidates without reference to the community of the voters or the candidate. But in Joint Electorate at least one seat is reserved for some particular community which means that the right to stand as a candidate for such reserved seat, is restricted to the members of that community.

(3) While the right to stand in Joint Electorate is restricted, the right to vote is unrestricted and all

voters in General Electorate, i.e., even voters of communities other than the one for which the seat is reserved are free to vote for the election of the candidate for the Reserved Seat.

(4) In declaring the result of the election to the reserved seat, there is no requirement that the successful candidate must have obtained a specified quantum of votes of the voters of his community. The rule is that the candidate of the community for which the seat is reserved if there is only one or if there be more than one candidate then the one who polls the highest number of votes must be declared to be elected even if another candidate belonging to the general community has secured a greater number of votes than the community's candidate.

Such is the Electoral System which obtains in India under the Government of India Act, 1935. The system made applicable to the Untouchables is the one referred to as the system of Joint Electorates with Reserved Seats and described under 7 above.

To give effect to the principle of reservation for the Untouchables what is done is to pick out a requisite number of General Electorates, convert them into plural member electorates and reserve in each such electorate one or two seats for the Scheduled Castes. Different Provinces have different number of such Joint Electorates. Their actual number is determined by the number of seats allotted to the Scheduled Castes in the Provincial Legislature and by the number of seats reserved for them in each Joint Electorate. Attention may also be drawn to some features of the plan, which from the point of view of results are of crucial character.

The Joint Electorate is a general electorate. But it must not on that account be supposed that it is a constituency consisting of the generality of voters. As has already been pointed out, the Muslims, Indian Christians, Anglo-Indians and Europeans have been given separate electorates and consequently, the Muslim, Indian Christian, Anglo-Indian and European voters are excluded from a joint Electorate. The result is that the Joint Electorate is a constituency in which the only voters who are included are those belonging to the Scheduled Castes, Hindus, Parsis and Jews. As the Parsis and

Jews are negligible except in Bombay, the Joint Electorate consists of Hindus and Scheduled Castes only.

Although the General Electorate selected for reserving a seat for the Untouchables may be bigger than a two-member constituency and although it is open to reserve more than one seat for the Untouchables in one General Electorate, in all provinces the general plan is to select a two-member General Electorate, and to reserve one seat for the Hindus and one seat for the Scheduled Castes. It is only in Bengal there are three constituencies in which two seats are reserved for the Scheduled Castes. The Joint Electorate is thus a linked constituency. Two features of this Joint Electorate should be noted: (1) The Hindu voters in a Joint Electorate are almost always in a majority, if not in an overwhelming majority and the Scheduled Castes voters are almost always in a minority, if not in a hopeless minority. (2) A Hindu voter can vote for the election of a Scheduled Caste candidate standing for the seat reserved for the Scheduled Castes and a Scheduled Caste voter can vote for the election of a Hindu candidate standing for the Hindu seat.

Under the system what are the probabilities? Will the Scheduled Castes be able to elect a Scheduled Caste candidate, who has their confidence, to the seat reserved for them, or will the Hindus be able to elect a Scheduled Caste candidate who is their tool and who has no confidence of the Scheduled Castes? The probabilities will be determined by two considerations: (1) by the number of seats reserved for the Hindus and (2) by the nature of the political organizations prevailing among the Hindus. If there is only one seat reserved for the Hindus and if the Hindus are so organized that they can prevent a contest for their seat and avoid frittering away their votes then it is absolutely certain that the Hindu nominee from the Scheduled Castes will win. The reason is that the Hindus who have a larger voting strength will find a surplus of votes which they do not need for election to their seat and which they can bestow upon their nominee from the Scheduled Castes and help him to win the seat reserved for the Scheduled Castes. The system of joint electorate and reserved seats which is in operation is a system of two member constituency. The Hindus under the Congress are so completely organized that there is no possibility of an electoral contest and consequent waste of votes. The result is that the system helps the Hindus to win the reserved seats and works against the Scheduled Castes. The Hindus are greatly aided in this matter by reason of the fact that for winning the seat reserved for the Scheduled Castes in a Joint Electorate it is not necessary that the majority of voters should belong to the Scheduled Castes for whom the seat is reserved.

How these weaknesses in the system of joint electorate were exploited by the Congress in the Elections which took place in 1937, will be explained later on. For the moment, I am only drawing attention to the Electoral plan devised for the purpose of giving representation to the Scheduled Castes and how vulnerable some of its features are.

III

We may now proceed to examine the Election Returns. It may be well to begin by asking a simple question : What do Congressmen mean when they say that the Election of 1937 shows that the Congress represents the Untouchables ? A clarification is necessary, because quite obviously the question can have two meanings. It may mean that those Untouchable candidates who stood on the Congress ticket for seats reserved for the Untouchables were elected as against those Untouchable candidates who did not stand on the Congress ticket. It may also mean that more votes were cast by the Untouchable voters in favour of those Untouchable candidates who stood on the Congress ticket than other Untouchable candidates. I propose to examine the returns from both points of view.

The results of the Election, in terms of seats won, have already been presented. It is not necessary to repeat those figures here. It was shown that out of 151 seats the Congress won 78. One cannot say that this result of the contest between the Congress and the Untouchables is a strong piece of evidence to support the Congress claim that it represents the Untouchables. If the Congress got 78 the Untouchables got 73. It was a neck to neck race.

Let us examine the claim of the Congress to represent the Untouchables in term of votes cast in favour of the Congress Untouchable candidates. The total number of votes cast by the Untouchable Voters in the election of 1937 numbered 1,586,456.

The following table shows how they were distributed, how many were cast in favour of the Congress Untouchable candidates and how many in favour of Non-Congress Untouchable candidates.

Table 11

Province	*In favour of Congress*	*Against Congress*	*Total of Untouchable Votes cast in the Election*
United Provinces	52,609	79,571	132,180
Madras	126,152	195,464	321,616
Bengal	59,646	624,797	684,443
Central Provinces	19,507	115,354	134,861
Bombay	12,971	158,076	171,047
Bihar	8,654	22,187	30,841
Punjab	*Nil.*	69,126	69,126
Assam	5,320	22,437	27,757
Orissa	5,878	8,707	14,585
Total ...	290,737	1,295,719	1,586,456

It is well-known that the number of seats captured by a party is not always in proportion to the number of votes cast in favour of the party and often a party carries a majority of seats with a minority of votes. This is particularly true where the single member constituency system prevails as it does in India. The real strength is measured by the number of votes secured by the party. Applying this test, it is clear that out of 1,586,456 votes only 290,737, i.e., eighteen per cent. have been cast in favour of the Congress. Eighty-two per cent. have been against the Congress. Can there be any evidence more conclusive against the Congress claim to represent the Untouchables? Congressmen may not accept voting strength as a measuring rod. They may continue to base the claim of the Congress to represent the Untouchables on the ground of seats captured. No sane man will look upon 78 out of 151 or majority of five as a victory worth talking about. As a matter of fact the Congress claim even on the basis of seats is futile. For, a further analysis of the Election Returns shows that the Congress far from capturing a majority of seats got only a minority of seats reserved for the Scheduled Castes.

If the credit side of the Congress is to be real and not bogus, then the following deductions must be made from the total of 78 which the Congress has won :

(1) Seats won by the Congress with the help of Hindu voters and which if left to be decided by the votes of the Untouchables only would have been lost by the Congress.

(2) Seats won by the Congress not by reason of an absolute majority but by reason of the splitting of the Untouchable votes due to too many Non-Congress Untouchable Candidates having stood to contest the seat against the Congress Untouchable candidate.

(3) Seats which, it was in the power of Untouchables to win, if they had used their votes in the election to the seats reserved for them and not cast them away in the election of candidates contesting the general or non-reserved seats.

I cannot see how a fair minded person can object to these deductions being made. A candidate whose majority is due to votes of persons other than Untouchables has no right to say that he is a representative of the Untouchables and the Congress cannot claim to represent the Untouchables through him merely because he belongs to the Untouchables and stood on a Congress ticket. An Untouchable candidate whose majority is the result of split in the camp of his opponents and who if there had been no split would have lost, cannot be taken as a real representative of the Untouchables and the Congress cannot claim to represent the Untouchables merely because he belongs to the Untouchables and stood on the Congress ticket. A candidate for a seat reserved for the Untouchables who succeeds in an election in which a large majority of the electors have not played their part cannot be a representative of the electors merely because the seat is an Untouchable seat. Untouchable seats captured by such Untouchable candidates must also be deducted from the total number of seats won by the Congress. The only Untouchable seats which the Congress can claim to have won are those which it has won exclusively by the votes of the Untouchable voters. All the rest must be deducted. The following table gives the distribution of the seats reserved for the Scheduled Castes and won by the Congress and the circumstances responsible for its success.

Table 12

Analysis of circumstances which helped the Congress to win the Seats it has captured

Province	Number of Seats won by the Congress				Total
	With Hindu Votes (1)	Without Hindu Votes (2)	Due to Splitting of Scheduled Castes Votes (3)	By want of interest shown by Scheduled Castes in the Election to Scheduled Castes Seats (4)	(5)
United Provinces ...	3	6	3	4	16
Madras	5	15	4	2	26
Bengal	—	4	—	2	6
Central Provinces ...	1	5	—	1	7
Bombay	1	1	1	1	4
Bihar	1	3	—	7	11
Punjab	—	—	—	—	—
Assam	1	2	—	1	4
Orissa	1	2	—	1	4
Total ...	13	38	8	19	78

These are the facts revealed by a study of the Election Returns. They are incontrovertible and must be accepted. Judged by the test of voting, the Congress far from representing the Untouchables, the Untouchables are proved to have repudiated the Congress. Judged by the test of seats, the Congress has only won 88 seats out of the total of 151. The account shows thet 78 seats it failed to win, 18 it won by Hindu Votes, 8 as a result of split due to too many Untouchables standing against the Congress Untouchable candidate and 19 on account of the foolishness of the Untouchables in not taking sufficient interest in the election to the seats reserved for them.

The following table specifies the Constituencies where such phenomena have occurred. They are classified under three heads and shown Province-wise and referred to by their serial number as shown in the Appendices XIV and XV.

Table 13

Provinces	*Analysis of Scheduled Castes Constituencies*		
	Serial Numbers of Constituencies in which Congress won with Hindu Votes	*Serial Numbers of Constituencies in which Congress won because of splitting of Scheduled Castes Votes*	*Serial Numbers of Constituencies in which Congress won because the Scheduled Castes were indifferent*
United Provinces ...	1, 3 & 4	8, 9 & 10	11, 13, 14 & 18
Madras	1, 22, 23, 24 & 25	8, 12, 15 & 17	4 & 21
Bengal	*Nil*	*Nil.*	6 & 7
Central Provinces ...	6	*Nil*	15
Bombay	1	14	3
Bihar	11	*Nil*	2, 6, 7, 8, 9, 10 & 13
Punjab	*Nil*	*Nil*	*Nil*
Assam	1	*Nil*	4
Orissa	6	*Nil*	2

The claim that the Congress represents the Untouchables is thus a false claim from beginning to end. It is a myth which in the light of the results of the election stands completely exploded.

The results of the election reveal other interesting facts which are summarised in the following two tables :—

Table 14

Election to Scheduled Castes Seats

Provinces	*Contested*	*Uncontested*	*Total*
United Provinces	15	5	20
Madras	26	4	30
Bengal	28	2	30
Central Provinces	19	1	20
Bombay	14	1	15
Bihar	6	9	15
Punjab	6	2	8
Assam	6	1	7
Orissa	4	2	6
Total ...	124	27	151

Table 15

Scheduled Castes Seats won by the Congress

Provinces	*On Contest*	*Without Contest*	*Total*
United Provinces	14	2	16
Madras	24	2	26
Bengal	6	*Nil*	6
Central Provinces	6	1	7
Bombay	3	1	4
Bihar	4	7	11
Punjab	*Nil*	*Nil*	*Nil*
Assam	4	1	4
Orissa	4	*Nil*	4
Total ...	64	14	78

Table 14 shows what keen interest the Untouchables have taken in the election to the seats reserved for them. Out of 151 as many as 124 were contested. This disproves the allegation that used to be made that it was n● use giving political rights to the Untouchables as they had neither political education nor political consciousness. Table 15 shows that the Untouchables far from looking upon the Congress as their friend and ally have regarded it as their political enemy No. 1. They have very seldom allowed the entry of the Congress in the election to the seat reserved for the Untouchables to go unchallenged. In most of the cases where the Congress had put up an Untouchable candidate on the Congress ticket for a seat reserved for the Untouchables, the Untouchables did not meekly surrender the seat to the Congress but came forward to contest the election by putting up their own candidate on a Non-Congress ticket. Out of the 78 candidates put up by the Congress for the Scheduled Castes seats as many as 64 were contested.

Table 16

Province	Number of Constituencies classified according to the ratio of Scheduled Castes Voters to every 100 of General, i.e., Hindu Voters											Remarks
	10 and Below	11—15	16—20	21—25	26—30	31—35	36—40	41—45	46—50	*Above 50*	*Total*	
United Provinces.	*Nil*	7	3	6	2	1	*Nil*	1	*Nil*	*Nil*	20	
Madras	*Nil*	5	6	10	3	3	1	1	1	*Nil*	30	
Bengal	*Nil*	*Nil*	*Nil*	3	1	3	1	3	*Nil*	14	25*	
Central Provinces.	5	5	1	2	1	*Nil*	1	1	1	3	20	
Bihar	4	5	2	2	2	*Nil*	*Nil*	*Nil*	*Nil*	*Nil*	15	
Punjab	1	1	*Nil*	1	2	*Nil*	*Nil*	1	*Nil*	2	8	
Orissa	2	*Nil*	*Nil*	2	*Nil*	2	*Nil*	*Nil*	*Nil*	*Nil*	6	
Assam	3	1	*Nil*	*Nil*	*Nil*	*Nil*	*Nil*	1	*Nil*	2	7	
Bombay	5	3	6	1	*Nil*	*Nil*	*Nil*	*Nil*	*Nil*	*Nil*	15	
Total ...	20	27	18	27	11	9	3	8	2	21	146	

* Five Constituencies have two seats reserved for Scheduled Castes which makes up the total of 30 Seats reserved for the Scheduled Castes of Bengal.

IV

To say that the elections of 1937 do not prove that the Congress was victorious over the Untouchables in the electoral fight is an understatement. In a real sense the Untouchables triumphed over the Congress. If not many are found to admit this, their inability or unwillingness to do so must be attributed to their ignorance of the difficulties which the Untouchables have had to face in their contest with the Congress. These difficulties were very real and very great. It is worthwhile to detail them so that people may know the courage and tenacity with which the Untouchables have fought to prove that they are independent of the Congress and that the Congress does not represent them.

These difficulties can be classified under two heads: (1) Organizational and (2) Electoral.

Under the first head special mention may be made of two :—

The first was the difference in the relative degree of resources at the command of the Congress and of the Untouchables. That the Congress is the richest political party goes without saying. No estimate has so far been made of the money the Congress spent in the elections of 1937. If an investigation was made it would be found that the money it spent in advertisement, in conveyance and in canvassing for the candidates who stood on its ticket was simply colossal. All these resources were placed by the Congress at the service of those Untouchables who stood on the Congress ticket. Not one millionth part of these resources were available to those Untouchable candidates who stood against the Congress. Some of them had even to borrow money to pay their deposits. They fought their elections without the help of advertisement, canvassing or conveyance.

The second is the existence of a party machine on the side of the Congress and the complete absence of it on the side of the Untouchables. The party machine as every one knows constitutes the real strength of the Congress. The credit for the creation of a party machine must be given to Mr. Gandhi. It has been in existence for the last 20 years and with the resources it possesses the Congress has kept the machine well oiled and in perfect order always ready to be put in motion by merely pressing the button. It is a vast machine which covers every town and every village in the country. There is no area in which there is no agent of the Congress to operate this machine. The Untouchables who stood on the Congress ticket had their electioneering done for them by this party machine of the Congress. Those Untouchables who stood against the Congress had no such party machine to help them. The scheme of separate representation was first introduced in Indian politics in the year 1909. The benefit of it was however given only to one community, namely, the Muslim. In 1920 the constitution was revised. In this revised constitution it was extended to the Non-Brahmins. The Untouchables were again left out. They were consoled in the matter of representation with one or two seats in the various Provincial Legislatures filled by nomination. It is for the first time in 1985 that they got the franchise and the right to representation through election. It is obvious that not having had any franchise the Untouchables had felt no need to set up a party machine of their own as there were no elections to be fought. They hardly had any time to organize themselves and to set up a party machine when suddenly in 1937 they were called upon to fight the elections. The fight between the Congress and the Untouchables was a fight between an army and a crowd.

The electoral difficulties in the way of the Untouchables were equally great. The first electoral difficulty arose from the unequal voting strength between the Hindus and the Untouchables in those General Electorates in which seats are reserved for the Untouchables. Table 16 contains figures showing the relative voting strength of the two.

This table shows how in the General Electorates the Scheduled Castes voters are outnumbered by the Hindu voters. Special attention should be paid to the proportion in which they are outnumbered by the Hindus. As the figures in the table show, in 20 constituencies the proportion of Scheduled Castes voters to Hindu voters is 10 to 100, in 27 constituencies between 11 and 15 to 100, in 18 constituencies between 16 and 20 to 100, in 27 constituencies between 21 and 25 to 100 and in 11 constituencies between 26 and 80 to 100. These instances will show how overwhelming is the majority of Hindu voters and by what a substantial margin the Hindus can overpower the Scheduled Caste voters. In this connection it must also be remembered that every Scheduled Caste Constituency is a Joint Electorate in which both classes of voters—those belonging to the Scheduled Castes and those belonging to the

Hindus—can vote for the Scheduled Castes seat and compete to capture it. In this game the relative disproportion in voting strength of the two becomes of immense importance. For, success in election in such a linked constituency primarily depends upon the relative voting strength of the competing groups.

The second electoral difficulty arose out of the number of seats fixed for the general constituencies in which seats were reserved for the Untouchables. The following table shows the system adopted in the different provinces.

Table 17

Classification of General Constituencies in which Seats for Untouchables are Reserved

Province	*No. of Seats Reserved for Untouchables*	*No. of Constituencies with 2 Seats*	*No. of Constituencies with 3 Seats*	*No. of Constituencies with 4 Seats*
Madras	30	30	*Nil*	*Nil*
Bombay	15	*Nil*	7	8
Bengal	30	20	5	*Nil*
United Provinces...	20	20	*Nil*	*Nil*
Punjab	8	8	*Nil*	*Nil*
Bihar	15	15	*Nil*	*Nil*
Central Provinces...	20	20	*Nil*	*Nil*
Assam	7	6	1	*Nil*
Orissa	6	6	*Nil*	*Nil*
Total ...	151	125	13	8

This table shows that out of 151 General Constituencies required to be declared as reserved for the Scheduled Castes as many as 125 were two-member constituencies in which one seat was reserved for the Scheduled Castes and the other was kept as a general seat. It is quite possible that many will not realize the electoral danger that is involved to the Untouchables in this two-member constituency system. But the danger is very real. How real it is, will become clear if it was considered along with the relative voting strength of the Hindus and the Untouchables in the General constituency to which attention has already been drawn. Where the constituency is a plural constituency of—say three or four members—one reserved for the Scheduled Castes and two or three left for the general community, the relatively higher voting strength of the Hindus is not so much a matter of danger as it is when under the two-member constituency the Hindus have only one candidate to elect. With more candidates to elect the voting strength of the Hindus is split as they become engaged in fighting out the election of their candidates to the general seat and there is no surplus of votes left with them, with the result that their excessive voting strength in the constituency does not become a menace to the Scheduled Castes. But, when they have only one seat to win, the chances of their votes being frittered away are remote. Under an organized party system such as that established by the Congress, they are nil. The excess of unused voting strength which they are thus able to retain becomes surplus and unnecessary for them, and which they are quite free to use in supporting a Scheduled Caste candidate of their choice, standing on their ticket as against another Scheduled Caste candidate who is independent and who is not prepared to be their tool. What havoc the Hindus played with their surplus votes is clear from the result of the elections.

When one considers the method of voting and the number of seats fixed and the distribution of the voting strength in the general constituencies one feels whether any better electoral system for deceiving the Untouchables could have been devised. The Joint Electorates to which the Scheduled Castes are tied are like the Rotten Boroughs which existed in England before the Reform Act of 1832. Under the Rotten Borough, the candidate elected was in fact nominated by the boss who controlled the Borough. Similarly, under the system of Joint Electorates the Scheduled Caste candidate who is elected to the Legislature is virtually nominated by the Hindus. That is the reason why Mr. Gandhi is so keenly devoted to the system of Joint Electorates.

One hears a great deal about the Muslim League having grown from strength to strength. But few realize how sheltered the Muslim League is by reason of the system of separate electorates. The Muslims are secure from the menace and mischief of the Congress. Not so are the Untouchables. They are open to the full blast of the Congress money, Congress votes and Congress propaganda. That the Untouchables overcame all these difficulties without resources, without a party machine and in spite of all electoral difficulties shows their triumph over the Congress and their desire to maintain their independent existence.

CHAPTER VII

A FALSE CHARGE

Are Untouchables the Tools of the British?

I

As I have said before, the Congress since the time it came under the auspices of Mr. Gandhi underwent a complete transformation. One of these transformations is noteworthy, for it is this which has made the Congress so famous and which has enabled it to capture the imagination of the people. Before Mr. Gandhi's time it did nothing more than meet annually at different places in India and pass certain and sometimes the same resolutions touching some flaw in the British Administration of India. After Mr. Gandhi took charge of the Congress in 1919, it became a party of action, or, as Congressmen like to put it, the Congress forged sanctions—a thing never thought of before. The sanctions, which make up the Congress armoury and which it has put into action one time or another are: (1) Non-co-operation; (2) Boycott; (3) Civil Disobedience and (4) Fast. The aim of non-co-operation was to make government useless by refusal to recognise or resort to Government schools, colleges, courts and to make it impossible by refusing to engage in Government service. Boycott was a weapon, the aim of which was to coerce individuals not prepared to follow the dictates of the Congress. It had two edges, social or economic. The social edge cut off all social intercourse even withdrawing the services of barbers, washermen, butchers, grocers, merchants, etc., in short, making life of the culprit impossible in every way. The economic edge cut off all business relations, such as buying and selling of goods. Its objective was the merchant class selling foreign goods. Civil Disobedience was intended to give a direct blow aimed at the British Government. It was a deliberate breach of law with a view to court imprisonment, fill gaols and thereby discredit Government. It is practised either as mass civil disobedience or individual civil disobedience. As to fasting Congressmen have not taken to it on a mass scale. It is still an individual activity. It is a weapon particularly reserved by Mr. Gandhi[1] for himself. Even he uses it for a term. These are the four weapons which the Congress forged to give sanction to its demand for India's freedom.

Having forged the sanctions, the Congress has gone on to give demonstrations of the use of these sanctions. Between 1920 and 1942, the country has witnessed demonstrations staged by Congressmen of one form or the other of these sanctions. The din and dust they raised filled the air and drew crowds to witness them. They have come to be described as "Fight for Freedom." What has been the use of such sanctions is a subject which demands serious consideration. But this is not the place for it. One must remain content with the observation that the old Congress could not have done worse. The use of sanctions has really been a tragedy. Swaraj is as far as it has been, but the reckless use of sanctions has made partition of India starker, surer and nearer. While it is not possible to discuss the gains resulting from the use of sanctions, the fact must be mentioned that this "Fight for Freedom" has been carried on mostly by the Hindus. It is only once that the Musalmans took part in it and that was during the short-lived Khilafat agitation. They soon got out of it. The other communities, particularly the Untouchables, never took part in it. A few stray individuals may have joined it for personal gain. But the community as such has stood out. This was particularly noticeable in the last campaign of the "Fight for Freedom," which followed the 'Quit India' resolution passed by the Congress in August 1942.

This is a glaring fact especially to a foreigner who comes to India and witnesses how more than half the population non-co-operates with the Congress in this "Fight for Freedom." Quite naturally he feels stupefied by this strange phenomenon. He asks: Why are the Muslims, Christians and Untouchables not participating in the "Fight for Freedom"? and turns to the Congress for an explanation. The Congress has a ready-made answer. It is that the Untouchables are the tools of British Imperialism and that is why they do not join the "Fight for Freedom." The echo of this charge was heard from the mouth of many foreigners whom one came across

[1] Mr. Gandhi has recently threatened to fast for the Untouchables—a thing he has never done before. He has also threatened to bring about a chain of fasts.—See *Hindustan Times* of 22-8-1945.

during the war. What is most disconcerting is the experience that most of these foreigners seemed to have accepted the allegation as being true. This simplicity and plausibility of the argument could be the only reason which can account for such an easy conversion. It serves a double purpose. It enables the Congress to account for a strange phenomenon and it gives an explanation to which circumstances lend an apparent plausibility.

Had it not been for the fact that even influential foreigners have been infected by this idea, one would hardly bestir oneself to take notice of such malicious propaganda. For, the explanation given by the Congress for the non-participation by the Untouchables in what is called " the Fight for Freedom " is an absurd explanation. It is an explanation which only a knave can venture to offer and which none but a fool can be expected to accept as satisfactory. But as it is almost certain that in the events that are coming, what foreigners think about India's problems will be a matter of some moment, I think it necessary to explain the correct situation and allow no room for such erroneous notions about the Untouchables to take roots in their mind especially when there can be no difficulty in proving that it is a false charge against the Untouchables and to prove that if the Untouchables have not joined the " Fight for Freedom " it is not because they are the tools of the British Imperialism but because they fear that freedom of India will establish Hindu domination, which is sure to close to them and for ever all prospect of life, liberty and pursuit of happiness and that they will be made the hewers of wood and drawers of water.

That the Untouchables should have refused to join the Congress in the " Fight for Freedom " is in itself a proof positive that their reason for non-co-operation with the Congress cannot be the puerile one suggested by the Congress. It must be something real and substantial. What is it ? The reason which has led the Untouchables to non-co-operate with the Congress has been popularly expressed by them when they say that they do not wish to be placed under *Hindu Raj* in which the governing class would be the *Bania* and the *Brahmin*, with low class Hindus as their policemen, all of whom have been the hereditary enemies of the Untouchables. This language is held to offend against good taste. That may be so. But it must not be supposed that because such slogans are offensive in their tone they are devoid of sense or that the outlook which they typify and the ideals which they embody have no compelling force or that they cannot be made to wear the garb of a true and respectable political philosophy.

Translated in the language of political science, what do these slogans mean? They mean that the Untouchables are not opposed to freedom from British Imperialism. But they refuse to be content with mere freedom from British Imperialism. What they insist upon is that free India is not enough. Free India should be made safe for democracy. Starting with this aim, they say that on account of the peculiar social formation in India there are minority communities pitted against a Hindu Communal Majority, that if no provisions are made in the Constitution to cut the fangs of the Hindu Communal Majority, India will not be safe for democracy. The Untouchables therefore insist on devising a constitution which will take note of the special circumstances of India and contain safeguards which will prevent this Hindu Communal Majority in Indian society from getting possession of political power to suppress and oppress the Untouchables and which will directly invest the Untouchables with at least a modicum of political power to prevent their suppression and exploitation, and to enable them at least to hold their own, in their struggle for existence against the Communal Majority. In short, what the Untouchables want are safeguards in the Constitution itself, which will prevent the tyranny of a Hindu Communal Majority from coming into being.

The Congress on the other hand regards the freedom of India from British Imperialism to be the be-all and end-all of Indian nationalism. Nothing more, it thinks, is necessary for the welfare of the Indian people in a free India. As to the question of a constitution for a free India, the Congress simply does not look upon it as a problem. Asked, what about the Constitution of a free India? the Congress reply is that it will be a democracy. What sort of democracy would it be? The Congress answer is that it will be based on adult franchise. Will there be any other safeguard, besides adult suffrage, for preventing the tyranny of a Hindu Communal Majority? The Congress reply is emphatically in the negative. Asked, why this opposition to safeguards? the Congress says that it is a vivisection of the nation—an argument the picturesqueness of which is intended to cover its stupidity and which has its origin in the genius of Mr. Gandhi, and for which the high class Hindus, who stand to lose by these safeguards, feel so grateful to him.

The Untouchables refuse to accept this silly sophism. They say that Indian social life has to be reckoned in terms of communities. There is no escape. Communities are such hard facts of Indian social life that it would be wrong to accept that communal impulse and communal prejudice do not dominate the relations of the communities. The social psychology of the Hindu Communal Majority is dominated by the dogma which recognizes not merely inequality but graded inequality as the rule governing the inter-relationship among the various communities. This dogma of graded inequality is absolutely inimical to liberty and fraternity. It cannot be believed that this graded inequality will vanish or that the Hindus will strive to abolish it. That is impossible. This graded inequality is not accidental or incidental. It is the religion of the Hindus. It is the official doctrine of Hinduism. It is sacred and no Hindu can think of doing away with it. The Hindu Communal Majority with its religion of graded inequality is not therefore a passing phase. It is a permanent fact and a menace for ever. In making a constitution for India the existence of a standing Communal Majority cannot be ignored and the problem of devising safeguards so as to reconcile it with political democracy must be faced. That is the reasoning of the Untouchables.

The constitutional safeguards which the Untouchables have been demanding are detailed in the Resolutions recently passed by the Working Committee of the All-India Scheduled Castes Federation and which are printed in Appendix XI. For purposes of argument I take three of them. (*i*) Guaranteed minimum representation in the Legislature; (*ii*) Guaranteed minimum representation in the Executive and (*iii*) Guaranteed minimum representation in the Public Services. These demands are ridiculed by the Congress as communalism and the leaders of the Untouchables are represented as job hunters. The Congress places its opposition to these guarantees on the high pedestal of nationalism, of which it holds itself as the guardian angel. The foreigner may find it difficult to see the absurdity of the Congress argument against safeguards. But if he were to take into account the purposes for which these guarantees are sought, he will find that the attempt of the Congress to represent them as a piece of communalism is arrant nonsense.

The purpose of these guarantees demanded by the Untouchables is not to fill the Legislature, the Executive and the Administration by the representatives of the Untouchables. These guarantees are really floorings below which the Untouchables will not fall under the crushing pressure of the Hindu Communal Majority. They are intended to keep the Hindu Communal Majority within bounds. For, if there were no such guarantees to the Untouchables, the result will be that the Hindu Communal Majority will not only capture the Legislature, the Executive and the Administration, but the Legislature, the Executive and the Administration will be over-run by the Hindu Communal Majority and these powerful organs of the State, instead of protecting the minorities, will become the tools of the Hindu Communal Majority doing its biddings.

In the light of this explanation there ought to be no difficulty for any outsider of average intelligence in understanding the issues between the Congress and the Untouchables. In the first place, he ought to be able to realize that the issue between them is created by the former refusing to recognize that in the existence of a Communal Majority there lies a great menace to political democracy and the latter maintaining the contrary and insisting that the Constitution should contain positive provisions to curb this menace. In other words, the Untouchables are anxious to make India safe for democracy, while the Congress, if it is not opposed to democracy, is certainly opposed to creating conditions which will make democracy real.

In the second place, the foreigner should be able to see that this demand by the Untouchables for safeguards is not a novel demand. His understanding will be facilitated if he were to regard these safeguards as another name for checks and balances and to bear in mind that there is no Constitution which does not contain such checks and balances to protect political democracy from being subverted and to note how the Constitution of the U.S.A. is full of such checks and balances, which are embodied in clauses relating to Fundamental Rights and Separation of Powers. Once the foreigner bears in mind that the principles of checks and balances is a sound one, then he need not feel puzzled if the safeguards demanded by the

Untouchables take a different form than they do in other countries. For, the nature of safeguards must differ with the nature of the forces which constitute a menace to political democracy and as these forces in India are of a different character, the safeguards must necessarily take a different form.

In the third place, the foreigner should have no difficulty in realizing that if anybody is communal it is the Congress and not the Untouchables, and that whatever the philosophic grounds advanced by the Congress, the real motive of the Congress in opposing the demand for constitutional guarantees is to keep the political field a free pasture for the Hindu Majority. He should be able to see, though the Congress does not openly say so, how natural it is for the Congress to be communal. The Hindu Communal Majority is the back-bone of the Congress. It is made up of the Hindus and is fed by the Hindus. It is this Majority which constitutes the clientele of the Congress and the Congress, therefore, is bound to protect the rights of its clients. If he realizes this, he will not be deceived by the arguments of the Congress that it is opposing these demands in the name of nationalism. On the other-hand, he will realize that the Congress is deceiving the world by using nationalism as a cloak for a free field for rank communalism.

Lastly, he will know why the representative character of the Congress has become an issue of such importance in Indian politics. He will realize that nobody would have cared to bother about the representative character of the Congress and to inquire, whom it represents and whom it does not, if the Congress were not to arrogate to itself the right to say what should be the constitution of a free India. But as it does, its right to speak in the name of the country forms a vital issue and those who do not accept this have no alternative but to challenge it.

II

With all this, foreigners have said—"Why not join the Congress in the 'Fight for Freedom'?; why make agreement on constitutional safeguards a condition precedent to co-operation with the Congress? After all, safeguards can come only after freedom is won." A foreigner who has followed the foregoing discussion as to matters which divide the Congress can be left to understand why the Untouchables have not thought it safe to co-operate with the Congress in this "Fight for Freedom." But there may be some who may not be able to imagine them and who would like to know what they are. Rather than leave them to find wrong reasons it is better to take the trouble to let them have the right ones. The reasons are various. Only the most important are set out below.

The first reason is founded in commonsense. The Untouchables say: "What harm is there in demanding from the Congress an agreement in advance? What is lost, if a guarantee is given by the Congress in advance?" They argue that if the Congress agreed to this demand for safeguards in advance it will have a double effect. In the first place, it will give an assurance to the Untouchables, who entertain so much dread, as to what their lot would be under a Hindu Communal Majority. Secondly, such an assurance would go a long way in inducing the Untouchables to co-operate with the Congress. After all, why are the Untouchables non-co-operating? Because, they are afraid that if this freedom is achieved it will enable the Hindu Majority once again to enslave them. Why not remove this fear if it can be done at so small a cost, namely, by an agreement in advance?

The second reason is founded in experience. The Untouchables say that the experience of the world does not justify the hope that when the "Fight for Freedom" ends, the stronger elements have shown the generosity to give security to the weaker elements.

Many examples of this betrayal could be cited. The most notorious one relates to the betrayal of the Negroes in the United States after the Civil War. Speaking of the part played by the Negroes in the Civil War, Mr. Herbert Apthekar says[1]:

> "One hundred and twenty-five thousand Negroes from the slave states served in the Federal armies. They, together with the eighty thousand from the North, fought in four hundred and fifty battles, with an inspiring and inspired courage that was of the utmost importance in bringing about the collapse of the Confederacy and the abolition of slavery.
>
> "Here were over two hundred thousand armed Negro men fighting within a state built upon and dedicated to the proposition that the Negro was, if at all a human being an innately and ineradicably inferior one, fit only to be a slave.

[1] The Negro in the Civil War, pp. 35-40.

> "And the Negro soldiers of the Republic fought notwithstanding shameful discriminations and disadvantages. White soldiers received thirteen dollars a month. Negroes received but seven dollars (until July 14, 1864, when the pay was equalized, retroactively to January 1, 1864); there were enlistment bounties for white recruits, none for Negroes (until June 15, 1864); and there was no possibility for advancement into the ranks of commissioned officers for Negroes . . . The Confederacy never recognised captured Negro soldiers who had been slaves as prisoners of war, and did not accord this status to captured free Negroes until October 1864. The Negroes were either killed, returned to slavery, or confined at hard labour.
>
> * * *
>
> "Here were these scores of thousands of hitherto enslaved and oppressed masses, armed, and sent forth into their own country, whose every creek and knoll was known to them, to maintain their newly obtained freedom, to prove their manhood and to liberate their own people, their own parents and children and wives, from a slavery that they know only too well . . . And let it always be remembered that in the war to save the republic thirty-seven thousand Negro soldiers were killed in action."

What happened to the Negroes after the Civil War was over? In the first flush of victory, the Republicans, who waged the war for saving the Union and obtained the help of the Negroes to win it, carried the Thirteenth Amendment to the Constitution. Under it the Negroes ceased to be slaves in the legal sense of the term. But did the Negroes get any right to participate in the Government as voters or officials? The Republicans did take some action in order to make the Southern States accept that the Negroes were to be treated as the political equals of the Whites. This was done by the Fourteenth Amendment which conferred citizenship, State as well as Federal, on all persons including the Negroes born or naturalized in the United States and subject to the jurisdiction thereof, forbade legislation by a State abridging the privileges or immunities of a citizen of the United States, and provided for reducing the representation in the Congress of any State in proportion to the number of its citizens excluded from the suffrage. The Southern States had no intention to respect the Fourteenth Amendment. All except Tennessee had rejected the amendment and had set up governments of the White inhabitants. The Republicans then proceeded (March 2, 1867) to pass the so-called Reconstruction Act (a Bill to provide efficient governments for the insurrectionary States) designed to create legitimate governments in the States not yet readmitted to the Union (ignoring the governments set up by the White inhabitants), and to determine the conditions proper for their readmission. By this Act these States, that is the whole seceding South except Tennessee, were divided into five military districts, each to be governed by a Brigadier-General of the Federal Army, until such time as (1) a State convention had framed a new constitution, (2) the Fourteenth Amendment had been ratified and (3) the States had been duly readmitted. The Republicans carried another amendment called the Fifteenth Amendment, forbidding the voting right of citizen to be denied or abridged on account of race, colour or previous condition of servitude which also became by similar acceptance part of the Constitution and binding on all the States.

The Whites in the South had no intention to admit the Negroes to equal citizenship. Disfranchisement of the Negro proceeded apace. It was undertaken as a solemn duty both by the State Governments of the South as well as by the Whites of the Southern States. To evade the Fifteenth Amendment the State Governments spent their ingenuity in framing franchise laws which denied the Negroes the right to vote on grounds other than race or colour. Most of them decided upon the grandfather clause[1] which effectively excluded the Negroes but fully included the Whites. On the people's side the process was carried out by the Ku Klux Klan. The Klan was in its origin a secret combination formed in Tennessee by youths for purposes of amusement. It was transferred into an organization to suppress the Negroes and prevent them from exercising their political rights. It started committing outrages upon Negroes, and (less frequently) upon Whites, supposed to be in sympathy with the Negroes, in the rural South. These gangmen were never discovered. This shows that the whole of the White population of the South supported the Klan men. No open resistance to the Federal troops was attempted; but neither their activity nor the penal laws passed by the Congress were effective in checking the flogging, house-burnings, and murders which during these years disgraced some districts.

The purposes of the Southern States and the Southern

[1] Grandfather clause is so-called because it restricted the right to vote to a person whose grandfather had enjoyed it.

Whites were facilitated by the decisions of the Supreme Court of the United States. The Supreme Court held that the State laws disfranchising the Negroes were valid, notwithstanding the Fifteenth Amendment because the disfranchisement was not based on race and colour. Similarly the Surpeme Court held that if the activities of the Ku Klux Klan prevented the Negro from exercising his electoral rights there was no redress: for, the Fifteenth Amendment, while it prevented the States from interfering with the electoral rights, did not prevent interference by private bodies.

What did the Republicans do? Instead of amending the Constitution to give better and more effective guarantees to the Negroes, they agreed to recognize the Southern States and admit them to the Union, to grant general amnesty to the rebels and to withdraw the troops stationed therein, leaving the Negroes to the tender mercy of their masters. As Mr. Apthekar says[1]:

> "But the heroic fight of the Negro people and their allies for democracy, land and civil rights in the South was defeated chiefly as a result of shameful betrayal by the industrial and financial bourgeoisie of the North. In 1877, the latter came to an understanding with the reactionary plantocracy of the South. Working through the reactionary wing of the Republican Party, the Northern big bourgeoisie sold out the Revolution by giving the old slave oligarchy a free hand (home rule) in the Southern States. This 'gentleman's agreement' meant disenfranchisement for the Negro, sharecropping peonage, lynch terrorism, and the loss of civil liberties and educational opportunities."

The story of the betrayal is not complete. It is necessary to add that if the Republicans were to carry their party opposition with the Democrats into the South, the Negro could still be saved from damnation. For it is the opinion of those who know that if the Whites of the South were divided into Republicans and Democrats as they are in the North there is hardly a State in the South which would not be largely controlled by the Negro voters. Even the Republicans will not do. The Republicans seem to have entered into a compact with the Democrats not to canvass for the votes of the Negroes. Indeed, the Republican Party in the South does not exist. It does not exist because it is afraid of having to take sides with the Negroes.

[1] The Negro in the Civil War, pp. 45-46.

The Untouchables cannot forget the fate of the Negroes. It is to prevent such treachery that the Untouchables have taken the attitude they have with regard to this "Fight for Freedom." What is wrong in this? Are they doing anything more than follow the advice of Burke, who has said that it is better to be accused of timidity than to be ruined by over-confident security?

The third argument is that there is no justification for the Congress to say that the "Fight for Freedom" must come first and the agreement about constitutional safeguards afterwards. The Untouchables feel that having regard to the attitude of the British Government to India's right to freedom, this fight, which the Congress loves so much, is uncalled for, at any rate, it is putting the cart before the horse. The attitude of the British towards India's claim for freedom has since the Mutiny of 1857 undergone a complete change. There was a time when the British Government held the view which was a complete negation of India's claim for freedom. It was proclaimed by Lawrence whose statue in Calcutta has the motto: "The British conquered India by the sword and they will hold it by the sword." This attitude is dead and buried and it is no exaggeration to say that every Englishman to-day is ashamed of it. This stage was followed by another in which the argument of the British Government against India's freedom was the alleged incapacity of Indians for Parliamentary institutions. It began with Lord Ripon's regime which was followed by an attempt to give political training to Indians, first in the field of Local Self-Government, and then under the Montagu-Chelmsford reforms in the field of Provincial Government. We have now entered the third or the present stage. The British Government is now ashamed to say that they will hold India by the sword. It no longer says that Indians have no capacity to run Parliamentary institutions. The British Government admits India's right to freedom, even to independence, if Indians so desire. The British Government admits the right of Indians to frame their own constitution. There can be no greater proof of this new angle of vision than the Cripps Proposals. The condition precedent laid down by the British Government for India's freedom is that Indians must produce a constitution which has the concurrence of the important elements in the national life of the country. Such is the stage we have reached. The Untouchables cannot therefore understand why the Congress, instead of trying to achieve agreement among Indians, should keep on talking in terms of a "Fight for Freedom" and maligning the Untouchables in not joining in it.

III

Why does the Congress oppose the proposal of the British Government? It seeks to justify its opposition on two grounds. It says that the condition prescribed by the British Government puts a veto on freedom of India in the hands of the Untouchables. This is a stupid argument and for two reasons. In the first place, the Untouchables in India have never made impossible demands. They have not even made unreasonable demands. They do not say as Carson did to Redmond: "Damn your safeguards. We don't wish to be ruled by you." The Untouchables are quite prepared to submit themselves to the rule of the Hindu Majority, notwithstanding the unsocial and the undemocratic character of its ethics, provided the constitution gives them reasonable safeguards. To say that the Untouchables will exercise a veto on India's freedom by raising impossible demands is thus a gross libel, for which there is not the slightest justification. Assuming the fear is well-founded, the Congress is not altogether without a remedy. For it is still open to the Congress to say that if there is no agreement between the Hindus and the Untouchables the dispute should be referred to an International Board of Arbitration. If the Congress took this stand, I am sure, neither the British Government nor the Untouchables will have the slightest objection to it. But when, instead of making an honest and sincere attempt to bring about an agreed constitution, the Congress goes on launching its campaigns for achieving freedom—not without occasional rests and retreats—the only conclusion, which the Untouchables can draw, is that the Congress wants to coerce the British Government to transfer its power or to use Mr. Gandhi's phrase "hand over the keys to the Congress," without being obliged to agree to the safeguards demanded by the Untouchables. In short, what the Congress wants is a free India with full, unrestricted freedom to the Hindus in a free India to dispose of the Untouchables in any way they liked. No wonder the Untouchables have refused to take part in such a dishonest agitation, elevated though it may be by such a high sounding name as "Fight for Freedom"!

The other ground urged by the Congress for not taking up the question of bringing about an agreement is that the British Government is not honest, and that notwithstanding its declarations it will not transfer power even if Indians agreed upon a constitution and that ultimately Indians will have to struggle with the British in order to wrest power from their hands. The reply of the Untouchables is that they see no reason why Indians should start with such complete distrust of the British intentions. After all, the British Government has moved in the direction of fulfilling Indian aspirations and is moving. If it is slow in moving it is due to Indians being content with small things. Right from the conquest of India by the British upto 1886, Indians never cared who ruled them nor how they were ruled. They were content to live without troubling themselves about these questions. In 1886 the Congress was organized and for the first time Indians began to take interest in the government of India. But even the Congress upto 1910 was content in agitating for good Government only. It was in 1910 that the Congress first demanded Self-Government. When in 1919 the Montagu-Chelmsford Reforms were on the anvil, Indians had an occasion to state the scope of their demand for Self-Government. What is known as the Memorandum of the Nineteen defined the aspirations of the Indians as they stood in 1917. Any one who knows it will remember that the best and the most radical Indians were content only with Dyarchy in the Provinces. Even this was regarded as a big jump by some Indian leaders such as Sir Dinshaw Watcha and Mr. Samarath[1]. In 1930 notwithstanding the Congress Resolution insisting on Independence, Mr. Gandhi at the R. T. C. was prepared[2] to be content with Provincial autonomy. The British granted more than that. If from 1939 there has been a halt, it is mainly because Indians are

---

[1] Mr. Montagu in his Indian Diary records that when they waited on him to discuss the question of political reforms they said "Give us the power to pass resolutions, to influence Government; we will use it in a spirit of sweet reasonableness; but we are not fit for responsible Government."—p. 147.

[2] This part of the story of what happened at the Round Table Conference has not been told. But everybody present at the Round Table Conference knows how Mr. Gandhi was won over to agree to Provincial autonomy. If the 1935 Government of India Act contains some elements of responsibility at the centre the credit goes to the representatives of the Non-Congress parties at the R. T. C.

not agreed on the sort of constitution they want for their country.

The Untouchables think that the stage, when the British were sitting upon the freedom of India, as the snake in the fable is said to sit on a treasure, not allowing anyone to come near it, is gone long past. India's Freedom is like property held by a receiver. The British Government has placed itself in the position of a receiver. As soon as the dispute is over and the right kind of constitution is settled, it has bound itself to hand over the property to its rightful owners, namely, the Indians. The Untouchables ask: Why not take advantage of this? Why not adopt the straight and honest course of arriving at an agreement among the important elements in the country and then make a joint application for the release of the property? That the Congress does not want to follow this line of action shows, say the Untouchables, that the Congress "Fight for Freedom" is nothing more than mere tactics, the object of which is to by-pass the necessity of an agreed constitution demanded by the Untouchables and made a condition precedent by the British Government for the grant of freedom.

The Untouchables do not say that they are out to underwrite the declarations made by the British Government. They do not say that if Indians are agreed it must necessarily be a case of "knock and it will open: ask and it shall be given unto you." They admit that the British may not act up to the declarations they have made. It may be that even when an agreed constitution is produced, they may not act up to their promises, and a fight for freedom may become necessary. The Untouchables do not overlook these possibilities. But what they do say is that the Indians have not put the British to the test. They can't be put to test unless they are presented with an agreed constitution. So long as the Congress does not adopt this course, the Untouchables feel that the Congress is not honest in its dealings with them. Who can say that the Untouchables have not sufficient justification for refusing to participate in the Congress "Fight for Freedom"?

CHAPTER VIII

THE REAL ISSUE

Aren't the Untouchables a Separate Element?

I

WHAT is the fundamental issue in the controversy between the Congress and the Untouchables? As I understand the matter, the fundamental issue is: *Are the Untouchables a separate element in the national life of India or are they not?*

This is the real issue in the controversy and it is on this issue that the Congress and the Untouchables have taken opposite sides. The answer of the Untouchables is "yes." They say, they are distinct and separate from the Hindus. The Congress on the other hand says 'No' and asserts that the Untouchables are a chip of the Hindu block. This is the attitude of the parties to the issue. The attitude of the British Government was made clear by Lord Linlithgow[1] in his statements as Viceroy and Governor-General of India in which he declared in quite explicit terms that the Untouchables were a separate element in the national life of India. Many people who regard the issue of constitutional safeguards as the fundamental issue will feel surprised that I should regard as fundamental an issue so apparently different from what they regard as fundamental. Really speaking there is no difference. It all depends upon what one regards as proximate and what as ultimate. Others regard the question of constitutional safeguards as ultimate. I regard it as proximate. What I have stated as fundamental I regard as ultimate from which the proximate follows, as the conclusion does from the premise in a logical syllogism. It may be as well for me to state why I have thought it necessary to make this difference. The evolution of the Indian Constitution appears to me to have established a sort of a logical syllogism. The major premise in the syllogism is that where there exists an element in the national life of India, which is definable as a separate and distinct element, it is entitled to constitutional safeguards. An element, making a claim for constitutional safeguards, must show that it is

[1] See Appendix VI, Items 9 and 12.

definable as separate and distinct from the rest. If it shows that it is separate and distinct, its right to constitutional safeguards is held admissible.

That is how the provisions for constitutional safeguards for Muslims, Indian Christians, Anglo-Indians, Europeans and Sikhs have come into being. It is true that the Constitution of India has not been framed in the light of principles. It has grown in an haphazard manner, more in answer to exigencies than in accordance with principles. Nevertheless, this silent postulate, if not a principle to which I have referred, seems to be working throughout. The right of a group to constitutional safeguards has come to be treated as consequential. It is deemed to follow automatically when the fundamental condition is satisfied, namely that they do constitute a separate and a distinct element in the national life of India. In dealing with this controversy, one must deal with it as one is required to do with a syllogism. In a syllogism both are fundamental, the conclusion as well as the premise and to close the argument it is not enough to deal with the conclusion. It is necessary to examine the premise also. Looking at the question from this angle, I think I ought not to close the case of the Untouchables with no more than a discussion of the constitutional safeguards. I feel that I ought to deal also with the premise, the ultimate or the fundamental proposition, from which the constitutional safeguards seem to follow, if not as a matter of course at least as a matter of precedent.

It will thus be seen that the decision I have taken to give a separate treatment to the ultimate, as distinguished from the proximate proposition, is not without justification. It also seems to be necessary to deal with it separately and substantially, because the Congress seems to be fully aware of the fact that this is the fundamental issue and knows that once it concedes that the Untouchables are a separate element it cannot prevent them from succeeding in their claim for constitutional safeguards. If the Congress has come forward to contest this proposition it is because it thinks that it is the first trench and if it fails to maintain it, it cannot save the situation.

II

It must be a matter of consideranle surprise to those who know the conditions in India that the Congress should come forward to controvert what is incontrovertible, namely, that the Untouchables are separate from the Hindus. But since the Congress has chosen to do so, I must deal with the issue as best as I can.

The grounds advanced by the Untouchables that they are separate from the Hindus are not difficult to comprehend. Nor do they require a long and an elaborate statement. The statement of their case can be fully covered by a simple question. In what sense are they Hindus ? In the first place, the word 'Hindu' is used in various senses and one must know in what sense it is used before one can give a proper answer to the question. It is used in a territorial sense. Everyone who is an inhabitant of Hindustan is a Hindu. In that sense it can certainly be claimed that the Untouchables are Hindus. But so are the Muslims, Christians, Sikhs, Jews, Parsis, etc. The second sense in which the word 'Hindu' is used is a religious one. Before one can draw any conclusion, it is necessary to separate the dogmas of Hinduism from the cults of Hinduism. Whether the Untouchables are Hindus in the religious sense of the word depends upon what tests one adopts, the dogmas or the cults. If the tests of Hinduism are the dogmas of Caste and Untouchability then every Untouchable would repudiate Hinduism and the assertion that he is a Hindu. If the test applied is the acceptance of a cult such as the worship of Rama, Krishna, Vishnu and Shiva and other Gods and Goddesses recognized by Hinduism the Untouchables may be claimed to be Hindus. The Congress as usual maintains a body of agents from among the Untouchables to shout when need be that the Untouchables are Hindus and that they will die as Hindus. But even these paid agents will not agree to be counted as Hindus if they are asked to proclaim themselves as Hindus, if Hinduism means belief in Caste and Untouchability.

One more point must be stressed. On the foregoing analysis, an Untouchable may be classed as a Hindu, only if the word Hindu is used in the religious but in the limited sense of a follower of a recognized cult. Even here, there is a necessity for giving a warning against concluding that the Hindu and the Untouchable have a common religion. The fact is that even as followers of recognized cults they cannot be said to have a common religion. The exact and appropriate expression would be to say that they have a similar religion. A common religion means a common cycle of participation. Now, in the observances of the cults there is no such common cycle of participation. The Hindus and the Untouchables practise their cults in segregation so that notwithstanding the similarity of their cults they remain as separate as two aliens do. Neither of these two senses of the word 'Hindu' can yield any result which can be of help in determining the political question, which alone can justify the discussion.

The only test which can be of use is its social sense as indicating a member of the Hindu Society. Can an Untouchable be held to be part of the Hindu Society? Is there any human tie that binds them to the rest of the Hindus? There is none. There is no *connubium*. There is no *commensalism*. There is not even the right to touch, much less to associate. Instead, the mere touch is enough to cause pollution to a Hindu. The whole tradition of the Hindus is to recognize the Untouchable as a separate element and insist upon it as a fact. The traditional terminology of the Hindus to distinguish Hindus and Untouchables furnishes the best evidence in favour of the contention of the Untouchables. According to this traditional terminology, the Hindus are called *Savarnas* and the Untouchables are called *Avarnas*. It speaks of the Hindus as *Chaturvarnikas* and of the Untouchables as *Panchamas*. Such a terminology could not have come into existence if separation had not become so prominent and its observance so necessary as to require coining of special terms to give expression to the fact.

There is thus hardly any substance in the Congress argument that the Untouchables are Hindus and that they cannot therefore demand the same political rights as the Muslims and others can. While the argument from tradition is a good and valid argument to prove that the Untouchables are not Hindus, it may appear to some to be a weak one. I do not wish to leave the field without directly meeting the Congress argument. For this purpose, I may grant that the Untouchables are Hindus by religion. But the question is: Does it matter if they are Hindus? Can it come in the way of their being recognized as a separate element in the national life of India? It is difficult to understand how the mere fact that they might be called Hindus by religion in such a limited sense, can be the basis of an argument that they are an integral part of the Hindu society.

Admitting for the sake of argument that they are Hindus by religion, can it mean anything more than what I have said, namely, that they worship the same Gods and Goddesses as the rest of the Hindus, go to the same places of pilgrimage, hold the same supernatural beliefs and regard the same stones, trees, mountains as sacred as the rest of the Hindus do ? Is this enough to conclude that the Untouchables and the Hindus are parts of one single community ? If that be the logic behind the contention of the Congress then, what about the Belgians, Dutch, Norwegians, Swedes, Germans, French, Italians, Slavs, etc. ? Are they not all Christians ? Do they not all worship the same God ? Do they not all accept Jesus as their Saviour ? Have they not the same religious beliefs ? Obviously, there is a complete religious unity between all of them in thought, worship and beliefs. Yet, who can dispute that the French, Germans and Italians and the rest are not a single community ? Take another case, that of the Whites and the Negroes in the U.S.A. They too have a common religion. Both are Christians. Can any one say that the two on that account form a single community ? Take a third case, that of the Indian Christians, Europeans and Anglo-Indians. They profess and follow the same religion. Yet it is admitted that they do not form one single Christian community. Take the case of the Sikhs. There are Sikhs, Mazbi Sikhs and Ramdasia Sikhs. All profess Sikhism. But it is accepted that they do not form one community. In the light of these illustrations it is obvious that the argument of the Congress is full of fallacies.

The first fallacy of the Congress lies in its failure to realize that the fundamental issue for settling the question whether to grant or not to grant constitutional safeguards is union *versus* separation of a social group in the population. Religion is only a circumstance from which unity or separation may be inferred. The Congress does not seem to have understood that the Musalmans and the Indian Christians have been given separate political recognition not because they are Musalmans or Christians but fundamentally because they form in fact separate elements from the Hindus.

The second fallacy of the Congress lies in its attempt to prove that where there is a common religion, social union must be presumed. It is on the basis of this reasoning that the Congress hopes to win. Unfortunately for the Congress, it cannot. For the facts are strongly against making a conclusive inference. If religion was a circumstance from which social union was made the only permissible inference, then the fact that the Italians, French, Germans and Slavs in Europe, the Negroes and the Whites in the U.S.A. and the Indian Christians, Europeans, and Anglo-Indians in India do not form a single community although they all profess the same religion, is enough to negative such a contention. The pity of the matter is that the Congress is so completely enamoured of its argument based on religion as an unifying factor, that it has failed to realize that there is no concomittance between the two and that there are cases where there is no separation although religions are separate, that there are cases where separation exists in spite of a common religion and what is worst, separation exists because religion prescribes it.

To give a quietus to the Congress argument, it may be desirable to give one illustration of each of these cases. Of the first case the best and the easiest illustration I can think of is that of the Sikhs and the Hindus. They differ in religion. But they are not socially separate. They dine together; they marry together; they live together. In a Hindu family one son may be a Sikh, another a Hindu. Religious difference does not break the social nexus. Of the second, the case of the Italians, French, Germans in Europe and Whites and Negroes in America are as good illustrations as one would want. This happens where religion is a binding force but is not powerful enough to withstand other forces tending to divide such as the sentiment of race. Hindus and Hinduism are the best and perhaps the only illustrations of the third case, where separation is the effect of religion itself. That there can be such a case, Hindus at any rate need not require to be told. For, it is well known that Hinduism preaches separation instead of union. To be a Hindu means not to mix, to be separate in everything. The language commonly used that Hinduism upholds Caste and Untouchability perhaps disguises and conceals its genius. The real genius of Hinduism is to divide. This is beyond dispute. What do Caste and Untouchability stand for? Obviously for separation. For Caste is another name for separation and Untouchability typifies the extremist form of separation of community from community. It is also beyond dispute that Caste and Untouchability are not innocuous dogmas to be compared with other dogmas relating to the condition of the soul after death. They are parts of the code of conduct which every Hindu is bound to observe during his life on earth. Caste and Untouchability far from being mere dogmas are among the foremost observances prescribed by Hinduism. It is not enough for a Hindu to believe in the dogmas of Caste and Untouchability. He must also observe Caste and Untouchability, in the conduct of his daily life.

The separation, which Hinduism has brought about, between the Hindus and the Untouchables by its dogma of Untouchability is not a mere imaginary line of separation, such as the one which the Pope once drew in a quarrel between the Portuguese and their rivals for Colonial possessions; it is not like the colour line which has length but no breadth and which one may observe or one may not observe; it is not like the race line, which involves distinction but no discrimination. It has both depth and width. Factually the Hindus and the Untouchables are divided by a fence made of barbed wire. Notionally it is *cordon sanitaire*, which the Untouchables have never been allowed to cross and can never hope to cross.

To put the matter in general terms, Hinduism and social union are incompatible. By its very genius Hinduism believes in social separation which is another name for social disunity and even creates social separation. If the Hindus wish to be one they will have to discard Hinduism. They cannot be one without violating Hinduism. Hinduism is the greatest obstacle to Hindu unity. Hinduism cannot create that longing to belong which is the basis of all social unity. On the contrary Hinduism creates an eagerness to separate.

The Congress does not seem to realize that the argument it is using goes against itself. Far from supporting the Congress contention, it is the best and the most effective argument that can be advanced to prove the contention of the Untouchables. For, if any conclusion is to be drawn from the hypothesis that the Untouchables are Hindus, it is that Hinduism has always insisted both in principle and in practice that the Untouchables are not to be recognized as a chip of the Hindu block but are to be treated as a separate element and segregated from the Hindus.

If therefore the Untouchables say that they are a separate element, nobody can accuse them of having invented a new theory for the sake of political advantages. They are merely pointing out what the facts are and how these facts are the heritage of Hinduism itself. The Congress cannot honestly and convincingly use Hinduism as an argument for refusing to recognise the Untouchables as a separate element. If it does, it is only because it is actuated by selfish motives. It knows that the recognition of the Untouchables as an element in the national life of India, as distinct and separate from the Hindus, must result in the apportionment of places in the Executive, in the Legislature, and in the Public Services between the Untouchables and the Hindus and thus limit the share of the Hindus. The Congress does not like that the Hindus should be deprived of the share of the Untouchables which the Hindus are in the habit of appropriating to themselves. That is the real reason why the Congress refuses to recognize that the Untouchables are a separate element in the national life of India.

The second argument of the Congress is that the political recognition of the Untouchables as a separate element in the national life of India should not be permitted on the ground that it will perpetuate the separation between the Untouchables and the Hindus.

This is hardly an argument worth consideration. It is the weakest of its kind and shows that the Congress has nothing better to advance. Besides contradicting its previous argument, it is entirely misconceived.

If there is a real separation between the Hindus and the Untouchables and if there is the danger of discrimination being practised by the Hindus against the Untouchables then the Untouchables must receive political recognition and must be given political safeguards to protect themselves against the tyranny of the Hindus. The possibility of a better future cannot be used as an argument to prevent the Untouchables from securing the means of protecting themselves against the tyranny of the present.

In the second place, this argument can be used only by those who believe in the social fusion of the Hindus and the Untouchables and are actively engaged in pursuing means and methods which will bring about such a fusion. Congressmen have often been heard to say that the problem of the Untouchables is social and political. But the point is, are Congressmen sincere when they say that it is a social problem? Or do they use it as an excuse with a view to avoid the consequences of having to share political power with the Untouchables? And, if they are sincere in holding that it is a social question, what proof is there of their sincerity in this matter? Have Congressmen sponsored Social Reform among Hindus? Have they carried on a crusade in favour of interdining and intermarriages? What is the record of Congressmen in the field of Social Reform?

III

It may be well to state what view the Untouchables take of the problem of Untouchables. Until the advent of the British, the Untouchables were content to remain Untouchables. It was a destiny preordained by the Hindu God and enforced by the Hindu State. As such there was no escape from it. Fortunately or unfortunately, the East India Company needed soldiers for their army in India and it could find none but the Untouchables. The East India Company's army consisted, at any rate in the early part of its history, of the Untouchables and although the Untouchables are now included among the non-martial classes and are therefore excluded from the Army, it is with the help of an army composed of Untouchables that the British conquered India. In the army of the East India Company there prevailed the system of compulsory education for Indian soldiers and their children, both male and female. The education received by the Untouchables in the army while it was open to them gave them one advantage which they never had before. It gave them a new vision and a new value. They became conscious that the low esteem in which they had been held was not an inescapable destiny but was a stigma imposed on their personality by the cunning contrivances of the priest. They felt the shame of it as they never did before and were determined to get rid of it. They too in the beginning thought their problem was social and struggled along the social lines for its solution. This was quite natural. For they saw that the outward marks of their social inferiority were prohibition of interdining and intermarriage between the Untouchables and the Hindus. They naturally concluded that for the removal of their stigma what was necessary was to establish social intercourse with the Hindus on terms of equality, which in its turn meant the abolition of rules against interdining and intermarriage. In other words, the first programme of action which the Untouchables launched out for their salvation after they became aware of their servile position was to bring about Social Equality among all those, who come within the fold of Hinduism by insisting upon the abolition of the Caste System.

In this, the Untouchables found an ally in a section of the Hindus. Like the Untouchables, the Hindus also by the contact with the British had come to realize that their social system was very defective and was the parent of many social evils. They too desired to launch forth a movement of Social Reform. It began with Raja Ram Mohan Roy in Bengal and from there had spread all over India and ultimately culminated in the formation of the Indian Social Reform Conference with its slogan of Social Reform before Political Reform. The Untouchables followed the Social Reform Conference and stood behind it as a body and gave it their full support. As every one knows, the Social Reform Conference is dead and buried and forgotten. Who killed it? The Congress. The Congress with its slogans "Politics First, Politics Last," "Politics by Each, Politics by All" regarded the Social Reform Conference as its rival. It denied the validity of the creed of the Conference that social reform was a necessary precursor of political reform. Under a constant and steady fire from the Congress platform and from individual Congress leaders, the Social Reform Conference was burnt down and reduced to ashes. When the Untouchables lost all hope of their salvation through social reform, they were forced to seek political means for protecting themselves. Now for Congressmen to turn round and say that the problem is social is nothing but hypocrisy.

It is wrong to say that the problem of the Untouchables is a social problem. For, it is quite unlike the problems of dowry, widow remarriage, age of consent, etc., which are illustrations of what are properly called social problems. Essentially, it is a problem of quite a different nature, in as much as it is a problem of securing to a minority liberty and equality of opportunity at the hands of a hostile majority, which believes in the denial of liberty and equal opportunity to the minority and conspires to enforce its policy on the minority. Viewed in this light, the problem of the Untouchables is fundamentally a political problem. Granting however for the sake of argument that it is a social problem, it is difficult to understand why political recognition of and political safeguards for the security of the Untouchables should retard their social unification with the Hindus if there is a genuine desire to set in motion processes which will bring about such a result. Congressmen appear to be arguing with no definite conception in their mind. They don't seem to have a clear idea of the inter-relation between political and social factors. This is well illustrated by its opposition to separate electorates and its preference to joint electorates. The process of reasoning is worth attention. In a joint electorate a Hindu votes for an Untouchable and an Untouchable votes for a Hindu. This builds up social solidarity. In a separate electorate a Hindu votes for a Hindu and an Untouchable votes for an Untouchable. This prevents social solidarity. This is not the point of view from which the Untouchables look at the question of electorates. Their point of view is, which of the two will enable the Untouchables to get an Untouchable of *their* choice elected. But I am interested in scrutinizing the Congress argument. I do not wish to enlarge upon and complicate the argument. The reasoning of the Congress appears to be correct. But it is only a superficial view of the matter. These elections take place once in five years. It may well be asked : How can social solidarity between the Hindus and the Untouchables be advanced by devoting one day out of five years to joint voting, if for the rest of the five years they are leading severely separate lives? Similarly, it may well be asked: How can one day devoted to separate voting in the course of five years make greater separation than what already exists or contrarywise how can one day in five years devoted to separate voting prevent those who wish to work for union from carrying out their purposes? To make it concrete: How can separate electorate for the Untouchables prevent intermarriage or interdining being introduced between them and the Hindus? Only a congenital idiot will say that they can. It is therefore puerile to say that the political recognition of the Untouchables as a separate element and granting them constitutional safeguards will perpetuate separation between them and the Hindus if the Hindus desire to put an end to it.

IV

There are other floating arguments against the claim of the Untouchables for political safeguards which must also be examined. One such argument is that there are social divisions everywhere, not merely in India but also in Europe; but they are not taken into account by the people of Europe in framing their constitutions. Why should they be taken into account in India? The thesis is general. But it may be extended to such a length that even the claim of the Untouchables may be enveloped by it. As such, I prefer to state why I think it is unsound.

In making my comments I propose to make a distinction between the statement and the argument founded on it and deal with them separately. The statement is good up to a point. In so far as it alleges that every society consists of groups it cannot be challenged. For even in European or American society there are groups associated together in various ways and for various purposes. Some are like the kindred closely bound together by blood or language. Some are of the nature of social classes differentiated on the basis of rank and status. Others are religious associations upholding particular dogmas, not to mention political parties and industrial corporations, criminal gangs and so on in an endless variety, with differing aims and bound together, some loosely some closely, by differing degrees of affinity. But when the statement goes beyond and says that the castes in India are not different from groups and classes in Europe and America it is nothing but an arrant nonsense. The groups and classes of Europe may be the same as the caste in India to look at. But fundamentally the two are quite different. The chief distinguishing feature is the isolation and exclusiveness which are the hall-marks of the castes in India and which are maintained as matter not of routine but of faith none of which characteristics is to be found in the group or the class system of Europe or America.

Turning to the thesis the social organization of India being different from what it is in Europe and America it follows that while Europe and America need not take into account the facts and circumstances of their social organization in framing their constitution, India cannot omit to take account of her Caste and Untouchability. For a fuller understanding of the matter I may explain why Europe need not and why India must. The danger to a society organized in groups is that each group develops what are called "its own interests" and the question of forging constitutional safeguards arises from the necessity of counteracting the mischief that such interest might cause to others outside it. Where there is a possibility of counteracting the mischief by non-political means there is no necessity for forging constitutional safeguards. If, on the other hand, non-political means of counteracting it do not exist then constitutional means must be forged. In Europe the possibility of counteracting mischief arising from a group seeking to maintain " its own interest " does exist. It exists because of the absence of isolation and exclusiveness among the various groups which allows free scope for interaction with the result that the dominant purpose of a group to stand out for its own interests and always seek to protect them as something inviolate and sacred gives way to a broadening and socialization of its aims and purposes. This endosmosis between groups in Europe affects dispositions and produces a society which can be depended upon for community of thought, harmony of purposes and unity of action. But the case of India is totally different. The caste in India is exclusive and isolated. There is no interaction and no modification of aims and objects. What a caste or a combination of castes regard "as their own interest" as against other castes remains as sacred and inviolate as ever. The fact that they mingle and co-operate does not alter their character. These acts of co-operation are mechanical and not social. Individuals use one another so as to get desired results, without reference to the emotional and intellectual disposition. The fact that they give and take orders modify actions and results. But it does not affect their dispositions. That being the case, the Indian constitution must provide safeguards to prevent castes with " their own interests " from doing mischief to other helpless castes.

There is another distinguishing feature of the Indian caste system, which justifies why the Indian Constitution must take account of it and provide against mischief arising from it. Every society consists of groups. But it must be recognized that the mutual relations of the groups are not the same everywhere. In one society groups may be only *non-social* in their attitude towards one another. But in another they may be *anti-social*. Where the spirit which actuates the various social groups is only non-social their existence may not be taken into account in framing a constitution. There is no cause for danger in a group which is only non-social. But where a group is actuated by an anti-social spirit towards another and to which alien is synonymous with enemy, the fact must be taken into account in framing the constitution and the class which has been the victim of anti-social spirit must be given protection by proper safeguards. In India the castes are not merely non-social. Often they are anti-social. This is particularly true of the Hindus towards the Untouchables. A few facts will suffice to show how anti-social the Hindus are towards the Untouchables. For instance, the Hindus will not allow the Untouchables to take water from a well. The Hindus will not allow the Untouchables entry in schools. The Hindus will not allow the Untouchables to travel in buses. The Hindus will not allow the Untouchables to travel in the same railway compartment. The Hindus will not allow Untouchables to wear clean clothes. The Hindus will not allow Untouchables to wear jewellery. The Hindus will not allow Untouchables to put tiles on the roofs of their houses. The Hindus will not tolerate Untouchables to own land. The Hindus will not allow Untouchables to keep cattle. The Hindus will not allow an Untouchable to sit when Hindu is standing. They are not isolated acts of a few bad men among the Hindus. They are the emanations of the permanent anti-social attitude of the Hindu community against the Untouchables.[1]

It is unnecessary to carry the matter further. It is enough to say that the thesis is full of fallacies and it would be a most shameful piece of chicanery, if it was used as a ground for opposing the demand of the Untouchables for constitutional safeguards.

V

There is another floating argument one sometimes comes across. The basis of the argument is that Untouchability is a vanishing thing and therefore there is no use recognizing the Untouchables as a separate element in the national life of India. Everything is vanishing and there is nothing that is permanent in human history. The point may be considered when Untouchability has gone root and branch. Until that state arrives, it is unnecessary to pay any regard to it. We must all hope for the disappearance of Untouchability. But we must be careful not to be misled by people who boast of being incorrigible optimists. An optimist is a good companion

1 For details, see my forthcoming volume—'*What The Hindus Have Done To Us.*'

to cheer up when one is in a state of depression. But he is not always a truthful witness of facts.

This argument is no argument at all. But since some people may be allured by it I wish to expose it and to show how futile it is. Those who raise this point do not seem to make a distinction between Untouchability as a touch-me-not-ism and Untouchability as a mental attitude manifesting itself in social discrimination. The two are quite different. It may be that Untouchability as a touch-me-not-ism may be gradually vanishing in towns, although I am doubtful if this is happening in any appreciable degree. But I am quite certain Untouchability as a propensity on the part of the Hindus to discriminate against the Untouchables will not vanish either in towns or in villages within an imaginable distance of time. Not only Untouchability as a discriminating propensity will not disappear but Untouchability as touch-me-not-ism will not disappear within a measurable distance of time in the vast number of villages in which the vast number of Hindus lives and will continue to live. You cannot untwist a two-thousand-year-twist of the human mind and turn it in the opposite direction.

I am quite aware that there are some protagonists of Hinduism who say that Hinduism is a very adaptable religion, that it can adjust itself to everything and absorb anything. I do not think many people would regard such a capacity in a religion as a virtue to be proud of just as no one would think highly of a child because it has developed the capacity to eat dung, and digest it. But that is another matter. It is quite true that Hinduism can adjust itself. The best example of its adjustability is the literary production called *Allahupanishad* which the Brahmins of the time of Akbar produced to give a place to his *Dine-Ilahi* within Hinduism and to recognize it as the Seventh system of Hindu philosophy. It is true that Hinduism can absorb many things. The beef-eating Hinduism (or strictly speaking Brahmanism which is the proper name of Hinduism in its earlier stage) absorbed the non-violence theory of Buddhism and became a religion of vegetarianism. But there is one thing which Hinduism has never been able to do—namely to adjust itself to absorb the Untouchables or to remove the bar of Untouchability. There have been many reformers who, long before Mr. Gandhi came on the scene, tried to remove the stain of Untouchability. But they have all failed. The reason for their failure appears to me to be very simple. Hindus have nothing to fear from the Untouchables, nor have they anything to gain by the abolition of Untouchability. Hindus gave up beef-eating because they were afraid that otherwise Buddhism would overpower Hinduism. Hindus wrote *Allah-upanishad* because they had everything to gain by helping Akbar to establish a new religion. The author gained money by pleasing the Emperor and by lending aid to establish a religion which promised less tyranny and oppression to the Hindus than Islam held out. Neither of these considerations exist for the most sanguine among the Untouchables to expect that the Hindus will readily put an end to this curse of Untouchability.

Not only have the Hindus nothing to fear and nothing to gain, they have in fact much to lose by the abolition of Untouchability. The system of Untouchability is a gold mine to the Hindus. In it the 240 millions of Hindus have 60 millions of Untouchables to serve as their retinue to enable the Hindus to maintain pomp and ceremony and to cultivate a feeling of pride and dignity befitting a master class, which cannot be fostered and sustained unless there is beneath it a servile class to look down upon. In it the 240 millions of Hindus have 60 millions of Untouchables to be used as forced labour and because of their state of complete destitution and helplessness can be compelled to work on a mere pittance and sometimes on nothing at all. In it the 240 millions of Hindus have 60 millions of Untouchables to do the dirty work of scavengers and sweepers which the Hindu is debarred by his religion to do and which must be done for Hindus by non-Hindus who could be no others than Untouchables. In it the 240 millions of Hindus have 60 millions of Untouchables who can be kept to lower jobs and prevented from entering into competition for higher jobs which are preserved for the Hindus. In it the 240 millions of Hindus have 60 millions of Untouchables who can be used as shock-absorbers in slumps and dead-weights in booms, for in slumps it is the Untouchable who is fired first and the Hindu is fired last and in booms the Hindu is employed first and the Untouchable is employed last.

Most people believe that Untouchability is a religious system. That is true. But it is a mistake to suppose that it is only a religious system. Untouchability is more than a religious system. It is also an economic system which is worse than slavery. In slavery the master at any rate had the responsibility to feed, clothe and house the slave and keep him in good condition lest the market value of the slave should decrease. But in the system of Untouchability the Hindu takes no responsibility for the maintenance of the Untouchable. As an economic system it permits exploitation without obligation. Untouchability is not only a system of unmitigated economic exploitation, but it is also a system of uncontrolled economic exploitation. That is because there is no independent public opinion to condemn it and there is no impartial machinery of administration to restrain it. There is no appeal to public opinion, for whatever public opinion there is it is the opinion of the Hindus who belong to the exploiting class and as such favour exploitation. There is no check from the police or the judiciary for the simple reason that they are all drawn from the Hindus, and take the side of the Exploiters.

Those who believe that Untouchability will soon vanish do not seem to have paid attention to the economic advantages which it gives to the Hindus. An Untouchable cannot do anything to get rid of his untouchability. It does not arise out of any personal fault on his part. Untouchability is an attitude of the Hindu. For Untouchability to vanish, it is the Hindu who must change. Will he change ?

Has a Hindu any conscience ? Is he ever known to have been fired with a righteous indignation against a moral wrong ? Assuming he does change so much as to regard Untouchability a moral wrong, assuming he is awakened to the sense of putting himself right with God and Man, will he agree to give up the economic and social advantages which Untouchability gives ? History, I am afraid, will not justify the conclusion that a Hindu has a quick conscience or if he has it is so active as to charge him with moral indignation and drive him to undertake a crusade to eradicate the wrong. History shows that where ethics and economics come in conflict, victory is always with economics. Vested interests have never been known to have willingly divested themselves unless there was sufficient force to compel them. The Untouchables cannot hope to generate any compelling force. They are poor and they are scattered. They can be easily suppressed should they raise their head.

On this analysis, Swaraj would make Hindus more powerful and Untouchables more helpless and it is quite possible that having regard to the economic advantages which it gives to the Hindus, Swaraj, instead of putting an end to Untouchability, may extend its life. That Untouchability is vanishing is therefore only wishful thinking and a calculated untruth. It would be most stupid—if not criminal—to take it into account in considering the demands of the Untouchables for constitutional safeguards and ignore the hard facts of the present and their certainty to continue in the indefinite future.

CHAPTER IX

A PLEA TO THE FOREIGNER

Let not Tyranny Have Freedom to Enslave

I

It is a matter of common experience that barring a few exceptions, almost all foreigners, who show interest in Indian political affairs, take the side of the Congress. This quite naturally puzzles and annoys the other political parties in the country, such as the Muslim League, claiming to represent the Musalmans, the Justice Party—now in a state of suspended animation but still—claiming to speak in the name of the non-Brahmins and the All-India Scheduled Castes Federation, claiming to represent the Untouchables, all of whom have been appealing to the foreigner for support but to whom the foreigner is not even prepared to give a sympathetic hearing. Why does the foreigner support the Congress and not the other political parties in India? Two reasons are usually assigned by the foreigner for his behaviour. One reason assigned by him for supporting the Congress is that it is the only representative political organization of the Indians and can speak in the name of India and even for the Untouchables. Is such a belief founded on facts?

It must be admitted that there have been circumstances which are responsible for creating such a belief. The first and foremost circumstance for the spread of this view is the propaganda by the Indian Press in favour of the Congress. The Press in India is an accomplice of the Congress, believes in the dogma that the Congress is never wrong and acts on the principle of not giving any publicity to any news, which is inconsistent with the Congress prestige or the Congress ideology. To the foreigner the Press is the principal medium of information about the Indian political affairs. The cry of the Indian Press being what it is, there is therefore no wonder if the people in England and America know one thing and only one thing, namely, that the Congress is the only representative body in India including even the Untouchables.

The effect of this propaganda is considerably heightened because of the absence of counter-propaganda on behalf of the Untouchables to advertise their case against the Congress claim. There are various explanations for this failure on the part of the Untouchables.

The Untouchables have no Press. The Congress Press is closed to them and is determined not to give them the slightest publicity. They cannot have their own Press and for obvious reasons. No paper can survive without advertisement revenue. Advertisement revenue can come only from business and in India all business, both high and small, is attached to the Congress and will not favour any Non-Congress organization. The staff of the Associated Press in India, which is the main news distributing agency in India, is entirely drawn from the Madras Brahmins—indeed the whole of the Press in India is in their hands and they, for well-known reasons, are entirely pro-Congress and will not allow any news hostile to the Congress to get publicity. These are reasons beyond the control of the Untouchables.

To a large extent the failure of the Untouchables to do propaganda, it must be admitted, is also due to the absence of will to do propaganda. This absence of will arises from a patriotic motive not to do anything, which will damage the cause of the country in the eyes of the world outside. There are two different aspects to the politics of India, which may be distinguished as foreign politics and constitutional politics. India's foreign politics relate to India's freedom from British Imperialism, while the constitutional politics of India centre round the nature of a constitution for a free India. For a discriminating student the two issues are really separate. But the Untouchables fear that though the two aspects of India's politics are separable, the foreigner, who counts in this matter and whose misunderstanding has to be guarded against, is not only incapable of separating them but is very likely to mistake a quarrel over constitutional politics for a disagreement over the ultimate purposes of India's foreign politics. This is why the Untouchables have preferred to remain silent and allowed the Congress propaganda to go unchallenged.

The Congressmen will not admit the patriotic motives of the Untouchables in keeping silent over Congress propaganda which is directed against them. The fact, however, remains that the silence and the desire to avoid open challenge on the part of the

Untouchables have been materially responsible for the general belief that the Congress represents all, even the Untouchables.

While, as explained above, there are circumstances which are responsible for creating the belief that Congress represents all including the Untouchables, such a belief is not warranted by the facts as disclosed by the elections that took place in 1937. How the claim of the Congress to represent all has been disproved by those elections has already been described in an earlier part of this book, both generally and also with particular regard to the claim of the Congress to represent the Untouchables. If the foreigner will make a note of it he will see how wide the propaganda is from the facts.

At a time when the representative character of the Congress was not put to test in an election it was excusable for a foreigner to be carried away by propaganda. But the matter has now been put to test in the elections that took place in 1937. With the results of the elections available to check the position, it may be hoped that the foreigners will revise their view that the Congress represents all, including the Untouchables, and that they will realize that the other parties are equally representative of elements in the social life of India which are outside the Congress and have therefore the right to be heard.

II

There is another reason why the foreigner lends his support to the Congress. It lies in the difference between the demonstrative activities of the Congress and the other political parties in the country. While he compares the activities of the different political parties, he sees Congressmen engaged in a conflict with the British Government, launching campaigns of civil disobedience, breaking laws made by a foreign Government, organizing movements for non-payment of taxes, courting prison, preaching non-co-operation with Government, refusing offices and exhibiting themselves in other ways as men out to sacrifice themselves for the freedom of the country. On the other hand, he sees the other political parties uninterested, passive and taking no part in such a struggle. From this, he concludes that the Congress is a body struggling for the freedom of India, while the other parties are indifferent, if not obstructive and as a lover of freedom feels bound to support the Congress as a body carrying on a 'Fight for Freedom' in preference to other parties.

This is quite natural. But a question arises which calls for attention. Is this partiality to the Congress the result of an infatuation for the 'Fight for Freedom' movement? Or, is it the result of a conviction that this 'Fight for Freedom' is going to make the people of India free? If it is the former, all I can do is to regret that what I have said in Chapter VII in explanation as to why the Untouchables have not joined with the Congress in this 'Fight for Freedom' has not produced the desired effect on the foreigner. But I cannot quarrel with him on that account. For it is quite understandable that many a foreigner on reading that chapter may say that while the reasons adduced by me as to why the Untouchables refuse to join the 'Fight for Freedom' are valid and good, I have shown no ground why he should not support a body which is carrying on a fight for freedom.

If the basis of his partiality to the Congress is of the latter sort then the matter stands on a different footing. It then becomes necessary to examine the rationale of his attitude and to save him from his error.

Ordinarily, no one trusts the word of a person who is not prepared to place all his cards on the table and commit himself to something clear and definite, so as to prove his *bona fides*, to inspire confidence and secure the co-operation of those who have doubts about his motives. The same rule must apply to the Congress. But as I have shown in Chapter VII the Congress has not produced its blue print of the sort of democracy it aims to establish in India, showing what place the servile classes and particularly the Untouchables will have in it. Indeed, it has refused to produce such a blue print, notwithstanding the insistent demand of the Untouchables and the other minority communities. In the absence of such a pronouncement it appears to be a strange sort of credulity on the part of the foreigner to give support to the Congress on the ground that it stood for democracy.

There is certainly no ground for thinking that the Congress is planning to establish democracy in India. The mere fact that the Congress is engaged in a 'Fight for Freedom' does not warrant such a conclusion. Before any such conclusion is drawn it is the duty of the foreigner to pursue the matter further and ask another question, namely, 'For whose freedom is the Congress fighting?' The question whether the Congress is fighting for freedom has very little importance as compared to the question, 'for whose freedom is the Congress fighting?' This is a pertinent and necessary inquiry and it would be wrong for any lover of freedom to support the Congress without further pursuing the matter and finding out what the truth is. But the foreigner who takes the side of the Congress does not care even to raise such a question. One should have thought that he would very naturally raise such a question and if he did raise it and pursue it, I am confident, he will find abundant proof that the Congress far from planning for democracy is planning to resuscitate the ancient form of Hindu polity of a hereditary governing class ruling a hereditary servile class.

The attitude of the foreigner to the cause of the servile classes and particularly to the cause of the Untouchables is a vital matter and no party can leave it out of consideration, as a case of idiosyncrasy. For any one representing the Untouchables it is necessary to take note of it and do his best to convince the foreigner that in supporting the Congress he is supporting a wrong party.

III

Apart from the question of likes and dislikes, the real explanation for this strange attitude of the foreigner towards the Congress seems to be in certain notions about freedom, self-government and democracy propounded by western writers on Political Science and which have become the stock-in-trade of the average foreigner.

As to freedom, the foreigner does not stop to make a distinction between the freedom of a country and the freedom of the people in the country. He takes it for granted that the freedom of a country is the same as the freedom of the people in the country and once the freedom of the country is secured the freedom of the people is also thereby assured.

As regards self-government he believes that all that is wanted in a people is a sense of constitutional morality, which Grote[1] defined as habits of "paramount reverence for the form of

[1] History of Greece, Vol. III, p. 347.

the constitution, enforcing obedience to the authorities acting under and within those forms, yet combined with the habit of open speech, of action subject only to definite legal control, and unrestrained censure of those very authorities as to all their public acts—combined, too, with a perfect confidence in the bosom of every citizen, admits the bitterness of party contest, that the forms of constitution will be not less sacred in the eyes of his opponents than in his own." If in a populace these habits are present, then according to the western writers on Politics, self-government can be a reality and nothing further need be considered. As to democracy he believes that what is necessary for achieving it is the establishment of universal adult suffrage. Other aids have been suggested such as recall, plebiscite and frequent elections and in some countries they have been brought into operation. But in a majority of countries nothing more than adult suffrage and frequent elections is deemed to be necessary for ensuring Government by the people, of the people and for the people.

I have no hesitation in saying that all these notions are fallacious and grossly misleading.

Not to make a distinction between the freedom of the country and the freedom of the people in the country is to allow oneself to be misled, if not deceived. For, words such as society, nation and country are just amorphous if not ambiguous terms. There is no gainsaying that 'nation' though one word means many classes. Philosophically, it may be possible to consider a nation as a unit but sociologically it cannot but be regarded as consisting of many classes and the freedom of the nation, if it is to be a reality, must vouchsafe the freedom of the different classes comprised in it, particularly of those who are treated as the servile classes.

Habits of constitutional morality may be essential for the maintenance of a constitutional form of Government. But the maintenance of a constitutional form of Government is not the same thing as a self-government by the people. Similarly, it may be granted that adult suffrage can produce government of the people in the logical sense of the phrase, i.e., in contrast to the government of a king. But it cannot by itself be said to bring about a democratic government, in the sense of the government by the people and for the people.

Anyone who knows the tragic fate of Parliamentary Democracy in Western Europe will not require more and better evidence to prove the fallacy underlying such notions of democracy[1]. If I may quote myself from what I have said in another place, the causes which have led to the failure of democracy in Western Europe may be summarized in the following words :

> " The Government of human society has undergone some very significant changes. There was a time when the government of human society had taken the form of autocracy by Despotic Sovereigns. This was replaced after a long and bloody struggle by a system of government known as Parliamentary Democracy. It was felt that this was the last word in the framework of government. It was believed to bring about the millennium in which every human being will have the right to liberty, property and pursuit of happiness. And there were good grounds for such high hopes. In parliamentary democracy there is the Legislature to express the voice of the people ; there is the executive which is subordinate to the Legislature and bound to obey the Legislature. Over and above the Legislature and the Executive there is the Judiciary to control both and keep them both within prescribed bounds. Parliamentary democracy has all the marks of a popular Government, a government of the people, by the people and for the people. It is therefore a matter of some surprise that there has been a revolt against parliamentary democracy although not even a century has elapsed since its universal acceptance and inauguration. There is revolt against it in Italy, in Germany, in Russia and in Spain, and there are very few countries in which there has not been discontent against parliamentary democracy. Why should there be this discontent and dissatisfaction against parliamentary democracy ? It is a question worth considering. There is no country in which the urgency of considering this question is greater than it is in India. India is negotiating to have parliamentary democracy. There is a great need of some one with sufficient courage to tell Indians: " Beware of parliamentary democracy, it is not the best product as it appears to be.
>
> Why has parliamentary democracy failed ? In the country of the dictators it has failed because it is a machine whose movements are very slow. It delays swift action. In a parliamentary democracy the Executive may be held up by the Legislature which may refuse to pass the laws which the Executive wants and if it is not held up by the Legislature it

---

[1] Labour and Parliamentary Democracy—A lecture delivered on 17th September 1943 to the All-India Trade Union Workers' Study Camp held in Delhi.

may be held up by the judiciary which may declare the laws as illegal. Parliamentary democracy gives no free hand to dictatorship and that is why it became a discredited institution in countries like Italy, Spain and Germany which readily welcomed dictatorships. If dictators alone were against parliamentary democracy it would not have mattered at all. Their testimony against parliamentary democracy would be welcomed for the reason that it can be an effective check upon dictatorship. But unfortunately there is a great deal of discontent against parliamentary democracy even in countries where people are opposed to dictatorship. That is the most regrettable fact about Parliamentary democracy. This is all the more regrettable because parliamentary democracy has not been at a standstill. It has progressed in three directions. It began with equality of political rights in the form of equal suffrage. There are very few countries having parliamentary democracy which have not adult suffrage. It has progressed by expanding the notion of equality of political rights to equality of social and economic opportunity. It has recognised that the State cannot be held at bay by corporations which are anti-social in their purpose. With all this, there is immense discontent against parliamentary democracy even in countries pledged to democracy. The reasons for discontent in such countries must obviously be different from those assigned by the dictator countries. There is no time to go into details. But it can be said in general terms that the discontent against parliamentary democracy is due to the realization that it has failed to assure to the masses the right to liberty, property or the pursuit of happiness. If this is true, it is important to know the causes which bave brought about this failure. The causes for this failure may be found either in wrong ideology or wrong organization or in both. I think the causes are to be found in both.

Of the erroneous ideologies which have been responsible for the failure of parliamentary democracy I have no doubt that the idea of freedom of contract is one of them. The idea became sanctified and was upheld in the name of liberty. Parliamentary democracy took no notice of economic inequalities and did not care to examine the result of freedom of contract on the parties to the contract, in spite of the fact that they were unequal in their bargaining power. It did not mind if the freedom of contract gave the strong the opportunity to defraud the weak. The result is that parliamentary democracy in standing out as protagonist of liberty has continuously added to the economic wrongs of the poor, the downtrodden and the disinherited class.

The second wrong ideology which has vitiated parliamentary democracy is the failure to realize that political democracy cannot succeed where there is no social and economic democracy. Some may question this proposition. To those who are disposed to question it, I will ask a counter-question. Why did parliamentary democracy collapse so easily in Italy, Germany and Russia? Why did it not collapse so easily in England and the U.S.A.? To my mind there is only one answer. It is that there was a greater degree of economic and social democracy in the latter countries than existed in the former. Social and economic democracy are the tissues and the fibre of a political democracy. The tougher the tissue and the fibre, the greater the strength of the body. Democracy is another name for equality. Parliamentary democracy developed a passion for liberty. It never made even a nodding acquaintance with equality. It failed to realize the significance of equality and did not even endeavour to strike a balance between liberty and equality with the result that liberty swallowed equality and has made democracy a name and a farce.

I have referred to the wrong ideologies which in my judgment have been responsible for the failure of parliamentary democracy. But I am equally certain that more than bad ideology it is bad organization which has been responsible for the failure of democracy. All political societies get divided into two classes—the Rulers and the Ruled. This is an evil. If the evil stopped here it would not matter much. But the unfortunate part of it is that the division becomes so stereotyped and stratified that Rulers are always drawn from the ruling class and the class that is ruled never becomes the ruling class. This happens because generally people do not care to see that they govern themselves. They are content to establish a government and leave it to govern them. This explains why parliamentary democracy has never been a government of the people or by the people and why it has been in reality a government of a hereditary subject class by a hereditary ruling class. It is this vicious organization of political life which has made parliamentary democracy such a dismal failure. It is because of this that parliamentary democracy has not fulfilled the hope it held out to the common man of ensuring to him liberty, property and pursuit of happiness."

If this analysis of the causes which have led to the failure of democracy is correct, it must serve as a warning to the protagonists of democracy that there are certain fundamental considerations which go to the root of democracy and which they cannot ignore without peril to democracy. For the sake of clarity these considerations may be set down in serial order.

First is the recognition of the hard fact of history that in every country there exist two classes,—the governing class and the servile class between whom there is a continuous struggle for power. *Second* is that by reason of its power and prestige the governing class finds it easy to maintain its supremacy over the servile class. *Third* is that adult suffrage and frequent elections are no bar against governing class reaching places of power and authority. *Fourth* is that on account of their inferiority complex the members of the servile classes regard the members of the governing class as their natural leaders and the servile classes themselves volunteer to elect members of the governing classes as their rulers. *Fifth* is that the existence of a governing class is inconsistent with democracy and self-government and that given the fact that where the governing class retains its power to govern, it is wrong to believe that democracy and self-government have become realities of life. *Sixth* is that self-government and democracy become real not when a constitution based on adult suffrage comes into existence but when the governing class loses its power to capture the power to govern. *Seventh* is that while in some countries the servile classes may succeed in ousting the governing class from the seat of authority with nothing more than adult suffrage, in other countries the governing class may be so deeply entrenched that the servile classes will need other safeguards besides adult suffrage to achieve the same end.

That there is great value in having these considerations drawn up and hung up, so to say on the wall, before every lover of democracy, so that he may see them and note them, goes without saying. For they will help, as nothing else can, to make him realize that in devising a constitution for democracy he must bear in mind: that the principal aim of such a constitution must be to dislodge the governing class from its position and to prevent it from remaining as a governing class for ever; that the machinery for setting up a democratic government cannot be a matter of dogma; that ousting the governing class from power being the main object the machinery for setting up a democratic government cannot be uniform and that variations in the machinery of Democracy must not merely be tolerated but accepted for the reason that the processes by which the governing classes obtain their mastery over the servile classes vary from country to country.

This is what democracy means and involves. But unfortunately Western writers on Politics from whom the foreigner draws his notions have failed to take such a realistic view of democracy. Instead, they have taken a very formal and a very superficial view of it by making constitutional morality, adult suffrage and frequent elections as the be-all and end-all of democracy.

Those who propound the view that democracy need involve no more than these three devices are probably unaware of the fact that they are doing nothing more than and nothing different from expressing the point of view of the governing classes. The governing classes know by experience that such mechanisms have not proved fatal to their power and their position. Indeed, they have helped to give to their power and prestige the virtue of legality and made themselves less vulnerable to attack by the servile classes.

Those who wish that democracy and self-government should come into their own, and should not remain as mere forms, cannot do better than start with the recognition of the crucial fact that the existence of a permanently settled governing class is the greatest danger to democracy. It is the only safe and realistic approach for a democrat to adopt. It is a fatal blunder to omit to take account of its existence in coming to a conclusion as to whether in a free country freedom will be the privilege of the governing class only or it will be the possession of all. In my view, therefore, what the foreigner who chooses to side with the Congress should ask is not whether the Congress is fighting for freedom. He should ask: For whose freedom is the Congress fighting? Is it fighting for the freedom of the governing class in India or is it fighting for the freedom of the people of India? If he finds that the Congress is fighting for the freedom of the governing class, he should ask Congressmen: Is the governing class in India fit to govern? This is the least he can do before siding with the Congress.

What are the answers which Congressmen have to give to these questions? I do not know. But I will give what I think are the only true answers to these questions.

IV

I cannot say if the foreigner will be impressed by what has been said in the foregoing section of this chapter. If he is he will no doubt ask for proof in support of the statement that the Congress in fighting for the freedom of the country is really fighting not to establish democracy but is planning to resuscitate the ancient Hindu polity of a hereditary governing class ruling a hereditary servile class. I am not certain that the foreigner will be satisfied with the evidence. But I am prepared to place it before him for what it is worth.

Who constitute the governing class in India? For Indians such a question is unnecessary. But for the foreigner it is a necessary preliminary and it must therefore be dealt with. The governing class in India consists principally of the Brahmins. Strangely enough some present-day Brahmins repudiate the allegation that they belong to the governing class though at one time they described themselves as *Bhudevas* (Gods on earth). What can this *volte face* be due to? The intellectual class in every community is charged by its moral code with one sacred duty, namely, to safeguard the interest of the community and not to sacrifice it to the interest of their own class. No intellectual class has so grossly violated this trust as have the Brahmins in India. When one finds the Brahmins repudiating their position as the governing class in India one begins to think whether it is due to a guilty conscience, born out of the realization that they have committed a criminal breach of this trust and therefore dare not stand before the bar of the world. Or is it due to their sense of modesty? It is not necessary to speculate as to what the truth is. For, it is hardly open to question that in India the Brahmins are a governing class. If necessary there are two tests which one could apply for the purpose of ascertaining the truth. First is the sentiment of the people and the second is the Brahmin's share in administration. Taking the attitude of the people towards the Brahmin, nobody can deny that the person of the Brahmin is regarded as sacred by every Hindu, high or low. He is the most "Worshipful Master" to whom everyone high and low must bow. In pre-British days he had immunities and privileges which were denied to the servile class. For instance he could not be hanged even if he committed murder. That was because he was a sacred person. There was a time when no person of the servile class could take his food without drinking the water in which the toes of the Brahmins were washed. Sir P. C. Ray once described how in his childhood, rows of children belonging to the servile classes used to stand for hours together in the morning on the roadside in Calcutta with cups of water in their hands waiting for a Brahmin to pass, ready to wash his feet and take the sacred liquid to their parents who would not take their food without having a sip of it first. He was entitled to first fruits. In Malabar, where the Sambandham form of marriage prevails, the servile classes, such as the Nairs, regard it an honour to have their females kept as mistresses by the Brahmins. Even kings invited Brahmins to deflower their queens on *prima noctis*.[1]

---

[1] The Traveller Ludovico Di Varthema who came to India in the middle of the 16th century and visited Malabar says:

"It is proper and at the same time a pleasant thing to know who these Brahmins are. You must know that they are the chief persons of the faith, as priests are among us. And when the king takes a wife he selects the most worthy and the most honoured of these Brahmins and makes him sleep the first night with his wife, in order that he may deflower her. Do not imagine that the Brahmin goes willingly to perform this operation. The king is obliged to pay him four hundred to five hundred ducats. The king only and no other person in Calicut adopts this practice."—*Voyages of Varthema* (Hakluyat Society), Vol. I, p. 141.

Other Travellers tell that the practice was widespread. Hamilton in his *Account of the East Indies* says:

"When the Samorin marries, he must not cohabit with his bride till the Nambourie (Nambudri) or chief priest, has enjoyed her, and if he pleases he may have three nights of her company, because the first fruits of her nuptials must be a holy oblation to the God she worships and some of the nobles are so complacent as to allow the clergy the same tribute; but the common people cannot have that compliment paid to them, but are forced to supply the priests places themselves."—Vol. I, p. 308.

Buchanan in his Narrative refers to the practice in the following terms:

"The ladies of the Tamuri family are generally impregnated by Nambudries; although if they choose they may employ the higher ranks of Nairs; but the sacred character of the Nambudries always procures them a preference."—*Pinkerton's Voyages*, Vol. VIII, p. 734.

Mr. C. A. Innes, I.C.S., Editor of the *Gazetteer* of Malabar and Anjengo, issued under the authority of the Government of Madras, says:

"Another institution found amongst all the classes following the *marukakkattayam* system, as well as amongst many of those who observe *makkattayam*, is that known as "Tali-tying wedding" which has been described as "the most peculiar, distinctive and unique" among Malayali marriage customs. Its essence is the tying of a *tali* (a small piece of gold or other metal, like a locket, on a string) on a girl's neck before she attains the age of puberty. This is done by a man of the same or of a higher caste (the usages of different classes differ), and it is only after it has been done that the girl is at liberty to contract a *sambandham*. It seems to be generally considered that the ceremony was intended to confer on the *tali tier* or *manavalan* (bridegroom) a right to cohabit with the girl; and by some the origin of the ceremony is found in the claim of the *Bhu-devas* or "Earth-Gods," (that is the Brahmins), and on a lower plane of Kshatriyas or ruling classes, to the first-fruits of lower caste womanhood, a right akin to the mediæval *droit de seigneurie*."—Vol. I, p. 101.

Under the British Government and by reason of its equalitarian jurisprudence these rights, immunities and privileges of the Brahmins have ceased to exist. Nonetheless the advantages they gave still remain and the Brahmin is still pre-eminent and sacred in the eyes of the servile classes and is still addressed by them as "Swami" which means 'Lord.'

The second test gives an equally positive result. To take only the Madras Presidency by way of illustration. Consider Table 18 (see page 213). It shows the distribution of gazetted posts between the Brahmins and the other communities in the year 1943. Similar data from the other provinces could also be adduced to support this conclusion. But it is unnecessary to labour the point. Whether the Brahmins accept or deny the status the facts that they control the State and that their supremacy is accepted by the servile classes, are enough to prove that they form the governing class.

It is of course impossible for the Brahmins to maintain their supremacy as a governing class without an ally to help them on account of their being numerically very small. Consequently, as history shows, the Brahmins have always had other classes as their allies to whom they were ready to accord the status of a governing class provided they were prepared to work with them in subordinate co-operation. In ancient and mediæval times they made such an alliance with the Kshatriyas or the warrior class and the two not merely ruled the masses, but ground them down to atoms, pulverized them so to say—the Brahmin with his pen and the Kshatriya with his sword. At present, Brahmins have made an alliance with the Vaishya class called Banias. The shifting of this alliance from the Kshatriya to the Bania is in the changed circumstances quite inevitable. In these days of commerce money is more important than sword. That is one reason for this change in party alignment. The second reason is the need for money to run the political machine. Money can come only from and is in fact coming from the Bania. If the Bania is financing the Congress it is because he has realized—and Mr. Gandhi has taught him—that money invested in politics gives large dividends. Those who have any doubt in the matter might do well to read what Mr. Gandhi told Mr. Louis Fischer on June 6, 1942. In his book *A Week with Mr. Gandhi*, Mr. Fischer

Table 18

Communities	Approximate Population in Lakhs	Percentage of Population	No. of Posts held out of Total No. Gazetted Posts (2,200)	Percentage of Appointments held	Non-Gazetted Posts: Over Rs. 100 Total No. 7,500 — No. held by	Over Rs. 100 — Percentage of Appointments held	Over Rs. 35 Total No. 20,782 — No. held by	Over Rs. 35 — Percentage of Appointments held
(1)	(2)	(3)	(4)	(5)	(6)	(7)	(8)	(9)
Brahmins	15	3	820	37	3,280	43.73	8,812	42.4
Christians	20	4	190	9	750	10	1,655	8.0
Muhammadans	37	7	150	7	497	6.63	1,624	7.8
Depressed Classes	70	14	25	1.5	39	.52	144	.69
Non-Brahmins: Forward Non-Brahmins	113	22	620	27	2,543	33.9	8,440	40.6
Non-Brahmins: Backward Classes ...	245	50	50	2				
Non-Asiatic and Anglo-Indians ...	—	—	—	—	372	5.0	83	.4
Other Communities	—	—	—	—	19	.5	24	.11

records very revealing answers to some of his most interesting and pertinent questions. Mr. Fischer writes[1] :

> " I said I had several questions to ask him (Mr. Gandhi) about the Congress Party. Very highly placed Britishers, I recalled, had told me that Congress was in the hands of big business and that Mr. Gandhi was supported by the Bombay Millowners who gave him as much money as he wanted. 'What truth is there in these assertions,' I asked, ' Unfortunately, they are true,' he declared simply. ' Congress hasn't enough money to conduct its work. We thought in the beginning to collect four annas (about eight cents) from each member per year and operate on that. But it hasn't worked.' ' What proportion of the Congress budget,' I asked, ' is covered by rich Indians ? ' ' Practically all of it,' he stated ' In this ashram, for instance, we could live much more poorly than we do and spend less money. But we do not and the money comes from our rich friends.' "

Being dependent on his money, it is impossible for the Brahmin to exclude the Bania from the position of a governing class. In fact, the Brahmin has established not merely a working but a cordial alliance with the Bania. The result is that the governing class in India to-day is a Brahmin-Bania instead of a Brahmin-Kshatriya combine as it used to be.

Enough has been said to show who constitute the governing class in India. The next inquiry must be directed to find out how the governing class fared in the elections to the Provincial Legislatures that took place in 1937.

The elections that took place in 1937 were based on a franchise which though it was neither universal nor adult was wide enough to include classes other than the governing class, certainly wider than any existing prior to 1937. The elections based on such a franchise may well be taken as a test to find out how the governing class fared as against the servile classes in this electoral contest.

Unfortunately, no Indian publicist has as yet undertaken to compile an Indian counterpart of Dodd's Parliamentary Manual. Consequently, it is difficult to have precise particulars regarding the caste, occupation, education and social status of members of the legislature elected on the Congress ticket. The matter is so important that I thought of collecting the

---

[1] *A Week With Gandhi* (1943), p. 41.

necessary information on these points relating to members of the Provincial Legislatures elected in 1937. I did not succeed in getting precise information about every member. There are many whom I have had to leave as unclassified. But the information I have been able to gather is I believe sufficient to warrant our drawing certain definite conclusions.

As an answer to the question as to how the governing class fared in the electoral contest of 1937, attention may be drawn to Table 19 (see page 216) which shows the proportion of Brahmins and Banias (landlords and moneylenders) representing the governing class and non-Brahmins and the Scheduled Castes representing the servile classes, that were elected to the Provincial Legislative Assemblies on the Congress ticket.

Those, who do not know how small is the proportion of the Brahmins to the total population of Hindus, may not be able to realize the degree of over-representation which the Brahmins have secured in the election. But there is no doubt that on comparison with their numbers the Brahmins have secured overwhelming representation.

Those, who wish to know what degree of representation the propertied classes, such as Banias, businessmen and landlords obtained, may see the figures given in Table 20 (see page 217). It shows how many Banias, businessmen and landlords were elected on the Congress ticket. Here again the representation secured by the Banias, landlords and businessmen is quite out of proportion to their numbers.

Such is the position of the governing class in the legislatures constituted under the elections that took place in 1937. Some may say that on the whole the governing classes were in a minority in the legislature. As against this, it must be pointed out that the supremacy of the governing class can be measured not by its position in the legislature but by its ability to get possession of executive authority. An inquiry into the class composition of the Ministers is therefore very pertinent. Information on this point will be found in Tables 21 and 22 (see pages 218 and 219). A glance at the tables[1] is enough to show that the Brahmins—the premier governing class—succeeded in capturing an overwhelming majority of seats in

[1] The facts summarized in these Tables are taken from the issue for July 15, 1939, of *Information*, an official publication issued by the Government of India.

Table 19

Classification of Congress Members of Provincial Assemblies by Castes

Province	*Brahmins*	*Non-Brahmins*	*Scheduled Castes*	*Not Stated*	*Total*
Assam	6	21	1	5	33
Bengal	15	27	6	6	54
Bihar	31	39	16	12	98
C. P.	28	35	7	—	70
Madras	38	90	26	5	159
Orissa	11	20	5	—	36
United Provinces	39	54	16	24	133

Table 20

Classification of the Congress Members of the Provincial Legislatures in terms of Occupation

Province	Lawyers	Medical Practitioners	Land-lords	Business-men	Private Officials	Money Lenders	Nil	Not Stated	Total
Assam	16	2	2	1	—	—	3	9	33
Bengal	9	2	16	5	2	—	16	4	54
Bihar	14	4	56	6	3	—	1	14	98
Central Provinces ...	20	2	25	10	—	—	8	5	70
Madras	52	2	45	18	2	1	3	36	159
Orissa	8	1	17	4	4	1	1	—	36

Table 21

Composition of the Cabinets in the Congress Provinces [f.6]

Province	Total No. of Cabinet Ministers	Total No. of Non-Hindu Ministers	Hindu Ministers in the Cabinet				Prime Minister
			Total	Brahmins	Non. Brahmins	Scheduled Castes	
Assam	8	3	5	1		Nil	Brahmin
Bihar	4	1	3	1	7	1	Brahmin
Bombay	7	2	5	3	2	Nil	Brahmin
Central Province	5	1	4	3	1	Nil	Brahmin
Madras	9	2	7	3	3	1	Brahmin
Orissa	3	Nil	3	7			Brahmin
United Provinces	6	2	4	4	Nit	Nil	Brahmin

Table 22

Classification of Parliamentary Secretaries in Congress Provinces*

Province	Total No. of Parliamentary Secretaries	Total No. of Non-Hindu Parliamentary Secretaries	Hindu Parliamentary Secretaries			
			Total	Brahmins	Non-Brahmins	Scheduled Castes
Assam	Nil	Nil	Nil	Nil	Nil	Nil
Bihar	8	Nil	8	2	5	1
Bombay	6	Nil	6	1	5	Nil
Central Provinces	Nil	Nlt	Nil	Nil	Nil	Nil

Madras	8	1	9	3	4	1
Orissa	3	Nil	3	1	?	Nil
United Province	12	1	11	1	8	1

Compiled from Indian Information Issue of July 15, 1939. Question mark indicate inability to classify whether Brahmin or non-Brahmin.

In all the Hindu Provinces, the Prime Ministers were Brahmins. In all Hindu provinces, if the non-Hindu ministers were excluded, the majority of ministers were Brahmins and even parliamentary secretaries were Brahmins.

What has been said so far makes two things as clear as daylight. First is that there is in India a well defined governing class, distinct and separate from the servile class. Second is that the governing class is so powerful that though small in number in the elections of 1987 it quite easily captured political power and established its supremacy over the servile classes. There remains only one more point for me to establish to be able to put my thesis across. It is to show how far Congress was responsible for the victory of the governing class in the elections of 1987. I know I must prove beyond reasonable doubt that the Congress is responsible for placing the governing class in the position of supremacy over the servile class. For it might be said that the Congress had nothing to do with this, that even if the Congress was responsible for it the result was an accident and that there was no intention on the part of the Congress to help the governing classes to win this position of supremacy.

the Cabinet. In all the Hindu Provinces, the Prime Ministers were Brahmins. In all Hindu provinces, if the non-Hindu ministers were excluded, the majority of ministers were Brahmins and even parliamentary secretaries were Brahmins.

What has been said so far makes two things as clear as daylight. First is that there is in India a well defined governing class, distinct and separate from the servile class. Second is that the governing class is so powerful that though small in number in the elections of 1937 it quite easily captured political power and established its supremacy over the servile classes. There remains only one more point for me to establish to be able to put my thesis across. It is to show how far Congress was responsible for the victory of the governing class in the elections of 1937. I know I must prove beyond reasonable doubt that the Congress is responsible for placing the governing class in the position of supremacy over the servile class. For it might be said that the Congress had nothing to do with this, that even if the Congress was responsible for it the result was an accident and that there was no intention on the part of the Congress to help the governing classes to win this position of supremacy.

V

The first line of these suggested defences can be easily disposed of. It is probable that those who raise this defence do not know the political colour of the province to which the figures given in Tables 19, 20, 21 and 22 relate. If they knew it they would give up this line of defence. For they relate to what are called the Congress Provinces. In these provinces the majority party was the Congress Party and the Cabinets were Congress Cabinets. Obviously, if in these Congress provinces the governing classes succeeded in establishing their rule over the servile classes it is difficult to see how the Congress could be absolved from responsibility for such a result. The Congress is a well disciplined party. It had a plan for fighting the elections. In every province there was established a Parliamentary Board, the functions of which were (1) to choose candidates for elections, (2) to decide upon the formation of Cabinets, and (3) to control the actions of ministers. Over and above these Provincial Parliamentary

Boards there was a Central Parliamentary Board to superintend and control the work of the Provincial Parliamentary Boards. It was an election which was planned and controlled by the Congress. It is therefore futile to argue that if the governing classes captured power in the elections of 1937 in the Congress Provinces the Congress is not responsible for the result.

The second line of defence is as fragile as the first. Those who wish to argue that the dominance of the governing class in the Congress provinces is accidental and not intentional should know that they are advancing an argument which will not stand. I would invite the attention of those who are inclined to treat it as an accident to consider the following circumstances.

First let them consider the mentality of the leading members of the Congress High Command who have guided the destiny of the Congress in the past and who are at present running the affairs of the Congress. It would be well to begin with Mr. Tilak. He is dead. But while he was alive he was the most leading man in the Congress and exercised the greatest sway over it. Mr. Tilak was a Brahmin and belonged to the governing class. Though he had acquired the reputation of being the father of the Swaraj movement his antipathy to the servile classes was quite well known. For want of space I will cite only one instance of his mentality towards the servile classes. In 1918, when the non-Brahmins and the Backward classes had started an agitation for separate representation in the legislature, Mr. Tilak in a public meeting held in Sholapur said that he did not understand why the oil pressers, tobacco shopkeepers, washermen, etc.—that was his description of the Non-Brahmins and the Backward classes—should want to go into the legislature. In his opinion, their business was to obey the laws and not to aspire for power to make laws.

Next after Tilak I may take Mr. Vallabhbhai Patel. Here again, I will cite only one instance to indicate his mentality. In 1942, Lord Linlithgow invited 52 important Indians representing different sections of the people to discuss the steps that might be taken to make the Central Government more popular and thereby enlist the sympathy and co-operation of all Indians in war effort. Among those that were invited were members belonging to the Scheduled Castes. Mr. Vallabhbhai Patel could not bear the idea that the Viceroy should have invited such a crowd of mean men. Soon after the event, Mr. Vallabhbhai Patel made a speech in Ahmedabad and said[1] :—

> " The Viceroy sent for the leaders of the Hindu Mahasabha, he sent for the leaders of the Muslim League and he sent for Ghanchis (oil pressers), Mochis (cobblers) and the rest."

Although Mr. Vallabhbhai Patel in his malicious and stinging words referred only to Ghanchis and Mochis his speech indicates the general contempt in which he holds the servile classes of his country.

It may be well to know the reactions of Pandit Jawaharlal Nehru. Pandit Jawaharlal Nehru is a Brahmin but he has the reputation of being non-communal in his outlook and secular in his beliefs. Facts do not seem to justify the reputation he carries. A person cannot be called secular if he, when his father dies, performs the religious ceremonies prescribed by orthodox Hinduism at the hands of Brahmin priests on the banks of the river Ganges as Pandit Jawaharlal did when his father died in 1931. As to his being non-communal it is stated by no less a person than Dr. Pattabhi Sitaramayya that Pandit Nehru is very conscious of the fact that he is a Brahmin.[2] This must come as a most astonishing fact to those who believe the Pandit to have the reputation of being the most nationally minded Hindu leader in India. But Dr. Sitaramayya must be knowing what he is talking about. More disturbing is the fact that in the United Provinces from which he hails and over which he exercises complete authority the ministers in the cabinet of the province were all Brahmins. Mrs. Vijaya Laxmi Pandit, the well-known sister of Pandit Jawaharlal Nehru, also seems to be conscious of herself being Brahmin by caste. It is said that at the All-India Women's Conference held in Delhi in December 1940, the question of not declaring one's caste in the Census Return was discussed. Mrs. Pandit disapproved[3] of the idea and said that she did not see any reason why she should not be proud of her Brahmin blood and declare herself as a Brahmin at the Census.

Who are these men? What is their status? Mr. Tilak

---

[1] Quoted by Mr. J. E. Sanjana in *Sense and Nonsense in Politics*—Serial No. XII in the *Rast Rahabar* (a Bombay Gujarati Weekly) of 14th January 1945.

[2] See his Invitation p. XVI to Jawaharlal Nehru by Y. G. Krishnamurti.

[3] Quoted by Sanjana in *Sense and Nonsense in Politics*—Serial No. XII in the *Rast Rahabar*, dated 14th January 1945.

has the reputation of being the father of the Swaraj movement. Mr. Patel and Pandit Nehru come next in command in the Congress hierarchy after Mr. Gandhi.

Some might think that these are the individual and private opinions of the members of the Congress High Command. But that would be an error. Several cases could be pointed out in which such opinions have been acted upon in election campaigns run by the Congress.

Ever since 1919 when Mr. Gandhi captured the Congress, Congressmen have looked upon the boycott of legislatures as one of the sanctions for making the British Government concede the demand for Swaraj. Under this policy, every time there was an election in which the Congress decided not to take part, the Congress would not only refuse to put candidates on the Congress ticket but would carry on propaganda against any Hindu proposing to stand for election as an independent candidate. One need not quarrel over the merits of such a policy. But what were the means adopted by the Congress to prevent Hindus standing on an independent ticket? The means adopted were to make the legislatures objects of contempt. Accordingly, the Congress in various Provinces started processions carrying placards with these significant and telling words: "Who will go in the legislatures? Only barbers, cobblers, potters and sweepers." In the processions one man would utter the question as part of the slogan and the whole Congress crowd would shout as answer the second part of the slogan. When the Congressmen found that this was not enough to deter persons from standing for the elections, they decided to adopt sterner measures. Believing that respectable people would not be prepared to stand for election if they felt certain that they would have to sit with barbers, potters and sweepers, etc., in the legislatures, the Congress actually went to the extent of putting up candidates from these despised communities on the Congress ticket and got them elected. A few illustrations of this outrageous conduct of the Congress may be mentioned. In the 1920 election, the Congress elected a cobbler[1] to the legislature of the Central Provinces. In the 1930 election, they elected in the Central

[1] Faguwa Rohidas.

Provinces two cobblers,[1] one milkman[2] and one barber,[3] and in the Punjab one sweeper.[4] In 1934, the Congress elected to the Central Legislature a potter.[5] It might be said that this is old history. Let me correct such an impression by referring to what happened in 1943, in the Municipal elections in Andheri—a suburb of Bombay. The Congress put up a barber to bring the Municipality in contempt.

What a mentality for a Governing class! What a brazen-facedness for a governing class to use the servile class for such an ignominious purpose and yet claim to be fighting for their freedom! What a tragedy for the servile class to take pride in its own disgrace and join in it voluntarily! The Sinn Fein Party in Ireland also boycotted the British Parliament. But did they make such hideous use of their own countrymen for effecting their purposes? The campaign of boycott of legislature which took place in 1930 is of particular interest. The elections to the Provincial legislatures in 1930 in which these instances occurred coincided with Mr. Gandhi's Salt Satyagraha campaign of 1930; I hope that the future (the official historian, Dr. Pattabhi Sitaramayya, has failed to do so) historian of Congress while recording how Mr. Gandhi decided to serve notice on the Viceroy, Lord Irwin, presenting him with a list of demands to be conceded before a certain date and on failure by the Viceroy in this behalf, how Mr. Gandhi selected Salt Act as a target for attack, how he selected Dandi as a scene of battle, how he decided to put himself at the head of the campaign, how he marched out from his Ashram in Ahmedabad with all pomp and ceremony, how the women of Ahmedabad came out with *Arthi* and applied *tilak* (saffron mark) to his forehead wishing him victory, how Mr. Gandhi assured them that Gujarat alone would win Swaraj for India, how Mr. Gandhi proclaimed his determination by saying that he would not return to Ahmedabad until he had won Swaraj, will not fail to record that while on the one hand Congressmen were engaged in fighting for Swaraj, which they said they wanted to win in the name of and for the masses, on the other

---

[1] Guru Gosain Agamdas and Babraj Jaiwar.
[2] Chunnu.
[3] Arjun Lal.
[4] Bansi Lal Caudhari.
[5] Bhagat Chandinial Gola.

hand and in the very year they were committing the worst outrages upon the very masses by exhibiting them publicly as objects of contempt to be shunned and avoided.

VI

This mentality of the Congress High Command towards the servile classes is enough to negative the theory that the supremacy of the governing classes in the Congress Provinces was an accident. There are other facts which also go to negative the theory of accident and which are set out in Table 23 (see page 226). They relate to the educational qualifications of the several classes of candidates selected by the Congress for fighting the elections. What does the table show ? It is crystal clear that in the case of the Brahmins the relative proportion of graduates to non-graduates is far higher than what it is in the case of non-Brahmins and the Scheduled Castes. Was this an accident or was this a matter of policy ? This sort of selection is marked by such a state of uniformity that it could hardly be doubted that the Congress High Command in selecting a candidate had a definite policy, namely, in the case of Brahmins, to give preference to a candidate who had the highest educational qualifications and in the case of the non-Brahmins and the Scheduled Castes, to give preference to a candidate who had the lowest educational qualifications. The difference in terms of graduates and non-graduates does not really reveal the real difference between the status and position of the Brahmin candidates and non-Brahmin candidates. The Brahmin candidates were not merely graduates but they were seasoned politicians of high repute, while the non-Brahmin graduates were raw graduates with nothing but the career of second class politicians behind them.

Why did the Congress select the best educated Brahmins as its candidates for election ? Why did the Congress select the least educated non-Brahmins and Scheduled Castes as its candidates for election ? To this question I can see only one answer. It was to prevent the non-Brahmins—the representatives of the servile classes—from forming a ministry. It cannot be that better educated non-Brahmins were not available. What the Congress seems to have done is deliberately

Table 23

Classification of Brahmin and Non-Brahmin Congress Partymen by Literacy

Provincial Assemblies	Castes	Total	Graduates	Non-Graduates	Matriculates	Illiterates	Not stated
Assam	Brahmin	6	5	1	—	—	—
	Non-Brahmin	21	15	2	—	1	9
Bengal	Brahmin	15	14	1	—	—	—
	Non-Brahmin	27	21	4	—	1	7
	Scheduled Castes ...	6	3	—	1	2	—
Bihar	Brahmin	31	11	5	8	4	3
	Non-Brahmin	39	23	4	3	8	13
	Scheduled Castes ...	—	1	1	4	10	—
Central Provinces...	Brahmin	39	15	—	2	9	2
	Non-Brahmin	54	15	—	2	17	1
	Scheduled Castes ...	—	1	—	—	6	—
Madras	Brahmin	38	16	2	3	4	13
	Non-Brahmin	90	31	3	1	7	61
	Scheduled Castes ...	26	1	1	1	14	—
	Backward Class ...	—	1	—	—	—	—
Orissa	Brahmin	11	6	1	—	3	1
	Non-Brahmin	20	7	3	2	7	1
	Scheduled Castes ...	5	—	—	—	5	—

to prefer an uneducated non-Brahmin to an educated non-Brahmin. And why? Because from the point of view of the governing class, the uneducated non-Brahmin has two definite advantages over an educated non-Brahmin. In the first place, he is likely to be more grateful to the Congress High Command for having got him elected than an educated non-Brahmin is likely to be. In the second place, the uneducated non-Brahmin is less likely to join hands with the educated non-Brahmins in the Congress Party and overturn the ministry of the governing classes and form a non-Brahmin ministry. In the third place, the greater the number of raw non-Brahmins in the Congress the lesser is the possibility of the non-Brahmins in the Congress forming a competent and alternative Ministry to the detriment of the governing class.

Given these circumstances, can there be any doubt that the Congress "Fight for Freedom" is for the freedom of nobody except that of the governing class? Is there any doubt that the Congress is the governing class and the governing class is the Congress? Is there any doubt that when Swaraj came in 1937 in the form of Provincial autonomy, the Congress deliberately and shamelessly put the governing class in places of power and authority?

VII

The facts set out above prove beyond cavil that the "Fight for Freedom" launched by the Congress has ended in perverting the aim and object of Indian freedom and that the Congress itself is a party to such a perversion. The result is an enormity, the character of which it would not be possible for the foreigner to realize unless he has an adequate idea of the social outlook and social philosophy of the Governing Classes in India.

Starting with the Brahmins who form a strong and powerful element in the governing class in India it is no exaggeration to say that they have been the most inveterate enemies of the servile classes, the Shudras (the old name for the non-Brahmins) and the Untouchables who together constitute about 80 or 90 per cent. of the total Hindu population of India. If the common man belonging to the servile classes in India is to-day so fallen, so degraded, so devoid of self-respect, hope or ambition, and so lifeless, it is entirely due to the Brahmins and their philosophy. The cardinal principles of this philosophy of the Brahmins were six—to use a correct expression, techniques of suppression—(1) graded inequality between the different classes; (2) complete disarmament of the Shudras and the Untouchables; (3) complete ban on the education of the Shudras and the Untouchables; (4) total exclusion of the Shudras and the Untouchables from places of power and authority; (5) complete prohibition against the Shudras and the Untouchables acquiring property, and (6) complete subjugation and suppression of women. Inequality is the official doctrine of Brahmanism and the suppression of the lower classes aspiring to equality has been looked upon by them and carried out by them, without remorse as their bounden duty. There are countries where education did not spread beyond a few. But India is the only country where the intellectual class, namely, the Brahmins not only made education their monopoly but declared acquisition of education by the lower classes, a crime punishable by cutting off of the tongue or by the pouring of molten lead in the ear of the offender. The result is that for centuries the Brahmins have denied the servile classes the right to education. Even to-day the Brahmins exhibit the same hostility to their education. Mr. Baines, the Census Commissioner for 1891 in discussing the causes why education was not spreading among the masses said :—

"The second influence antagonistic to a more general spread of literacy is the long continued existence of a hereditary class whose object it has been to maintain their own monopoly of all book-learning as the chief buttress of their social supremacy. Sacerdotalism knows that it can reign over none but an ignorant populace. The opposition of the Brahmin to the rise of the writer castes has been already mentioned, and the repugnance of both, in the present day, to the diffusion of learning amongst the masses can only be appreciated after long experience. It is true that the recognition by the British Government of the virtue and necessity of primary education has met with some response on the part of the literate castes, but it is chiefly in the direction of academic utterances, which cannot, in the circumstances, be well avoided. It is welcome too, in its capacity of affording the means of livelihood to many of these castes, as they have to be engaged as teachers, and are bound accordingly to work up to the State standard of efficient tuition. The real interest of the castes in question is centred on secondary education, of which they almost exclusively are in a position to reap the advantage."

The Congress politicians complain that the British are ruling India by a wholesale disarmament of the people of India. But they forget that disarmament of the Shudras and the Untouchables was the rule of law promulgated by the Brahmins. Indeed, so strongly did the Brahmins believe in the disarmament of the Shudras and the Untouchables that when they revised the law to enable the Brahmins to arm themselves for the protection of their own privileges, they maintained the ban on the Shudras and the Untouchables as it was without lessening its rigour. If the large majority of people of India appear to-day to be thoroughly emasculated, spiritless, with no manliness, it is the result of the Brahmanic policy of wholesale disarmament to which they have been subjected for the untold ages. There is no social evil and no social wrong to which the Brahmin has not given his support. Man's inhumanity to man, such as the feeling of caste, untouchability, unapproachability and unseeability is a religion to him. It would, however, be a mistake to suppose that only the wrongs of man are a religion to him. The Brahmin has given his support to some of the worst wrongs that women have suffered from in any part of the world. In India widows were burnt alive as suttees and the Brahmin gave his fullest support to the practice. Widows were not allowed to remarry. The Brahmins upheld the doctrine. Girls were required to be married before 8 and the husbands were permitted to claim the right to consummate the marriage at any time thereafter whether she had reached puberty or not. The Brahmin defended the system. The record of the Brahmins as law givers for the Shudras, for the Untouchables and for women is the blackest as compared with the record of the intellectual classes in other parts of the world. For no intellectual class has prostituted its intelligence for the sole purpose of inventing a philosophy to keep his uneducated countrymen in a perpetual state of servility, ignorance and poverty as the Brahmins have done in India. Every Brahmin to-day believes in this philosophy of Brahmanism propounded by his forefathers. He is an alien element in the Hindu Society. The Brahmin *vis-a-vis* the Shudras and the Untouchables is as foreign as the German is to the French, as the

Jew is to the Gentile or as the White is to the Negro. There is a real gulf between him and the lower classes of Shudras and Untouchables. He is not only alien to them but he is also hostile to them. In relationship with them, there is in him no room for conscience and no call for justice.

The Bania is the worst parasitic class known to history. In him the vice of money-making is unredeemed by culture or conscience. He is like an undertaker who prospers when there is an epidemic. The only difference between the undertaker and the Bania is that the undertaker does not create an epidemic while the Bania does. He does not use his money for productive purposes. He uses it to create poverty and more poverty by lending money for unproductive purposes. He lives on interest and as he is told by his religion that money-lending is the occupation prescribed to him by the divine Manu, he looks upon money-lending as both right and righteous. With the help and assistance of the Brahmin judge who is ready to decree his suits, the Bania is able to carry on his trade with the greatest ease. Interest, interest on interest, he adds on and on, and thereby draws millions of families perpetually into his net. Pay him as much as he may, the debtor is always in debt. With no conscience to check him there is no fraud, and there is no chicanery which he will not commit. His grip over the nation is complete. The whole of poor, starving, illiterate India is irredeemably mortgaged to the Bania.

In every country there is a governing class. No country is free from it. But is there anywhere in the world a governing class with such selfish, diseased and dangerous and perverse mentality, with such a hideous and infamous philosophy of life which advocates the trampling down of the servile classes to sustain the power and glory of the governing class ? I know of none. It is true that the governing classes in other countries do not readily admit into their society those who do not belong to their class. But they do not refuse admission to those who have risen to their level. Nor do they prevent any person from rising to their level. In India the governing class is a close corporation unwilling to admit anyone who does not belong to it by birth and ready to use every means to prevent the servile classes from rising to their level.

VIII

There was a governing class in France before the French Revolution. There was a governing class in Japan before the seventies of the nineteenth century when Japan decided to modernize its constitution. In both countries the governing classes realizing that it was an hour of national crisis decided to shed their ancient rights and privileges in order to make the transition from oligarchy to democracy smooth and easy.

In France, when the Revolution broke out and demanded equality the governing class in France voluntarily came forward to give up its powers and its privileges and to merge itself in the mass of the nation. This is clear from what happened when the States-General was called. The Commons got 600 representatives, while the clergy and the Nobles got 300 each. The question arose how were the 1,200 members to sit, debate and vote. The Commons insisted upon the union of all the estates in one Chamber and 'vote by head.' It was impossible to expect the clergy and the Nobles to accept this position. For it meant the surrender of their most ancient and valuable privileges. Yet a good part of them agreed to the demand of the Commons and gave France a constitution based upon liberty, equality and fraternity.

The attitude of the governing classes in Japan during the period between 1855 to 1870—a period in which the Japanese people were transformed from a feudal society into a modern nation—was even more self-sacrificing than the attitude of the governing classes in France. As students of Japanese history know, there were four classes in Japanese Society: (1) The *Damiyos*, (2) The *Samurai*, (3) The *Hemin* or the Common folk and (4) The *Eta* or the outcasts, standing one above the other in an order of graded inequality. At the bottom were the *Eta* numbering a good many thousands. Above the *Eta* were the *Hemin* numbering about 25/30 millions. Over them were the *Samurai* who numbered about 2 millions and who had the power of life and death over the *Hemin*. At the apex were the *Damiyos* or the Feudal Barons who exercised sway over the rest of the three classes and who numbered only 300. The *Damiyos* and the *Samurai* realized that it was impossible to transform this feudal society with its class composition and class rights into a modern nation with equality of citizenship. Accordingly the *Damiyos* charged with the spirit of nationalism and anxious not to stand in the way of national unity, came forward to surrender their privileges and to merge themselves in the common mass of people. In a memorial submitted to the Emperor on the 5th March 1869 they said[1] :—

> "The Place where we live is the Emperor's land. The food that we eat is grown by the Emperor's men. How then can we claim any property as our own? We now reverently offer up our possessions and also our followers (Samurai as well as 'common folk') with the prayer that the Emperor will take good measures for rewarding those to whom reward is due, and for fining such as do not deserve reward. Let imperial orders be issued for altering and remodelling the territories of the various clans. Let the civil and penal codes, the military laws down to the rules for uniform and for the construction of engines of war, all proceed from the Emperor. Let all affairs of the Empire, both great and small, be referred to him."

How does the governing class in India compare in this behalf with the governing class in Japan? Just the opposite. Unfortunately, the history of the struggle of the servile classes in India against the governing class has not yet been written. But those who know anything about it will know that the governing class in India has no intention of making any sacrifice not even on the altar of Indian Freedom for which it is thirsting. Instead, the governing class is using every means to retain them. For this it is using two weapons. First is the weapon of nationalism. Whenever the servile classes ask for reservations in the legislatures, in the Executive and in Public Services, the governing class raises the cry of 'nationalism in danger.' What are these reservations for? To put it briefly they are intended to provide floorings below which the governing class will not be able to push down the servile classes in their struggle for existence. There is nothing sinister and nothing wrong in this demand for reservations. How does the governing class react to them? It loses no occasion to deprecate them and to ridicule them. People are led to believe that if they are to achieve national freedom, they must maintain unity, that all questions regarding reservations in the Legislatures, Executives and the Public Services are inimical to national unity and that, therefore, for anyone interested in national freedom it is a sin to support those who ask for such

[1] Quoted in *Romance of Japan* by James A. B. Scherer.

reservations. That is the attitude of the governing class in India. It stands in glaring contrast with that of the governing class in Japan. It is a misuse of nationalism. But the governing class does not feel any compunction for such misuse.

The second means employed by the governing class is the writing of the lampoons and parodies calculated to pour ridicule on the demand for reservations. Such lampoons are by no means few and far between. Even the most respectable members of the governing class do not mind indulging in such compositions. Even Dr. R. P. Paranjpe, now India's High Commissioner for Australia, who stands for an advanced type of liberalism, could not withstand the temptation of trying his hand in writing such a parody.[1] Among the parodies composed by members of the governing class his was the most colourful and had, when it appeared, excited the greatest resentment among the servile classes.

The argument used by the governing classes to oppose the demand of the servile classes for reservations is based on the doctrine of efficiency. To give a patriotic look to the stand taken by the governing classes it is represented that what

---

[1] The parody written by Dr. R. P. Paranjpe appeared in a magazine called *Gujarathi Punch* for May 1926 under the heading "A Peep into the Future." As a specimen of this class of writing by members of the governing class it is worth perusal. It is a satire based on certain incidents which are imagined to have occurred under the principle of communal reservations. As the magazine is not easily available, I reproduce it below with a view to rescue it from oblivion :—

'A PEEP INTO THE FUTURE'

The following extracts are taken from reports of Commissions, records of police courts cases, judicial trials, Council Proceedings, Administration Reports, etc., issued between the year 1930-50 and are published for the exclusive benefit of the readers of the *Gujarati Punch*.

I

Report of the Royal Commission on the Government of India, 1930 :

We have given our closest consideration to the representations made on behalf of several communities in India. Taking the figures of the last Census as our basis we can only give an approximate satisfaction to all the claims made before us, for it is not possible to give an absolutely accurate solution to the problem of constructing a machinery of Government unless every single person in the country is made a member thereof, as the numbers of the several communities do not possess a common measure. We lay down the number 2375 as the fundamental number in the constitution and this number is divided into parts attached to the several communities as shown in the schedule attached to our report. The claims of each community will henceforward be represented by its proper number, and all appointments, memberships of various bodies, and in fact everything in the country will be awarded according to the proportion given in the schedule wherever possible. The Viceroy's Executive Council will consist of 475 members selected as far as may be according to one-fifth the numbers belonging to each community and three members will hold

Indians must aim at is to maintain in India an efficient body politic and that this can be done only by insisting that every place of power and authority should be filled by none but the best man available. It is this argument which seems to impress the foreigner and which makes him a critic if not an adversary of the demand for reservation. It is therefore

---

office for one year so that each community will have attained its exact share of membership in five years. There will be 125 Judges in each High Court, each judge holding office for one year, though according to this arrangement, each section will have obtained its exact share only after the lapse of 19 years. The number of other kinds of appointments will be determined on the same basis for the accurate adjustment of all claims.

To allow for the proper functioning of all bodies with these numbers as many existing Government buildings as may be necessary may be pulled down and rebuilt so as to be of the proper size.

II

(*Notification of the Government of India*, 1932)

In accordance with the provisions of the Government of India Act, 1931, His Majesty the King Emperor has been pleased to appoint the following 475 gentlemen as members of the Executive Council of the Governor-General :

267. Matadin Ramdin (caste Barber) member in charge of the Surgical Branch of the Medical Department.

372. Allabux Peerbux (Mahomedan Camel driver) in charge of the camel transport division of the Army Department.

433. Ramaswamy (caste, Andhra Sweeper) in charge of the road cleaning branch of the P.W.D.

437. Jagannath Bhattacharya (Kulin Brahmin Priest) in charge of the domestic section of the Registration Department.

IV

(*Letter to all Local Governments*, 1934)

In response to a resolution passed by the Legislative Assembly, with which the Government of India are in full agreement, I am directed to say that henceforward every appointment under Government should go by rotation to each community irrespective of the merits of the applicants.

V

(*Notification in the Bombay Government Gazette*, 1934)

The Government of Bombay will proceed to make the following appointments in December. The applicants for the several appointments should belong to the castes mentioned against each according to the rotation fixed by Government Order No. , dated November 30th, 1934.

1. Chief Engineer for Irrigation (Sind) : Kunbi from North Kanara.
2. Professor of Sanskrit, Elphinstone College, Bombay : Baluchi Pathan from Sind.
3. Commandant of His Excellency's Bodyguard : Marwari from North Gujarat.
4. Consulting Architect to Government : Wadari (wandering gypsy) from the Deccan.
5. Director of Islamic Culture : Karhada Brahmin.
6. Professor of Anatomy : (Grant Medical College) Mahomedan Butcher.
7. Superintendent of Yeravda Jail : Ghantichor.
8. Two organizers of prohibition : Dharala (Kaira District Bhil) (Panch Mahals).

necessary to examine the validity of the argument and the sincerity of those who use it.

Nobody will have any quarrel with the abstract principle that nothing should be done whereby the best shall be superseded by one who is only better and the better by one who is merely good and the good by one who is bad. But the argument completely fails to carry conviction when in practice one finds that having regard to the historical circumstances of India every time the 'best man' is chosen he turns out to be a man from the governing class. This may be alright from the point of view of the governing class. But can it be right from the point of view of the servile class? Could the 'best' German be the 'best' for the French? Could the 'best' Turk be 'best' for the Greeks? Could the 'best' Pole be regarded

---

VI

(Report of a Case from the High Court, 1935)

A.B. (caste Teli) was charged with the cold-blooded murder of his father while he was asleep. The judge summing up against the accused, the jury brought in a verdict of guilty. Before passing sentence the judge asked the pleader for the accused if he had to say anything. The pleader, Mr. Bomanji, said he agreed with the verdict but that according to Law the accused could not be sentenced at all, much less sentenced to death, as during the current year seven Telis had already been convicted and sentenced two of them with death, that several other communities had not yet reached their quota of convictions as given in the Government of India Act, while the Telis had already reached theirs. His Lordship accepted the contention of the defence pleader and acquitted the accused.

VII

(Extract from the 'Indian Daily Mail,' 1936)

Annaji Ramchandra (Chitpavan Brahmin) was found wandering in the streets of Poona with a long knife attacking whomsoever he met. When brought up before the Magistrate he was shown by the police to have been recently let off from the Mental Hospital. The Superintendent of the Hospital in his evidence said that Annaji had been in the hospital as a dangerous insane for three years, but as there was the quota for the Chitpavanas and as the inmates belonging to other communities had not finished their year-quotas he could not keep him any longer and show any special favouritism to the Chitpavans and he had therefore let him off according to Government Order No. ... in the Medical Department. The Magistrate ordered Annaji to be discharged.

VIII

(Extract from the Report of the Administration of Jails in the Bombay Presidency, 1937)

In spite of every precaution the numbers in the jails did not correspond to the quotas fixed for each community. The Superintendent had already asked for instructions from Government with a view to remedying the discrepancy.

Resolution of Government: Government view with serious displeasure this grave dereliction of duty on the part of the I. G. of prisons. Immediate steps should be taken to arrest and put in jail as many members of the various com-

'best' for the Jews? There can hardly be any doubt as to the correct answer to these questions.

In answering this question two things cannot be overlooked. One is that a great man is not necessarily a good man. The other is that man is not a mere machine without any feelings. This is even true of the 'best' man. He too is charged with the feelings of class sympathies and class antipathies. Having regard to these considerations the 'best' man from the governing class may well turn out to be the worst from the point of view of the servile classes.

Mere efficiency can never be accepted as a test. If it was accepted as the only test the result would be that the affairs of the French might well be run by the Germans, of Turks by the Russians and of Chinese by the Japanese. Those who hold out the theory of naked efficiency and nothing but efficiency as the test of good Government should ask the French, the Turks and the Chinese as to what they have to say about it and how they like the result which follows from its application.

---

munities as are required to bring their quotas up to the proper level. If enough persons required cannot be caught, a sufficient number of inmates should be let off to bring down all to the same level.

IX

(*Proceedings of the Legislative Council*, 1940)

Mr. Chennappa asked: Has the attention of Government been called to the fact that class list of the recent M.A. Examination in Pali do not show the proper quota for mang-garudis?

The Hon. Mr. Damu Shroff (Minister of Education): The University Registrar reports that no candidate from among Mang-garudis offered himself for examination.

Mr. Chennappa: Will Government be pleased to stop this examination until such a candidate offers himself and if the University disobeys the order of Government to take away the University grant and amend the University Act?

The Hon. Member: Government will be pleased to consider the suggestion favourably. (Cheers).

X

(*Extract from 'The Times of India*,' 1942)

The Coroner Mr. . . . was suddenly called last evening to inquire into the death of Ramji Sonu at the J. J. Hospital as the result of a surgical operation. Dr. Tanu Pandav (caste Barber) deposed that he had conducted the operation. He wished to open an abscess in the abdomen but his knife pierced the heart and the patient expired. Asked whether he had ever carried out any operation of this nature before, he said that he was appointed as the principal surgeon to the hospital only one day before as it was then the turn of his community and that he had never held a surgical instrument in his hand before except a razor for shaving. The jury returned a verdict of death by misadventure.

Even a simpleton can imagine what answer they are likely to return. I am sure that a theory which produces such a result will be regarded as an absurd one on all hands without exceptions. How then can such a theory be applied to India where the difference between the governing class and the servile class is the same both in degree and in kind as the difference between French and Germans, Turks and Russians or Chinese and Japanese? The fact is that the governing class in India blinded by self-interest is unmindful of the absurdity of the argument of naked efficiency and being conscious that it has the power to convert its opinion into law does not bother what the servile classes have to say on the point.

The governing class does not bother to inquire into the ways and means by which it has acquired its supremacy. It does not feel the necessity of doing so, partly because it believes that it acquired its supremacy by dint of merit and partly because it believes that no matter how it acquired its power it is enough that it is in a position to dictate its policy on the servile classes. Assuming that the governing class did not find it necessary to examine the ways and means by which it obtained its supremacy what would it find? Strange as it may seem the governing class has obtained its power by the same system of reservations which it is now opposing on the ground of communalism. Many may find it difficult to accept the truth of this statement. Those who have any doubt need do no more than read the Manu Smriti, the Bible of the Hindus. What will they find in it? They will find and will no doubt be shocked to know that the Brahmins, the chief and the leading element in the governing class, acquired their political power not by force of intellect—for intellect is nobody's monopoly—but by sheer communalism. According to the Laws of Manu Smriti the post of the Purohit, King's Chaplain and Lord Chancellor, the posts of the Chief Justice and Judges of the High Court and the post of Ministers to the Crown were all reserved for the Brahmins. Even for the post of the Commander-in-Chief the Brahmin was recommended as a fit and a proper person though it was not in terms reserved for him. All the strategic posts having been reserved for the Brahmins it goes without saying that all ministerial posts came to be reserved for the Brahmins. This is not all. The Brahmin was not content with reserving places of profit and power for his class. He knew that mere reservation will not do. He must prevent rivals shooting up from other non-Brahmin communities equally qualified to hold the posts and agitate and blow up the system of reservations. In addition to reserving all executive posts in the State for Brahmins a law was made whereby education was made the monopoly and privilege of Brahmins. As has already been pointed out the law made it a crime for the Shudra, i.e., the lower orders of Hindu Society to acquire learning, the infringement of which was followed by not only heavy but cruel and inhuman punishment such as cutting the tongue of the criminal and filling his ear with hot molten lead. It is true that these reservations do not exist under the British rule. But it must be admitted that though the reservations made by Manu have gone, the advantages derived from their continuance over several centuries have remained. In asking for reservations the servile classes are not asking for anything new or anything extraordinary. The demand for reservation is a demand for protection against the aggressive communalism of the governing class, which wants to dominate the servile class in all fields of life and without imposing on the governing class any such ignominious conditions as was done by the Brahmins for their own aggrandisement and for the perpetuation of their own domination on the Shudra, namely, to make it a crime for the governing class to learn or to acquire property.

This argument of naked efficiency has also to be considered from the point of view of public welfare. It was said by Campbell Bannerman in the course of a debate in the House of Commons on Ireland, that self-government is better than good government. The statement had become so popular in India that it had become more than a mere slogan. It had become a maxim. As it stands the statement is quite absurd. Campbell Bannerman was not contrasting self-government with good government. He was contrasting self-government with efficient government or rather with "resolute government" to use the phrase of his opponent Lord Salisbury. There is no denying that self-government must be good government, otherwise it is not worth having. The question is, how is good government to be had. Some people seem to be under the impression that as self-government is a sovereign government it is bound to result in good government. This is one of the greatest delusions from which most people in dependent countries are suffering. Those who are living in such a delusion had better read what Prof. Dicey has to say on this point. Discussing the question what persons and bodies with full sovereign powers can do Dicey has the following observations to make :—

> " The actual exercise of authority by any sovereign whatever and notably by Parliament, is bounded or controlled by two limitations. Of these the one is an external, the other is an internal limitation.
>
> " The external limit to the real power of a sovereign consists in the possibility or certainty that his subjects or a large number of them, will disobey or resist his laws.
>
> " This limitation exists even under the most despotic monarchies. A Roman Emperor, or a French King during the middle of the eighteenth century, was (as is the Russian Czar at the present day) in strictness a ' sovereign ' in the legal sense of that term. He had absolute legislative authority. Any law made by him was binding, and there was no power in the empire or kingdom which could annul such law . . . But it would be an error to suppose that the most absolute ruler who ever existed could in reality make or change every law at his pleasure . . .
>
> " The authority, that is to say, even of a despot, depends upon the readiness of his subjects or of some portion of his subjects to obey his behests ; and this readiness to obey must always be in reality limited. This is shown by the most notorious facts of history. None of the early Cæsars could at their pleasure have subverted the worship of fundamental institutions of the Roman world . . . The Sultan could not abolish Mahomedanism. Louis the Fourteenth at the height of his power could revoke the Edict of Nantes, but he would have found it impossible to establish the supremacy of Protestantism, and for the same reason which prevented James the Second from establishing the supremacy of Roman Catholicism . . . What is true of the power of a despot or of the authority of a constituent assembly is specially true of the sovereignty of Parliament ; it is limited on every side by the possibility of popular resistance. Parliament might legally tax the Colonies ; Parliament might without any breach of law change the succession to the throne or abolish the monarchy ; but everyone knows that in the present state of the world the British Parliament will do none of these things. In each case widespread resistance would result from legislation which,

though legally valid, is in fact beyond the stretch of Parliamentary power.

* * *

"There is an internal limit to the exercise of sovereign power itself. Even a despot exercises his powers in accordance with his character, which is itself moulded by the circumstances under which he lives, including under that head the moral feelings of the time and the society to which he belongs. The Sultan could not if he would, change the religion of the Mahommedan world, but if he could do so it is in the very highest degree improbable that the head of Mahommedanism should wish to overthrow the religion of Mahomet; the internal check on the exercise of the Sultan's power is at least as strong as the external limitation. People sometimes ask the idle question why the Pope does not introduce this or that reform? The true answer is that a revolutionist is not the kind of man who becomes a Pope, and that the man who becomes a Pope has no wish to be a revolutionist . . ."

I have already pointed out that it is not enough for the servile classes to be content with the mere fact that their country has become an independent and a sovereign state. It is necessary for them to go further and to find out who are likely to be the instruments of the State, in other words who is going to be the governing class. Dicey's observations and the profound truth which underlies them no one can question—add a further point namely that for good government, ability and efficiency of the governing class are not enough. What is necessary is to have in the governing class the will to do good or to use Dicey's language, freedom from internal limitations arising out of selfish class interests. Efficiency combined with selfish class interests instead of producing good government is far more likely to become a mere engine of suppression of the servile classes.

In selecting the instrumentalities of the State considerations of class bias in the instrumentalities cannot be overlooked. It is in fact fundamental to good government. It is unfortunate that the importance of this fact is not generally recognized even by those who regard themselves as the champions of democracy. Karl Marx was the first to recognize it and take account of it in the administration of the Paris Commune. It is unnecessary to say that it is to-day the basis of Government in Soviet Russia. The demand for reservations put forth by the servile classes in India is essentially based upon the same considerations pointed out by Dicey, advocated by Marx and adopted by Russia. Only those who belong to the servile class can be trusted to protect the interest of that class. This consideration is so important that the principle of efficiency cannot be allowed to altogether override it. If the governing class in India stands on the principle of efficiency and efficiency alone it is because it is actuated by the selfish motive of monopolizing the instrumentalities of Government.

IX

The foregoing discussion has extended over such length that the foreigner is likely to miss the points which it is intended to bring out. It may therefore be well to assemble them together with a view to underline them.

The main problems, which those desirous of establishing democracy in India must face, are:—(1) the position of the governing class of India, (2) the aims and objects of the governing class towards the servile classes, (3) the *raison d'etre* of the demands of the servile classes for constitutional safeguards and (4) the relation of the governing class to the Congress.

Regarding the first point the argument is that the position of the governing class in India is quite different from the position of the governing classes in other countries of the world. It is not easy to understand this difference, nor is it easy to state it in expressive terms. Perhaps the illustration of a bar and a hyphen may help to give a clear idea of what the difference is. Nobody can mistake the difference between a hyphen and a bar. A bar divides but does not link. A hyphen does both. It divides but it also links. In India the governing classes and the servile classes are divided by a bar. In other countries there exists between them only a hyphen. The resultant difference is a very crucial one. In other countries, there is a continuous replenishment of the governing class by the incorporation of others who do not belong to it but who have reached the same elevation as the governing class. In India, the governing class is a close corporation in which nobody, not born in it, is admitted. In other countries where the governing class is not a close preserve, where there is social endosmosis between it and the rest, there is a mental assimilation and accommodation which makes the governing class less antagonistic in its composition and less antagonistic to the servile classes in its social philosophy. In other words, the governing class in countries outside India is not anti-social. It is only non-social. In India where the governing class is a close corporation, tradition, social philosophy and social outlook which are antagonistic to the servile classes remain unbroken in their depth and their tenor and the distinction between masters and slaves, between the privileged and the unprivileged continues for ever hard in substance and fast in colour. In other words the governing class in India is not merely non-social. It is positively anti-social.

As to the demand for reservations by the servile classes the reason behind it is to put a limit on the power of the governing classes to have control over the instrumentalities of government. The governing classes are bent on giving the reservations a bad name in order to be able to hang those who are insisting upon them. The real fact is that the reservations are only another name for what the Americans call checks and balances which every constitution must have, if democracy is not to be overwhelmed by the enemies of democracy. That the reservations demanded by the servile classes are different in form from the American sort of checks and balances does not alter their character. The forms of checks and balances must be determined by two considerations. The first is the necessity of establishing a correlation between the political constitution and social institutions of the country if democracy is to be real. As the social institutions of countries differ in their form the checks and balances in its political constitutions must also differ. For instance, where a country is ridden by the caste system the checks and balances will have to be of a different sort from what they need be in a country pervaded by a spirit of social democracy. The second is the necessity of providing a firm flooring to the servile classes against the possibility of their being pressed down by the governing classes by reason of their superior power. In some countries adult suffrage may be quite enough for the servile classes to hold their own against the governing classes. In India unlike other countries the governing class is so omnipotent and omnipresent that other remedies besides adult suffrage will be necessary to give adequate power to the servile classes to protect themselves against exploitation by the governing classes. Looked at in the light of these observations, the reservations demanded by the servile classes, though different in form from the checks and balances embodied in the American Constitution, are fundamentally checks and balances, and must be considered as such by the foreigner before he forms an adverse opinion against them.

The facts bearing on the last point namely the relation of the Congress to the governing classes have also been fully set out. From these facts the foreigner should be able to see how intimate is the connection between the two. The same facts will explain why the governing class in India has placed itself in the vanguard of the Congress movement and why it strives to bring everybody within the Congress fold. To put it briefly the governing class is aware that a political campaign based on class ideology and class conflicts will toll its death knell. It knows that the most effective way of side-tracking the servile classes and fooling them is to play upon the sentiment of nationalism and national unity. It clings to the Congress because it realizes that the Congress platform is the only platform that can most effectively safeguard the interest of the governing class. For if there is any platform from which all talk of conflict between rich and poor, Brahmin and non-Brahmin, landlord and tenant, creditor and debtor, which does not suit the governing class, can be effectually banned, it is the Congress platform which is not only bound to preach nationalism and national unity,—this is what the governing class wants, as it is on this that its safety entirely depends—but which prohibits any other ideology inconsistent with nationalism being preached from its platform.

If the foreigner bears in mind these points he will realize why the servile classes of India are not attracted by the Congress brand of Swaraj. What good can the Congress brand of Swaraj bring to them? They know that under the Congress brand of Swaraj the prospect for them is really very bleak. The Congress brand of Swaraj will either be materialization of what is called Gandhism or it will be what the governing class would want to make of it. If it is the former it will mean the spread of charkha, village industries, the observance of caste, Bramhcharya (continence), reverence for the cow and things of that sort. If it is left to governing classes to make what it likes of Swaraj the principal item in it will be the suppression of the servile classes by withdrawing the facilities given by the

British Government in the matter of education and entry in public services.

Some people hope that under Swaraj there will be a reform of tenancy laws, factory legislation, compulsory primary education, prohibition and construction of roads and canals, improvement of currency, regulation of weights and measures, dispensaries and introduction of other measures for the servile classes. I am not quite sure that these hopes are well-founded. Most people forget that what leads the Congress to-day to mouth such a programme is the desire to show that the Congress is better than the British bureaucracy. But once the bureaucracy is liquidated, will there be the same incentive to better the lot of the masses ? That is the question. Firstly, I entertain very grave doubts as to how far this will materialize. Secondly, there is nothing very great in it. In the world of to-day, no governing class can omit to undertake reforms, which are necessary to maintain society in a civilized state. Apart from this, is social amelioration the be-all and end-all of Swaraj ?. Knowing the servile classes as I do that is certainly not the fault of the servile classes. They certainly do not intend to follow the teaching that 'the meek shall eat and be satisfied.' The want and poverty which has been their lot for centuries is nothing to them as compared to the insult and indignity which they have to bear as a result of the vicious social order. Not bread but honour, is what they want. That can happen only when the governing classes disappear and cease to have control over their destiny. The question for the servile classes is not whether this reform or that reform will be undertaken. The question is : Will the governing classes in India having captured the machinery of the State, undertake a programme for the reform of the social order whereby the governing class will be liquidated, as distinguished from a programme of social amelioration ? The answer to this depends upon whether the future constitution of India will be with safeguards or without safeguards for the protection of the servile classes. If it will have safeguards it will be possible for the servile classes to liquidate the governing classes in course of time. If the constitution is without safeguards the governing class will continue to maintain its dominance over the servile classes. This being the issue, the foreigner should note that the much-advertised representative character of the Congress is absolutely irrelevant. The Congress may be a representative body and the Congress may be the body which is engaged in what is called the Fight for Freedom ; but these things have nothing to do with the decision of the issue. A true lover of democracy before he befriends the Congress will demand that it should produce its blue print of the constitution and be satisfied that its constitution does contain unequivocal and positive provisions for the safety, security for the life, liberty and the pursuit of happiness for the servile classes.

X

The foreigners who take interest in Indian politics fall into two classes. The first class includes those who are travellers and tourists who come ' to do ' India for a short while and who are not equipped with a knowledge of the intricacies of the Indian Political problems, the theoretical apparatus to pronounce a correct opinion on the attitude of the different parties to these problems. Those who fall into the second class are the leaders of democratic public opinion such as Louis Fischer in America, Kingsley Martin, Brailsford and Laski whose knowledge and equipment none can question. I would have had no regrets if the foregoing discussion had been called for by the needs of correcting the unthinking bias of the tourists and traveller class of foreigners in favour of the Congress. But unfortunately the same sort of bias is also to be found in those foreigners who fall into the second class.

That there should be foreigners of the tourist sort who cannot understand the intricacies of Indian politics and who therefore support the Congress on no other ground except that which Mr. Pickwick gave to Sam Weller—to shout with the biggest crowd—is quite understandable. But what annoys most is the attitude of the leaders of the British Labour Party, heads of radical and leftist groups in Europe and America, represented by men like Laski, Kingsley Martin, Brailsford and editors of journals like the *Nation* in America, and the *New Statesman* in England championing the cause of the oppressed and the suppressed people in other parts of the world. How can these men support the Congress it is difficult to understand. Do they not know that the Congress means the governing class and that the governing class in India is a Brahmin-Bania combine ? That masses are drawn in the Congress only to be camp followers with no say in the making of Congress policy ?

Do they not realize that for the reasons for which the Sultan could not abolish Islam or the Pope could not repudiate Catholicism, the governing class in India will not decree the destruction of Brahmanism and that so long as the governing class remains what it is, Brahmanism, which preaches the supremacy of Brahmins and the allied castes and which recognises the suppression and degradation of the Shudras and the Untouchables as the sacred duty of the State, will continue to be the philosophy of the State even if India became free? Do they not know that this governing class in India is not a part of the Indian people, is not only completely isolated from them, but believes in isolating itself, lest it should be contaminated by them, has implanted in its mind by reason of the Brahmanic philosophy, motives and interests which are hostile to those who are outside its fold and therefore does not sympathise with the living forces operating in the servile masses whom it has trodden down, is not charged with their wants, their pains, their cravings, their desires, is inimical to their aspirations, does not favour any advance in their education, promotion to high office and disfavours every movement calculated to raise their dignity and their self-respect? Do they not know that in the Swaraj of India is involved the fate of 60 millions of Untouchables?

It would be impossible to say that the leaders of the British Labour Party, that Kingsley Martin, Brailsford and Laski whose writings on liberty and democracy are a source of inspiration to all suppressed people, do not know these facts. Yet if they refer to India, it is always to support the Congress. It is very, very seldom that they are found to discuss the problem of the Untouchables which ought to make the strongest appeal to all radicals and democrats. Their exclusive attention to Congress activities and their utter neglect of other elements in the national life of India show how misguided they have been. One could well understand their support to the Congress if the Congress was fighting for political democracy. But is it? As every one knows, the Congress is only fighting for national liberty and is not interested in political democracy. The party in India who is fighting for political democracy is the party of the Untouchables who fear that this Congress fight for liberty, if it succeeds, will mean liberty to the strong and the powerful to suppress the weak and the down-trodden unless they are protected by constitutional safeguards. It is they who ought to receive the help of these radical leaders. But the Untouchables have been waiting in vain for all these years even for a gesture of goodwill and support from them. These radicals and leftists in Europe and America have not even cared to know the forces behind the Congress.

Ignorant or unmindful one does not know, but the fact remains that these leftists and radical leaders have been giving blind and unquestioning support to the Congress which admittedly is run by capitalists, landlords, money-lenders and reactionaries, only because the Congress calls its activities by the grandiloquent name of "Fight for Freedom." All battles for freedom are not on equal moral plane for the simple reason that the motives and purposes behind these battles of freedom are not always the same. To take only a few illustrations from English History. The Barons' Rebellion against John which resulted in the *Magna Charta* could be called a battle for freedom. But could any democrat in modern times give it the same support which he would give—say to the Levellers' Rebellion or to the Peasants' Revolt in English History, merely because it could logically be described as a battle for freedom? To do so will be to respond to a false cry of freedom. Such crude conduct would have been forgivable, had it proceeded from groups not intelligent enough to make a distinction between freedom to live and freedom to oppress. But it is quite inexcusable in radical and leftist groups led by Messrs. Laski, Kingsley Martin, Brailsford, Louis Fischer and other well-known champions of democracy.

When pressed to explain why they don't support Indian Parties which stand for true democracy, they are reported to meet the charge by a counter question. Are there any such parties in India? Insist that there are such parties and they turn round and say: If such parties exist, how is it the Press does not report their activities? When told that the Press is a Congress Press, they retort: How is it that the foreign correspondents of the English Papers do not report them? I have shown why nothing better can be expected from these foreign correspondents. The Foreign Press Agency in India is not better than the Indian Press. Indeed it cannot be better. There are in India what are called foreign correspondents. In a large majority of cases they are Indians. Only a very few are foreigners. The selection of Indians as foreign correspondents is so made that they are almost always from the Congress camp. The foreign correspondents who are foreigners fall into two groups. If they are Americans they are just Anti-British and for that reason pro-Congress. Any political party in India which is not madly anti-British does not interest them. Those who are not in the Congress will testify how hard it was for them to persuade the American War Correspondents who trooped into this country in 1941-42, even to entertain the possibility of the Congress not being the only party, much less to induce them to interest themselves in other political parties. It took a long time before they recovered their sanity and when they did, they either abused the Congress as an organization led by impossible men or just lost interest in Indian politics. They never got interested in other political parties in India and never cared to understand their point of view. The situation is no better in the case of foreign correspondents who are Britishers. They too are interested only in that kind of politics which is first and foremost anti-British. They are uninterested in those political parties in India whose foremost concern is to make a are India safe for democracy. The result is that the foreign press provides the same kind of news about Indian politics as does the Indian Press.

These reasons cannot be beyond the ken of these radicals. Correspondents or no correspondents, is it not the duty of radicals to keep in touch with their kindred in other parts of the world to encourage them, to help them and to see that true democracy lives everywhere? It is a most unfortunate thing that the Radicals of England and America should have forgotten the class to whom they owe a duty to help and have become the publicity agents of Indian Tories who are just misusing the slogan of liberty to befool and befog the world.

The sooner they get out of this fog created by the Congress and realize that democracy and self-government in India cannot be real unless freedom has become the assured possession of all, the better for them and the better for the people of India. But if they persist in giving their blind support to the Congress on the basis of an empty slogan without examining its relation to facts and intentions, I for one will have no hesitation in saying that far from being the friends of India they are a positive menace to the freedom of the Indian masses. It is a pity that they do not seem to distinguish the case of a tyrant who is held down and who pleads for liberty because he wants to regain his right to oppress and the case of an oppressed class seeking to be free from the oppression of the tyrant. In their hurry to bring freedom to India they have no time to realize that by siding with the Congress what they are doing is not to make India safe for democracy but to free the tyrant to practise his tyrannies. Is it necessary to tell them that to support Congress is to let tyranny have freedom to enslave? It is to save their own reputation as the champions of the oppressed and suppressed classes that they should reconsider their attitude towards the Congress.

CHAPTER X

WHAT DO THE UNTOUCHABLES SAY?

Beware of Mr. Gandhi

I

CONGRESSMEN never hesitate to impress upon the Untouchables that Mr. Gandhi is their saviour. Not only do Congressmen all over India hold out Mr. Gandhi as a real saviour but they go forth to persuade the Untouchables to accept the fact that he is their only saviour. When pressed for evidence, they tell the Untouchables that if any one ever took a vow to go on a fast unto death for the sake of the Untouchables it was Mr. Gandhi and none else. Indeed, without any compunction they tell the Untouchables that whatever political rights the Untouchables have got under the Poona Pact, they are the result of Mr. Gandhi's efforts. As an illustration of such propaganda, I refer to what one Rai Bahadur Mehrchand Khanna is reported[1] to have said at a meeting of the Untouchables held at Peshawar on April 12, 1945, under the auspices of the Depressed Classes League:

> "Your best friend is Mahatma Gandhi who even resorted to a fast for your sake and brought about the Poona Pact under which you have been enfranchised and given representation on local bodies and legislatures. Some of you, I know, have been running after Dr. Ambedkar, who is just a creation of the British Imperialists and who uses you to strengthen the hands of the British Government in order that India may be divided and the Britishers continue to retain power. I appeal to you in your interests, to distinguish between self-styled leaders and your real friends."

If I refer to the statement of Rai Bahadur Mehrchand Khanna, it is not because he is worth taking notice of. For, there cannot be any one guilty of bigger blackguardism in Indian politics than this man. In the course of one year—not in very remote time but in 1944—he successfully played three different roles. He started as Secretary of the Hindu

---

1. *Free Press Journal*, dated 14-4-45.

Mahasabha, turned agent of British Imperialism, went abroad to explain India's war effort to the British and American people and is now agent of the Congress in N.W.F. Province. The opinion of a man like Rai Bahadur Khanna, who, to use Dryden's language, is so various as to be everything by starts, and nothing long, and who in the course of one revolving moon, can be a chemist, fiddler, statesman and buffoon, must be beneath contempt. If I refer to him it is only because I wish to illustrate what sort of propaganda[1] friends of Mr. Gandhi are carrying on in order to beguile the Untouchables.

I do not know how many Untouchables will be found prepared to swallow such a lie. But this much I think has been proved by the Nazis that if a lie is a big lie—too big for the common man's intelligence to scrutinize—and if it is repeated continuously, the lie has all the chances of being accepted as truth, and if not accepted as truth has all the chances of growing upon the victims of propaganda and win their acquiescence. It is, therefore, necessary for me to expose the part played by Mr. Gandhi in the movement of the Untouchables and to warn the Untouchables against succumbing to this propaganda.

II

In making a survey of the part played by Mr. Gandhi, it is well to begin by ascertaining when Mr. Gandhi for the first time realized that Untouchability was an evil. On this point, we have the direct testimony of Mr. Gandhi himself. In an address delivered as President of the Suppressed Classes Conference, held at Ahmedabad on the 14th and 15th April 1921, Mr. Gandhi said :—

> "I was hardly yet twelve when this idea had dawned on me. A scavenger named Ukha, an Untouchable, used to attend our house for cleaning latrines. Often I would ask my mother why it was wrong to touch him, why I was forbidden to touch him. If I accidentally touched Ukha, I was asked to perform ablutions, and though I naturally obeyed, it was not without

[1] Another illustration of such propaganda is that carried on by one Parsi gentleman by name Prof. A. R. Wadia. The views of Prof. Wadia have been critically examined and exposed by Mr. E. J. Sanjana in a series of articles in the *Rast-Rahabar*—a Gujarati Weekly published in Bombay from 29th October 1944 to 15th April 1945 under the heading of "Sense and Nonsense in Politics."

smilingly protesting that untouchability was not sanctioned by religion, that it was impossible that it should be so. I was a very dutiful and obedient child and so far as it was consistent with respect for parents. I often had tussles with them on this matter. I told my mother that she was entirely wrong in considering physical contact with Ukha as sinful.

"While at school I would often happen to touch the 'Untouchables' and as I never would conceal the fact from my parents, my mother would tell me that the shortest cut to purification after the unholy touch was to cancel the touch by touching any Musalman passing by. And simply out of reverence and regard for my mother I often did so, but never did so believing it to be a religious obligation. After some time we shifted to Porebandar, where I made my first acquaintance with Sanskrit. I was not yet put to an English School, and my brother and I were placed in charge of a Brahmin, who taught us Ram Raksha and Vishnu Punjar. The texts 'Jale Vishnuh' 'Sthale Vishnuh' (there is the Lord (present) in water, there is the Lord (present) in earth, have never gone out of my memory. A motherly old dame used to live close by. Now it happened that I was very timid then, and would conjure up ghosts and goblins whenever the lights went out, and it was dark. The old mother, to disabuse me of fears, suggested that I should mutter the Ramraksha texts whenever I was afraid, and all evil spirits would fly away. This I did and, as I thought with good effect. I could never believe then that there was any text in the Ramraksha pointing to the contact of the 'untouchables' as a sin. I did not understand its meaning then, or understood it very imperfectly. But I was confident that Ramraksha which could destroy all fear of ghosts, could not be countenancing any such things as fear of contact with the 'untouchables.'

"The Ramayana used to be regularly read in our family. A Brahmin called Ladha Maharaj used to read it. He was stricken with leprosy, and he was confident that a regular reading of the Ramayana would cure him of leprosy, and indeed, he was cured of it. 'How can the Ramayana,' I thought to myself 'in which one is regarded nowadays as an 'untouchable,' took Rama across the Ganges in his boat, countenance the idea of any human beings being 'untouchables' on the ground that they were polluted souls? The fact that we addressed God as the 'purifier of the polluted' and by similar appellations, shows that it is a sin to regard any one born in Hinduism as polluted or untouchable—that it is satanic to do so. I have hence been never tired of repeating that it is a great sin. I do not pretend that this thing had crystallised as a conviction in me at the age of twelve, but I do say that I did then regard untouchability as a sin. I narrate this story for the information of the Vaishnavas and orthodox Hindus."

It is no doubt very interesting to know that in that age of blind orthodoxy, Mr. Gandhi should have become aware that Untouchability was a sin and that too at so early an age as 12. What the Untouchables, however, want to know is: What did Mr. Gandhi do to remove the evil. I give below an extract from a biographical note about Mr. Gandhi by the publishers, Tagore & Co., of Madras, to their volume called *Young India*, issued in 1922, to show the principal activities, which Mr. Gandhi launched since the time he started his public career. This is what the note says :—

"Mohandas Karamchand Gandhi was born on October 5, 1869. Caste Bania; son of Karamchand Gandhi, Dewan of Porebunder, Rajkote, and some other Kathiawar States; He was educated at the Kathiawad High School, later at London University and the Inner Temple. On return from London was enrolled as advocate of the Bombay High Court. Went to Natal and thence to the Transvaal on a legal mission. Was enrolled as advocate of the Natal Supreme Court. Decided to remain there. Founded the Natal Indian Congress, 1894. Returned to India, 1895. Agitation in India on behalf of the Natal and Transvaal Indians. Return to Durban. On landing attacked by the mob and narrowly escaped death; led an Indian Ambulance Corps in the Anglo-Boer War, 1899; Returned to India in 1901 to recoup his health. Again returned to South Africa to lead the Indian deputation to place the Indian view of the South African Indian trouble before Mr. Chamberlain. Enrolled as attorney of the Supreme Court of Transvaal and founded the Transvaal British Indian Association and was its Honorary Secretary and Principal legal adviser. Founded the *Indian Opinion* in 1903 and the "Phoenix" Settlement. Led a Stretcher Bearer Corps in the native rebellion in 1906; Agitation against the Anti-Asiatic Act, 1906; Deputation to England for the repeal of the Act; Passive Resistance movement begun against the Act; Negotiations between General Smuts and Mr. Gandhi and compromise. Smuts later denying the promise of repeal of the law, and again commenced passive resistance. Imprisoned twice for breaking the law. Again went to England in 1909 to lay the Indian case before the British public; Provisional Settlement in 1911 Mr. Gokhale's visit to South Africa. On the Government declining to fulfil the settlement of 1911 organized a revival of the passive resistance movement. Final settlement in 1914. Visit to England; Raised an Indian Ambulance Corps in 1914."

From this biographical note, it is clear that Mr. Gandhi began his public life in 1894 when he founded the Natal Indian Congress. From 1894 to 1915, he was in South Africa. During this period, he never thought of the Untouchables and never even inquired after Ukha.

Mr. Gandhi returned to India in 1915. Did he then take up the cause of the Untouchables? Let me again quote from the same biographical note which says :—

> " Returned to India 1915; Founded the Satyagraha Ashram at Ahmedabad. Took part in the Settlement of the Champaran Labour troubles in 1917 and Kaira famine and Ahmedabad mill strike, 1918; Recruiting Campaign 1918; Agitation against the Rowlatt Act and the inauguration of the Satyagraha movement, 1919; Arrested at Kosi on his way to Delhi and sent back to Bombay; Punjab disorders and the official atrocities 1919; Was member of the Congress Committee of Enquiry into the Punjab atrocities; Took part in the Khilafat Agitation. Inauguration of the Non-Co-operation campaign, 1920; Interview with Lord Reading May 1921; appointed sole executive authority of the Congress in 1921 Session of the Congress; Civil Disobedience Programme, February 1922; Suspension of Civil Disobedience campaign on account of Chauri Chaura riots, February 1922; Arrested on March 10, 1922, tried and sentenced to six years simple imprisonment."

This note is obviously incorrect. It omits some very significant and quite well-known events in the life of Mr. Gandhi. To make it complete, the following items must be added :—

> " 1919 declared readiness to welcome Afghan invasion of India to free India from British Imperialism; 1920 put before the country the Bardoli Programme of Constructive work; 1921 started Tilak Swaraj Fund and collected one crore and 25 lakhs to be used for preparing the country for winning swaraj."

In these five years, Mr. Gandhi was completely absorbed in transforming the Congress into a militant organization—a war machine fit to fight and shake British Imperialism. He took up the cause of the Khilafat with a view to make the Muslims join the Congress and did his level best to rally the Hindus for the support of the Khilafat,

What did Mr. Gandhi do for the Untouchables during this period? Congressmen will of course refer to the Bardoli Programme. It is true that in the Bardoli Programme the uplift of the Untouchables was an item. But what is important is to know what happened to it. For the Hindus, the Bardoli Programme[1] was easy to carry out. For it was not for the removal of Untouchability. It was a programme of amelioration which was defined by Disraeli as a combination of ancient institutions and modern improvements. The programme openly recognized Untouchability and planned to do no more than to provide separate wells and separate schools for the Untouchables. The Sub-Committee appointed to draw up a programme for the uplift of the Untouchables consisted of persons, who had never shown any interest in the Untouchables and some of them were even hostile to them. Swami Shraddhanand, the one and only person in the Sub-Committee who can be said to be charged with the desire to do something substantial for the Untouchables, was forced to resign. A paltry sum of money was allotted for carrying on the work of the Committee. The Committee was dissolved without meeting even once. The work of the uplift of the Untouchables was declared to be a work best suited to the Hindu Mahasabha. Mr. Gandhi took no interest in that part of the Bardoli Programme, which related to the Untouchables. On the contrary instead of siding with Swami Shraddhanand he sided with the reactionaries and opponents of Swami Shraddhanand, knowing full well that they did not want anything on a big scale done for the Untouchables.

So much for what Mr. Gandhi did in 1921 in connection with the Bardoli Programme.

What did Mr. Gandhi do after 1922? The publication from which the previous extract from the biographical note was taken is dated 1922. It is necessary to make the following additions[2] to bring the biographical note up to date :—

1924 was released from prison; Forged a compromise between the two wings of the Congress who in his absence were fighting over the issue of Council Entry *versus* Constructive programme; 1929 proclaimed complete independence as the political goal of India; 1930 launched Civil Disobedience

[1] For details see Chapter II.

[2] These additions are mine. I am sure I have not omitted any noteworthy incident in Mr. Gandhi's life.

movement; 1931 went to London to represent Congress at the Round Table Conference. 1932 was imprisoned. Declared fast unto death against the Communal Award of His Majesty's Government and saved his life agreeing to the Poona Pact; 1933 planned a campaign in favour of temple-entry for Untouchables and established the Harijan Sevak Sangh; 1934 ceased to be a member of the Congress; 1942 planned 'Quit India' movement and was imprisoned; 1943 went on fast and was released; 1944 engaged in correspondence with Lord Wavell and in issuing statements explaining away the 8th August 1942 Resolution; 1945 occupied with Kasturba Fund.

The year 1924 gave Mr. Gandhi another opportunity to push forth his campaign for the removal of Untouchability and make it effective. What did Mr. Gandhi do?

The years between 1922 and 1944 have a special significance in the history of the Congress politics. The programme of non-co-operation was accepted by the Congress at the Special Session held in Calcutta in September 1920. The programme included the well-known five boycotts: the boycott of the Legislature, boycott of foreign cloth, etc. The resolution on non-co-operation was opposed by the leaders of the intellectual classes, namely, Messrs. Bepin Chandra Pal, C. R. Das and Lala Lajpat Rai to mention only a few names, but was passed notwithstanding their opposition. The regular Annual Session of the Congress was held in Nagpur in December 1920. The resolution on non-co-operation again came up for discussion. Strange as it may seem, the same resolution was moved by Mr. C. R. Das[1] and seconded by Lala Lajpat Rai and confirmed. The result was that 1921 saw non-co-operation galore. On 19th March 1922, Mr. Gandhi was tried for sedition and sentenced to six years' imprisonment. Immediately Mr. Gandhi was put behind the prison bars, Mr. C. R. Das seems to have recovered his balance and started a campaign to lift the boycott of the Legislature. In this he was joined by Mr. Vithalbhai Patel, Pandit Motilal Nehru and Pandit Malaviya. This move was opposed by the followers of Mr. Gandhi, who were not

[1] This is notwithstanding the fact reported by Mr. Pattabhi Sitaramayya, the Official Historian of the Congress namely that:—

"Mr. C. R. Das brought a contingent of about 250 delegates from East Bengal and Assam, bore their expenses to and fro, and spent Rs. 36,000 from his pocket to undo what was done in Calcutta. There was even a small fight between his men and those of Jitendralal Banerjee, his opponent."
The History of the Congress, p. 347.

prepared to abate a jot or a tittle from the terms of the resolution on non-co-operation passed in Calcutta and confirmed in Nagpur. This led to a schism in the Congress. In 1924, Mr. Gandhi on account of his illness was released from gaol before his time. When he came out, Mr. Gandhi found that the Congress was divided into two warring camps on the issue of the boycott of the Legislature. The quarrel was a bitter one and both sides were engaged in slinging mud at each other. Mr. Gandhi knew that if the quarrel continued the Congress would be weakened and wanted to patch it up. Neither side was prepared to give in. There were statements and counter-statements. Ultimately, Mr. Gandhi made certain proposals for restoring peace between the two wings which were accepted by both sides. The proposals were intended to please both sides. To please the protagonists of Council Entry he proposed that the Congress should recognize entry in the Legislatures as legitimate part of the Congress activity and the opponents of Council Entry should stop their propaganda against it. To please the opponents of Council Entry he proposed that the Congress should accept a new basis for franchise, namely, (*i*) the Congress franchise instead of being 4 annas per annum should be a tender of 2,000 yards of hand-spun and self-spun yarn with the penalty clause attached to it by which any default in this behalf would automatically disqualify a person from being a member of the Congress and (*ii*) the observance of five boycotts of foreign cloth, Government law courts, schools and colleges, and of titles should be deemed as a qualification for a post within the Congress organization and any person who did not believe in the principle of boycott and who did not carry them out in his own person must be deemed to be disqualified as a candidate.

Here was an opportunity for Mr. Gandhi to advance his anti-Untouchability campaign. He could have proposed that if a Hindu wishes to enroll himself as a member of the Congress he should prove that he does not observe untouchability and that the employment of an Untouchable in his household should be adduced in support of his claim in this behalf and that no other evidence would be allowed to be tendered. Such a proposal could not have been impracticable for almost every Hindu, certainly every high Caste Hindu, keeps more than one servant in his household. If Mr. Gandhi could make the Hindu accept spinning and boycott as a franchise for membership of the Congress he could also make acceptable the employment of an Untouchable in a Hindu household a franchise for membership of the Congress. But Mr. Gandhi did not do it.

After 1924 till 1930 there is a complete blank. Mr. Gandhi does not appear to have taken any active steps for the removal of Untouchability or got himself interested in any activity beneficial to the Untouchables during this period. While Mr. Gandhi was inactive, the Untouchables had started a movement called the *satyagraha* movement. The object of the movement was to establish their right to take water from public wells and public temples. The *satyagraha* at the Chowdar Tank situated in Mahad, a town in the Kolaba District of the Bombay Presidency, was organised to establish the right of the Untouchables to take water from public watering places. The *satyagraha* at the Kala Ram Temple situated in Nasik, a town in the Nasik District of the Bombay Presidency, was organised to establish the right of the Untouchables to enter Hindu temples. There were many minor *satyagrahas*. These were, however, the two principal ones over which the efforts of the Untouchables and their opponents, the Caste Hindus, were concentrated. The din and noise caused by them were heard all over India. Thousands of men and women from the Untouchables took part in these *satyagrahas*. Both men and women belonging to the Untouchables were insulted and beaten by the Hindus. Many were injured and some were imprisoned by Government on the ground of causing breach of the peace. This *satyagraha* movement went on for full six years when it was brought to a close in 1935 at a Conference held in Yeola in the Nasik District in which the Untouchables as a result of the adamantine attitude of the Hindus in refusing to give them equal social rights resolved to go out of the Hindu fold. This *satyagraha* movement was no doubt independent of the Congress. It was organised by the Untouchables, led by the Untouchables and financed by the Untouchables. Yet the Untouchables were not without hope of getting the moral support of Mr. Gandhi. Indeed, they had very good ground for getting it. For the weapon of *satyagraha* —the essence of which is to melt the heart of the opponent by suffering—was the weapon which was forged by Mr. Gandhi, and who had led the Congress to practise it against the British Government for winning Swaraj. Naturally the Untouchables expected full support from Mr. Gandhi to their *satyagraha* against the Hindus the object of which was to establish their right to take water from public wells and to enter public Hindu temples. Mr. Gandhi however did not give his support to the *satyagraha*. Not only did he not give his support, he condemned it in strong terms.

In this connection reference may be made to two novel weapons invented or discovered by Mr. Gandhi for redressing human wrongs. Mr. Gandhi claims exclusive credit for forging and perfecting them. First is *satyagraha*. Mr. Gandhi has put into action this weapon of *satyagraha* many a time against the British Government for the removal of political wrongs. But Mr. Gandhi has never used the weapon of *satyagraha* against Hindus to get them to throw open wells and temples to the Untouchables. Fasting is another weapon of Mr. Gandhi. It is said that there have been altogether 21 fasts to the credit of Mr. Gandhi. Some were for the sake of Hindu-Muslim unity and quite a number as atonements for the immoralities committed by the inmates of his Ashram. One was against the order of the Government of Bombay refusing to give the work of a scavenger in the gaol to a prisoner by name Mr. Patwardhan although he demanded it. In these 21 fasts there is not one undertaken for the removal of Untouchability. These are very significant facts.

In 1930 came the Round Table Conference. Mr. Gandhi joined the deliberations of the Conference[1] in 1931. The Conference was concerned with a vital question of framing a constitution for a self-governing India. It was unanimously held that if India was to be a self-governing country then the government must be a government of the people, by the people and for the people. Everybody agreed that only when a government is in a real sense a government *by* the people that it could be a government of the people and for the people. The problem was how to make it a government *by* the people in a country rent into communities, majorities and minorities, who are charged not merely with social cleavages but also with social antagonisms. Having regard to these circumstances, it was agreed that in India there was no possibility of government by the people unless the Legislature and the Executive were framed on the basis of communal representation.

[1] For details see Chapter III.

The problem of the Untouchables loomed large at the Conference. It assumed a new aspect. The question was: Should the Untouchables be left as they were to the tender mercies of the Hindus or should they be given the means to protect themselves by extending to them the principle of communal representation ? The Untouchables strongly objected to be left to the pleasure of the Hindus and demanded the same protection as was given to the other minorities. The contention of the Untouchables was accepted by all. It was just and logical. They contended that the chasm between the Hindus and the Muslims, between the Hindus and the Sikhs, between the Hindus and the Christians is nothing as compared with the chasm between the Hindus and the Untouchables. It is the widest and the deepest. The chasm between the Hindus and the Muslims is religious and not social. That between the Hindus and the Untouchables is both religious *and* social. The antagonism arising out of the chasm existing between the Hindus and the Muslims cannot spell political disaster to the Muslims because the relationship between the Hindus and the Muslims is not that of master and slave. It is one of mere estrangement. On the other hand, the chasm between the Hindus and the Untouchables must spell political disaster for the Untouchables because the relationship between the two is that of master and slave. The Untouchables contended that the attempts to close the gap between them and the Hindus by means of social process had been tried for ages. They had all failed. There was no hope of their success. Since power is being transferred into the hands of the Hindu majority they must have political safeguards of the same sort as, if not better, than those conceded to the Muslims and other minorities.

Here was an opportunity to Mr. Gandhi to show his sympathy to the Untouchables by lending his support to their demand and thereby strengthen their power of resistance against the tyranny and oppression of the Hindus. Instead of showing his sympathy, Mr. Gandhi used every means in his power to defeat them. He made a pact with the Muslims with a view to isolate the Untouchables. Failing to win the Musalmans to his side, he went on a fast unto death to compel the British Government to withdraw their decision to give to the Untouchables the same political rights as given to the Muslims and other minority communities. When the fast failed and Mr. Gandhi was obliged to sign a pact—called the Poona

Pact—which conceded the political demands of the Untouchables he took his revenge by letting the Congress employ foul electioneering tactics to make their political rights of no avail.

In 1933, Mr. Gandhi took up two movements. First was the Temple-entry Movement.[1] He took personal responsibility for seeing through these two measures. One was the opening of the Guruvayur temple. The other was the passing of the Temple-entry Bill sponsored by Mr. Ranga Iyer in the Central Legislature. Mr. Gandhi said that he would fast unto death if the trustee of the Guruvayur temple did not throw it open to the Untouchables by a certain date. The Guruvayur temple still remains closed to the Untouchables but Mr. Gandhi has not fulfilled his vow of going on fast. Surprising as it may be he has done nothing to get the temple declared open to the Untouchables although it is now thirteen years since he took the vow. Mr. Gandhi virtually coerced the Governor-General to give his sanction to the introduction of the Temple-entry Bill. The Congress part in the Central Legislature which was pledged to carry through the Bill refused to support it when the stage of referring it to a Select Committee came on the ground that the Bill gave offence to the Hindus and in the election that was pending the Hindus would seek revenge on the Congress and defeat it at the poll if the Congress supported the Bill. To the great chagrin of Mr. Ranga Iyer, the Congress party let him down by leaving the Bill to die. Mr. Gandhi did not mind this. He even went to the length of justifying the conduct of the Congress Party.

The other movement which Mr. Gandhi sponsored in 1933 was the establishment of the Harijan Sevak Sangh[2] with a net-work of branches all over India. There were three motives which lay behind the organization of the Sangh. First was to prove that Hindus had enough charitable spirit towards the Untouchables and that they would show it by their generous contributions towards their uplift. The second motive was to serve the Untouchables by helping them in the many difficulties with which they were faced in their daily life. The third motive was to create in the minds of the Untouchables a sense of confidence in the Hindus from whom they were

---

[1] For details see Chapter IV.

[2] For details see Chapter V.

estranged in matters political. None of the three objects has been realized. In the first flush the Hindus contributed a total of about 8 lakhs of rupees for the Sangh which is of course nothing as compared to the crores they have contributed for general political purposes. After that they have gone dry. The Sangh is now depending for its finances either on the Government grants or on the income derived from the sale of Mr. Gandhi's autographs or on the munificence of some wealthy merchant who makes a contribution to the Sangh, not because he loves the Untouchables but because he thinks it profitable to please Mr. Gandhi. The branches of the Sangh are being closed every year. The Sangh is contracting and contracting so rapidly that very soon it will have only a centre and no circumference. That the Hindus have lost interest in the Sangh is not the only regrettable aspect of this activity of Mr. Gandhi. The Sangh has not been able to secure the good will and the co-operation of the Untouchables for whose benefit it is supposed to have been started. This is due to various reasons. The work of the Sangh is of the most inconsequential kind. It does not catch anyone's imagination. It neglects most urgent purposes for which the Untouchables need help and assistance. The Sangh rigorously excludes the Untouchables from its management. The Untouchables are no more than beggars—mere recipients of charity. The result is that the Untouchables feel no concern for the Sangh. They look upon it as a foreign body set up by the Hindus with some ulterior motive. Here was an opportunity for Mr. Gandhi to make the Sangh a real bridge between the Hindus and the Untouchables. He could make it a virile institution by improving its programme of work and by allowing the Untouchables to participate in its working. Mr. Gandhi has done nothing of the kind. He has allowed the Sangh to languish. It is dying peacefully and may perish even during the life-time of Mr. Gandhi.

There need be no surprise if this survey of Mr. Gandhi's anti-Untouchability campaign, of his sayings and his doings baffles and puzzles the reader. There need be no wonder if the reader were to pause and ask a few questions on the lines set out below to clear his own mind :

(1) In 1921, Mr. Gandhi collected 1 crore and 85 lakhs of rupees for the Tilak Swaraj Fund. Mr. Gandhi insisted that there was no possibility of winning swaraj unless Untouch-

ability was removed. Why did he not protest when only a paltry sum of Rs. 43,000 was given to the cause of the Untouchables?

(2) In 1922, there was drawn up the Bardoli Programme of constructive work. Uplift of the Untouchables was an important item in it. A Committee was appointed to work out the details. The Committee never functioned and was dissolved and the uplift of the Untouchables as an item in the constructive programme was dropped. Only Rs. 500 were allotted to the Committee for working expenses. Why did Mr. Gandhi not protest against this niggardly and step-motherly treatment of the Committee by the Congress Working Committee? Why did not Mr. Gandhi support Swami Shradhanand who was fighting with the Congress Working Committee for large funds being assigned to the Committee? Why did not Mr. Gandhi protest against the dissolution of the Committee? Why did not Mr. Gandhi appoint another Committee? Why did he allow the work for the Untouchables to drop out as though it was of no importance?

(3) Mr. Gandhi had at the very outset of his campaign for Swaraj insisted that there were five conditions precedent for winning swaraj, namely: (*i*) Hindu-Moslem Unity: (*ii*) Removal of Untouchability; (*iii*) Universal adoption of hand-spun and hand-woven *khadi*; (*iv*) absolute non-violence and (*v*) complete non-co-operation. Mr. Gandhi had not only laid down these conditions but had told Indians that without the fulfilment of these conditions there could be no Swaraj. In 1922, he fasted for the sake of Hindu-Moslem unity. In 1924, he made production of hand-spun yarn the basis of franchise for Congress membership. Why did he not make non-observance of Untouchability the basis of Congress franchise in 1924 or at any time subsequent thereto?

(4) Mr. Gandhi has gone on fast many a time to achieve a variety of objects which are dear to him. Why has Mr. Gandhi not fasted even once for the sake of the Untouchables?

(5) Mr. Gandhi has devised satyagraha as a weapon to redress wrongs and to win freedom and has practised it against the British Government. Why has Mr. Gandhi not started satyagraha even once against the Hindus on behalf of the Untouchables for securing admission to wells, temples and other public places to which access is denied by the Hindus?

(6) Following Mr. Gandhi's lead the Untouchables started satyagraha from 1929 onwards against the Hindus for admission to wells and temples. Why did Mr. Gandhi condemn their satyagraha ?

(7) Mr. Gandhi declared that he would fast if the Guruvayur temple was not thrown open to the Untouchables by the Zamorin. The temple has not been thrown open. Why did not Mr. Gandhi go on fast ?

(8) Mr. Gandhi in 1932 threatened the British Government with dire consequences if the Governor-General did not give permission to Mr. Ranga Iyer to introduce his Temple-entry Bill on behalf of the Congress Party in the Central Legislature. As fresh elections to the Central Legislature were announced the Congress Party withdrew its support to the Bill and Mr. Ranga Iyer had to drop it. If Mr. Gandhi was earnest and sincere about Temple-entry, why did Mr. Gandhi support the action of the Congress Party ? What was more important—Temple-entry for the Untouchables or electoral victory to the Congress ?

(9) Mr. Gandhi knows that the difficulty of the Untouchables does not lie in their not having civic rights. Their difficulty lies in the conspiracy of the Hindus who threaten them with dire consequences if the Untouchables dare to exercise them. The real way of helping the Untouchables is to have some organization for the protection of civic rights which will undertake the duty of prosecuting those Hindus who assault the Untouchables or proclaim social and economic boycott against them and thereby prevent them from exercising their civic rights. Why did not Mr. Gandhi include this as one of the objects of the Harijan Sevak Sangh ?

(10) Before Mr. Gandhi came on the scene, the Depressed Classes Mission Society was formed by the caste Hindus for the uplift of the Untouchables. The moneys were subscribed by the Hindus. Yet the Society's affairs were conducted by Joint Boards consisting of the Hindus and the Untouchables. Why has Mr. Gandhi excluded the Untouchables from the management of the Harijan Sevak Sangh ?

(11) If Mr. Gandhi is the real friend of the Untouchables, why did he not leave it to the Untouchables to decide whether political safeguards were the best means for their protection ? Why did he go to the length of making a pact with the Muslims in order to isolate and defeat the Untouchables ? Why did

Mr. Gandhi declare a fast unto death the object of which was to deprive the Untouchables of the benefit of the Communal Award by this extreme form of coercion ?

(12) After having accepted the Poona Pact, why did not Mr. Gandhi keep faith with the Untouchables by telling the Congress not to despoil the politics of the Untouchables by contesting the seats reserved for the Untouchables by getting such Untouchables elected as were prepared to become the tools of the Hindus ?

(13) After having accepted the Poona Pact why did not Mr. Gandhi keep up the gentleman's agreement and instruct the Congress High Command to include representatives of the Untouchables in the Congress Cabinets ?

(14) Why did Mr. Gandhi disapprove of the appointment by Dr. Khare of Mr. Agnibhoj—a member of the Scheduled Castes—as a minister in the Congress Cabinet in the C. P. when Mr. Agnibhoj was in every way qualified to be a Minister ? Did Mr. Gandhi say that he was opposed to the creation of such high ambitions among persons belonging to the Scheduled Castes ?

III

What is the explanation that Mr. Gandhi has to offer ? What is the explanation that Mr. Gandhi's friends have to offer ? Mr. Gandhi's anti-untouchability campaign is marked by so many twists and turns, inconsistencies and contradictions, attacks and surrenders, advances and retreats that the whole campaign has become a matter of mystery. Few have a belief in its efficacy and quite a large number hold that there is not enough earnestness and sincerity behind it. Some explanation is therefore necessary. It is more for the sake of Mr. Gandhi's reputation for earnestness and sincerity than for the sake of giving a clear understanding of Mr. Gandhi's aims and methods to the reader that one would like Mr. Gandhi and his friends to explain the points raised in the foregoing questions.

It would no doubt be interesting to know what Mr. Gandhi and his friends may have to say in reply to these questions. Everybody interested in this question will naturally be looking forward to it. It will not however do for anyone else to anticipate the reply and then deal with it. They must be left to frame it in their own way and select their own time to do so.

In the meantime one may well ask what the Untouchables have to say about Mr. Gandhi and his anti-untouchability campaign. It is not difficult to state what view the Untouchables take of Mr. Gandhi's anti-untouchability campaign.

Do the Untouchables regard Mr. Gandhi as being in earnest ? The answer is in the negative. They do not regard Mr. Gandhi as being in earnest. How can they ? How can they look upon a man being in earnest who, when in 1921 the whole country was aroused to put the Bardoli programme in action, remained completely indifferent to the anti-untouchability part of it ? How could they look upon a man as being in earnest who, when he found that out of 1 crore and 25 lakhs of Swaraj Fund, only 43 thousand rupees were allotted to the cause of the Untouchables, did not raise any protest at this niggardly treatment of a long neglected cause ? How can they regard a man as being in earnest who, when in 1924 he got an opportunity to impose upon the Hindus the obligation to remove Untouchability, did not do so even though he had the power and the occasion to enforce it ? Such a step would have served three purposes. It would have put the nationalism of Congressmen to test. It would have helped to remove Untouchability. It would have proved that Mr. Gandhi was sincere in his talks about the evil of Untouchability and its being a sin and a stigma on Hinduism. Why did not Mr. Gandhi do it ? Does this not show that Mr. Gandhi was more interested in the spread of spinning than in the removal of Untouchability ? Does this not show that removal of Untouchability was the least part of Mr. Gandhi's programme and that it was not even last ? Does it not show that the statements by Mr. Gandhi that Untouchability is a blot on Hinduism and that there will be no Swaraj without the removal of Untouchability, were just empty phrases with no earnestness behind them ? How could they believe in the earnestness of a person who takes a vow to fast if the Guruvayur temple is not opened to the Untouchables but will not go on fast even when the temple remains closed ? How could they accept a man to be in earnest when he sponsors a Bill for securing Temple-entry and subsequently becomes a party to dropping it ? How could they accept the earnestness of a man who contents himself with saying that he will not go into a temple if it is not open to the Untouchables when what is required of him is to adopt every means to get the temples thrown open to the Untouchables ? How could they believe in the earnestness of a man who is ready to fast for everything but will not fast for the Untouchables? How can they believe in the earnestness of a man who is prepared to practise satyagraha for everything and against everybody but who will not practise it against the Hindus for the sake of the Untouchables? How can they believe in the earnestness of a man who does nothing more than indulge in giving sermons on the evils of Untouchability?

Do they regard Mr. Gandhi as honest and sincere? The answer is that they do not regard Mr. Gandhi as honest and sincere. At the outset of his campaign for Swaraj, Mr. Gandhi told the Untouchables not to side with the British. He told them not to embrace Christianity or any other religion. He told them that they could find salvation in Hinduism. He told the Hindus that they must remove Untouchability as a condition precedent to Swaraj. Yet in 1921 when only a paltry sum out of the Tilak Swaraj Fund was allotted to the Untouchables, and when the Committee to plan the uplift of the Untouchables was unceremoniously wound up, he did not even raise a word of protest.

Mr. Gandhi had under his command a sum of Rs. 1 crore and 25 lakhs belonging to the Tilak Swaraj Fund. Why did Mr. Gandhi not insist upon a substantial portion of this amount being ear-marked for the uplift of the Untouchables? That Mr. Gandhi showed almost complete indifference to the cause of the Untouchables is beyond dispute. What is surprising is the explanation which Mr. Gandhi offered for his indifference. He said that he was busy in planning a campaign to win swaraj and that he had no time to spare for the cause of the Untouchables. He not only did not blush at his explanation but he offered a moral justification for his indifference to the cause of the Untouchables. He took the stand that there was nothing wrong in his devoting himself entirely to the political cause of India to the exclusion of the cause of the Untouchables for in his opinion the good of the whole includes the good of the part and that as the Hindus are slaves of the British, slaves cannot emancipate slaves. Phrases such as 'slaves of slaves' and 'greater includes the less' may be admirable dialectics, though they cannot have more truth than the saying that because the country's wealth has increased, therefore everybody's wealth has increased. But we are not considering Mr. Gandhi's ability as a dialectician. We are testing his sincerity. Can we accept the sincerity of a man who evades his responsibility and contents himself with an excuse? Can the Untouchables believe that Mr. Gandhi is the champion of their cause?

How can they regard Mr. Gandhi as honest and sincere if they consider Mr. Gandhi's conduct towards them and towards the Muslims and Sikhs in the matter of constitutional safeguards?

Mr. Gandhi used to justify his discrimination between the Scheduled Castes and the other Minorities in the matter of constitutional safeguards by another plea. The plea was that there were historical reasons, which compel him to recognize the Muslims and the Sikhs. He has never explained what those reasons are. They cannot be other than those, which hold the Muslims and the Sikhs as the fragments of the old ruling communities. One does not mind Mr. Gandhi having succumbed to such puerile and undemocratic arguments, though he could have insisted that he would treat all minorities on equal basis and would not give any weight to such illogical and irrelevant considerations. The question is: How could the admission of such a plea have prevented Mr. Gandhi from opposing the demand of the Scheduled Castes? Why did Mr. Gandhi regard himself as bound by no other reasons except the historical reasons? Why did not Mr. Gandhi think that if historical reasons were decisive in the case of the Muslims and the Sikhs, moral reasons were decisive in the case of the Untouchables? The fact is that the plea of historical reasons is a hollow plea. It was not a plea at all. It was an excuse for not conceding the demand of the Untouchables.

IV

Mr. Gandhi is never so much disgusted as he is when he is confronted with the question of Majority *versus* Minority. He would like to forget it and ignore it. But circumstances will not let him do either and he is often forced to deal with the issue. The last time he dealt with it was on the 21st October 1939 in the form of an Editorial in the *Harijan* under the heading "The Fiction of Majority." The article is full of venom and Mr. Gandhi has not hesitated to pour all the ridicule he could on those who were constantly raising the question. In the article he vehemently denied that the Muslims are a Minority. He denied that the Sikhs are a Minority. He denied that the Indian Christians are a Minority. His contention was that they were not minorities in the technical sense of Oppressed Communities, they were minorities in the numerical sense only, which meant that they were no minorities at all. What did Mr. Gandhi have to say about the Scheduled Castes? Could he deny their contention that they are a Minority? Let me quote Mr. Gandhi's own words. Mr. Gandhi said :—

> "I have endeavoured to show that there is no such things as real minorities in India whose rights can be endangered by India becoming independent. With the exception of the Depressed Classes there is no minority which is not able to take care of itself."

Here is an admission on the part of Mr. Gandhi that the Scheduled Castes are a minority in the real sense of the word and that they are the only minority in India who will not be able to take care of themselves in a free India governed by a Hindu communal majority. Notwithstanding this inner conviction Mr. Gandhi maintained in a most vehement manner that he would not concede any political safeguards to the Untouchables. How can the Untouchables accept such a man as sincere and honest?

Mr. Gandhi opposed the demands of the Untouchables for political safeguards at the Round Table Conference. He did everything to defeat the object of the Untouchables. To weaken the force behind their demand and isolate them he tried to buy over the Muslims by offering to concede the whole of their fourteen demands. Mr. Gandhi at the meeting of the Minorities Sub-Committee had said: "Who am I to oppose the demand of the Untouchables if the Committee gave it its approval." It was wrong for Mr. Gandhi to have tried to defeat the verdict of the Committee by offering to give the Muslims their full demand formulated in Mr. Jinnah's fourteen points in return for their agreeing to oppose the demands of the Scheduled Castes. His was a most subtle piece of strategy. He offered the Musalmans a most difficult choice between having their 14 points and withdrawing their support to the demand of the Untouchables or siding with the Untouchables and losing their 14 points. In the end, Mr. Gandhi's strategy failed and neither did the Musalmans lose their 14 points nor did the Untouchables lose their case. But the episode remains as a witness to Mr. Gandhi's perfidy. What else can be the appropriate description of the conduct of a man who offers criminal inducement to another for getting him to break his promise and who calls a person his friend and then contrives to stab him in the back ? How can such a man be regarded by the Untouchables as honest and sincere ?

Mr. Gandhi left the decision of the communal question to the arbitration of the British Prime Minister. Notwithstanding Mr. Gandhi's efforts to defeat the Untouchables, His Majesty's Government conceded them their political demands. As a party to the arbitration Mr. Gandhi was bound to abide by the decision. But Mr. Gandhi decided to defy it and he did it by going on a fast unto death. Mr. Gandhi shook India and the world outside by his "Fast unto Death." The object of the fast was to compel the British Government to withdraw the constitutional safeguards which the British Prime Minister had proposed in his Award for the protection of the Untouchables under the new Constitution. One of Mr. Gandhi's disciples has described the fast as an Epic Fast. Why it should be described as an Epic Fast it is not easy to follow. There was nothing heroic about it. It was the opposite of heroic. It was an adventure. It was launched by Mr. Gandhi because he believed that both the Untouchables and the British Government would quake before his threat of fast unto death, and surrender to his demand. Both were prepared to call off his bluff and as a matter of fact did call it off. All his heroism vanished, the moment Mr. Gandhi found that he had overdone the trick. The man who started by saying that he would fast unto death unless the safeguards to the Untouchables were completely withdrawn and the Untouchables reduced to the condition of utter helplessness without rights and without recognition was plaintively pleading : "My life is in your hands, will you save me ? " Mr. Gandhi's over-impatience to sign the Poona Pact—though it did not cancel the Prime Minister's Award as he had demanded but only substituted another and a different system of constitutional safeguards—is the strongest evidence that the hero had lost his courage and was anxious to save his face and anyhow save his life.

There was nothing noble in the fast. It was a foul and filthy act. The fast was not for the benefit of the Untouchables. It was against them and was the worst form of coercion against a helpless people to give up the constitutional safeguards of which they had become possessed under the Prime Minister's Award and agree to live on the mercy of the Hindus. It was a vile and wicked act. How can the Untouchables regard such a man as honest and sincere?

After having gone on a fast unto death, he signed the Poona Pact. People say that Mr. Gandhi sincerely believed that political safeguards were harmful to the Untouchables. But how could an honest and sincere man, who opposed the political demands of the Untouchables, who was prepared to use the Muslims to defeat them and who went on a fast unto death, in the end accept the very same demands—for there is no difference between the Poona Pact and the Communal Award—when he found that there was no use opposing, as opposition would not succeed? How can an honest and sincere man accept as harmless the demands of the Untouchables which once he regarded as harmful?

Do the Untouchables regard Mr. Gandhi as their friend and ally? The answer is in the negative. They do not regard him as their friend. How can they? It may be that Mr. Gandhi honestly believes that the problem of the Untouchables is a social problem. But how can they believe him to be their friend when he wishes to retain caste and abolish Untouchability it being quite clear that Untouchability is only an extended form of caste and that therefore without abolition of caste there is no hope of abolition of Untouchability? It may be that Mr. Gandhi honestly believes that the problem of Untouchables can be solved by social processes. But how can the Untouchables regard a man as their friend who develops a fanatic and frantic opposition to political processes being employed when everyone was agreed that the use of political processes cannot mar the effect of social processes and may be depended upon to help and accelerate the solution of the problem? How could a man be regarded as the friend of the Untouchables, when he does not believe the Untouchables reaching to places of power and authority in the State?

In this controversy over political safeguards, Mr. Gandhi could have pursued any of the following courses. He could have been the champion of the Untouchables. As such, he should not only have welcomed their demand for safeguards but he should have proposed them himself without waiting for the Untouchables to do so. Not only should he have proposed them himself but he should have fought for them. For, what could give greater happiness to a genuine champion of the Untouchables than to see that provision was made to enable them to become members of the Legislature, ministers in the executive, and occupants of high offices in the State? Surely, if Mr. Gandhi is a champion of the Untouchables these are the very provisions he should have fought for. Secondly, if he did not wish to be the champion of the Untouchables, he could have been their ally. He could have helped them by giving them his moral and material support. Thirdly, if Mr. Gandhi did not like to play the part of a champion and was averse to be even an ally of the Untouchables, the next thing he could have done, consistent with his proclaimed and much advertised sympathies for the Untouchables, was to be their friend. Again, as a friend he could have taken up the attitude of benevolent neutrality—declining to fight but ready to render all help for getting the demand for safeguards accepted. Failing benevolent neutrality, he could have taken the attitude of strict neutrality and could have told the Untouchables to get the safeguards if the Round Table Conference was prepared to give them and that he would neither help nor hinder. Abandoning all these sober considerations, Mr. Gandhi came out as an open enemy of the Untouchables. How can the Untouchables regard such a man as their friend and ally?

V

That Mr. Gandhi's anti-untouchability campaign has failed is beyond cavil.

On 17th August 1939, Mr. B. K. Gaikwad, a member of the Scheduled Castes in the Bombay Legislative Assembly, asked a question as to how many temples in the Bombay Presidency were thrown open to the Untouchables since 1932 when Mr. Gandhi started his Temple-entry movement. According to the figures given by the Congress Minister the total number of temples thrown open was 142. Of these 121 were ownerless temples standing on the wayside, which were under the care of nobody in particular and which nobody used as places of worship. Another fact revealed was that not a single temple was thrown open to the Untouchables in Gujarat, the district which is the home of Mr. Gandhi.

Even the Congress papers admit it. I give on the next page a few quotations from some of them.

Writing on 10th March 1940, the *Harijan Bandu*, Mr. Gandhi's Gujarati paper, said :

> "The Untouchability of the 'Harijans' in the matter of entry into schools persists nowhere so much still as in Gujarat."[1]

The *Bombay Chronicle* in its issue of 27th August 1940 reproduced an extract from a monthly letter of the Harijan Sevak Sangh. It states :—

> "Harijans of Godhavi in Ahmedabad District were so persecuted by caste Hindus for sending their children to Local Board School that ultimately 42 Harijan families left that place . . . and went to the Taluka town of Sanand."

On 27th August 1943, Mr. M. M. Nandgaonkar, a leader of the Untouchables residing in Thana in the Bombay Presidency and ex-Vice President of Thana Municipality was refused tea in a Hindu hotel. The *Bombay Chronicle* commenting upon this incident in its issue dated 28th August 1943 said :

> "When Gandhiji fasted in 1932, some feverish attempts were made to have some temples and hotels opened to Harijans. Now the actual position is nearly what it used to be before with regard to temple entry and access to hotels. The cleanest Harijan is not admitted to temples and hotels. Yet many anti-Untouchability workers take a complacent view of these disabilities and patronisingly talk of 'uplift first' for Harijans, saying that when Harijans learn to be clean, their civic disabilities will fall off automatically. This is rank nonsense."

Writing on the proceedings of the All-India Scheduled Castes Federation held in Cawnpore in January 1944, the *Bombay Chronicle* in its issue of 4th February 1944 said :

> "But such is the passivity of Hindu society that both caste and Untouchability still thrive. Nay, several Hindu leaders... misguided by the interested propaganda by certain Britishers, still plead that there is some mysterious virtue in caste because Hindu culture has remained today. Else, they argue, caste would not have survived the shocks of centuries . . . It is most tragic to find that, in spite of all that Gandhiji and other reformers . . . have done, Untouchability still persists to no small extent. It is most rampant in villages . . . Even in a city like Bombay, a person known to be a sweeper, let alone a scavenger, however clean dressed he may be, is not allowed to enter a caste Hindu restaurant, nay, even an Irani's restaurant for tea."

---

[1] Quoted from Sanjana's *Sense and Nonsense in Politics*.

The Untouchables have always said that Mr. Gandhi's anti-Untouchability campaign has failed. After 25 years of labour, hotels have remained closed, wells have remained closed, temples have remained closed and in very many parts of India—particularly in Gujarat—even schools have remained closed. The extracts produced from the papers form therefore a very welcome testimony especially because the papers are Congress papers. As they fully corroborate what the Untouchables have been saying on the point, nothing further need be said on the subject except to ask one question :

Why has Mr. Gandhi failed ? According to me, there are three reasons which have brought about this failure.

The first reason is that the Hindus to whom he makes his appeal for the removal of Untouchability do not respond. Why is this so ? It is a common experience that the words a man uses and the effect they produce are not always commensurate. What he says has its momentum indefinitely multiplied, or reduced to nullity, by the impression that the hearer for good reason or bad happens to have formed of the spirit of the speaker. This gives a clue to know why Mr. Gandhi's sermons on Untouchability have completely failed to move the Hindus, why people hear his after-prayer sermons for few minutes and then go to the comic opera and why there is nothing more to it. The fault is not entirely of the Hindu public. The fault is of Mr. Gandhi himself. Mr. Gandhi has built up his reputation of being a Mahatma on his being an harbinger of political freedom and not on his being a spiritual teacher. Whatever may be his intentions, Mr. Gandhi is looked upon as an apostle of Swaraj. His anti-Untouchability campaign is looked upon as a fad if not a side-show. That is why the Hindus respond to his political biddings but never to his social or religious preaching. The momentum of his anti-Untouchability campaign must therefore remain a nullity. Mr. Gandhi is a political shoe-maker. He must stick to his political last. He thought he could take up the task of solving the social question. That was a mistake. A politician is not the man for it. That is why the hope held out to the Untouchables that Mr. Gandhi's sermons will do the trick has failed.

The second reason is that Mr. Gandhi does not wish to antagonize the Hindus even if such antagonism was necessary to carry out his anti-Untouchability programme. A few instances will illustate Mr. Gandhi's mentality.

Most of Mr. Gandhi's friends give credit to him for sincerity and earnestness for the cause of the Untouchables and expect the Untouchables to believe in it on the mere ground that Mr. Gandhi is the one man who keeps on constantly preaching to the Hindus the necessity of removing Untouchability. They have lost sight of the old proverb that an ounce of practice is worth a ton of preaching and have never cared to ask Mr. Gandhi to explain why does he not cease to preach to the Hindus the necessity of removing Untouchability and launch a campaign of satyagraha or start a fast. If they would ask for such an explanation they would know why Mr. Gandhi merely contents himself with sermons on Untouchability.

The true reasons why Mr. Gandhi will not go beyond sermons were revealed to the Untouchables for the first time[1] in 1929 when the Untouchables in the Bombay Presidency opened a campaign of satyagraha against the Hindus for establishing their civic rights in the matter of temple-entry and taking water from public wells. They hoped to get the blessings of Mr. Gandhi in as much as satyagraha was Mr. Gandhi's own weapon to get wrongs redressed. When appealed to for support, Mr. Gandhi surprised the Untouchables by issuing a statement condemning their campaign of satyagraha against the Hindus. The argument urged by Mr. Gandhi was very ingenious. He stated that satyagraha was to be used only against foreigners; it must not be used against one's own kindred or countrymen and as the Hindus were the kindred and countrymen of the Untouchables by rules of satyagraha the latter were debarred from using the weapon against the former. What a fall from the sublime to the ridiculous! By this Mr. Gandhi made nonsense of satyagraha. Why did Mr. Gandhi do this? Only because he did not want to annoy and exasperate the Hindus.

As a second piece of evidence, I would refer to what is known as the Kavitha incident. Kavitha is a village in the Ahmedabad District in Gujarat. In 1935, the Untouchables of the village demanded from the Hindus of the village that their children should be admitted in the common school of the village along with other Hindu children. The Hindus were enraged at this

[1] In 1924 in the Satyagraha at Vaikom the object of which was to get a public road in Travancore open to the Untouchables, Mr. Gandhi objected to the Sikhs opening a kitchen for the satyagrahis. The reason given by Mr. Gandhi was not stated quite so explicitly.

outrage and took their revenge by proclaiming a complete social boycott. The events connected with this boycott were reported by Mr. A. V. Thakkar, who went to Kavitha to intercede with the Hindus on behalf of the Untouchables. The story told by him runs as follows :—

"The Associated Press announced on the 10th inst. that the Caste Hindus of Kavitha agreed to admit Harijan boys to the village school in Kavitha and that matters were amicably settled. This was contradicted on the 13th instant by the Secretary of the Ahmedabad Harijan Sevak Sangh, who said in his statement that the Harijans had undertaken (privately of course) not to send their children to the school. Such an undertaking was not given voluntarily, but was extorted from them by the Caste Hindus, in this case the Garasias of the village, who had proclaimed a social boycott against poor Harijans—weavers, chamars and others, who number over 100 families. They were deprived of agricultural labour, their animals of grazing in the pasture land, and their children of buttermilk. Not only this, but a Harijan leader was compelled to take an oath by Mahadev that he and others would not hereafter even make an effort to reinstate their children in the school. The so-called settlement was brought about in this way.

"But even after the bogus settlement reported on the 10th and the complete surrender by poor Harijans, the boycott was not lifted up to the 19th and partly up to the 22nd from the weavers. It was lifted somewhat earlier from the head of the chamars, as Garasias themselves could not remove the carcasses of their dead animals, and thus had to come to terms with the Chamars earlier. As if the enormities perpetrated so far were not enough, kerosene was poured into the Harijans' well, once on the 15th instant and again on the 19th instant. One can imagine what terrorism was thus practised on poor Harijans because they had dared to send their children to sit alongside of the 'princely' Garasia boys.

"I met the leaders of the Garasias on the morning of the 22nd. They said they could not tolerate the idea of boys of Dheds and Chamars sitting by the side of their own boys. I met also the District Magistrate of Ahmedabad on the 23rd with a view to finding out if he would do something to ease the situation, but without any result.

"Harijan boys are thus practically banned from the village school with nobody to help them. This has caused despondency among the Harijans to such an extent that they are thinking of migrating in a Body to some other village."

This was a report made to Mr. Gandhi. What did Mr. Gandhi do? The following[1] is the advice Mr. Gandhi gave to the Untouchables of Kavitha :—

> "There is no help like self-help. God helps those who help themselves. If the Harijans concerned will carry out their reported resolve to wipe the dust of Kavitha off their feet, they will not only be happy themselves but they will pave the way for others who may be similarly treated. If people migrate in search of employment how much more should they do so in search of self-respect? I hope that well-wishers of Harijans will help these poor families to vacate inhospitable Kavitha."

Mr. Gandhi advised the Untouchables of Kavitha to vacate. But why did he not advise Mr. Thakkar to prosecute the Hindus of Kavitha and help the Untouchables to vindicate their rights? Obviously, he would like to uplift the Untouchables if he can but not by offending the Hindus. What good can such a man do to promote the cause of the Untouchables? All this shows that Mr. Gandhi is most anxious to be good to the Hindus. That is why he opposes satyagraha against the Hindus. That is why he opposed the political demands of the Untouchables as he believed that they were aimed against them. He is anxious to be so good to the Hindus that he does not care if he is thereby becoming good for nothing for the Untouchables. That is why Mr. Gandhi's whole programme for the removal of Untouchability is just words, words and words and why there is no action behind it.

The third reason is that Mr. Gandhi does not want the Untouchables to organize and be strong. For he fears that they might thereby become independent of the Hindus and weaken the ranks of the Hindus. This is best illustrated by the activities of the Harijan Sevak Sangh. The whole object of the Sangh is to create a slave mentality among the Untouchables towards their Hindu masters. Examine the Sangh from any angle one may like and the creation of slave mentality will appear to be its dominant purpose.

The work of the Sangh reminds one of the mythological demoness *Putana* described in the Bhagvat—a companion to the Mahabharat. *Kamsa*, the king of Mathurra, wanted to kill *Krishna*, as it was predicted that *Kamsa* will die at the hands of *Krishna*. Having come to know of the birth of *Krishna*, *Kamsa*

---

[1] *Harijan*, dated 5th October, 1935.

asked *Putana* to undertake the mission to kill *Krishna* while he was yet a baby. *Putana* took the form of a beautiful woman and went to *Yashoda*, the foster-mother of *Krishna* and having applied liquid poison to her breast pleaded to be employed as a wet nurse for suckling the baby *Krishna* and thus have the opportunity to kill it. The rest of the story it is unnecessary to pursue. The point of the story is that the real purpose is not always the same as the ostensible purpose and a nurse can be a murdress. The Sangh is to the Untouchables what *Putana* was to *Krishna*. The Sangh under the pretence of service is out to kill the spirit of independence from among the Untouchables. The Untouchables, in the early stages of their agitation, had taken the support of some well-meaning Hindus and had followed their leadership. By the time of the Round Table Conference, the Untouchables had become completely self-reliant and independent. They were no longer satisfied with charity from the Hindus. They said they wanted rights. There is no doubt that it is to kill this spirit of independence among the Untouchables that Mr. Gandhi started the Harijan Sevak Sangh. The Harijan Sevak Sangh by its petty services has collected a swarm of grateful Untouchables who are employed to preach that Mr. Gandhi and the Hindus are the saviours of the Untouchables. Daniel O'Connel, the Irish leader, once said that no man can be grateful at the cost of his honour, no woman can be grateful at the cost of her chastity and no country can be grateful at the cost of its liberty. The Untouchables are too simple-minded to know that the cost of the service which the Harijan Sevak Sangh offers to render, is loss of independence. This is exactly what Mr. Gandhi wants.

The worst part of the activities of the Harijan Sevak Sangh is the help rendered to the Untouchable students kept in the hostels maintained by the Sangh. These Untouchable students remind me of *Bhishma* and *Kacha*, two prominent characters which figure in the Mahabharata. *Bhishma* proclaimed with great show that the *Pandavas* were right and the *Kauravas* wrong. Yet when it came to a war between the two he fought on the side of the *Kauravas* and against the *Pandavas*. When asked to justify his conduct, he was not ashamed to say that he fought for the *Kauravas* because they fed him. *Kacha* belonged to the community of the *Devas* who were engaged in a war against the *Rakshasas*. The spiritual head of the *Rakshasas* knew a *mantra* (incantation) by which he could revive a dead *Rakshasa*. The *Devas* were losing the battle since their head did not know the *mantra* and could not revive their dead. The *Devas* planned to send *Kacha* to the head of the *Rakshasas* with instructions somehow to learn the *mantra* and come back. *Kacha* in the beginning could not succeed. Ultimately he entered into an agreement with *Devayani*, the daughter of the spiritual head of the *Rakshasas*, that if she helped him to acquire the *mantra* he would be prepared to marry her. *Devayani* succeeded in fulfilling her part of the contract. But *Kacha* refused to perform his part alleging that the interests of his community were more important than his promise to her.

Bhishma and *Kacha*, in my opinion, are typical of the morally depraved characters who know no other purpose but to serve their own interests for the time being. The Untouchable students in the Harijan hostels are acting the part of both *Bhishma* and *Kacha*. During their stay in the hostels they play the part of *Bhishma* by singing the praises of Mr. Gandhi and the Congress. When they come out of the hostels they play the part of *Kacha* and denounce Mr. Gandhi and the Congress. I am extremely pained to see this. Nothing worse could happen to the youth of the Untouchables than this moral degeneration. But this is the greatest disservice which his Harijan Sevak Sangh has done to the Untouchables. It has destroyed their character. It has destroyed their independence. This is what Mr. Gandhi wants to happen.

Take a fourth illustration. The Sangh is run by the Caste Hindus. There are some Untouchables who have demanded that the institution should be handed over to the Untouchables and should be run by them. Others have demanded that the Untouchables should have representation on the governing Board. Mr. Gandhi has flatly refused to do either on two very ingenious grounds which no man with the greatest cunning could improve. Mr. Gandhi's first argument is that the Harijan Sevak Sangh is an act of penance on the part of the Hindus for the sin of observing Untouchability. It is they who must do the penance. Therefore[1] the Untouchables can have no place in running the Sangh. Secondly Mr. Gandhi says the money collected by him is given by the Hindus and not by the Untouchables and as the money is not of the

[1] Mr. Gandhi has repeated this view of his only recently.

Untouchables, the Untouchables have no right to be on the Governing Body. The refusal of Mr. Gandhi may be tolerated, but his arguments are most insulting and a respectable Untouchable will be forgiven if he refuses to have anything to do with the Sangh. One should have thought that the Harijan Sevak Sangh was a Trust and the Untouchables its beneficiaries. Any trio in law would admit that the beneficiaries have every right to know the aims and objects of the Trust, its funds and whether the objects are properly carried out or not. The beneficiaries have even the right to have the Trustees removed for breach of trust. On that basis it would be impossible to deny the claim of the Untouchables for representation on the Managing Board. Evidently, Mr. Gandhi does not wish to accept this position. A self-respecting Untouchable, who has no desire to cringe and who does not believe in staking the future of the Untouchables on the philanthropy of strangers, cannot have any quarrel with Mr. Gandhi. He is quite prepared to say that if meanness is a virtue then Mr. Gandhi's logic is superb and Mr. Gandhi is welcome to the benefit of it. Only he must not blame the Untouchables if they boycott the Sangh.

These however could not be the real reasons for not allowing the Untouchables to run the Sangh. The real reasons are different. In the first place, if the Sangh was handed over to the Untouchables, Mr. Gandhi and the Congress will have no means of control over the Untouchables. The Untouchables will cease to be dependent on the Hindus. In the second place, the Untouchables having become independent will cease to be grateful to the Hindus. These consequences will be quite contrary to the aims and objects, which have led Mr. Gandhi to found the Sangh. He wants to create among the Untouchables what is known among Indian Christians as the mission compound mentality. That is why Mr. Gandhi does not wish to hand over the Sangh to the control and management of the Untouchables. Is this consistent with a genuine desire for the emancipation of the Untouchables ? Can Mr. Gandhi be called a liberator of the Untouchables ? Does this not show that Mr. Gandhi is more anxious to tighten the tie which binds the Untouchables to the apron strings of the Hindus than to free them from the thraldom of the Hindus ?

These are the reasons why Mr. Gandhi's anti-Untouchability campaign has failed.

VI

To sum up, can it be said that Mr. Gandhi has recovered the title deeds to humanity which the Untouchables have lost? Obviously not. Those title deeds are still with the Hindus. He has done nothing to recover them. Nor has he helped the Untouchables to recover them. On the contrary, Mr. Gandhi has put every obstacle in their way. The Untouchables feel that their title deeds to humanity—which means their emancipation from their thraldom of the Hindus—can be secured by them by political power, and by nothing else. Mr. Gandhi, on the other hand, believes that his preaching and the charity and zeal of the Hindus are sufficient panacea for all the ills of the Untouchables. Can the Untouchables rely on a sustained flow of Hindu charity and Hindu zeal? Charity which has its fury is worth talking about. Zeal which has its vengeance is worth building upon. But which friend of the Untouchables can ask them to depend upon the miserable measure of Hindu charity and Hindu zeal? Untouchability has been in existence for the last two thousand years, during which period the Hindus have day in and day out sucked the very blood of the Untouchables and have mutilated them and trodden upon them in every way. During these two thousand years what amount of charity have the Hindus done to the Untouchables? Only 8 lakhs and that too when Mr. Gandhi personally went round the country with a begging bowl! Having put his programme to test, Mr. Gandhi might have shown his willingness to concede the Untouchables' demand for political power as their only means of salvation. Indeed, so obvious is the justice of this demand that a man with no more than commonsense could have understood that executive power in the hands of the Untouchables could do more in a year than the whole order of preaching friars could be relied upon to do in a century. But the very idea of political power to the Untouchables is hateful to Mr. Gandhi. Why should not the Untouchables say 'Beware of Mr. Gandhi' when they know that he would not allow the use of political processes for the emancipation of the Untouchables though Mr. Gandhi is fully alive to the fact that the social processes on which he laid so much store for helping them have completely failed?

In this connection one is reminded of the attitude of President Lincoln in the American Civil War towards the two questions of union and slavery. This attitude is well revealed by the correspondence[1] that passed in 1862 between Mr. Horace Greeley and President Lincoln. In a letter addressed to the President entitled " The Prayer of Twenty Millions," Mr. Greeley said :

> " On the face of this wide earth, Mr. President, there is not one disinterested, determined, intelligent champion of the Union cause who does not feel that all attempts to put down the rebellion and at the same time uphold its inciting cause (namely slavery) are preposterous and futile."

To this, President Lincoln's reply was :

> " If there be those who would not save the Union unless they could at the same time save slavery, I do not agree with them.
>
> " If there be those who would not save the Union unless they could at the same time destroy slavery, I do not agree with them.
>
> " My paramount object is to save the Union, and not either to save or to destroy slavery.
>
> " If I could save the Union without freeing any slave, I would do it. If I could save it by freeing all the slaves, I would do it—and if I could do it by freeing some and leaving others alone, I would also do that."

These were the views of President Lincoln about Negro slavery and its relation to the question of Union. They certainly throw a very different light on one who is reputed to be the liberator of the Negroes. As a matter of fact he did not believe in the emancipation of the Negroes as a categorical imperative. Obviously, the author of the famous Gettysberg oration about Government of the people, by the people and for the people, would not have minded if his statement had taken the shape of government of the black people by the white people and for the white people provided there was union. Mr. Gandhi's attitude towards Swaraj and the Untouchables resembles very much the attitude of President Lincoln towards the two questions of the Negroes and the Union. Mr. Gandhi wants Swaraj as did President Lincoln want Union. But he does not want Swaraj at the cost of disrupting the structure of Hinduism, which is what political emancipation of the Untouchables means as President Lincoln did not want to free the slaves, if it was not necessary to do so for the sake of the

[1] *Works of Abraham Lincoln*, Vol. XI, pp. xii-xiii.

Union. There is of course this difference between Mr. Gandhi and President Lincoln. President Lincoln was prepared to emancipate the Negro slaves if it was necessary to preserve the Union. Mr. Gandhi's attitude is in marked contrast. He is not prepared for the political emancipation of the Untouchables even if it was essential for winning Swaraj. Mr. Gandhi's attitude is that let Swaraj perish if the cost of it is the political freedom of the Untouchables.

Some Untouchables are probably under the impression that all this is a matter of the dead past and that Mr. Gandhi having accepted the Poona Pact cannot now oppose the political demands of the Untouchables, for, as a party to the Poona Pact, Mr. Gandhi must be assumed to have conceded that the Untouchables are a separate element in the national life of India. This is a complete misunderstanding. For there are grounds to believe that the Poona Pact has made no difference in Mr. Gandhi's view and he still maintains the same attitude to the Untouchables' claim for political safeguards as he did, at the Round Table Conference and before the Poona Pact.[1] These grounds have their foundation in the fact that when His Majesty's Government declared in 1940 that the Untouchables are a separate element in the National life of India and that their consent to the Constitution is necessary Mr. Gandhi came out with a protest. When the Viceroy Lord Linlithgow referred to the Untouchables as a separate element and said that their consent to the Constitution was necessary, Mr. Gandhi said[2] :—

> " I felt that the putting up by the Viceroy, and then the Secretary of State of want of agreement by the Congress with the Princes, the Muslim League and even the Scheduled Classes as a barrier to the British recognition of India's right to freedom was more than unjust to the Congress and the people."

* * *

> " The introduction of the Scheduled Classes in the controversy has made the unreality of the case of the British Government doubly unreal. They know that these are the special care of the Congress, and that the Congress is infinitely more capable of guarding their interests than the British Government. Moreover, the Scheduled Classes are divided into

[1] See Chapter III.

[2] *Harijan*, dated 13th October 1940.

as many castes as the Caste Hindu Society. No single Scheduled classes member could possibly and truthfully represent the innumerable castes."

The argument advanced by Mr. Gandhi is puerile. It may be pointed out that in the hurry he made in stating his opposition to the position assigned to the Scheduled Castes by the Viceroy, Mr. Gandhi forgot that if the Scheduled Castes are divided into many castes and no single caste could represent them all, the case of the Muslims and the Indian Christians is in no way different. The Muslims are divided into three groups : (1) Sunnis ; (2) Shias and (3) Momins each of which consists of many castes who interdine but do not intermarry. Indian Christians are divided into (1) Catholics, and (2) Protestants. Catholics are again sub-divided into (1) Caste Christians and (2) Non-caste Christians. Both Catholics and Protestants have castes which do not intermarry and caste Christians and Non-caste Christians do not even interdine or go to the same church. This shows that Mr. Gandhi notwithstanding his being a party to the Poona Pact is determined not to allow the Scheduled Castes being given the status of a separate element and that he is prepared to adopt any argument however desperate to justify his attitude of opposition.

In short, Mr. Gandhi is still on the war-path so far as the Untouchables are concerned. He may start the trouble over again. The time to trust him has not arrived. The Untouchables must still hold that the best way to safeguard themselves is to say 'Beware of Mr. Gandhi.'

CHAPTER XI

GANDHISM

The Doom of the Untouchables

I

HITHERTO when Indians have been talking about the reconstruction of Indian social and economic life they have been talking in terms of individualism *versus* collectivism, capitalism *versus* socialism, conservatism *versus* radicalism and so on. But quite recently, a new 'ism' has come on the Indian horizon. It is called Gandhism. It is true that very recently Mr. Gandhi had denied that there is such a thing as Gandhism. This denial is nothing more than the usual modesty, which Mr. Gandhi wears so well. It does not disprove the existence of Gandhism. There have been quite a number of books with the title of Gandhism without any protest from Mr. Gandhi. It has already caught the imagination of some people, both inside and outside India. Some have so much faith in it that they do not hesitate to offer it as an alternative to Marxism.

The followers of Gandhism, who may happen to read what is said in the foregoing pages, may well ask : Mr. Gandhi may not have done what the Untouchables expected him to do ; but does not Gandhism offer any hope to the Untouchables ? The followers of Gandhism may accuse me of remembering only the short, slow, intermittent steps taken by Mr. Gandhi for the sake of the Untouchables and of forgetting the potential length of the principles enunciated by him. I am prepared to admit that it does sometimes happen that a person who enunciates a long principle takes only a short step and that he may be forgiven for the short step in the hope that some day the principle will, by its native dynamic force, take a long step covering all who were once left out. Gandhism is in itself a very interesting subject for study. But to deal with Gandhism after having dealt with Mr. Gandhi is bound to be a tedious task and therefore my first reaction was to leave out the consideration of Gandhism and the Untouchables. At the same time, I could hardly remain indifferent to the facts that the effect of my omission to consider the subject might be very unfortunate. For

Gandhists, notwithstanding my exposure of Mr. Gandhi, might take advantage of it and continue to preach that if Mr. Gandhi has failed to solve the problem of the Untouchables still the Untouchables will find their salvation in Gandhism. It is because I wish to leave no room for such propaganda that I have overcome my original disinclination and engage upon discussion of Gandhism.

II

What is Gandhism? What does it stand for? What are its teachings about economic problem? What are its teachings about social problem?

At the outset, it is necessary to state that some Gandhists have conjured up a conception of Gandhism which is purely imaginary. According to this conception, Gandhism means return to the village and making the village self-sufficient. It makes Gandhism a mere matter of regionalism. Gandhism, I am sure, is neither so simple nor so innocent as regionalism is. Gandhism has a much bigger content than regionalism. Regionalism is a small insignificant part of it. It has a social philosophy and it has an economic philosophy. To omit to take into account the economic and social philosophy of Gandhism is to present deliberately a false picture of Gandhism. The first and foremost requisite is to present a true picture of Gandhism.

To start with Mr. Gandhi's teachings on social problem. Mr. Gandhi's views on the caste system—which constitutes the main social problem in India—were fully elaborated by him in 1921-22 in a Gujarati Journal called *Nava-Jivan*. The article[1] is written in Gujarati. I give below an English translation of his views as near as possible in his own words. Says Mr. Gandhi:

> "1. I believe that if Hindu Society has been able to stand it is because it is founded on the caste system.
>
> "2. The seeds of Swaraj are to be found in the caste system. Different castes are like different sections of military division. Each division is working for the good of the whole . . .
>
> "3. A community which can create the caste system must be said to possess unique power of organization.

[1] It is reprinted in Vol. II of the series called *Gandhi Sikshan* as No. 18.

"4. Caste has a ready made means for spreading primary education. Every caste can take the responsibility for the education of the children of the Caste. Caste has a political basis. It can work as an electorate for a representative body. Caste can perform judicial functions by electing persons to act as judges to decide disputes among members of the same caste. With castes it is easy to raise a defence force by requiring each caste to raise a brigade.

"5. I believe that interdining or intermarriage are not necessary for promoting national unity. That dining together creates friendship is contrary to experience. If this was true there would have been no war in Europe . . . Taking food is as dirty an act as answering the call of nature. The only difference is that after answering call of nature we get peace while after eating food we get discomfort. Just as we perform the act of answering the call of nature in seclusion so also the act of taking food must also be done in seclusion.

"6. In India children of brothers do not intermarry. Do they cease to love because they do not intermarry? Among the Vaishnavas many women are so orthodox that they will not eat with the members of the family nor will they drink water from a common water pot. Have they no love? The Caste system cannot be said to be bad because it does not allow interdining or intermarriage between different Castes."

"7. Caste is another name for control. Caste puts a limit on enjoyment. Caste does not allow a person to transgress caste limits in pursuit of his enjoyment. That is the meaning of such caste restrictions as interdining and intermarriage.

"8. To destroy caste system and adopt Western European social system means that Hindus must give up the principle of hereditary occupation which is the soul of the caste system. Hereditary principle is an eternal principle. To change it is to create disorder. I have no use for a Brahmin if I cannot call him a Brahmin for my life. It will be a chaos if every day a Brahmin is to be changed into a Shudra and a Shudra is to be changed into a Brahmin.

"9. The caste system is a natural order of society. In India it has been given a religious coating. Other countries not having understood the utility of the Caste System it existed only in a loose condition and consequently those countries have not derived from Caste system the same degree of advantage which India has derived.

These being my views I am opposed to all those who are out to destroy the Caste System."

In 1922, Mr. Gandhi was a defender of the caste system. Pursuing the inquiry, one comes across a somewhat critical view of the caste system by Mr. Gandhi in the year 1925. This is what Mr. Gandhi said on 3rd February 1925 :—

"I gave support to caste because it stands for restraint. But at present caste does not mean restraint, it means limitations. Restraint is glorious and helps to achieve freedom. But limitation is like chain. It binds. There is nothing commendable in castes as they exist to-day. They are contrary to the tenets of the shastras. The number of castes is infinite and there is a bar against intermarriage. This is not a condition of elevation. It is a state of fall."

In reply to the question : What is the way out ? Mr. Gandhi said :

"The best remedy is that small castes should fuse themselves into one big caste. There should be four such big castes so that we may reproduce the old system of four varnas."

In short, in 1925 Mr. Gandhi became an upholder of the Varna system.

The old *Varna* system prevalent in ancient India had the society divided into four orders : (1) Brahmins, whose occupation was learning ; (2) Kshatriyas, whose occupation was warfare ; (3) Vaishyas, whose occupation was trade and (4) Shudras, whose occupation was service of the other classes. Is Mr. Gandhi's *Varna* system the same as this old *Varna* system of the orthodox Hindus ? Mr. Gandhi explained his *Varna* system in the following terms[1] :

"1. I believe that the divisions into *Varna* is based on birth.

"2. There is nothing in the *Varna* system which stands in the way of the *Shudra* acquiring learning or studying military art of offence or defence. Contra it is open to a Kshatriya to serve. The *Varna* system is no bar to him. What the *Varna* system enjoins is that a Shudra will not make learning a way of earning a living. Nor will a Kshatriya adopt service as a way of earning a living. [Similarly a Brahmin may learn the art of war or trade. But he must not make them a way of earning his living. Contra a Vaishya may acquire learning or may cultivate the art of war. But he must not make them a way of earning his living.]

[1] The extracts are taken from an article by Mr. Gandhi on the subject and is reproduced in the *Varna Vayavastha*—a book which contains Mr. Gandhi's writings in original Gujarati.

"3. The *varna* system is connected with the way of earning a living. There is no harm if a person belonging to one *varna* acquires the knowledge or science and art specialized in by persons belonging to other *varnas*. But as far as the way of earning his living is concerned he must follow the occupation of the *varna* to which he belongs which means he must follow the hereditary profession of his forefathers.

"4. The object of the *varna* system is to prevent competition and class struggle and class war. I believe in the *varna* system because it fixes the duties and occupations of persons.

"5. *Varna* means the determination of a man's occupation before he is born.

"6. In the *Varna* system no man has any liberty to choose his occupation. His occupation is determined for him by heredity."

Turning to the field of economic life, Mr. Gandhi stands for two ideals.

One of these is the opposition to machinery. As early as 1921, Mr. Gandhi gave vent to his dislike for machinery. Writing in the *Young India* of 19th January 1921, Mr. Gandhi said :

"Do I want to put back the hand of the clock of progress ? Do I want to replace the mills by hand-spinning and hand-weaving ? Do I want to replace the railway by the country-cart ? Do I want to destroy machinery altogether ? These questions have been asked by some journalists and public men. My answer is : I would not weep over the disappearance of machinery or consider it a calamity."

His opposition to machinery is well evidenced by his idolization of *charkha* (the spinning wheel) and by insistence upon hand-spinning and hand-weaving. His opposition to machinery and his love for *charkha* are not a matter of accident. They are a matter of his philosophy of life. This philosophy Mr. Gandhi took special occasion to propound in his presidential address at the Kathiawad Political Conference held on 8th January 1925. This is what Mr. Gandhi said :

"Nations are tired of the worship of lifeless machines multiplied *ad infinitum*. We are destroying the matchless living machines, viz., our own bodies by leaving them to rust and trying to substitute lifeless machinery for them. It is a law of God that the body must be fully worked and utilised. We dare not ignore it. The spinning wheel is the auspicious symbol of Sharir Yajna—body labour. He who eats his food without offering this sacrifice steals it. By giving up this sacrifice we became traitors to the country and banged the door in the face of the Goddess of Fortune."

Anyone who has read Mr. Gandhi's booklet on *Hind Swaraj* (Indian Home Rule) will know that Mr. Gandhi is against modern civilization. The book was first published in 1908. But there has been no change in his ideology. Writing in 1921 Mr. Gandhi said[1]:

> "The booklet is a severe condemnation of 'modern civilization.' It was written in 1908. My conviction is deeper to-day than ever. I feel that, if India would discard 'Modern civilization' she can only gain by doing so."

In Mr. Gandhi's view [2]:

> "Western civilization is the creation of satan."

The second ideal of Mr. Gandhi is the elimination of class-war and even class struggle in the relationship between employers and employees and between landlords and tenants. Mr. Gandhi's views on the relationship between employers and employees were set forth by him in an article on the subject, which appeared in the *Nava-Jivan* of the 8th June 1921 and from which the following is an extract:

> "Two paths are open before India, either to introduce the Western principle of 'Might is right' or to uphold the Eastern principle that truth alone conquers, that truth knows no mishap, that the strong and the weak have alike a right to secure justice. The choice is to begin with the labouring class. Should the labourers obtain an increment in their wages by violence? Even if that be possible, they cannot resort to anything like violence, howsoever legitimate may be their claims. To use violence for securing rights may seem an easy path, but it proves to be thorny in the long run. Those who live by sword die also by sword. The swimmer often dies by drowning. Look at Europe. No one seems to be happy there, for not one is contented. The labourer does not trust the capitalist and the capitalist has no faith in the labourer. Both have a sort of vigour and strength but even the bulls have it. They fight to the very bitter end. All motion is not progress. We have got no reason to believe that the people of Europe are progressing. Their possession of wealth does not argue the possession of any moral or spiritual qualities.

* * *

---

[1] *Young India*, 26th January 1921.
[2] *Dharma Manthan*, p. 65.

"What shall we do then? The labourers in Bombay made a fine stand. I was not in a position to know all the facts. But this much I could see that they could fight in a better way. The millowner may be wholly in the wrong. In the struggle between capital and labour, it may be generally said that more often than not the capitalists are in the wrong box. But when labour comes fully to realise its strength, I know it can become more tyrannical than capital. The millowners will have to work on the terms dictated by labour, if the latter could command intelligence of the former. It is clear, however, that labour will never attain to that intelligence. If it does, labour will cease to be labour and become itself the master. The capitalists do not fight on the strength of money alone. They do possess intelligence and tact.

"The question before us is this: When the labourers, remaining what they are, develop a certain consciousness, what should be their course? It would be suicidal if the labourers rely upon their numbers or brute-force, i.e., violence. By so doing, they will do harm to industries in the country. If, on the other hand, they take their stand on pure justice and suffer in their person to secure it, not only will they always succeed but they will reform their masters, develop industries and both master and men will be as members of one and the same family."

Referring to the same theme on another occasion Mr. Gandhi said[1]:

"Nor was it otherwise before. India's history is not one of strained relations between capital and labour."

Particularly noteworthy are the views of Mr. Gandhi on strike as a weapon in the hand of the workers to improve their economic condition. Mr. Gandhi says[2]:

"Speaking, therefore, as one having handled large successful strikes, I repeat the following maxims, already stated in these pages, for the guidance of all strike leaders:

(1) There should be *no strike without a real grievance.*

(2) There should be no strike, if the persons concerned are not able to support themselves out of their own savings or by engaging in some temporary occupation, such as carding, spinning and weaving. *Strikers should never depend upon public subscriptions or other charity.*

(3) *Strikers must fix an unalterable minimum demand, and declare it before embarking upon their strike.*

[1] *Young India*, February 23, 1922.

[2] *Young India*, 11th August, 1921. Italics not in the original.

"A strike may fail in spite of a just grievance and the ability of strikers to hold out indefinitely, if there are workers to replace them. A wise man, therefore, will not strike for increase of wages or other comforts, if he feels that he can be easily replaced. But a philanthropic or patriotic man will strike in spite of supply being greater than the demand, when he feels for and wishes to associate himself with his neighbour's distress. Needless to say, there is no room in a civil strike of the nature described by me for violence in the shape of intimidation, incendiarism or otherwise . . . Judged by the tests suggested by me, it is clear that friends of the strikers could never have advised them to apply for or receive Congress or any other public funds for their support. The value of the strikers' sympathy was diminished to the extent, that they received or accepted financial aid. The merit of a sympathetic strike lies in the inconvenience and the loss suffered by the sympathisers."

Mr. Gandhi's view on the relationship between landlords and tenants were expounded by him in the *Young India* of 18th May 1921 in the form of instructions[1] to the tenants of U.P. who had risen against their landlords. Mr. Gandhi said :

"Whilst the U. P. Government is crossing the bounds of propriety, and intimidating people, there is little doubt that the Kisans too are not making wise use of their newly found power. In several Zamindaries, they are said to have overstepped the mark, taken the law into their own hands and to have become impatient of anybody who would not do as they wish. They are abusing social boycott and are turning it into an instrument of violence. They are reported to have stopped the supply of water, barber and other paid services to their Zamindars in some instances and even suspended payment of the rent due to them. The Kisan movement has received an impetus from Non-co-operation but it is anterior to and independent of it. *Whilst we will not hesitate to advise the Kisans when the moment comes, to suspend payment of taxes to Government, it is not contemplated that at any stage of Non-co-operation we would seek to deprive the Zamindars of their rent. The Kisan movement must be confined to the improvement of status of the Kisans and the betterment of the relations between the Zamindars and them.* The Kisans must be advised scrupulously to abide by the terms of their agreement with the Zamindars, whether such is written or inferred from custom. Where a custom or even a written contract is bad, they may not try

---

[1] Italics are not in the original. Kisan means a tenant and zamindar means landlord.

to uproot it by violence or without previous reference to the Zamindars. In every case there should be a friendly discussion with the Zamindars and an attempt made to arrive at a settlement."

Mr. Gandhi does not wish to hurt the propertied class. He is even opposed to a campaign against them. He has no passion for economic equality. Referring to the propertied class Mr. Gandhi said quite recently that he does not wish to destroy the hen that lays the golden egg. His solution for the economic conflict between the owners and the workers, between the rich and the poor, between the landlords and the tenants and between the employers and the employees is very simple. The owners need not deprive themselves of their property. All that they need do is to declare themselves Trustees for the poor. Of course, the Trust is to be a voluntary one carrying only a spiritual obligation.

III

Is there anything new in the Gandhian analysis of economic ills? Are the economics of Gandhism sound? What hope does Gandhism hold out to the common man, to the down and out? Does it promise him a better life, a life of joy and culture, a life of freedom, not merely freedom from want but freedom to rise, to grow to the full stature which his capacities can reach?

There is nothing new in the Gandhian analysis of economic ills, in so far as it attributes them to machinery and the civilization that is built upon it. That machinery and modern civilization help to concentrate management and control into relatively few hands, and with the aid of banking and credit facilitate the transfer into still fewer hands of all materials and factories and mills in which millions are bled white in order to support huge industries thousands of miles away from their cottages, or that machinery and modern civilization cause deaths, maimings and cripplings far in excess of the corresponding injuries by war, and are responsible for disease and physical deterioration due directly and indirectly to the development of large cities with their smoke, dirt, noise, foul air, lack of sunshine and out-door life, slums, prostitution and unnatural living which they bring about, are all old and worn out arguments. There is nothing new in them. Gandhism is merely repeating the views of Rousseau, Ruskin, Tolstoy and their school.

The ideas which go to make up Gandhism are just primitive. It is a return to nature, to animal life. Their only merit is their simplicity. As there is always a large corps of simple people who are attracted by them, such simple ideas do not die, and there is always some simpleton to preach them. There is, however, no doubt that the practical instincts of men—which seldom go wrong—have found them unfruitful and which society in search of progress has thought it best to reject.

The economics of Gandhism are hopelessly fallacious. The fact that machinery and modern civilization have produced many evils may be admitted. But these evils are no argument against them. For the evils are not due to machinery and modern civilization. They are due to wrong social organization, which has made private property and pursuit of personal gain, matters of absolute sanctity. If machinery and civilization have not benefited everybody, the remedy is not to condemn machinery and civilization but to alter the organization of society so that the benefits will not be usurped by the few but will accrue to all.

In Gandhism, the common man has no hope. It treats man as an animal and no more. It is true that man shares the constitution and functions of animals, nutritive, reproductive, etc. But these are not distinctively human functions. The distinctively human function is reason, the purpose of which is to enable man to observe, meditate, cogitate, study and discover the beauties of the Universe and enrich his life and control the animal elements in his life. Man thus occupies the highest place in the scheme of animate existence. If this is true what is the conclusion that follows? The conclusion that follows is that while the ultimate goal of a brute's life is reached once his physical appetites are satisfied, the ultimate goal of man's existence is not reached unless and until he has fully cultivated his mind. In short, what divides the brute from man is culture. Culture is not possible for the brute, but it is essential for man. That being so, the aim of human society must be to enable every person to lead a life of culture, which means the cultivation of mind as distinguished from the satisfaction of mere physical wants. How can this happen?

Both for society as well as for individual there is always a gulf between merely living and living worthily. In order that one may live worthily one must first live. The time and energy spent upon mere life, upon gaining of subsistence detracts from that available for activities of a distinctively human nature and which go to make up a life of culture. How then can a life of culture be made possible ? It is not possible unless there is sufficient leisure. For, it is only when there is leisure that a person is free to devote himself to a life of culture. The problem of all problems, which human society has to face, is how to provide leisure to every individual. What does leisure mean ? Leisure means the lessening of the toil and effort necessary for satisfying the physical wants of life. How can leisure be made possible ? Leisure is quite impossible unless some means are found whereby the toil required for producing goods necessary to satisfy human needs is lessened. What can lessen such toil ? Only when machine takes the place of man. There is no other means of producing leisure. Machinery and modern civilization are thus indispensable for emancipating man from leading the life of a brute, and for providing him with leisure and for making a life of culture possible. The man who condemns machinery and modern civilization simply does not understand their purpose and the ultimate aim which human society must strive to achieve.

Gandhism may be well suited to a society which does not accept democracy as its ideal. A society which does not believe in democracy may be indifferent to machinery and the civilization based upon it. But a democratic society cannot. The former may well content itself with a life of leisure and culture for the few and a life of toil and drudgery for the many. But a democratic society must assure a life of leisure and culture to each one of its citizens. If the above analysis is correct then the slogan of a democratic society must be machinery, and more machinery, civilization and more civilization. Under Gandhism the common man must keep on toiling ceaselessly for a pittance and remain a brute. In short, Gandhism with its call of back to nature, means back to nakedness, back to squalor, back to poverty and back to ignorance for the vast mass of the people.

The division of life into separate functions and of society into separate classes may not be altogether obliterated. In spite of many social and economic changes and in spite of the abolition of legal serfdom, legal slavery and the spread of the notion of democracy, with the extension of science, of general education through books, newspapers, travel and general intercourse in schools and factories there remains and perhaps will remain enough cleavage in society into a learned and an ignorant class, a leisure and a labouring class.

But Gandhism is not satisfied with only *notional* class distinctions. Gandhism insists upon class structure. It regards the class structure of society and also the income structure as sacrosanct with the consequent distinctions of rich and poor, high and low, owners and workers, as permanent parts of social organization. From the point of view of social consequences, nothing can be more pernicious. Psychologically, class structure sets in motion influences which are harmful to both the classes. There is no common plane on which the privileged and the subject classes can meet. There is no endosmosis, no give and take of life's hopes and experiences. The social and moral evils of this separation to the subject class are of course real and obvious. It educates them into slaves and creates all the psychological complex which follows from a slave mentality. But those affecting the privileged class, though less material and less perceptible, are equally real. The isolation and exclusiveness following upon the class structure creates in the privileged classes the anti-social spirit of a gang. It feels it has interests 'of its own' which it makes its prevailing purpose to protect against everybody even against the interests of the State. It makes their culture sterile, their art showy, their wealth luminous and their manners fastidious. Practically speaking in a class structure there is, on the one hand, tyranny, vanity, pride, arrogance, greed, selfishness and on the other, insecurity, poverty, degradation, loss of liberty, self-reliance, independence, dignity and self-respect. Democratic society cannot be indifferent to such consequences. But Gandhism does not mind these consequences in the least. It is not enough to say that Gandhism is not satisfied with mere class distinctions. It is not enough to say that Gandhism believes in a class structure. Gandhism stands for more than that. A class structure which is a faded, jejune, effete thing—a mere sentimentality, a mere skeleton is not what Gandhism wants. It wants class structure to function as a living faith. In this there is nothing to be surprised at. For, class structure in Gandhism is not a mere accident. It is its official doctrine.

The idea of trusteeship, which Gandhism proposes as a panacea and by which the moneyed classes will hold their properties in trust for the poor, is the most ridiculous part of it. All that one can say about it is that if anybody else had propounded it the author would have been laughed at as a silly fool, who had not known the hard realities of life and was deceiving the servile classes by telling them that a little dose of moral rearmament to the propertied classes—those who by their insatiable cupidity and indomitable arrogance have made and will always make this world a vale of tears for the toiling millions—will recondition them to such an extent that they will be able to withstand the temptation to misuse the tremendous powers which the class structure gives them over servile classes.

IV

The social ideal of Gandhism is either *caste* or *varna*. Though it may be difficult to say which, there can be no doubt that the social ideal of Gandhism is not democracy. For, whether one takes for comparison *caste* or *varna* both are fundamentally opposed to democracy. It would have been something if the defence of caste system which Gandhism offers was strong and honest. But his defence of the caste system is the most insensible piece of rhetoric one can think of. Examine Mr. Gandhi's arguments in support of caste and it will be found that everyone of them is specious, if not puerile.

To run through the arguments summarized earlier in this Chapter[1]. The first three arguments call for pity. That the Hindu Society has been able to stand while others have died out or disappeared is hardly a matter for congratulation. If it has survived it is not because of caste but because the foreigner, who conquered the Hindus did not find it necessary to kill them wholesale. There is no honour in mere survival. What matters is the plane of survival. One can survive by unconditional surrender. One can survive by beating a cowardly retreat and one can survive by fighting. On what plane have the Hindus survived? If they can be said to have survived after fighting and beating their enemies the virtue ascribed to the caste system by Mr. Gandhi could be admitted. The history of the Hindus has been one of surrender—abject

[1] See pages 286-288.

surrender. It is true, others have surrendered to their invaders. But in their case surrender is followed by a revolt against the foreign ruler. The Hindus have not only never withstood the onslaught of the foreign invader, but they have never even shown the capacity to organize a rebellion to throw off the foreign yoke. On the other hand, the Hindus have tried to make slavery comfortable. On this, one may well argue the contrary namely that this helpless condition of the Hindus is due entirely to the caste system.

Argument in para 4 of Mr. Gandhi's statement is plausible. But it cannot be said that caste is the only machinery for discharging such functions as the spread of primary education or the judicial settlement of disputes. Caste is probably the worst instrument for the discharge of such functions. It can be easily influenced and easily corrupted. Such functions have been discharged in other countries much better than they have been in India although they have had no caste system. As to using the caste as basis for raising military units, the idea is simply fantastic. Under the occupational theory underlying the caste system this is unthinkable. Mr. Gandhi knows that not a single caste in his own Province of Gujarat has ever raised a military unit. It did not do it in the present World War. But it did not do so even in the last World War, when Mr. Gandhi toured through Gujarat as a recruiting agent of British Imperialism. In fact, under the caste system a general mobilization of the people for defence is impossible since mobilization requires a general liquidation of the occupational theory underlying the caste system.

Arguments contained in paras 5 and 6 are as stupid as they are revolting. The argument in para 5 is hardly a good argument. It is quite true the family is an ideal unit in which every member is charged with love and affection for another member although there is no intermarriage among members of a family. It may even be conceded that in a Vaishnava family members of the family do not interdine and yet they are full of love and affection for one another. What does all this prove? It does not prove that interdining and intermarrying are not necessary for establishing fraternity. What it proves is that where there are other means of maintaining fraternity —such as consciousness of family tie—interdining and intermarriage are not necessary. But it cannot be denied that where—as in the caste system—no binding force exists intermarriage and interdining are absolutely essential. There is no analogy between family and caste. Inter-caste dinner and inter-caste marriage are necessary because there are no other means of binding the different castes together while in the case of a family there exist other forces to bind them together. Those who have insisted upon the ban against interdining and intermarriage have treated it as a question of relative values. They have never elevated it to the level of a question of absolute value. Mr. Gandhi is the first one to do it. Interdining is bad and even if it was capable of producing good it should not be resorted to and why? Because eating is a filthy act, as filthy as answering the call of nature! The caste system has been defended by others. But this is the first time I have seen such an extraordinary, if not a shocking, argument used to support it. Even the orthodox may say, "Save us from Mr. Gandhi." It shows what a deep-dyed Hindu Mr. Gandhi is. He has outdone the most orthodox of orthodox Hindus. It is not enough to say that it is an argument of a cave man. It is really an argument of a mad man.

The argument in favour of the caste system outlined in para 7 is not worth much in terms of building up moral strength. The caste system no doubt prohibits a man from satisfying his lust for a woman who is not of his caste. The caste system no doubt prohibits a man from satisfying his craving for food cooked in the house of a man who is not of his caste. If morality consists of observing restraints without regard to the sense or sensibility of restraints then the caste system may be admitted to be a moral system. But Mr. Gandhi does not see that these easy restraints are more than balanced by the vast liberties permitted by Hinduism. For, Hinduism places no restraint upon a man marrying hundred women and keeping hundred prostitutes within the ambit of his caste. Nor does it stop him from indulging in his appetite with his castemen to any degree.

The argument in para 8 begs the whole question. The hereditary system may be good or may not be good. It may be agreeable to some. It may be disagreeable to others. Why elevate it into an official doctrine? Why make it compulsory? In Europe, it is not an official doctrine and it is not compulsory. It is left to the choice of an individual most of whom do follow the profession of their ancestors and some don't. Who can say that compulsory system has worked better than the voluntary system? If a comparison of the economic condition of the people in India and the people of Europe is any guide there would be very few rationally-minded people who would be found to support the caste system on this ground. As to the difficulty in changing nomenclature to keep pace with frequent changes in occupation it is only artificial. It arises out of the supposed necessity of having labels for designating persons following a particular profession. The class labels are quite unnecessary and could well be abolished altogether without causing difficulty. Besides, what happens to-day in India? Men's callings and their class labels are not in accord. A Brahmin sells shoes. Nobody is disturbed because he is not called a Chamar. A Chamar becomes an officer of the State. Nobody is upset because he is not called a Brahmin. The whole argument is based on a misunderstanding. What matters to society is not the label by which the individual's class is known but the service he offers.

The last argument set out in para 9 is one of the most astounding arguments I have heard in favour of the caste system. It is historically false. No one who knows anything about the Manu Smriti can say that the caste system is a natural system. What does the Manu Smriti show? It shows that the caste system is a legal system maintained at the point of a bayonet. If it has survived it is due to (1) prevention of the masses from the possession of arms; (2) denying to the masses the right to education and (3) depriving the masses of the right to property. The caste system far from natural is really an imposition by the ruling classes upon the servile classes.

That Mr. Gandhi changed over from the caste system to the *varna* system does not make the slightest difference to the charge that Gandhism is opposed to democracy. In the first place, the idea of *varna* is the parent of the idea of *caste*. If the idea of caste is a pernicious idea it is entirely because of the viciousness of the idea of *varna*. Both are evil ideas and it matters very little whether one believes in *varna* or in *caste*. The idea of *varna* was most mercilessly attacked by the Buddhists who did not believe in it. Orthodox or the Sanatan Vedic Hindus had no rational defence to offer. All that they could say was that it was founded on the authority of the Vedas and that as the Vedas were infallible so was the *varna* system. This argument was not enough to save the *varna* system against the rationalism of the Buddhists. If the idea of the *varna* survived it was because of the Bhagvat Gita, which gave a philosophical foundation to the *varna* system by arguing that the *varna* was based on the innate qualities of man. The Bhagvat Gita made use of the Sankhya philosophy to bolster and buttress the *varna* idea which would have otherwise petered away by making sense of a thing that is absolute nonsense. Bhagvat Gita had done enough mischief by giving a fresh lease of life to the *varna* system by basing it upon a new and plausible foundation, namely, that of innate qualities.

The *varna* system of the Bhagvat Gita has at least two merits. It does not say that it is based on birth. Indeed, it makes a special point that each man's *varna* is fixed according to his innate qualities. It does not say that the occupation of the son shall be that of the father. It says that the profession of a person shall be according to his innate qualities, the profession of the father according to the father's innate quality and that of the son according to the son's innate qualities. But Mr. Gandhi has given a new interpretation of the *varna* system. He has changed it out of recognition. Under the old orthodox interpretation, *caste* connoted hereditary occupation but *varna* did not. Mr. Gandhi by his own whim has given a new connotation to the *varna*. With Mr. Gandhi *varna* is determined by birth and the profession of a *varna* is determined by the principle of heredity so that *varna* is merely another name for *caste*. That Mr. Gandhi changed from *caste* to *varna* does not indicate the growth of any new revolutionary ideology. The genius of Mr. Gandhi is elvish, always and throughout. He has all the precocity of an elf with no little of its outward guise. Like an elf he can never grow up and grow out of the caste ideology.

Mr. Gandhi sometimes speaks on social and economic subjects as though he was a blushing Red. Those who will study Gandhism will not be deceived by the occasional aberrations of Mr. Gandhi in favour of democracy and against capitalism. For, Gandhism is in no sense a revolutionary creed. It is conservatism in excelsis. So far as India is concerned, it is a reactionary creed blazoning on its banner the call of Return to Antiquity. Gandhism aims at the resuscitation and reanimation of India's dread, dying past.

V

Gandhism is a paradox. It stands for freedom from foreign domination, which means the destruction of the existing political structure of the country. At the same time, it seeks to maintain intact a social structure which permits the domination of one class by another on a hereditary basis which means a perpetual domination of one class by another. What is the explanation of this paradox? Is it a part of a strategy by Mr. Gandhi to win the whole-hearted support of the Hindus, orthodox and unorthodox, to the campaign of Swaraj? If it is the latter, can Gandhism be regarded as honest and sincere? Be that as it may there are two features of Gandhism, which are revealing but to which unfortunately no attention has so far been paid. Whether they will make Gandhism more acceptable than Marxism is another matter. But as they do help to distinguish Gandhism from Marxism, it may be well to refer to them.

The first special feature of Gandhism is that its philosophy helps those who want to keep what they have and to prevent those who have not from getting what they have a right to get. No one who examines the Gandhian attitude to strikes, the Gandhian reverence for caste and the Gandhian doctrine of Trusteeship by the rich for the benefit of the poor can deny that this is an upshot of Gandhism. Whether this is the calculated result of a deliberate design or whether it is a matter of accident may be open to argument. But the fact remains that Gandhism is the philosophy of the well-to-do and the leisure class.

The second special feature of Gandhism is to delude people into accepting their misfortunes by presenting them as best of good fortunes. One or two illustrations will suffice to bring out the truth of this statement.

The Hindu sacred law penalized the Shudras (Hindus of the fourth class) from acquiring wealth. It is a law of enforced poverty unknown in any other part of the world. What does Gandhism do? It does not lift the ban. It blesses the Shudra for his moral courage to give up property. It is well worth quoting Mr. Gandhi's own words. Here they are[1]:

> "The Shudra who only serves (the higher caste) as a matter of religious duty, and who will never own any property, who

[1] Quoted from *Varna Vyavastha*, p. 51

indeed has not even the ambition to own anything, is deserving of thousand obeisances . . . The very Gods will shower down flowers on him.

Another illustration in support is the attitude of Gandhism towards the scavenger. The sacred law of the Hindus lays down that a scavenger's progeny shall live by scavenging. Under Hinduism scavenging was not a matter of choice, it was a matter of force. What does Gandhism do? It seeks to perpetuate this system by praising scavenging as the noblest service to society! Let me quote Mr. Gandhi: As a President of a Conference of the Untouchables, Mr. Gandhi said[1]:

"I do not want to attain *Moksha.* I do not want to be reborn. But if I have to be reborn, I should be born an untouchable, so that I may share their sorrows, sufferings and the affronts levelled at them, in order that I may endeavour to free myself and them from that miserable condition. I, therefore prayed that if I should be born again, I should do so not as a Brahmin, Kshatriya, Vaishya, or Shudra, but as an Atishudra...

"I love scavenging. In my Ashram, an eighteen years old Brahmin lad is doing the scavenger's work in order to teach the Ashram scavenger cleanliness. The lad is no reformer. He was born and bred in orthodoxy . . . But he felt that his accomplishments were incomplete until he had become also a perfect sweeper, and that, if he wanted the Ashram sweeper to do his work well, he must do it himself and set an example.

"You should realize that you are cleaning Hindu Society."

Can there be a worse example of false propaganda than this attempt of Gandhism to perpetuate evils which have been deliberately imposed by one class over another? If Gandhism preached the rule of poverty for all and not merely for the Shudra the worst that could be said about it is that it is a mistaken idea. But why preach it as good for one class only? Why appeal to the worst of human failings, namely, pride and vanity in order to make him voluntarily accept what on a rational basis he would resent as a cruel discrimination against him? What is the use of telling the scavenger that even a Brahmin is prepared to do scavenging when it is clear that according to the Hindu Shastras and the Hindu notions even if a Brahmin did scavenging he would never be subject to the disabilities of one who is a born scavenger? For in India a man is not a scavenger because of his work. He is a scavenger

[1] *Young India*, 27th April 1921.

because of his birth irrespective of the question whether he does scavenging or not. If Gandhism preached that scavenging is a noble profession with the object of inducing those who refuse to engage in it, one could understand it. But why appeal to the scavenger's pride and vanity in order to induce him and him only to keep on to scavenging[1] by telling him that scavenging is a noble profession and that he need not be ashamed of it? To preach that poverty is good for the Shudra and for none else, to preach that scavenging is good for the Untouchables and for none else and to make them accept these onerous impositions as voluntary purposes of life, by appeal to their failings is an outrage and a cruel joke on the helpless classes which none but Mr. Gandhi can perpetuate with equanimity and impunity. In this connection one is reminded of the words of Voltaire who in repudiation of an 'ism' very much like Gandhism said: "Oh! mockery to say to people that the suffering of some brings joy to others and works good to the whole! What solace is it to a dying man to know that from his decaying body a thousand worms will come into life?"

Criticism apart, this is the technique of Gandhism, to make wrongs done appear to the very victim as though they were his privileges. If there is an 'ism' which has made full use of religion as an opium to lull the people into false beliefs and false security, it is Gandhism. Following Shakespeare, one can well say: Plausibility! Ingenuity! Thy name is Gandhism.

VI

Such is Gandhism. Having known what is Gandhism the answer to the question, 'Should Gandhism become the law of the land what would be the lot of the Untouchables under it?' cannot require much scratching of the brain. How would it compare with the lot of the lowest Hindu? Enough has been said to show what would be his lot should the Gandhian social order come into being. In so far as the lowest Hindu and the Untouchable belong to the same disinherited class, the Untouchable's lot cannot be better. If anything it might easily be worse. Because, in India even the lowest man

[1] Some of the Provinces of India have laws which make refusal by a scavenger to do scavenging a crime for which he can be tried and punished by a criminal court.

among the Caste Hindus—why even the aboriginal and the Hill Tribe man—though educationally and economically not very much above the Untouchables is still superior to the Untouchables. It is not that he regards himself as superior to the Untouchables. The Hindu society accepts his claim to superiority over the Untouchables. The Untouchable will therefore continue to suffer the worst fate as he does now namely, in prosperity he will be the last to be employed and in depression the first to be fired.

What does Gandhism do to relieve the Untouchables from this fate? Gandhism professes to abolish Untouchability. That is hailed as the greatest virtue of Gandhism. But what does this virtue amount to in actual life? To assess the value of this anti-Untouchability which is regarded as a very big element in Gandhism, it is necessary to understand fully the scope of Mr. Gandhi's programme for the removal of Untouchability. Does it mean anything more than that the Hindus will not mind touching the Untouchables? Does it mean the removal of the ban on the right of the Untouchables to education? It would be better to take the two questions separately.

To start with the first question. Mr. Gandhi does not say that a Hindu should not take a bath after touching the Untouchables. If Mr. Gandhi does not object to it as a purification of pollution then it is difficult to see how Untouchability can be said to vanish by touching the Untouchables. Untouchability centres round the idea of pollution by contact and purification by bath to remove the pollution. Does it mean social assimilation of the Untouchables with the Hindus? Mr. Gandhi has most categorically stated that removal of Untouchability does not mean inter-dining or intermarriage between the Hindus and the Untouchables. Mr. Gandhi's anti-Untouchability means that the Untouchables will be classed as Shudras instead of being classed as Ati-Shudras.[1] There is nothing more in it. Mr. Gandhi has not considered the question whether the old Shudras will accept the new Shudras into their fold. If they don't then the removal of Untouchability is a senseless proposition for it will still keep the Untouchables as a separate social category. Mr. Gandhi probably knows that the abolition of Untouchability will not

[1] *Young India*, 5th February 1925.

bring about the assimilation of the Untouchables by the Shudras. That seems to be the reason why Mr. Gandhi himself has given a new and a different name to the Untouchables. The new name registers by anticipation what is likely to be the fact. By calling the Untouchables *Harijans*, Mr. Gandhi has killed two birds with one stone. He has shown that assimilation of the Untouchables by the Shudras is not possible. He has also by his new name counteracted assimilation and made it impossible.

Regarding the second question, it is true that Gandhism is prepared to remove the old ban placed by the Hindu Shastras on the right of the Untouchables to education and permit them to acquire knowledge and learning. Under Gandhism the Untouchables may study law, they may study medicine, they may study engineering or anything else they may fancy. So far so good. But will the Untouchables be free to make use of their knowledge and learning? Will they have the right to choose their profession? Can they adopt the career of lawyer, doctor or engineer? To these questions the answer which Gandhism gives is an emphatic 'no.[1]' The Untouchables must follow their hereditary professions. That those occupations are unclean is no excuse: That before the occupation became hereditary it was the result of force and not volition does not matter. The argument of Gandhism is that what is once settled is settled for ever even if it was wrongly settled. Under Gandhism the Untouchables are to be eternal scavengers. There is no doubt that the Untouchables would much prefer the orthodox system of Untouchability. A compulsory state of ignorance imposed upon the Untouchables by the Hindu Shastras made scavenging bearable. But Gandhism which compels an educated Untouchable to do scavenging is nothing short of cruelty. The grace in Gandhism is a curse in its worst form. The virtue of the anti-Untouchability plank in Gandhism is quite illusory. There is no substance in it.

VII

What else is there in Gandhism which the Untouchables can accept as opening a way for their ultimate salvation? Barring this illusory campaign against Untouchability, Gandhism is

---

[1] See *supra*, pages 286-88 for Mr. Gandhi's views on the subject.

simply another form of Sanatanism which is the ancient name for militant orthodox Hinduism. What is there in Gandhism which is not to be found in orthodox Hinduism ? There is caste in Hinduism, there is caste in Gandhism. Hinduism believes in the law of hereditary profession, so does Gandhism. Hinduism enjoins cow-worship. So does Gandhism. Hinduism upholds the law of *karma*, predestination of man's condition in this world, so does Gandhism. Hinduism accepts the authority of the Shastras. So does Gandhism. Hinduism believes in *avatars* or incarnations of God. So does Gandhism. Hinduism believes in idols. So does Gandhism.[1] All that Gandhism has done is to find a philosophic justification for Hinduism and its dogmas. Hinduism is bald in the sense that it is just a set of rules which bear on their face the appearance of a crude and cruel system. Gandhism supplies the philosophy which smoothens its surface and gives it the appearance of decency and respectability and so alters it and embellishes it as to make it even attractive. What philosophy does Gandhism propound to cover the nudity of Hinduism ? This philosophy can be put in a nutshell. It is a philosophy which says : " All that is in Hinduism is well, all that is in Hinduism is necessary for public good." Those who are familiar with Voltaire's *Candide* will recognize that it is the philosophy of Master Pangiloss and recall the mockery Voltaire made of it. The Hindus are of course pleased with it. No doubt it suits them and accords with their interest. Prof. Radhakrishnan—whether out of genuine feeling or out of sycophancy we need not stop to inquire—has gone to the length of describing Mr. Gandhi as 'God on earth.' What do the Untouchables understand this to mean ? To them it means : " This God by name Gandhi came to console an afflicted race : He saw India and changed it not saying all is well and will be, if the Hindus will only fulfil the law of caste. He told the afflicted race, 'I have come to fulfil the law of caste.' Not a tittle, not a jot shall I allow to abate from it."

What hope can Gandhism offer to the Untouchables ? To the Untouchables, Hinduism is a veritable chamber of horrors. The sanctity and infallibility of the Vedas, Smritis and Shastras, the iron law of caste, the heartless law of karma and the senseless

---

[1] Mr. Gandhi's articles of faith have been outlined by him in *Young India* of 6th October 1921.

law of status by birth are to the Untouchables veritable instruments of torture which Hinduism has forged against the Untouchables. These very instruments which have mutilated, blasted and blighted the life of the Untouchables are to be found intact and untarnished in the bosom of Gandhism. How can the Untouchables say that Gandhism is a heaven and not a chamber of horrors as Hinduism has been ? The only reaction and a very natural reaction of the Untouchables would be to run away from Gandhism.

Gandhists may say that what I have stated applies to the old type of Gandhism. There is a new Gandhism, Gandhism without caste. This has reference to the recent statement[1] of Mr. Gandhi that caste is an anachronism. Reformers were naturally gladdened by this declaration of Mr. Gandhi. And who would not be glad to see that a man like Mr. Gandhi having such terrible influence over the Hindus, after having played the most mischievous part of a social reactionary, after having stood out as the protagonist of the caste system, after having beguiled and befooled the unthinking Hindus with arguments which made no distinction between what is fair and foul should have come out with this recantation ? But is this really a matter for jubilation ? Does it change the nature of Gandhism ? Does it make Gandhism a new and a better 'ism' than it was before. Those who are carried away by this recantation of Mr. Gandhi, forget two things. In the first place, all that Mr. Gandhi has said is that caste is an anachronism. He does not say it is an evil. He does not say it is anathema. Mr. Gandhi may be taken to be not in favour of caste. But Mr. Gandhi does not say that he is against the *Varna* system. And what is Mr. Gandhi's *varna* system ? It is simply a new name for the caste system and retains all the worst features of the caste system.

The declaration of Mr. Gandhi cannot be taken to mean any fundamental change in Gandhism. It cannot make Gandhism acceptable to the Untouchables. The Untouchables will still have ground to say : "Good God ! Is this man Gandhi our Saviour ?"

---

[1] *Hindustan Times*, 15th April 1945.

APPENDIX I

SHRADHANAND ON BARDOLI PROGRAMME FOR UNTOUCHABLES

Correspondence between Swami Shradhanand and Pandit Motilal Nehru, General Secretary of the Congress, on the Congress Sub-Committee appointed in 1922 to frame a Scheme for the uplift of the Untouchables.

(1) SWAMIJI'S LETTER

The General Secretary,
All-India Congress Committee,
Camp, Delhi.

I acknowledge, with thanks, receipt of your letters Nos. 331 and 332 embodying resolutions of the Working Committee and of the All-India Congress Committee about Untouchability. I observe with pain, that the resolution of the All-India Congress Committee, as at present worded, does not include the whole of what was passed by the Committee.

The facts are these : I sent the following letter to Mr. Vithalbhai Patel (the then) General Secretary on 23rd May 1922, which was also published by the principal dailies of the country.

"MY DEAR MR. PATEL,

There was a time (vide *Young India* of 25th May, 1921) when Mahatmaji put the question of Untouchability in the forefront of the Congress programme. I find now that the question of raising the Depressed Classes has been relegated to an obscure corner. While Khadi claims the attention of some of our best workers and a liberal sum has been earmarked for it, for the year, while a strong sub-committee has been appointed to look after national education and a special appeal for fund is to be made for the same, the question of the removal of Untouchability has been shelved by making small grants to Ahmedabad, Ahmednagar and Madras. I am of opinion that with a majority of 6 crores of our brethren set against us by the bureaucracy, even the Khadi Scheme cannot succeed completely. The Members of the Working Committee, perhaps, do not know that on this side, our suppressed brethren are leaving off khadi and taking to buying cheap foreign cloth. I want to move the following resolution in the meeting of the All-India Congress Committee which comes off on the 7th of June next at Lucknow: "that a sub-committee consisting of three members of the All-India Congress Committee be appointed to give effect to the resolution about the so-called Depressed Classes, that a sum of five lakhs of rupees be placed at their disposal for propaganda work and that in future all applications for grants be referred to the said sub-committee for disposal." My proposal was amended by the Working Committee and ran as follows :—

"This Committee hereby appoints a committee consisting of Swami Shradhanand, Mrs. Sarojini Naidu and Messrs. G. B. Deshpande and I. K. Yajnik to formulate a scheme embodying practical measures to be adopted for bettering the condition of the so-called Untouchables throughout the country and to place it for consideration before the next meeting of the Working Committee, the amount to be raised for the scheme to be Rs. 2 lakhs for the present."

Mr. Patel asked me to accept the Working Committee's proposed resolution *in toto*. I refused to accept the Working Committee's resolution and in the very first sitting of the All-India Congress Committee substituted 5 lakhs for 2 lakhs with the condition that one lakh of the same be allotted by the All-India Congress Committee out of the funds in its hands, in cash and an appeal be made for the balance.

Mr. Rajagopalachariar, on behalf of the Working Committee, proposed that instead of fixing the amount to be allotted out of the Congress funds now, it should be provided that when the Scheme was accepted by the Working Committee that Committee should allot as much cash as it could then spare for this purpose. I do not recollect the exact words but the purport of the amendment as given above is, to my knowledge, true.

On this an uproar arose and the query was pressed from all sides that the cash balance in the hands of the All-India Congress Committee ought to be announced. The President called me aside and told me in confidence that the Congress possessed very little cash balance and if pressed to disclose the true state of affairs it would harm the movement, as outsiders and even C.I.D. people were also present. On this I accepted the amendment of Mr. Rajagopalachariar in spite of protests from my seconder and supporters. But my surprise was great when I found the resolution in the dailies, as reported by the Associated Press, shorn of Mr. Rajagopalachariar's amendment.

After the above resolution was passed, some members suggested that a convener of the sub-committee ought to be appointed and several members proposed me as the convener. On this, Mr. Vithalbhai Patel (the then General Secretary) got up and said: "As Swami Shradhanand's name occurs first, naturally he will be the convener and therefore there was no need of moving any fresh resolution at all."

Members from all parts of the country began to give information to me about Untouchability in their provinces and pressed me to visit their parts. On this, I made some promises. Then I thought that without some cash for preliminary expenses, no enquiries on the spot could be made and hence no proper scheme could be formulated. I also learnt that Rs. 25,000 had been voted by the Working Committee for "the Independent" of Allahabad and that an application for grant of Rs. 10,000 to the Urdu daily *Congress* of Delhi had been placed by Hakim Ajmal Khan and Dr. Ansari before the Working Committee. So, considering that after all, the Congress might not be so hard pressed for cash, I wrote a letter addressed to the President, asking him to give the Untouchability Sub-Committee an advance of Rs. 10,000 for preliminary expenses.

After all this, the following resolution of the Working Committee forwarded by your letter No. 331 presents a very interesting reading :—

"Read letter from Swami Shradhanand, dated 8th June 1922 for an advance for drawing up a scheme for Depressed Class work—Resolved that Mr. Gangadharrao B. Deshpande be appointed convener of the sub-committee appointed for the purpose and he be requested to convene a meeting at an early date, and that Swami Shradhanand's letter be referred to the Sub-Committee."

There is another matter which is inexplicable. After my first letter had been acknowledged, I addressed the following letter from Hardwar on 3rd June 1922 :—

"My Dear Mr. Patel,

I shall leave Hardwar the day after to-morrow and reach Lucknow on the morning of June 6th. You know by now, that I feel the most for the so-called Depressed Classes. Even in the Punjab I find that no attention worth the name has been paid to this item of the constructive programme. In the U. P. of course it will be an uphill work. But there is another very serious difficulty.

The Bardoli programme in its note under item (4) lays down that where prejudice is still strong, separate wells and separate schools must be maintained out of the Congress Funds. This leaves a loophole for those Congress workers who are either prejudiced against the Depressed Classes or are weak and no work can be done in inducing people to agree to allow the Untouchables to draw water from common wells. In the Bijnoor District, I learn there was no restriction and the Untouchables drew water freely from common wells. But in some places, fresh prejudice is being engendered under the aegis of the Bardoli resolution note. In my recent visits to Ambala Cant., Ludhiana, Batala, Lahore, Amritsar and Jandiala, I found that the question of the removal of disabilities of the Untouchables is being ignored. In and near Delhi, it is the Dalitodhar Sabha, of which I am the president, rather than the Congress which is doing appreciable work. I think that unless item (4) of the Bardoli constructive programme is amended in proper form, the work which I consider to be the most important plank in the Congress programme, will suffer.

Kindly place the following proposal before the President and if he allows it to be placed before the next meeting of the All-India Congress Committee, I shall move it there—" Instead of the Note under item (4) of the Bardoli resolution substitute the following note :—

" The following demands of the Depressed Classes ought to be complied with at once, namely that (*a*) they are allowed to sit on the same carpet with citizens of other classes ; (*b*) they get the right to draw water from common wells and (*c*) their children get admission into National schools and Colleges and are allowed to mix freely with students drawn from the so-called higher castes."

I want to impress upon the members of the All-India Congress Committee the great importance of this term. I know of cases where the Depressed Classes are in open revolt against tyranny of the so-called upper castes and unless the above demands are conceded to them, they will succumb to the machine of the bureaucracy.

After my first proposals were passed in the All-India Congress Committee Meeting on June 7th at Lucknow, I asked Mr. Patel to put my proposed amendment of Note to item (4) of Bardoli resolution before the meeting. He told me that the Working Committee would refer it to the Sub-Committee and asked me not to press it there. I agreed. But I have not received copy of my resolution of the Working-Committee, referring my proposal to the Untouchability Sub-Committee.

The Untouchability question is very acute in and near Delhi and I have to grapple with it at once. But the Sub-Committee cannot begin work off-hand because the Working Committee has to take several other political situations in the country into consideration before deciding upon any scheme of practical measures to be adopted for uprooting Untouchability on behalf of the Congress. Under these circumstances, I cannot be of any use to the Sub-Committee and beg to resign from membership.

Yours sincerely,

Delhi, Jan. 30. SHRADHANAND SANYASI.

(2) SECRETARY'S REPLY

DEAR SWAMIJI,

Your letter, dated June 1922 received in my office on the 30th of that month, has by a resolution of the Working Committee passed in Bombay on the 18th instant been referred to me with instructions to explain facts and request you to be good enough to reconsider your resignation from the Depressed Classes Sub-Committee.

As you are aware, I have no personal knowledge of the facts which happened prior to my release from the jail. But I was present at the meeting of the Working Committee which passed the resolution dated 10th June 1922, appointing Mr. Deshpande as the Convener of the Sub-Committee. It was not then mentioned that there was any understanding about any particular member acting as the convener of the Sub-Committee and the whole resolution was passed merely to complete the necessary formalities in regard to the payment of money. It was felt that a formal resolution of the Sub-Committee was necessary before any expenditure could be sanctioned. Mr. Deshpande was accordingly appointed as the convener and a sum of Rs. 500/- was voted for the expense of these preliminary steps. By an oversight, the resolution as drafted omitted to mention the sanction of Rs. 500/-. You will thus observe that it was not due to the unwillingness of the Working Committee to sanction Rs. 10,000/- for Untouchability, but the true reason for framing the resolution in the manner it was framed was that I have explained above. Nothing could be farther from the intention of the Working Committee than a desire to under-rate the importance of the work your Sub-Committee was called upon to do or in any way to ignore the valuable advice tendered by you. On your letter being placed before the last meeting of the Working Committee, the omission of the grant of Rs. 500/- was supplied and I was instructed to communicate with you on the subject. It will be a great pity if the Sub-Committee is deprived of the benefit of your experience and special knowledge of the whole question of Untouchability and I will ask you, therefore, in public interest, to reconsider your decision and wire to my office at Allahabad withdrawing your resignation from the Sub-Committee. I need hardly add that any resolutions arrived at by your Sub-Committee will receive all the consideration they deserve at the hands of the Working Committee.

As to the alteration in the Working Committee's resolution in regard to separate wells and schools, the best course would be for your Sub-Committee to recommend the change and for the Working Committee to adopt it.

I am afraid you are under a misapprehension as regards the grant to *The Independent*, of Allahabad, and *The Congress* of Delhi. In reference to the former, all that has been done is to sanction the application of the U. P. Provincial Committee to advance as a loan to the "Nationalist Journals" Ltd., Rs. 25,000/- from the funds already granted to that committee and in reference to the latter, the application for a grant of a loan was wholly rejected.

Yours sincerely,

MOTILAL NEHRU,

General Secretary.

Bombay, July 23, 1922.

(3) Swamiji's Rejoinder

Dear Pandit Motilalji,

I received your letter of 23rd July 1922 addressed from Bombay about my resignation from the Untouchability Sub-Committee, I am sorry I am unable to reconsider it because some of the facts brought out by me in my first letter have simply been ignored.

(1) Kindly enquire of Mr. Rajagopalachariar whether I did not first propose that at least one lakh should be given in cash out of the funds in the hands of the All-India Congress Committee, whether he did not move an amendment substituting words for the above which purported to promise that when the plan of work formulated by the Sub-Committee was accepted by the Working Committee, that Committee would allot as much money for Untouchability department as it could then spare and whether I did not accept his amendment when the President called me aside and explained the exact financial position at the time. If this is the fact, then why did the amendment not appear with the resolution?

(2) Did you enquire of Mr. Vithalbhai J. Patel whether the members of the All-India Congress Committee did not propose me as the convener of the Sub-Committee and whether he did not then say—"As Swami Shradhanand's name occurs first naturally he will be the convener and therefore there was no need of moving any fresh resolution at all?" I enquired about this from Dr. Ansari and he wrote back to me on June 17th, 1922, saying that I was appointed convener. Dr. Ansari is with you and you can verify it from him. I hope Mr. Patel has not forgotten all about it.

(3) Then the immediate work among the Untouchables here is very urgent and I cannot delay it for any reason whatsoever. Kindly have my resignation accepted in the next meeting of the Working Committee, so that I may be free to work out my own plan about the removal of Untouchability. This was my position at the end of July last. My experience in the Amritsar and Mianwali Jails and the information I gathered there have confirmed me in the belief that unless sexual purity (Brahmacharya) is revived on the ancient Aryan lines and the curse of Untouchability is blotted out of the Indian Society, no efforts of the Congress nor of other patriotic organisations out of the Congress will avail in their efforts for the attainment of Swaraj. And as national self-realization and virile existence is impossible without Swaraj, I, as a Sanyasi, should devote the rest of my life to this sacred cause—the cause of sexual purity and true national unity.

Yours, etc.

Delhi, July 23, 1922. Shradhanand Sanyasi.

Appendix II

POLITICAL SAFEGUARDS FOR DEPRESSED CLASSES

Supplementary Memorandum on the claims of the Depressed Classes for Special Representation, submitted to the R. T. C. by Dr. Bhimrao R. Ambedkar and Rao Bahadur R. Srinivasan.

In the memorandum that was submitted by us last year dealing with the question of political safeguards for the protection of the Depressed Classes in the constitution for a self-governing India, and which forms Appendix III to the printed volume of Proceedings of the Minorities Sub-Committee, we had demanded that special representation of the Depressed Classes must form one of such safeguards. But we did not then define the details of the special representation we claimed as being necessary for them. The reason was that the proceedings of the Minorities Sub-Committee came to an end before the question was reached. We now propose to make good the omission by this supplementary memorandum so that the Minorities Sub-Committee, if it comes to consider the question this year, should have the requisite details before it.

(1) Extent of Special Representation

A. Special Representation in Provincial Legislatures.

(*i*) In Bengal, Central Provinces, Assam, Bihar and Orissa, Punjab and the United Provinces, the Depressed Classes shall have representation in proportion to their population as estimated by the Simon Commission and the Indian Central Committee.

(*ii*) In Madras, the Depressed Classes shall have twenty-two per cent. representation.

(*iii*) In Bombay :

(*a*) in the event of Sind continuing to be a part of the Bombay Presidency, the Depressed Classes shall have sixteen per cent. representation ;

(*b*) in the event of Sind being separated from the Bombay Presidency the Depressed Classes shall enjoy the same degree of representation as the Presidency Muslims, both beng equal in population.

B.—Special Representation in the Federal Legislature.

In both Houses of the Federal Legislature, the Depressed Classes shall have representation in proportion to their *population in India.*

Reservations

We have fixed this proportion of representation in the Legislatures on the following assumptions :—

(1) We have assumed that the figures for the population of the Depressed Classes given by the Simon Commission (Vol. I, p. 40) and the Indian Central Committee (Report, p. 44) will be acceptable as sufficiently correct to form a basis for distributing seats.

(2) We have assumed that the Federal Legislature will comprise the whole of India, in which case the population of the Depressed Classes in Indian States, in Centrally Administered Areas, and in Excluded Territories, besides their population in Governor's Provinces, will form very properly an additional item in calculating the extent of representation of the Depressed Classes in the Federal Legislature.

(3) We have assumed that the administrative areas of the Provinces of British India will continue to be what they are at present.

But if the assumptions regarding figures of population are challenged, as some interested parties threaten to do, and if under a new census the Depressed Classes show a lower proportion, or if the administrative areas of the Provinces are altered, resulting in disturbing the existing balance of population, the Depressed Classes reserve their right to revise their proportion of representation and even to claim weightage. In the same way, if the All-India Federation does not come into being, they will be willing to submit to readjustment in their proportion of representation calculated on that basis in the Federal Legislature.

(2) Method of Representation

1. The Depressed Classes shall have the right to elect their representatives to the Provincial and Central Legislature through separate electorates of their voters.

For their representation in the Upper House of the Federal or Central Legislature, if it is decided to have indirect election by members of the Provincial Legislatures, the Depressed Classes will agree to abandon their right to separate electorates so far as their representation to the Upper House is concerned subject to this: that in any system of proportional representation arrangement shall be made to guarantee to them their quota of seats.

2. Separate electorates for the Depressed Classes shall not be liable to be replaced by a system of joint electorates and reserved seats, except when the following conditions are fulfilled :—

(*a*) A referendum of the voters held at the demand of a majority of their representatives in the Legislatures concerned and resulting in an absolute majority of the members of the Depressed Class having the franchise.

(*b*) No such referendum shall be resorted to until after twenty years and until universal adult suffrage has been established.

(3) Necessity of Defining the Depressed Classes

The representation of the Depressed Classes has been grossly abused in the past inasmuch as persons other than the Depressed Classes were nominated to represent them in the Provincial Legislatures, and cases are not wanting in which persons not belonging to the Depressed Classes got themselves nominated as representatives of the Depressed Classes. This abuse was due to the fact that while the Governor was given the power to nominate persons to represent the Depressed Classes, he was not required to confine his nomination to persons belonging to the Depressed Classes. Since nomination is to be substituted by election under the new constitution, there will be no room for this abuse. But in order to leave no loophole for defeating the purpose of their special representation we claim :

(*i*) That the Depressed Classes shall not only have the right to their own separate electorates, but they shall also have the right to be represented by their own men.

(*ii*) That in each Province the Depressed Classes shall be strictly defined as meaning persons belonging to communities which are subjected to the system of Untouchability of the sort prevalent therein and which are enumerated by name in a schedule prepared for electoral purposes.

(4) Nomenclature

In dealing with this part of the question we would like to point out that the existing nomenclature of Depressed Classes is objected to by members of the Depressed Classes who have given thought to it and also by outsiders who take interest in them. It is degrading and contemptuous, and advantage may be taken of this occasion for drafting the new constitution to alter for official purposes the existing nomenclature. We think that they should be called "Non-Caste Hindus," "Protestant Hindus," or "Non-Conformist Hindus," or some such designation, instead of "Depressed Classes." We have no authority to press for any particular nomenclature. We can only suggest them, and we believe that if properly explained the Depressed Classes will not hesitate to accept the one most suitable for them.

We have received a large number of telegrams from the Depressed Classes all over India supporting the demands contained in this Memorandum.

Nov. 4th, 1931.

APPENDIX III

MINORITIES PACT

Provisions for a Settlement of the Communal Problem, put forward jointly by Muslims, Depressed Classes, Indian Christians, Anglo-Indians and Europeans.

CLAIMS OF MINORITY COMMUNITIES

1. No person shall by reason of his origin, religion, caste or creed, be prejudiced in any way in regard to public employment, office of power or honour, or with regard to enjoyment of his civic rights and the exercise of any trade or calling.

2. Statutory safeguards shall be incorporated in the constitution with a view to protect against enactments of the Legislature of discriminatory laws affecting any community.

3. Full religious liberty, that is, full liberty of belief, worship observances, propaganda, associations and education, shall be guaranteed to all communities subject to the maintenance of public order and morality.

No person shall merely by change of faith lose any civic right or privilege, or be subject to any penalty.

4. The right to establish, manage and control, at their own expense, charitable, religious and social institutions, schools and other educational establishments with the right to exercise their religion therein.

5. The constitution shall embody adequate safeguards for the protection of religion, culture and personal law, and the promotion of education, language, charitable institutions of the minority communities and for their due share in grants-in-aid given by the State and by the self-governing bodies.

6. Enjoyment of civic rights by all citizens shall be guaranteed by making any act or omission calculated to prevent full enjoyment an offence punishable by law.

7. In the formation of Cabinets in the Central Government and Provincial Governments, so far as possible, members belonging to the Mussalman community and other minorities of considerable number shall be included by convention.

8. There shall be Statutory Departments under the Central and Provincial Governments to protect minority communities and to promote their welfare.

9. All communities at present enjoying representation in any Legislature through nomination or election shall have representation in all Legislatures through separate electorates and the minorities

shall have not less than the proportion set forth in the Annexure but no majority shall be reduced to a minority or even an equality. Provided that after a lapse of ten years it will be open to Muslims in Punjab and Bengal and any minority communities in any other Provinces to accept joint electorates, or joint electorates with reservation of seats, by the consent of the community concerned. Similarly after the lapse of ten years, it will be open to any minority in the Central Legislature to accept joint electorates with or without reservation of seats with the consent of the community concerned.

With regard to the Depressed Classes, no change to joint electorates and reserved seats shall be made until after 20 years' experience of separate electorates and until direct adult suffrage for the community has been established.

10. In every Province and in connection with the Central Government, a Public Services Commission shall be appointed, and the recruitment to the Public Services, except the proportion, if any, reserved to be filled by nomination by the Governor-General and the Governors, shall be made through such commission in such a way as to secure a fair representation to the various communities consistently with the considerations of efficiency and the possession of the necessary qualifications. Instructions to the Governor-General and the Governors in the Instrument of Instructions with regard to recruitment shall be embodied to give effect to this principle, and for that purpose to review periodically the composition of the Services.

11. If a Bill is passed which, in the opinion of two-thirds of the members of any Legislature representing a particular community, affects their religion or social practice based on religion, or in the case of fundamental rights of the subjects if one-third of the members object, it shall be open to such members to lodge their objection thereto, within a period of one month of the Bill being passed by the House, with the President of the House who shall forward the same to the Governor-General or the Governor, as the case may be, and he shall thereupon suspend the operation of that Bill for one year, upon the expiry of which period he shall remit the said Bill for further consideration by the Legislature. When such Bill has been further considered by the Legislature and the Legislature concerned has refused to revise or modify the Bill so as to meet the objection thereto, the Governor-General or the Governor, as the case may be, may give or withhold his assent to it in the exercise of his discretion, provided, further, that the validity of such Bill may be challenged in the Supreme Court by any two members of the denomination affected thereby on the ground that it contravenes one of their fundamental rights.

Special Claims of Mussulmans

A.—The North-West Frontier Province shall be constituted a Governor's Province on the same footing as other Provinces with due regard to the necessary requirements for the security of the Frontier.

In the formation of the Provincial Legislature, the nominations shall not exceed more than 10 per cent. of the whole.

B.—Sind shall be separated from the Bombay Presidency and made a Governor's Province similar to and on the same footing as other Provinces in British India.

C.—Mussulman representation in the Central Legislature shall be one-third of the total number of the House, and their representation in the Central Legislature shall not be less than the proportion set forth in the Annexure.

Special Claims of the Depressed Classes

A.—The constitution shall declare invalid any custom or usage by which any penalty or disadvantage or disability is imposed upon or any discrimination is made against any subject of the State in regard to the enjoyment of the civic rights on account of Untouchability.

B.—Generous treatment in the matter of recruitment to Public Services and the opening of enlistment in the Police and Military Service.

C.—The Depressed Classes in the Punjab shall have the benefit of the Punjab Land Alienation Act extended to them.

D.—Right of Appeal shall lie to the Governor or Governor-General for redress of prejudicial action or neglect of interest by any Executive Authority.

E.—The Depressed Classes shall have representation not less than set forth in the Annexure.

Special Claims of the Anglo-Indian Community

A.—Generous interpretation of the claims admitted by Sub-Committee No. VIII (Services) to the effect that in recognition of the peculiar position of the community, special consideration should be given to the claim for public employment, having regard to the maintenance of an adequate standard of living.

B.—The right to administer and control its own educational institutions, i.e., European education, subject to the control of the Minister.

Provisions for generous and adequate grants-in-aid and scholarship on the basis of present grants.

C.—Jury rights equal to those enjoyed by other communities in India unconditionally of proof of legitimacy and descent and the

ANNEXURE—*Representation in Legislatures.*

Figures in brackets = Population basis 1931 figures and depressed percentages as per Simon Report

—	*Strength of Chamber*	*Hindu*			*Muslims*	*Christians*	*Sikhs*	*Anglo-Indians*	*Tribal, etc.*	*Europeans*	*Remarks*
		Caste	*Depressed*	*Total*							
CENTRE All India (1931) Upper ...	200	(47.5) 101	(19)* 20	(66.5) 121	(21.5) 67	1	6	1	—	4	*Represents percentage in Governor's Provinces of B.I.
Lower	300	123	45	168	100	7	10	3	—	12	
Assam ...	*100	(48.9) 38	(13.4) 13	(62.3) 51	(34.8) 35	3	—	1	—	10	*Pop. figures exclude Tribal Areas.
Bengal ...	200	(18.3) 38	(24.7) 35	(43) 73	(54.9) 102	2	—	3	—	20	
Bihar & Orissa	100	(67.8) 51	(14.5) 14	(82.3) 65	(11.3) 25	1	—	1	3	5	
Bombay ...	200	(68) 88	(8) 28	(76) 116	(20) 66	2	—	3	—	13	On Sind being separated weightage to Mussulmans in Bombay to be on the same footing as to the Hindus in the N.W.F.P.
C. P.	100	(63.1) 58	(23.7) 20	(86.8) 78	(44) 15	1	—	2	2	2	
Madras ...	200	(71.3) 102	(15.4) 40	(86.7) 142	(7.1) 30	(3.7) 14	—	4	2	8	
Punjab ...	100	(15.1) 14	(13.5) 10	(28.6) 24	(56.5) 51	1.5	(13) 20	1.5	—	2	
U. P.	100	(58.1) 44	(26.4) 20	(84.5) 64	(14.8) 30	1	—	2	—	3	

Sind & N.W.F.P. Weightage similar to that enjoyed by the Mussulmans in the Provinces in which they constitute a minority of the population, shall be given to the Hindu minority in Sind and to the Hindu and Sikh minorities in the N.W.F.P.

right of accused persons to claim trial by either a European or an Indian jury.

SPECIAL CLAIMS OF THE EUROPEAN COMMUNITY

A.—Equal rights and privileges to those enjoyed by Indian-born subjects in all industrial and commercial activities.

B.—The maintenance of existing rights in regard to procedure of criminal trials, and any measure or bill to amend, alter, or modify such a procedure cannot be introduced except with the previous consent of the Governor-General.

Agreed by :—

HIS HIGHNESS THE AGA KHAN (Muslims)
DR. AMBEDKAR (Depressed Classes)
RAO BAHADUR PANNIR SELVAM (Indian Christians)
SIR HENRY GIDNEY (Anglo-Indians)
SIR HUBERT CARR (Europeans).

APPENDIX IV

STATEMENT BY B. R. AMBEDKAR ON GANDHI'S FAST

Statement on Mr. Gandhi's attitude at the Round Table Conference to the Untouchables and their demand for Constitutional Safeguards, 19th September 1932.

I need hardly say that I was astounded to read the correspondence between Mahatma Gandhi, Sir Samuel Hoare and the Prime Minister, which was published recently in the Papers, in which he has expressed his determination to starve himself unto death till the British Government of its own accord or under pressure of public opinion revise their opinion and withdraw their scheme of communal representation for the Depressed Classes. The unenviable position, in which I have been placed by the Mahatma's vow of self-immolation, can easily be imagined.

It passes my comprehension why Mr. Gandhi should stake his life on an issue arising out of the communal question which he, at the Round Table Conference, said was one of a comparatively small importance. Indeed, to adopt the language of those of Mr. Gandhi's way of thinking, the communal question was only an appendix to the book of India's constitution and not the main chapter. It would have been justifiable, if Mr. Gandhi had resorted to this extreme step for obtaining independence for the country on which he was so insistent all through the R. T. C. debates. It is also a painful surprise that Mr. Gandhi should single out special representation for the Depressed Classes in the Communal Award as an excuse for his self-immolation. Separate electorates are granted not only to the Depressed Classes, but to the Indian Christians, Anglo-Indians, Europeans, as well as to the Mahomedans and the Sikhs. Also separate electorates are granted to landlords, labourers and traders. Mr. Gandhi had declared his opposition to the special representation of every other class and creed except the Mahomedans and the Sikhs. All the same, Mr. Gandhi chooses to let everybody else except the Depressed Classes retain the special electorates given to them.

The fears expressed by Mr. Gandhi about the consequences of the arrangements for the representation of the Depressed Classes are, in my opinion, purely imaginary. If the nation is not going to be split up by separate electorates to the Mahomedans and the Sikhs, the Hindu society cannot be said to be split up if the Depressed Classes are given separate electorates. His conscience is not aroused if the nation is split by the arrangements of Special Electorates for classes and communities other than the Depressed Classes.

I am sure many have felt that if there was any class which deserved to be given special political rights in order to protect itself against the tyranny of the majority under the Swaraj constitution it was the Depressed Classes. Here is a class which is undoubtedly not in a position to sustain itself in the struggle for existence. The religion to which they are tied, instead of providing for them an honourable place, brands them as lepers, not fit for ordinary intercourse. Economically, it is a class entirely dependent upon the high-caste Hindus for earning its daily bread with no independent way of living open to it. Nor are all ways closed by reason of the social prejudices of the Hindus but there is a definite attempt all throughout the Hindu Society to bolt every possible door so as not to allow the Depressed Classes any opportunity to rise in the scale of life. Indeed it would not be an exaggeration to say that in every village the caste Hindus, however divided among themselves, are always in a standing conspiracy to put down in a merciless manner any attempt on the part of the Depressed Classes who form a small and scattered body of an ordinary Indian citizen.

In these circumstances, it would be granted by all fair-minded persons that as the only path for a community so handicapped to succeed in the struggle for life against organised tyranny, some share of political power in order that it may protect itself is a paramount necessity.

I should have thought that a well-wisher of the Depressed Classes would have fought tooth and nail for securing to them as much political power as might be possible in the new Constitution. But the Mahatma's ways of thinking are strange and are certainly beyond my comprehension. He not only does not endeavour to augment the scanty political power which the Depressed Classes have got under the Communal Award, but on the contrary he has staked his very life in order to deprive them of little they have got. This is not the first attempt on the part of the Mahatma to completely dish the Depressed Classes out of political existence. Long before, there was the Minorities Pact. The Mahatma tried to enter into an agreement with the Muslims and the Congress. He offered to the Muslims all the fourteen claims which they had put forth on their behalf, and in return asked them to join with him in resisting the claims for social representation made by me on behalf of the Depressed Classes.

It must be said to the credit of the Muslim delegates that they refused to be a party to such a black act, and saved the Depressed Class from what might as well have developed into a calamity for them as a result of the combined opposition of the Mahommedans and Mr. Gandhi.

I am unable to understand the ground of hostility of Mr. Gandhi to the Communal Award. He says that the Communal Award has separated the Depressed Classes from the Hindu Community. On the other hand, Dr. Moonje, a much stronger protagonist of the Hindu case and a militant advocate of its interests, takes a totally different view of the matter. In the speeches which he has been delivering since his arrival from London, Dr. Moonje has been insisting that the Communal Award does not create any separation between the Depressed Class and the Hindus. Indeed, he has been boasting that he has defeated me in my attempt to politically separate the Depressed Class from the Hindus. I am sure that Dr. Moonje is right in his interpretation of the Communal Award although, I am not sure that the credit of it can legitimately go to Dr. Moonje. It is therefore surprising that Mahatma Gandhi who is a nationalist and not known to be a communalist should read the Communal Award, in so far as it relates to the Depressed Class, in a manner quite contrary to that of a communalist like Dr. Moonje. If Dr. Moonje does not sense any separation of the Depressed Classes from the Hindus in the Communal Award the Mahatma ought to feel quite satisfied on that score.

In my opinion, that Communal Award should not only satisfy the Hindus, but also satisfy those individuals among the Depressed Classes such as Rao Bahadur Rajah, Mr. Baloo or Mr. Govai, who are in favour of Joint Electorates. Mr. Rajah's fulminations in the Assembly have amused me considerably. An intense supporter of Separate Electorates and the bitterest and the most vehement critic of caste Hindu tyranny, now professes faith in the Joint Electorates and love for the Hindus! How much of that is due to his natural desire to resuscitate himself from the oblivion in which he was cast by his being kept out of the Round Table Conference and how much of it is to his honest change of faith, I do not propose to discuss.

The points on which Mr. Rajah is harping by way of criticism on the Communal Award are two: One is that the Depressed Classes have gained lesser number of seats than they are entitled to on the population basis, and the other is that the Depressed Classes have been separated from the Hindu fold.

I agree in his first grievance, but when the Rao Bahadur begins to accuse those who represented the Depressed Classes at the R. T. C. for having sold their rights, I am bound to point out what Mr. Rajah did as a member of the Indian Central Committee. In that Committee's report, the Depressed Classes were given in Madras 10 seats out of 150; in Bombay 8 seats out of 14; in Bengal 8 seats out of 200; in U. P. 8 seats out of 182; in the Punjab 6 seats out of 150; in Bihar and Orissa 6 out of 150; in C. P. 8 out of 125 and in Assam, 9 seats for the Depressed Classes and the indigenous and primitive races out of 75. I do not wish to overburden this statement by pointing out how this distribution compares with the population ratio. But there can be no doubt that this meant a terrible under-representation of the Depressed Classes. To this distribution of seats Mr. Rajah was a party. Surely, Mr. Rajah, before he criticises the Communal Award and accuses others, should refresh his memory of what he accepted as Member of the Indian Central Committee on behalf of the Depressed Classes without any protest. If the population ratio of representation was to him a natural right of Depressed Classes and its full realisation was a necessity for their protection, why did not Mr. Rajah insist upon it in the Central Committee when he had an opportunity to do so?

As to his contention that in the Communal Award, the Depressed Classes have been separated from the caste Hindus, it is a view to which I cannot subscribe. If Mr. Rajah has any conscientious objection to separate Electorates, there is no compulsion on him to stand as a candidate in the Separate Electorates. The opportunity to stand as a candidate in the general electorate as well as the right to vote in it are there, and Mr. Rajah is free to avail himself of the same. Mr. Rajah is crying at the top of his voice to assure to the Depressed Classes that there is a complete change of heart on the part of the Caste Hindus towards the Depressed Class. He will have the opportunity to prove that fact to the satisfaction of the Depressed Class, who are not prepared to take his word by getting himself elected in the general constituency. The Hindus, who profess love and sympathy for the Depressed Classes, will have also an opportunity to prove their *bona fides* by electing Mr. Rajah to the legislature.

The Communal Award, therefore, in my opinion, satisfied both those who want separate Electorates and those who want joint Electorates. In this sense, it is already a compromise and should be accepted as it is. As to the Mahatma, I do not know what he wants. It is assumed that although Mahatma Gandhi is opposed to the system of separate electorates, he is not opposed to the system of Joint Electorates and Reserved Seats. That is a gross error. Whatever his views are today, while in London he was totally opposed to any system of Special representation for the Depressed Classes whether by joint Electorates or by Separate Electorates. Beyond the right to vote in a general electorate based upon Adult Suffrage, he was not prepared to concede anything to the Depressed Classes by way of securing their representation in the legislatures. This was the position he had taken at first. Towards the end of the R. T. C. he suggested to me a scheme, which he said, he was prepared to consider. The scheme was purely conventional without any constitutional sanction behind it and without any single seat being reserved for the Depressed Classes in the electoral law.

The scheme was as follows :

Depressed Class candidates might stand in the general electorate as against other high caste Hindu candidates. If any Depressed Class Candidate was defeated in the election, he should file an election petition and obtain the verdict that he was defeated because he was an Untouchable. If such a decision was obtained, the Mahatma said he would undertake to induce some Hindu members to resign and thus create a vacancy. There would be then another election in which the defeated Depressed Class candidate or any other Depressed Class candidate might again try his luck as against the Hindu candidates. Should he be defeated again, he should get similar verdict that he was defeated because he was an Untouchable and so on *ad infinitum*. I am disclosing these facts as some people are even now under the impression that the Joint Electorates and Reserve Seats would satisfy the conscience of the Mahatma. This will show why I insist that there is no use discussing the question until the actual proposals of the Mahatma are put forth.

I must, however, point out that I cannot accept the assurances of the Mahatma that he and his Congress will do the needful. I cannot leave so important a question as the protection of my people to conventions and understandings. The Mahatma is not an immortal person, and the Congress, assuming it is not a malevolent force, is not to have an abiding existence. There have been many Mahatmas in India whose sole object was to remove Untouchability and to elevate and absorb the Depressed Classes, but every one of them has failed in his mission. Mahatmas have come and Mahatmas have gone. But the Untouchables have remained as Untouchables.

I have enough experience of the pace of Reform and the faith of Hindu reformers in the conflicts that have taken place at Mahad and Nasik, to say that no well-wisher of the Depressed Classes will ever consent to allow the uplift of the Depressed Classes to rest upon such treacherous shoulders. Reformers who in moments of crises prefer to sacrifice their principles rather than hurt the feelings of their kindred can be of no use to the Depressed Classes.

I am therefore bound to insist upon a Statutory guarantee for the protection of my people. If Mr. Gandhi wishes to have the Communal Award altered, it is for him to put forth his proposals and to prove that they give a better guarantee than has been given to us under the Award.

I hope that the Mahatma will desist from carrying out the extreme step contemplated by him. We mean no harm to the Hindu society when we demand separate electorates. If we choose separate electorates, we do so in order to avoid the total dependence on the sweet will of the Caste Hindus in matters affecting our destiny. Like the Mahatma we also claim our right to err, and we expect him not to deprive us of that right. His determination to fast himself unto death is worthy of a far better cause. I could have understood the propriety of the Mahatma contemplating such extreme step for stopping riots between Hindus and Mohammedans or between the Depressed Classes and the Hindus or any other national cause. It certainly cannot improve the lot of the Depressed Classes. Whether he knows it or not, the Mahatma's act will result in nothing but terrorism by his followers against the Depressed Classes all over the country.

Coercion of this sort will not win the Depressed Classes to the Hindu fold if they are determined to go out. And if the Mahatma chooses to ask the Depressed Classes to make a choice between Hindu faith and possession of political power, I am quite sure that the Depressed Classes will choose political power and save the Mahatma from self-immolation. If Mr. Gandhi coolly reflects on the consequences of his act, I very much doubt whether he will find this victory worth having. It is still more important to note that the Mahatma is releasing reactionary and uncontrollable forces, and is fostering the spirit of hatred between the Hindu Community and the Depressed Classes by resorting to this method and thereby widening the existing gulf between the two. When I opposed Mr. Gandhi at the R. T. C., there was a hue and cry against me in the country and there was a conspiracy in the so-called nationalist press to represent me as a traitor to the nationalist cause, to suppress correspondence coming from my side and to boost the propaganda against my party by publishing exaggerated reports of meetings and conferences, many of which were never held. "Silver bullets" were freely used for creating divisions in the ranks of the Depressed Classes. There have been also a few clashes ending in violence.

If the Mahatma does not want all this to be repeated on a larger scale, let him, for God's sake, reconsider his decision and avert the disastrous consequences. I believe the Mahatma does not want this. But if he does not desist, in spite of his wishes these consequences are sure to follow as night follows the day.

Before concluding this statement, I desire to assure the public that although I am entitled to say that I regard the matter as closed, I am prepared to consider the proposals of the Mahatma. I however trust the Mahatma will not drive me to the necessity of making a choice between his life and the rights of my people. For I can never consent to deliver my people bound hand and foot to the Caste Hindus for generations to come.

B. R. AMBEDKAR.

APPENDIX V

TEMPLE ENTRY IN TRAVANCORE

His Highness the Maharaja of Travancore issued a Proclamation on the 12th November 1936 opening the Temples in the State to the Untouchables. The Proclamation reads as follows :—

" Profoundly convinced of the truth and validity of our religion, believing that it is based on divine guidance and on all-comprehending toleration, knowing that in its practice it has throughout the centuries adapted itself to the need of the changing times, solicitous that none of our Hindu subjects should, by reason of birth, caste or community, be denied the consolation and solace of the Hindu faith, we have decided and hereby declare, ordain and command that, subject to such rules and conditions as may be laid down and imposed by us for preserving their proper atmosphere and maintaining their rituals and observances, there should henceforth be no restriction placed on any Hindu by birth or religion on entering or worshipping at temples controlled by us and our Government."

A great lot has been made by the Congressmen and by Mr. Gandhi about this Proclamation. It is regarded as heralding the birth of a new conscience in the Hindu world. I don't feel quite so sure of this. At any rate there are facts on the other side, which are worth bearing in mind.

The proclamation was issued by the Maharaja of Travancore in his name. But the real active force behind the scene was the Prime Minister, Sir C. P. Ramaswami Iyer. It is his motives that we must understand. In 1932, Sir C. P. Ramaswami Iyer was also the Prime Minister of Travancore. In 1932, when Mr. Gandhi had raised a controversy over the entry of the Untouchables into the

Guruvayur Temple, Sir C. P. Ramaswami Iyer had taken part in the controversy on the side of those who were against Temple Entry. In the course of this controversy, Sir C. P. Ramaswamy Iyer issued a statement[1] to the Press. This is what he said :

" Personally I do not observe caste rules. I realise there are strong, though not very articulate, feelings in this matter in the minds of men who believe that the present system of temple worship and its details are based on divine ordinances. The problem can be permanently solved only by a process of mutual adjustment and by the awakening of religious and social leaders of Hindu society to the realities of the present situation and to the need for preserving the solidarity of the Hindu community.

" Shock tactics will not answer the purpose and direct action will be even more fatal in this sphere than in the political. I have the misfortune to differ from Mr. Gandhi when he says that the problem of temple-entry can be divorced from such topics as interdining and I agree with Dr. Ambedkar that the social and economic uplift of the Depressed Classes should be our immediate and urgent programme."

This statement shows that in 1933 spiritual considerations did not move Sir C. P. Ramaswamy Iyer. Spiritual considerations have become operative after 1933. What made Sir C. P. Ramaswamy Iyer take a different view in 1936? What had happened in Travancore in 1936 to compel this change of opinion ? It may be recalled that in 1936, there was held in Travancore a Conference of the Yezawa Community. The Yezawas are an Untouchable community spread over Malabar. It is an educated community and economically quite strong. It is also a vocal community and has been carrying on agitation in the State against social and religious disabilities. The Conference was held to consider whether the Yezawas should not abandon the Hindu Religion in favour of some other religion.[2] The Yezawas form a very large community. The cessation of so large a community would be death-knell to the Hindus and the Conference had made the danger real.

It may not be far-fetched to say that the Proclamation was issued to forestall this danger. If this is correct, there is very little spiritual substance behind the proclamation. It must not be forgotten that Sir C. P. Ramaswamy Iyer has his own way of giving spiritual colouring to a material act. The Brahmins have been, in accordance with the Hindu Law, exempt from capital punishment which applied to all Brahmins. This was a very glaring case of discrimination. Sir C. P. Ramaswami Iyer very recently announced the abolition

[1] *Times of India* dated November 10, 1932.

[2] This was in pursuance of the decision taken at Yeola in 1935 under my chairmanship.

of capital punishment in Travancore State and took credit for having carried out a great humanitarian Reform. As a matter of fact, the object was really preventing the Brahmin from being brought under the guillotine in obedience to the principle of equality before law.

How far did this Proclamation change facts and how far it has remained a show? It is not possible to get real facts as they exist in Travancore. In the course of the discussion on the Malabar Temple Entry Bill in the Madras Legislative Assembly, certain facts relating to Travancore were mentioned by Sir T. Pannirselvam which, if true, would show that the whole thing is hollow.

Sir T. Pannirselvam said :—

"One of the arguments advanced by the Premier in support of the measure was that temples in Travancore had been thrown open to the 'Untouchables.' A Maharaja vested with autocratic powers did so by an order. But how was it working there? From representations received, he was led to believe that after the first flush of enthusiasm, Harijans had left off going to temples, and people who used to worship previously before Harijans were allowed to enter the temples, had stopped worshipping in temples. He would ask the Government to tell them if the measure was really a success in Travancore."

On the third reading of the Bill, Sir T. Pannirselvam made a statement which must have come as a surprise to many. He said:

"He wanted to know whether it was a fact that the private temples of the Senior Maharani were excluded from the Proclamation. What was the reason for it? Again during the celebration of the marriage of the daughter of the Senior Maharani, it was found necessary, so he was told, to perform purificatory ceremony of the temple. If such a purification of temples took place, what happened to the Proclamation?"

These facts were not challenged by anybody, either by Sir C. P. Ramaswami Iyer or C. Rajagopalachariar. Evidently, they cannot be challenged. If they are incontrovertible, then the less said about the Malabar Temple Entry Proclamation as a spiritual testament, the better.

Is this Temple Entry in Travancore the be-all and end-all of the social reform in Travancore? Is there to be just Temple Entry and no further or is it going to lead to equality in the matter of religious status? Will, for instance, the Devastan Department be placed in the hands of the Untouchables and the Shudras? Nine years since the Proclamation have passed, there has been no move in democratization of religion in Travancore.

Will the Untouchables of Travancore have to pay for Temple Entry? I am not in a position to say. But I like to reproduce below a letter addressed to me by Sri Narayan Swami of the All-Travancore Pulayar Cheramar Aykia Maha Sangham. It is dated 24th November 1938.

"Camp Mayyanad,
Quilon, 24-11-1938.

To
Dr. Ambedkar,
Bombay.

RESPECTED SIR,

I have unaffected pleasure to draw your attention to the following facts for obtaining the valuable advice from you. Being the leader of a Harijan Community of the Travancore State, I think it is my paramount duty to suggest you definitely all the grievances that the Harijans of this State are enduring.

1. The Temple Entry Proclamation issued by His Highness The Maharaja is indeed a boon to Harijans; but the Harijans are enjoying all the other social disabilities except the temple Entry. The Government do not take any step for the amelioration of the Harijans.

2. Among 15 lakhs of Harijans, there are a few graduates, half a dozen undergraduates and 50 school finals and more than 200 vernacular certificate holders. Though the Government have appointed a Public Service Commission, appointments to the Harijans are very few. All the appointments are given to Savarnas. If a Harijan is appointed, it will be for one week or two weeks. According to the rules of the recruitment in Public Service, the applicant is allowed to apply only after a year again. While a Savarna will be appointed for a year or more. When the list of the appointments is brought before the Assembly, the number of appointments will be equal to the communal representation; but the duration of the post of all the Harijans will be equal to one Savarna. This kind of fraud is associating with the officials. Thus the public service is a common property of the Savarnas. No Harijan is benefited by it.

3. There was a proclamation from H. H. The Maharaja, a few years ago that three acres of ground should be given to each Harijan to live in; but the officials are Savarnas who are always unwilling to carry out the proclamation. Even though the Government is willing to grant large extent of ground for pasturing near towns, not a piece of the ground is given to the Harijans. The Harijans are still living in the compounds of the Savarnas and are undergoing manifold difficulties. Though large extents of ground lay in "Reserve," the applications of the Harijans for granting grounds are not at all regarded with importance or listened to. The most parts of the lands are benefited by the Savarnas.

4. The Government nominates every year, for the election of members of the Assembly, one member from each Harijan Community. Though they are elected to present the grievances of the Harijans before the Assembly, they are found to be the machinery of the Government, viz., the toys of the Savarna officers, who are benefited by them. Thus the grievances of the Harijans cannot be redressed any way.

5. All the Harijans of Travancore are labourers in the fields and compounds. They are the servants of the Savarnas who behave with them as beasts—nobody to look after for protection. Every Harijan gets only 2 chs (one anna) as the wage in most parts of the State. The social disabilities are the same to them even after the Temple Entry. The workers in the factories in various parts of the State of Travancore and the Officers of the State are all Savarnas and they are at present agitating for responsible Government. Now the Harijans are demanding jobs in Government and in factories but the agitation in Travancore is a Savarna agitation by which the Savarnas are making arrangements to get aid of Harijans in Public Service and factories. They plead for higher salaries and more privileges. They pay the least care to the Harijan labourers while the people of Travancore are maddened with the agitation of the workers in the factories. The standard of salary of Harijan worker is very low while the standard of a factory worker is thrice the former.

6. Due to starvation and want of proper means of livelihood, the heads of the children of Harijans are heated as a result of which they are likely to fail in school. Before proclamation, the duration of Concession in high schools was for 6 years; now, it has been reduced to three years by which a good number of students stopped their education after their failure.

7. There is a department for the Depressed Classes, the head of which is Mr. C. O. Damodaran (the protector of the Backward Communities). Though every year a big amount is granted for the expenditure, at the end of the year, two-thirds of the sum is lapsed by his sagacity. He used to submit reports to the Government that there is no way of spending the amount. Ninety-five per cent. of the sum allotted for the Depressed Class is spent as the salary of officials who are always Savarnas and 5 per cent. is benefited. Now the Government is going to make some colonies in three parts of Travancore. The officers are Savarnas. This scheme is, in my opinion, not a success for the Government do not pay greater attention to it. I regret that Travancore Government spends one anna for the Harijan cause, while Cochin State spends a rupee for the same.

8. The majority of the subjects of Travancore are now agitating strongly for Responsible Government under an organisation 'The

State Congress.' The leaders of this popular organisation belong to the four major communities of the State, namely, the Nair, Mahomedan, Christian and Ezhava community. The President of the State Congress Mr. Thanu Pillai issued a statement in which he stressed that special concessions would be given to the Depressed Class. All the leaders of the Depressed Class have been awaiting for a time to see the attitude of the State Congress. Now we come to understand that there is no reality in the promise of these leaders.

9. Now I am sure that the leaders have neglected the cause of the Depressed Class. The State Congress was started on the principles of nationalism and now it has become an institution of communalism. Communal spirit is now working among the leaders. In every public speech, statement or article, the leaders mention only these four major communities, while they have no thought on us. I fear, if this is the case of the leaders of the political agitation of Travancore, the situation of the Depressed Class will be more deplorable when the Responsible Government is achieved, for the entire possession of the Government will be then within the clutches of the above mentioned communities and the Depressed Classes' rights and privileges will be devoured by the former. In the meetings of the working committee of the States Congress, two-thirds of the time was devoted in discussion concerning the strike of the Alleppey Coir Factories; but nothing was mentioned in the meeting about the Harijan workers who are undergoing manifold difficulties. The workers in Factories are Savarnas and the agitation for obtaining Responsible Government is a kind of anti-Harijan movement. The motive of every leader of the State Congress is to improve the situation (circumstance) of the Savarna. The leaders of the major communities have some mercenary attitude who are going to sacrifice the Depressed for their progress.

10. These are the conditions of the Depressed Class of the State. What are the ways by which we have to establish our rights in the State ? I humbly request you to be good enough to render me your advice at this occasion. I am awaiting for the reply.

Excuse me for the trouble,

Yours faithfully,
SRINARAYANASWAMI."

If the plan of Temple Entry is ultimately to deprive the Untouchables of their statutory rights, then the movement is not only not spiritual but it is positively mischievous and it would be the duty of all honest people to warn the Untouchables.

APPENDIX VI

RECOGNITION OF UNTOUCHABLES AS A SEPARATE ELEMENT

Pronouncements of the British Government on the position of the Untouchables in the Constitution of India.

INTRODUCTION

The necessity for recalling the pronouncements of the Viceroys and of the Secretaries of State has arisen because of the recent criticism in the Press against the reply of 15th August 1944 given by Lord Wavell to Mr. Gandhi stating that the Scheduled Castes are a separate element in the national life of India and that their consent to the new Constitution was essential before power is transferred to Indian hands. This criticism is based upon the supposition that the Cripps's proposals did not recognize the Scheduled Castes as a separate element and did not make their consent necessary. Reliance is placed upon the fact that the Cripps's proposals spoke of "racial and religious minorities" only and it is argued that the Scheduled Castes are neither a racial nor a religious minority.

It is hardly necessary to point out how ignorant this criticism is. The Scheduled Castes are really a religious minority. The Hindu religion by its dogma of untouchability has separated the Scheduled Castes from the main body of the Hindus in a manner which makes the separation far more real and far wider than the separation which exists either between Hindus and Muslims or Hindus and Sikhs or Hindus and Christians. It is difficult to conceive of a more effective method of separation and segregation than the principle of untouchability and it is only those who are actuated by malicious spirit of finding excuses to deny the Scheduled Castes their claim to political rights would indulge in this kind of jugglery. Those who regard the statement of Lord Wavell as a new departure have completely forgotten what attitude His Majesty's Government has taken in the matter of the Scheduled Castes from the very beginning when the transfer of political power from British to Indian hands was thought of. Ever since 1917 when the Montagu-Chelmsford Report advocated responsible Government, the British Government have taken a definite stand that they would, under no circumstances, transfer power to Indian hands until they were satisfied that the position of the Scheduled Castes was safeguarded by adequate Constitutional provisions. A few of the many declarations made by Secretaries of State and Viceroys of India from 1917 to 1941 are collected together in the following pages. It will be found that the recognition that the Scheduled Castes are a separate and important element in the national life of the country and that their consent is necessary are in no way new proposals. Both the statements have been made by responsible representatives of His Majesty's Government, viz., the Secretary of State and the Viceroy long before the Cripps's proposals came into being. Particular attention is drawn to Mr. Amery's statement on 14th August 1940 and Lord Linlithgow's statement on 10th January 1940. It is hoped that a perusal of these declarations will enable those who are trying to negative the claim of the Scheduled Castes for political rights to realise that their propaganda is both foolish and malicious.

(1)

Extract from the Montagu-Chelmsford Report on Indian Constitutional Reform—1917.

155. . . . . . . We have shown that the political education of the ryot cannot be a very rapid, and may be a very difficult process. Till it is complete, he must be exposed to the risk of oppression by people who are stronger and cleverer than he is : and until it is clear that his interests can safely be left in his own hands or that the legislative councils represent and consider his interest, we must retain power to protect him. So with the depressed classes. We intend to make the best arrangements that we can for their representation, in order that they too may ultimately learn the lesson of self-protection. But if it is found that their interests suffer and that they do not share in the general progress, we must retain the means in our own hands of helping them.

* * *

(2)

Extract from the Fifth Despatch of the Government of India dated 23rd April 1919 on the Report of the Southborough Committee on Franchise.

13. We have analysed in the statement (printed at the top of the next page) the interests which in the committee's opinion should be represented by non-official nomination.

We accept these proposals generally. But there is one community whose case appears to us to require more consideration than the committee gave it. The Report on Indian Constitutional Reforms clearly recognizes the problem of the depressed classes and gave a pledge respecting them. "We intend to make the best arrangements that we can for their representation." The castes described as "Hindus—others" in the committee's report, though they are defined in varying terms, are broadly speaking all the same kind of people. Except for differences in the rigidity of their

Name of Province	Depressed Classes	Anglo-Indians	Indian Christians	Labour	Excluded Tracts	Military Interest	Industrial Interest other than Planting & Mining	Aborigines	Domiciled Bengalis	Others	Total	Percentage of total Membership
1	2	3	4	5	6	7	8	9	10	11	12	13
Madras	2	—	—	—	2	—	—	—	—	2	6	5
Bombay	—	1	1	1	—	—	—	—	—	2	6	5
Bengal	1	—	1	1	—	—	—	—	—	2	5	4
United Provinces ...	1	1	1	—	—	—	—	—	—	2	5	4
Punjab	—	2*	1	—	—	1	—	—	—	2	6	7
Bihar and Orissa ...	1	1	1	1	—	—	1	1	1	2	9	9
Central Provinces ...	1	1*	—	—	2	—	—	—	—	1	5	7
Assam	—	1*	1	1	1	—	—	—	—	1	5	9
Total	7	7	6	4	5	1	1	1	1	14	47	—

* Europeans and Anglo-Indians.

exclusion they are all more or less in the position of the Madras Panchamas, definitely outside that part of the Hindu community which is allowed access to their temples. They amount to about one-fifth of the total population, and have not been represented at all in the Morley-Minto Councils. The committee's report mentions the depressed classes twice, but only to explain that in the absence of satisfactory electorates they have been provided by nomination. It does not discuss the position of these people or their capacity for looking after themselves. Nor does it explain the amount of nomination which it suggests for them. Para 24 of the report justifies the restriction of the nominated seats on grounds which do not suggest that the committee were referring to the Depressed Classes. The measures of representation which they propose for this community is as follows :—

—	Total Population	Population of Depressed Classes	Total Seats	Seats for Depressed Classes
	(millions)	(millions)		
Madras	39.8	6.3	120	2
Bombay	19.5	.6	113	1
Bengal	45.0	9.9	127	1
United Provinces ...	47.0	10.1	120	1
Punjab	19.5	1.7	85	—
Bihar and Orissa ...	32.4	9.3	100	1
Central Provinces ...	12.2	3.7	72	1
Assam	6.0	0.3	54	—
Total	221.4	41.9	791	7

These figures speak for themselves. It is suggested that one-fifth of the entire population of British India should be allotted seven seats out of practically eight hundred. It is true that in all the councils there will be roughly a one-sixth proportion of officials who may be expected to bear in mind the interests of the depressed; but that arrangement is not, in our opinion, what the Report on reforms aims at. The authors stated that the depressed classes also should learn the lesson of self-protection. It is surely fanciful to hope that this result can be expected from including a single member of the community in an assembly where there are sixty or seventy caste Hindus. To make good the principles of paras 151, 152, 154 and 155 of the Report we must treat the outcasts more generously. We think there should be in each council enough representatives of the depressed classes to save them from being entirely submerged, and at the same time to stimulate some capacity for collective action. In the case of Madras, we suggest that they should be given six seats; in Bengal, the United Provinces and Bihar and Orissa, we would give them four; in the Central Provinces and Bombay two and elsewhere one. In these respects we think that the committee's report clearly requires modification.

* * *

(3)

Extract from Lord Birkenhead's speech as Secretary of State for India in the House of Lords on the 30th March 1927 on the appointment of Statutory Commission.

* * *

... ... Let me take the case of the depressed classes. There is in India a vast population even in relation to the numbers with which we are dealing, a population of sixty millions of the depressed classes. Their condition is not quite as terrible, quite as poignant as it has been in the past, but it is still terrible and poignant. They are repelled from all social intercourse. If they come between the gracious light of the sun and one who despised them the sun is disfigured for that man. They cannot drink at the public water-supply. They must make diversions of miles in order to satisfy thirst and they are tragically known and they have been known for generations as the "untouchables." There are sixty millions of them in India. Am I to have a representative of them upon this Commission ? Never, never would I form a Commission nor would anyone in a democratic country, nor would my friends opposite recommend it, from which you have excluded a member of this class which more than any other requires representation if you are indeed to put the matter to a mixed jury of the kind I am indicating.

(4)

Extract from the Report of the Simon Commission, Vol. II.

* * *

78. ... ... In no other province has it been possible to get an estimate of the number of the depressed classes who are qualified to vote. It is clear that even with a considerable lowering of the franchise—which would no doubt increase the proportion of the depressed class voters—there would be no hope of the depressed classes getting their own representatives elected in general constituencies without special provision being made to secure it. In the long run the progress of the depressed classes, so far as it can be secured by the exercise by them of political influence, will depend on their getting a position of sufficient importance for other elements to seek their support and to consider their needs.

* * *

80. ... ... It will be seen, therefore. that we do not recommend allocating seats to the depressed classes on the basis of their full population ratio. The scale of reserved representation suggested will secure a substantial increase in the number of the M.L.C's. drawn from the depressed classes. The poverty and want of education which so widely prevail amongst them make it extremely doubtful whether a large number of adequately equipped members could be at once provided, and it is far better that they should be represented by qualified spokesmen rather than by a larger number of ineffectives who are only too likely to be subservient to higher castes. The re-distribution of seats which is now being attempted among different kinds of representatives cannot be permanent, and provision must be made for its revision. But we think that our proposal is adequate for the present, especially as the representation of opinion by reservation of seats does not exclude the possibility of the capture of other seats not so reserved.

* * *

(5)

Extract from the Government of India's Despatch on Proposals for Constitutional Reform (as set out by the Simon Commission).

* * *

35. *The Representation of the Depressed Classes.*—The suggestions made by the Commission for the representation of the depressed classes have been much criticized by the provincial Governments. The difficulty of framing for each province a definition of the "depressed classes" is probably inherent in any scheme for the special representation of this class other than by nomination ; but the

Commission's proposals place a peculiarly embarrassing duty on the Governor to certify candidates authorised to stand for the depressed classes; and the proportion of representation which the Commission suggest, namely, in the ratio of three-quarters of the proportion of the depressed classes population to the total population of the electoral area of the provinces, seems likely to be unduly high. The Government of the United Provinces have calculated that in that province the Commission's proposal would result in the return to the provincial legislature of no less than forty members in place of the single nominated member who at present represents the community. The whole problem of the representation of the depressed classes will require careful investigation by the Franchise Committee; and at this stage we only wish to make plain that in our view their adequate representation should be secured by the best means that may be found practicable. Though there are some differences of opinion within the community, recent meetings of depressed classes associations have re-affirmed their belief in separate electorates.

* * *

(6)

Extract from the Terms of Reference to the Lothian Committee (on Franchise) 1932.

* * *

3. You are aware that the present electorate in Indian provinces amounts to less than 3 per cent. of the population of the areas returning members to provincial Councils, and it is obvious that under this limited franchise, the majority of the people and many large and important sections of the community can enjoy no effective representation in the Legislatures. The principle of a responsible Federal Government, subject to certain reservations and safeguards, has been accepted by His Majesty's Government while it has been decided that the Governors' provinces are to become responsibly governed units, enjoying the greatest possible measure of freedom from outside interference and dictation in carrying out their own policies in their own sphere. In these circumstances, it is clearly necessary so to widen the electorate that the legislatures to which responsibility is to be entrusted should be representative of the general mass of the population and that no important section of the community may lack the means of expressing its needs and its opinions.

* * *

6. It is evident from the discussions which have occurred in various connections in the Conference that the new Constitution must make adequate provision for the representation of the Depressed

Classes and that the method of representation by nomination is no longer regarded as appropriate. As you are aware, there is difference of opinion whether the system of separate electorates should be instituted for the Depressed Classes and your Committee's investigations should contribute towards the decision of this question by indicating the extent to which the Depressed Classes would be likely, through such general extension of the franchise as you may recommend, to secure the right to vote in ordinary electorates. On the other hand, should it be decided eventually to constitute separate electorates for the Depressed Classes, either generally or in those provinces in which they form a distinct and separate element in the population, your committee's inquiry into the general problem of extending the franchise should place you in possession of facts which would facilitate the devising of a method of separate representation for the Depressed Classes.

* * *

(7)

Extract from the Statement issued by H. E. Lord Linlithgow, the Viceroy and Governor-General of India, dated 17th October 1939.

* * *

"Be that as it may, His Majesty's Government recognise that when the time comes to resume consideration of the plan for the future federal Government of India, and of the plan destined to give effect to the Assurance given in Parliament by the late Secretary of State, to which I have just referred, it will be necessary to reconsider in the light of the then circumstances to what extent the details of the plan embodied in the Act of 1935 remain appropriate.

And I am authorised now by His Majesty's Government to say that at the end of the war they will be very willing to enter into consultation with representatives of the several communities, parties and interests in India, and with the Indian Princes, with a view to securing their aid and co-operation in the framing of such modifications as may seem desirable."

* * *

(8)

Extract from a Statement made on 7th November 1939 by Lord Zetland, Secretary of State for India, in the House of Lords.

* * *

"The Congress have further consistently taken the line, which they still maintain, that the fact that there are racial and religious minorities in India is of no relevance in that connexion, and that it has always been the intention of the Congress to secure, through the Constitution to be framed by Indians themselves, such protection for their rights as may prove acceptable to the minorities.

His Majesty's Government find it impossible to accept this position. The long-standing British connexion with India has left His Majesty's Government with obligations towards her which it is impossible for them to shed by disinteresting themselves wholly in the shaping of her future form of Government. Moreover, one outstanding result of the recent discussions in which the Governor-General has been engaged with representatives of all parties and interests in India has been to establish beyond doubt the fact that a declaration in the sense proposed, with the summary abandonment by His Majesty's Government of their position in India, would be far from acceptable to large sections of the Indian population."

* * *

(9)

Extract from the Speech made by H. E. Lord Linlithgow, Viceroy and Governor-General, at the Orient Club, Bombay, on January 10, 1940.

" Nor must we forget the essential necessity, in the interests of Indian unity, of the inclusion of the Indian States in any Constitutional scheme.

There are the insistent claims of the minorities.

I need refer only to two of them—the great Muslim minority and the Scheduled Castes—there are the guarantees that have been given to the minorities in the past; the fact that their position must be safeguarded, and that those guarantees must be honoured.

* * *

(10)

Extract from a Speech made by the Right Hon'ble Mr. L. S. Amery, Secretary of State for India, in the House of Commons on August 14, 1940.

* * *

" Congress leaders . . . have built up a remarkable organization, the most efficient political machine in India . . . if only they had succeeded, if the Congress could, in fact speak, as it professes to speak, for all the main elements in India's national life, then however advanced their demands, our problem would have been in many respects far easier than it is to-day. It is true that they are numerically the largest single party in British India, but their claim in virtue of that fact to speak for India is utterly denied by very important elements in India's complex national life. These others assert their right to be regarded not as mere numerical minorities but as separate constituent factors in any future Indian policy. The foremost among these elements stands the great Muslim community. They will have nothing to do with a constitution framed by a constituent assembly elected by a majority vote in geographical constituencies. They claim the right in any constitutional discussions to be regarded as an entity against the operations of a mere numerical majority. The same applies to the great body what are known as the Scheduled Castes who feel, in spite of Mr. Gandhi's earnest endeavours on their behalf, that, as a community, they stand outside the main body of the Hindu community which is represented by the Congress.

* * *

(11)

Extract from the Speech of the Right Hon'ble Mr. L. S. Amery, Secretary of State for India, in the House of Commons on 23rd April 1941.

* * *

"India's future Constitution should be devised by Indians for themselves and not by the British Government. India's future Constitution should be essentially an Indian Constitution, framed in accordance with the Indian conception of Indian conditions and Indian needs. The only essential condition is that the Constitution itself and the body which is to frame it must be the outcome of agreement between principal elements in India's national life.

* * *

(12)

Extract from a Statement by H. E. Lord Linlithgow, Viceroy and Governor-General of India, on 8th August 1940.

* * *

"These are two main points which have emerged. On these two points, His Majesty's Government now desire me to make their position clear. The first is as to the position of the minorities in relation to any future Constitutional scheme . . . It goes without saying that they (H. M. Government) could not contemplate the transfer of their present responsibilities for the peace and welfare of India to any system of Government whose authority is directly denied by large and powerful elements in India's national life. Nor could they be parties to the coercion of such elements into submission to such a Government."

APPENDIX VII

MINORITIES AND WEIGHTAGE

Views of the Montagu-Chelmsford Report and of the Simon Commission on the inequitous distribution of weightage.

(1)

MONTAGU-CHELMSFORD REPORT.

Extract from the Montagu-Chelmsford Report on Indian Constitutional Reforms.

* * *

Minority representation.

163. Important minorities, it is proposed, should be represented by election. This appears to point to a system of which latter are specified only for Muhammadans, who are no longer to be allowed to vote in the general electorates as well as in their own special ones. We have elsewhere touched upon the difficulty of denying to certain other communities, such as the Sikhs in the Punjab, a concession which is granted to Muhammadans. The authors of the scheme have also agreed upon, and set forth the proportions of the seats to be reserved for the special Muslim electorates in the various provinces. We are not aware on what basis, other than that of negotiation, the figures were arrived at. Separate electorates are proposed in all provinces even where Muhammadans are in a majority: and wherever they are numerically weak, the proportion suggested is in excess of their numerical strength or their present representation. At the same time, nearly all the Muslim associations which addressed us urged upon us that it should be still further increased. Now a privileged position of this kind is open to the objection, that if any other community hereafter makes good a claim to separate representation, it can be satisfied only by deduction from the non-Muslim seats, or else by a rateable deduction from both Muslim and non-Muslim; and Hindu and Muslim opinions are not likely to agree which process should be adopted. While, therefore, for reasons that we explain subsequently, we assent to the maintenance of separate representation for Muhammadans, we are bound to reserve our approval of the particular proposals set before us until we have ascertained what the effect upon other interests will be, and have made fair provision for them. We agree with the authors of the scheme that Muhammadans should not have votes both in their own special, and in the general electorates—and we welcome the Muslim League's assent to the revision in this respect of existing arrangements."

(2)

Extract from the Report of the Indian Statutory Commission, Vol. II.

*   *   *

Number of Muhammadan Seats

Para 85. We now take up the question of the proportion of seats in the various provincial councils to be set aside for Muhammadan members.

The Lucknow Pact, as we have already pointed out, included an agreement between Hindus and Moslems as to the proportion of Indian elected seats allotted in each province to the Muhammadan community, and its terms have been followed closely in the allocation of Muhammadan seats in the existing provincial legislatures. The Pact is no longer accepted by either side as offering a fair basis of representation and the rival contentions now put forward are indicated in paragraph 70 above. It is very much to be hoped that a renewed effort will be made between the two communities themselves to arrive at a fresh accommodation : but in the absence of agreement, a decision will have to be reached by others, on the assumption that separate electorates remain. Our own opinion is that in view of the existing position and of the weakness of the Moslem minority in six out of the eight[1] provinces, the present scale of weightage in favour of Muhammadans in those provinces might properly be retained. Thus, the proportion to be allotted to them, of seats filled from the "general" constituencies (other than the European general constituencies) would be determined as at present. But a claim has been put forward for a guarantee of Muhammadan representation which goes further than this—see paragraph 70 above and Appendix VII at the end of this chapter. This claim goes to the length of seeking to preserve the full security for representation now provided for Moslems in these six provinces and at the same time to enlarge in Bengal and the Punjab the present proportion of seats secured to the community by separate electorates to figures proportionate to their ratio of population. This would give Muhammadans a fixed and unalterable majority of the "general constituency" seats in both provinces. We cannot go so far. The continuance of the present scale of weightage in the six provinces could not—in the absence of a new general agreement between the communities—equitably be combined with so great a departure from the existing allocation in Bengal and the Punjab.

It would be unfair that Muhammadans should retain the very considerable weightage they now enjoy in the six provinces, and that there should at the same time be imposed, in face of Hindu-Sikh opposition, a definite Moslem majority in the Punjab and in

---

[1] Burma is not in question.

Bengal unalterable by any appeal to the electorate. On the other hand, if by agreement separate electorates in Bengal were abandoned, so that each community in that province was left to secure such seats as it could gain by appeal to a combined electorate, we should not, on that account, seek to deprive the Moslem community of its existing weightage in the six provinces where they are in a minority. In the same way in the Punjab, if Moslems, Sikhs and Hindus were prepared to seek election through a joint electorate covering all three communities, here again we should still be prepared to see this combined with the preservation of the present numerical proportion secured to the Muhammadans by separate electorates in the six other provinces.

We make this last suggestion, which really involves giving the Moslem community the advantage of a choice between two courses to follow, because we sincerely desire to see all practicable means attempted for reducing the extent of separate electorates and for giving the other system a practical trial.

Appendix VIII

CRIPPS PROPOSALS

DRAFT DECLARATION FOR DISCUSSION WITH INDIAN LEADERS

The conclusions of the British War Cabinet set out below are those which Sir Stafford Cripps has brought with him for discussion with Indian Leaders, and the question as to whether they will be implemented will depend upon the outcome of those discussions which are now taking place.

His Majesty's Government having considered the anxieties expressed in this country and in India as to the fulfilment of promises made in regard to the future of India have decided to lay down in precise and clear terms, the steps which they propose shall be taken for the earliest possible realisation of self-government in India. The object is the creation of a new Indian Union which shall constitute a Dominion associated with the United Kingdom and other Dominions by a common allegiance to the Crown but equal to them in every respect, in no way subordinate in any aspect of its domestic or external affairs.

His Majesty's Government, therefore, make the following Declaration :—

(*a*) Immediately upon cessation of hostilities, steps shall be taken to set up in India, in manner described hereafter, an elected body charged with the task of framing a new Constitution for India.

(*b*) Provision shall be made, as set out below, for participation of Indian States in the Constitution-making body.

(*c*) His Majesty's Government undertake to accept and implement forthwith the Constitution so framed subject only to :—

(*i*) The right of any Province of British India that is not prepared to accept the new Constitution, to retain its present constitutional position, provision being made for its subsequent accession if it so decides.

With such non-acceding Provinces, should they so desire, His Majesty's Government will be prepared to agree upon a new Constitution giving them the same full status as the Indian Union and arrived at by a procedure analogous to that here laid down.

(*ii*) The signing of a Treaty which shall be negotiated between His Majesty's Government and the Constitution-making body. This Treaty will cover all necessary matters arising out of the complete transfer of responsibility from British to Indian hands; it will make provision, in accordance with undertakings given by His Majesty's Government, for the protection of racial and religious minorities; but will not impose any restriction on the power of the Indian Union to decide in future its relationship to other Member States of the British Commonwealth.

Whether or not an Indian State elects to adhere to the Constitution, it will be necessary to negotiate a revision of its Treaty arrangements so far as this may be required in the new situation.

(*d*) The Constitution-making body shall be composed as follows unless the leaders of Indian opinion in the principal communities agree upon some other form before the end of hostilities :—

Immediately upon the result being known of Provincial Elections which will be necessary at the end of hostilities, the entire membership of the Lower Houses of Provincial Legislatures shall as a single electoral college proceed to the election of the Constitution-making body by the system of proportional representation. This new body shall be in number about 1/10th of the number of the electoral college.

Indian States shall be invited to appoint representatives in the same proportion to their total population as in the case of representatives of British India as a whole and with the same powers as British Indian Members.

(*e*) During the critical period which now faces India and until the New Constitution can be framed, His Majesty's Government must inevitably bear the responsibility for and retain the control and direction of the defence of India as part of their world war effort, but the task of organising to the full the military, moral and material resources of India must be the responsibility of the Government of India with the co-operation of the peoples of India. His Majesty's Government desire and invite the immediate and effective participation of the leaders of the principal sections of the Indian people in the counsels of their country, of the Commonwealth and of the united nations. Thus they will be enabled to give their active and constructive help in the discharge of a task which is vital and essential for the future freedom of India.

APPENDIX IX

OBJECTIONS TO CRIPPS PROPOSALS

Statement by B. R. Ambedkar showing how the Cripps Proposals would affect the Untouchables

The War Cabinet proposals show a sudden *Volte Face* on the part of His Majesty's Government. The putting forth of these proposals, which were denounced by them as an invasion of minority rights, is an indication of their complete surrender of right to win might. This is Munich mentality, the essence of which is to save oneself by sacrificing others, and it is this mentality which is writ large on these proposals. It is reported that the American and English people are annoyed at Indians not welcoming the proposals of His Majesty's Government relating to the constitutional advancement of India and thereby allowing the mission of Sir Stafford Cripps to fail. One can forgive the Americans for their attitude, but surely the English people and Sir Stafford Cripps ought to know better. It does not seem to have been sufficiently realised that the proposals of His Majesty's Government now put forth as the best are the very proposals which have been rejected and condemned by His Majesty's Government as the worst, only a few months previously. Those who realise this cannot but help saying that this is the ugliest part of the whole business of constitutional advance, which His Majesty's Government is now suddenly and contrary to its previous declarations, rushing to undertake. The proposals fall into three parts: (1) There is to be a constituent assembly with a right to frame the Constitution for India. This Assembly is to have the fullest power to frame such constitution as the majority in the Assembly may choose to decide; (2) The new Constitution is not to include all of the present Provinces of India but only such Provinces as may be willing to be bound by it. For this the Provinces have been given a right to decide whether they shall join the new Constitution or stay out of it. This is left to be done by a plebiscite in which a bare majority is declared enough to decide the issue; (3) The Constituent Assembly shall be required to enter into a treaty with the British Government. The treaty is to contain provisions for the safety and security of racial and religious minorities. After such a treaty is signed, the British Government is to withdraw its sovereignty and the Constitution framed by the Constituent Assembly is to come into operation.

Such, in brief outline, is the scheme of His Majesty's Government.

The proposal regarding Constituent Assembly is not a new proposal. It was put forth by the Congress when the war broke out and what is important is that this proposal of the Congress was rejected by His Majesty's Government. This is what Mr. Amery said in the House of Commons on August 14, 1940, regarding Constituent Assembly :—

> "Congress leaders . . . have built up a remarkable organization, the most efficient political machine in India . . . If only they had succeeded, if the Congress could, in fact speak, as it professes to speak, for all the main elements in India's national life, then however advanced their demands, our problem would have been in many respects far easier than it is to-day. It is true that they are numerically the largest single party in British India, but their claim in virtue of that fact to speak for India is utterly denied by very important elements in India's complex national life. These others assert their right to be regarded not as mere numerical minorities but as separate constituent factors in any future Indian policy. The foremost among these elements stands the great Muslim community. They will have nothing to do with a Constitution framed by a Constituent Assembly elected by a majority vote in geographical constituencies. They claim the right in any constitutional discussions to be regarded as an entity

and are determined only to accept a Constitution whose actual structure will secure their position as an entity against the operations of a mere numerical majority. The same applies to the great body of what are known as the *Scheduled Castes* who feel, in spite of Mr. Gandhi's earnest endeavours on their behalf, that, as a community, they stand outside the main body of the Hindu Community which is represented by the Congress."

This statement was made by Mr. Amery when he was elucidating the announcement made by the Viceroy on 8th August 1941 in which he had given the following pledge to the minorities on behalf of His Majesty's Government :—

"There are two main points which have emerged. On these two points, His Majesty's Government now desire me to make their position clear. The first is as to the position of the minorities in relation to any future constitutional scheme . . . It goes without saying that they (H.M. Government) could not contemplate the transfer of their present responsibilities for the peace and welfare of India to any system of government whose authority is directly denied by large and powerful elements in India's national life. Nor could they be parties to the coercion of such elements into submission to such a government."

Again on the 23rd April 1941, Mr. Amery referred to the demand of the Constituent Assembly and expressed himself in the following terms :—

"India's future Constitution should be devised by Indians for themselves and not by the British Government. India's future Constitution should be essentially an Indian Constitution, framed in accordance with the Indian conception of Indian conditions and Indian needs. The only essential condition is that the Constitution itself and the body which is to frame it, must be the outcome of agreement between principal elements in India's national life."

Such were the views and pledges given by H. M. Government regarding Constituent Assembly, which is now conceded. Regarding the demand for Pakistan, it was a demand put forward by the Muslim League. This demand was also rejected by His Majesty's Government. This is what Mr. Amery said in regard to it in the House of Commons on 1st August, 1940 :—

"This reaction against the dangers of what is called the Congress Raj or Hindu Raj has gone so far as to lead to a growing demand from Muslim quarters for a complete breaking up of India into separate Hindu and Muslim dominions. I need say nothing to-day of the manifold and to my mind, insuperable objections to such a scheme, at any rate in its extreme form. I would only note that it merely shifts the problem of permanent minorities to somewhat smaller areas, without solving it."

Again on 23rd April, 1941, he referred to it in his speech in the House of Common and spoke about it in the following terms :—

> " I am not concerned here to discuss the immense practical difficulties in the way of this so-called Pakistan project nor need I go back to the dismal record of India's history in the 18th century or to the disastrous experience of the Balkan countries before our eyes, to-day, in order to point out the terrible dangers inherent in any break up of the essential unity of India, at any rate in its relation to the outside world. After all, there is no British achievement in India of which we have reason to be proud than the unity . . . we have given her."

Such were the views of His Majesty's Government only a year ago regarding Constituent Assembly and Pakistan.

It is quite obvious that the proposal for a Constituent Assembly is intended to win over the Congress, while the proposal for Pakistan is designed to win over the Muslim League. How do the proposals deal with the Depressed Classes ? To put it shortly, they are bound hand and foot and handed over to the caste Hindus. They offer them nothing ; stone instead of bread. For the Constituent Assembly is nothing short of a betrayal of the Depressed Classes. There can be no doubt as to what the position of the Depressed Classes will be in the Constituent Assembly ; nor can there be any doubt regarding the political programme of the Constituent Assembly. In the Constituent Assembly, there may be no representatives of the Depressed Classes at all because no communal quotas are fixed by these proposals. If they are there, they cannot have a free, independent and decisive vote. In the first place, the representatives of the Depressed Classes will be in a hopeless minority. In the second place, all decisions of the Constituent Assembly are not required to be by a unanimous vote. A majority vote is enough to decide any question no matter what its constitutional importance is. It is clear that under this system the voice of the Depressed Classes in the Constituent Assembly cannot count. In the third place, the present system of proportional representation by which the members to the Constituent Assembly are to be elected under the terms contained in His Majesty's proposals cannot but result in the caste Hindus having virtually the right to nominate the representatives of the Depressed Classes to the Constituent Assembly. Such representatives of the Depressed Classes will be the tools of the caste Hindus. In the fourth place, the Constituent Assembly will be filled with the Congressites who will form the dominant majority party able to carry out its own programme. There is no doubt that Mr. Gandhi, whatever may be said about his endeavours in the matter of the social uplift of the Depressed Classes, is totally opposed to giving political recognition to the Depressed Classes in the Constitution as a separate and distinct element in the national life of India. That being the case, the programme of the majority party in the Constituent Assembly will be to wipe out the political safeguards already granted to the Depressed Classes in the present Constitution. Any one, who realises what is implied in the Constituent Assembly, will admit that His Majesty's Government by their proposals have literally thrown the Depressed Classes to the wolves. It may be said that while there is the Constituent Assembly which may deny constitutional safeguards to the Depressed Classes, His Majesty's Government have been careful to include in their proposals the provisions for a treaty with the Constituent Assembly the object of which is to secure the interests of the Depressed Classes. This proposal of a treaty is evidently borrowed from the plan adopted by His Majesty's Government for the settlement of the Irish dispute. The proposal regarding the treaty does not say what are the safeguards His Majesty's Government will decide to include in the treaty. This is an important point because there may be a difference of opinion between His Majesty's Government and the Depressed Classes on the nature, number and method of the political safeguards that may be necessary to protect the interests of the Depressed Classes under the new Constitution. The second and equally important question about the treaty is what is going to be the sanction behind the treaty. Will the treaty be a part of the Constitution framed by the Constituent Assembly, so that any provision in the Constitution which is repugnant with the treaty will be null and void? Or, will the treaty be just a treaty between the two governments; the Indian National Government and His Majesty's Government, as any trade treaty? If the treaty is to be of the former kind, it will be the law of the land and will have legal sanction of the Indian Government behind it. If, on the other hand, the treaty is to be of the latter kind, it is obvious it will not be the law of the land and will have no legal sanction behind it. Its sanction will be political sanction. Now a treaty cannot override the Constitution framed by the National Government for the obvious reason that such a thing, as was found in the case of Irish Free State, is incompatible with Dominion Status. The only sanction behind such a treaty will be political sanction. It is obvious that the use of such sanction must depend upon the colour of the Government and the state of public opinion. Given this fact, the questions that arise are two: (1) What are the means which His Majesty's Government will have at its disposal to enforce the treaty obligations? (2) Secondly, will His Majesty's Government be prepared to use these means to coerce the Indian National Government to abide by the terms of the treaty? With regard to the first question, it is obvious that the means for enforcing the treaty are twofold—use of force and trade war. As to the military force, the Indian army will not be available. It will be entirely transferred to the control of the new Indian National Government. His Majesty's Government will have therefore lost this means of enforcing the treaty. It is impossible to believe that His Majesty's Government will send its own army to compel the National Government to obey the treaty. A trade war is not possible. It is a suicidal policy and the experience of the Irish war with the Irish Free State for the recovery of land annuities shows that a nation of shopkeepers will not sanction it even though it may be for their interest and honour. The treaty therefore is going to be an empty formula, if not a cruel joke, upon the Depressed Classes. His Majesty's Government has sent out these proposals to be welcomed by Indians. But neither His Majesty's Government nor Sir Stafford Cripps have offered any explanation as to why they are offering to Indians the very proposals which His Majesty's Government had been condemning in seathing terms only a few months ago. A year ago, His Majesty's Government said that they would not grant Constituent Assembly because that would be a coercion of the minorities. His Majesty's Government is now prepared to grant Constituent Assembly and to coerce the minorities. A year ago, His Majesty's Government said that they will not allow Pakistan because that is Balkanization of India. To-day, they are prepared to allow the partition of India. How can the Government of a Great Empire lose all sense of principle? The only explanation is that His Majesty's Government has, as a result of the course of the war, become panic-stricken. The proposals are the result of loss of nerve. How great is the panic that has overtaken His Majesty's Government can be easily seen if one compared the demands made by the Congress and the Muslim League and the concessions made to them by these proposals. The Congress demanded that the Constitution should be framed by a Constituent Assembly by a mere majority vote. On the other hand, when the Viceroy announced that the British Government will not be a party to the coercion of the minorities involved in the demand by the Congress, the Working Committee of the Congress as its meeting at Wardha held on August 22, 1940, passed the following resolution:—

> "The Committee regrets that although the Congress has never thought in terms of coercing any minority, much less of asking the British Government to do so, the demand for a settlement of a Constitution though through a Constituent Assembly of duly elected representatives has been misrepresented as coercion and the issue of minorities has been made into an insuperable barrier to Indian progress."

The Working Committee added :—

> " The Congress had proposed that minority rights should be amply protected by agreement with the elected representatives of the minorities concerned."

This shows that even the Congress did not demand that the decision of minority rights should be included in the purview of the Constituent Assembly. His Majesty's Government has, however, given them the additional right to decide this minority rights issue by a bare majority vote. With regard to the question of Pakistan, the same attitude is noticeable. The Muslim League did not demand that Pakistan must be conceded immediately. All that the Muslim League had asked for was that at the next revision of the Constitution, the Mussulmans should not be prevented from raising the question of Pakistan. The present proposals have gone a step beyond and distinctly give to the Muslim League the right to create Pakistan. These are constitutional proposals. They are intended to lead India to wage a total war in which Hindus, Mussalmans, Depressed Classes and Sikhs are called upon wholeheartedly to participate. Yet Sir Stafford Cripps, either with the consent or without the consent of His Majesty's Government, has been making discrimination between major parties and minor parties. The major parties are those whose consent is necessary. Minor parties are those with whom consultation is believed to be enough. This is a new distinction. Certainly it was never made in the prior pronouncements either of His Majesty's Government or of the Viceroy. The pronouncement spoke of the " consent of the principal elements in the national life of India."

So far as the Depressed Classes are concerned, I am not aware of any pronouncement in which the Depressed Classes were placed on a lower plane than the one given to the Mussalmans. I quote the following from the speech of the Viceroy made in Bombay on January 10, 1941, from which it will be seen that the Depressed Classes were bracketed with the Mussalmans ;

> " There are insistent claims of the minorities. I need refer only to two of them ; the great Muslim minority and the Scheduled Classes—there are the guarantees that have been given to the minorities in the past, the fact that their position must be safeguarded and that those guarantees must be honoured."

This invidious distinction now sought to be made is a breach of faith with those minorities whose position has been lowered by this discrimination. From a constitutional point of view of total war, it is bound to cause more disaffection and disloyalty in the country. It is for the British to consider whether in this attempt to win the friendship of those who have probably already decided to choose other friends, they should lose those who are their real friends. The proposals show a sudden *volte face* on the part of His Majesty's Government. The putting forth of those proposals which were denounced by them as an invasion of minorities' rights is an indication of their complete surrender of right to win might. This is Munich Mentality the essence of which is to save oneself by sacrificing others and it is this mentality which is writ large on those proposals. My advice to the British Government is that they should withdraw these proposals. If they cannot fight for right and justice and their plighted word they should better make peace. They can thereby at least save their honour.

Appendix X

CORRESPONDENCE BETWEEN LORD WAVELL AND MR. GANDHI, 1944.

1. *Letter from Mr. Gandhi to Viceroy on July 15th, 1944.*

"Dear Friend,

You have no doubt seen the authentic copies, now published in the Indian Press, of the statements given by me to Mr. Gelder of the *News Chronicle.* As I have said to the Press, they were meant primarily to be shown to you. But Mr. Gelder, no doubt with the best of motives, gave the interview premature publicity. I am sorry. The publication will nevertheless be a blessing in disguise, if the interview enables you to grant at least one of my requests contained in my letter of June 17, 1944.

I am yours, etc.,
(Sd.) M. K. Gandhi."

2. *Viceroy's reply to Mr. Gandhi, dated 22nd July 1944.*

"Dear Mr. Gandhi,

Thank you for your letter of July 15. I have seen the statements you have made to Mr. Gelder, and your subsequent explanation of them. I do not think I can usefully comment at present, except to repeat what I have said in my last letter that if you will submit to me a definite and constructive policy, I shall be glad to consider it.

Yours sincerely,
(Sd.) Wavell."

3. *Gandhi's letter to the Viceroy, dated 27th July 1944.*

"DEAR FRIEND,

I must admit my disappointment over your letter of 22nd instant. But I am used to work in the face of disappointment. Here is my concrete proposal.

I am prepared to advise the Working Committee to declare that in view of changed conditions, mass civil disobedience envisaged by the resolution of August 1942, cannot be offered and that full co-operation in the war effort should be given by the Congress, if a declaration of immediate Indian independence is made and a National Government responsible to the Central Assembly be formed subject to the proviso that, during the pendency of the war, the military operations should continue as at present but without involving any financial burden on India. If there is a desire on the part of the British Government for a settlement, friendly talks should take the place of correspondence. But I am in your hands. I shall continue to knock so long as there is the least hope of an honourable settlement.

After the foregoing was written, I saw Lord Munster's speech in the House of Lords. The summary given by him in the House of Lords fairly represents my proposal. This summary may serve as a basis for mutual friendly discussion.

I am,

Yours sincerely,

(Sd.) M. K. GANDHI."

4. *Viceroy's reply to Mr. Gandhi, dated 15th August 1944.*

"DEAR MR. GANDHI,

Thank you for your letter of July 27. Your proposals are :—

(*i*) that you should undertake to advise the Working Committee : (*a*) " that in view of changed conditions mass civil disobedience envisaged by the resolution of August 1942, cannot be offered " and (*b*) " that full co-operation in the war effort should be given by the Congress" provided

(*ii*) that His Majesty's Government (*a*) declare immediate Indian independence, and (*b*) form a " National Government responsible to the Central Assembly subject to the proviso that during the pendency of the war the military operations should continue as at present but without involving any financial burden on India."

2. His Majesty's Government remain most anxious that a settlement of the Indian problem should be reached. But proposals such as those put forward by you are quite unacceptable to His Majesty's

Government as a basis for discussion and you must realise this if you have read Mr. Amery's statement in the House of Commons on July 28th last. They are indeed very similar to the proposals made by Maulana Abul Kalam Azad to Sir Stafford Cripps in April 1942 and His Majesty's Government's reasons for rejecting them are the same as they were then.

3. Without recapitulating all these reasons in detail, I should remind you that His Majesty's Government at that time made it clear :

(*a*) That their offer of unqualified freedom after the cessation of hostilities was made conditional upon the framing of a Constitution agreed by the main elements of India's national life and the negotiation of the necessary treaty arrangements with His Majesty's Government :

(*b*) That it is impossible during the period of hostilities to bring about any change in the Constitution by which means alone a "National Government" such as you suggest could be made responsible to the Central Assembly.

The object of these conditions was to ensure the fulfilment of their duty to safeguard the interests of the racial and religious minorities of the Depressed Classes and their treaty obligations to the Indian States.

4. It was upon the above conditions that His Majesty's Government invited Indian leaders to take part in an interim Government which would operate under the existing Constitution. I must make it quite clear that until the war is over responsibility for defence and military operations cannot be divided from the other responsibilities of Government and that until hostilities cease and the new Constitution is in operation, His Majesty's Government and the Governor-General must retain their responsibility over the entire field. So far as the question of India's share of the cost of the war is concerned, this is essentially a matter for settlement between His Majesty's Government on the one hand and the Government of India on the other, and existing financial arrangements can only be reopened at the instance of one or the other.

5. It is clear in these circumstances that no purpose will be served by discussion on the basis which you suggest. If however the leaders of the Hindus, the Muslims and the important minorities were willing to co-operate in a transitional Government established and working within the present constitution, I believe good progress might be made. For such a transitional Government to succeed, there must before it is formed, be agreement in principle between Hindus and Muslims and all important elements as to the method by which the new Constitution should be framed. This agreement is a matter for Indians themselves.

Until Indian leaders have come closer together than they are now, I doubt if I myself can do anything to help. Let me remind you too that minority problems are not easy. They are real and can be solved only by mutual compromise and tolerance.

6. The period after the termination of hostilities for which the transitional Government would last, would depend on the speed with which the new constitution could be framed. I see no reason why preliminary work on that Constitution should not begin as soon as the Indian leaders are prepared to co-operate to that end. If they can arrive at a genuine agreement as to the method of framing the Constitution, no unnecessary time need be spent after the war in reaching final conclusions and in agreeing treaty arrangements with His Majesty's Government. There again the primary responsibility rests on the Indian leaders.

Yours sincerely,
(Sd.) WAVELL."

APPENDIX XI

POLITICAL DEMANDS OF SCHEDULED CASTES

Resolutions passed by the Working Committee of the All-India Scheduled Castes Federation held in Madras on the 23rd September 1944 under the Presidentship of Rao Bahadur N. Shiva Raj, B.A., B.L., M.L.A., outlining the safeguards for the Untouchables in the new Constitution.

RESOLUTION No. 1

SUBJECT :—*Recognition of the Scheduled Castes as a separate element.*

The Working Committee of the All-India Scheduled Castes Federation has found a section of the Press in India making the allegation, that the statement made by H. E. the Viceroy in his letter to Mr. Gandhi dated the 15th August 1944 to the effect that the Scheduled Castes are one of the important and separate elements in the national life of India and requiring that the consent of the Scheduled Castes to the Constitution of India was a necessary condition precedent for transfer of power to Indians, is a departure from the position of His Majesty's Government as defined in the Cripps Proposals. The Committee cannot help expressing its indignation at this propaganda and takes this occasion to state in most emphatic and categorical terms that the Scheduled Castes are a distinct and separate element in the national life of India and that they are a religious minority in a sense far more real than the Sikhs and Muslims can be and within the meaning of the Cripps Proposals. The Working Committee desires to point out that what has been stated by Lord Wavell in his letter to Mr. Gandhi has been the position of His Majesty's Government from the very beginning and was enunciated in clear terms as early as 1917 by the authors of the Montagu-Chelmsford Report simultaneously with the enunciation by them of Responsible Government as the goal of India's political evolution and has been confirmed by subsequent action of His Majesty's Government such as the grant of separate representation to the Scheduled Castes at the Round Table Conference, Joint Parliamentary Committee and in the Government of India Act, 1935, as a recognized minority, separate from the Hindus. The Working Committee has, therefore, no hesitation in saying that it is a false and malicious propaganda to allege that this is a departure from the policy of His Majesty's Government and regards it as a manœuvre on the part of the enemies of the Scheduled Castes to defeat their just claims for constitutional safeguards and calls upon Indian political leaders and particularly the Hindu leaders to accept this fact, in the interests of peace and good-will between the Hindus and the Scheduled Castes, and for the speedy realization of India's political goal.

Resolution No. 2

SUBJECT :—*Declaration by His Majesty's Government relating to the Scheduled Castes and the Constitution.*

The Working Committee of the All-India Scheduled Castes Federation welcomes the declaration made by His Majesty's Government and recently reiterated by His Excellency the Viceroy that His Majesty's Government regards the consent of the Scheduled Castes, among others, to the Constitution of a free India, as a matter of vital importance and as a necessary condition precedent to the transfer of power to Indian hands. At the same time, the Working Committee wishes to draw the attention of His Majesty's Government to the attitude of the Congress and other political organizations in the country which treats this declaration of His Majesty's Government as not being a *bona fide* declaration and made without any intention to honour it and as a mere matter of tactics adopted to postpone transfer of power, and which is in all probability responsible for the unwillingness of the Majority Community to seek for a settlement with the Scheduled Castes. The Working Committee regards this allegation as baseless and calls upon His Majesty's Government not to give any ground for such suspicion and make it clear that they will stand by the declaration at all times and under all circumstances.

Resolution No. 3

Subject :—*Nature of Constitutional Safeguards.*

The Working Committee declares that no Constitution shall be acceptable to the Scheduled Castes unless :—

(*a*) it has the consent of the Scheduled Castes.

(*b*) it recognizes the Scheduled Castes as distinct and separate element ;

(*c*) it contains within itself provisions for securing the following purposes :

(1) For earmarking a definite sum in the Budgets of the Provincial and Central Governments for the Secondary, University and Advanced Education of the Scheduled Castes.

(2) For reservation of Government lands for separate settlements of the Scheduled Castes through a Settlement Commission.

(3) For Representation of the Scheduled Castes according to their needs, numbers and importance :—

(*i*) in the Legislatures,
(*ii*) in the Executive,
(*iii*) in Municipalities and Local Boards,
(*iv*) in the Public Services;
(*v*) on the Public Service Commissions.

(4) For the recognition of the above provisions as fundamental rights beyond the powers of the Legislature or the Executive to amend or alter or abrogate.

(5) For the appointment of an Officer similar in status to that of the Auditor-General appointed under Section 166 of the Government of India Act of 1935 and removable from office in like manner and on the like grounds as a judge of the Federal Court to report on the working of the provisions relating to Fundamental Rights.

Resolution No. 4

Subject :—*Communal Settlement.*

The Working Committee of the All-India Scheduled Caste Federation, while it is most eager for a settlement of the Communal problem, wholly disapproves of the secret negotiations which are being carried on by Mr. Gandhi and Mr. Jinnah for a settlement between the Hindus and the Muslims. The Working Committee is of opinion that Communal settlement of a sectional character is harmful in every way. It is harmful because it ignores the vital interests of other communities. It is harmful because it creates a feeling of suspicion in other communities that dishonest deal is being made between two communities to defeat their interests. It is also harmful to the general interests of the country, inasmuch as the singling out of one special community from others for conferring special privileges, not necessary for its protection but demanded on the basis of prestige, creates differences in status which from the point of view of maintaining equal citizenship for all, are unjustifiable and must be deplored. The Working Committee is surprised that Mr. Gandhi who has time and again proclaimed himself as an opponent of secrecy in public life should have entered into secret diplomacy to bring about Hindu-Moslem Settlement. The Committee expresses its emphatic opinion that the proper procedure to settle the communal question, which would give a sense of security and ensure fair and equal treatment to all is to discuss the demands put forth by each interest in public and in the presence of and with the representatives of other interests.

Resolution No. 5

Subject :—*Revision of the Constitution.*

The Working Committee of the All-India Scheduled Castes Federation is of opinion that the provisions in the existing Constitution relating to minority representation are not based on any intelligible principle. The Committee finds that as the system now stands, some minorities have not received even their population ratio of representation, while other minorities have been given weightage over and above their population ratio as a concession to their claims based on historical and military importance. The Working Committee regards the recognition of such claims to be harmful to the interests of other minorities and inconsistent with the ideal of social and political democracy, which is the goal of all Indians and that they should never be tolerated. In this connection, the Committee wishes to draw attention to the fact that the principle of giving weightage to specially selected minorities has been condemned by the authors of the Montagu-Chelmsford Report and also by the Simon Commission. The Committee demands that in view of the fact that the next Constitution of India will be for India as a Dominion, the provisions of the Constitution relating to minorities should be revised and should be brought in accord with the principle of equal treatment of all minorities.

Resolution No. 6

Subject :—*Representation in the Legislatures and in the Executive.*

The Working Committee of the All-India Scheduled Castes Federation desires to state in categorical and emphatic terms that the Scheduled Castes will not tolerate any discrimination between one community and another in the matter of representation and will insist upon their claim for seats in the Provincial and Central Legislatures and in the Provincial and Central Executive being adjudged in the same manner and by the same principles that may be made applicable to the claims of the Muslim Community.

Resolution No. 7

Subject :—*Electorates.*

The Working Committee of the All-India Scheduled Castes Federation is of opinion that the experience of the last elections held under the Government of India Act has proved that the system of joint electorates has deprived the Scheduled Castes of the right to send true and effective representatives to the Legislatures and has given the Hindu Majority the virtual right to nominate members of the Scheduled Castes who are prepared to be the tools of the Hindu Majority. The Working Committee of the Federation therefore demands that the system of joint electorates and reserved seats should be abolished and the system of separate electorates be introduced in place thereof.

Resolution No. 8

Subject :—*Framework of Executive Government.*

The working Committee of the All-India Scheduled Castes Federation takes note of the fact that not only all wealth, property, trade and industry are in the hands of the Majority Community, but even the whole administration of the State is controlled by the Majority Community whose members have monopolized all posts in the State services both superior and inferior. The Working Committee of the All-India Scheduled Castes Federation regards this as the most dangerous situation which cannot but cause great apprehension to the minority communities since the combination of these circumstances gives the majority the fullest power to establish its stranglehold upon the minorities. This fear of a stranglehold is greatly augmented by the Constitutional provisions relating to the Executive contained in the Government of India Act of 1935 which permits the majority in the Legislature to form a Government without reference to the wishes of the minorities.

The Working Committee of the All-India Scheduled Castes Federation feels that while, in the absence of an alternative system, the Parliamentary system of Government may have to be accepted, the Committee is definitely opposed to the system of Parliamentary cabinet inasmuch as it automatically vests the Executive authority in the Majority Community and thereby strengthens the hold of the Majority Community which has entered into the steel frame of the administration and thus has become a source of great danger to the Minorities. The Working Committee has, therefore, come to the conclusion that the system of Parliamentary Cabinet is not suited to Indian conditions and that a different system under which Executive Government would be formed in consultation with the wishes of the Minorities must be designed to give them a better sense of security.

The Working Committee insists that the Executive in the Provinces as well as in the Centre should be constituted in the following manner :—

(*i*) The Executive should consist of a Prime Minister and other ministers drawn from general community and from minority communities in a proportion to be specified in the Constitution.

(*ii*) The Prime Minister and Ministers drawn from the general community shall be elected to the Executive by the whole house by single transferable vote.

(*iii*) The Ministers representing the minority communities shall be chosen by the members representing the different communities by single transferable vote.

(*iv*) The Members of the Executive shall be members of the Legislature, shall answer questions, vote and take part in debates.

(*v*) Any vacancy in the Executive shall be filled in accordance with rules governing the original appointments.

(*vi*) The period for which the Executive shall hold office shall be co-terminus with the life of the Legislature.

Resolution No. 9

Subject :—*Public Services.*

While it is desirable to plan for a Government which will be a Government of Laws and not of men, it cannot be forgotten that no matter how Government is organized, it must remain a Government of men. That being so, whether Government is good or bad—as distinguished from a merely efficient Government—and how far the administration of public affairs will be non-political and impartial must depend upon the spirit and outlook and sense of justice of the men who are appointed to administer the Law. The Working Committee of the All-India Scheduled Castes Federation is convinced that the Scheduled Castes can never get protection, justice or sympathy from the present administration which is controlled by men full of caste consciousness, narrow-mindedness, absence of sense of justice and having a hatred and contempt for the Scheduled Castes. The Working Committee, therefore, demands that the Constitution must recognize the right of the Scheduled Castes to reservation in the Public Services in the same proportion as may be applied to the claims of the Muslim Community.

RESOLUTION No. 10

SUBJECT :—*Provision for Education.*

The Working Committee of the All-India Scheduled Castes Federation feels that unless persons belonging to the Scheduled Castes are able to occupy posts which carry executive authority, the Scheduled Castes must continue to suffer, as they have been doing in the past all the injustices and indignities from the hands of the Government and the Public. The Working Committee, therefore, regards the spread of higher and advanced education among the Scheduled Castes as of vital importance to them. But, it cannot be denied that such advanced education is beyond the means of the Scheduled Castes. The Committee regards it as essential that a definite liability in this behalf should be imposed on the State to provide funds for that purpose and demands that the Constitution should impose an obligation upon the Provincial Governments and the Central Government to set apart adequate sums, as may be specified by the Constitution, exclusively for advanced education of the Scheduled Castes in their annual budgets and to accept such provisions as a first charge on their revenues.

RESOLUTION No. 11

SUBJECT :—*Separate Settlements.*

The Working Committee of the All-India Scheduled Castes Federation holds :—

(*a*) that so long as the Scheduled Castes continue to live on the outskirts of the Hindu village, as an alien people, with no source of livelihood and in small numbers as compared to Hindus, they will continue to remain Untouchables and subject to the tyranny and oppression of the Hindus and will not be able to enjoy free and full life, and (*b*) that for the better protection of the Scheduled Castes from the tyranny and oppression of the Caste Hindus, which may take a worse form under Swaraj, and to enable the Scheduled Castes to develop to their fullest manhood, to give them economic and social security as also to pave the way for the removal of untouchability, the Working Committee demands that the Constitution should provide—

(1) For the transplantation of the Scheduled Castes from their present habitations and form separate Scheduled Caste villages away from and independent of Hindu villages ;

(2) For the settlement of the Scheduled Castes in new villages a provision shall be made by the Constitution for the establishment of a Settlement Commission ;

(3) All Government land which is cultivable and which is not occupied and land which may be reclaimed shall be handed over to the Commission to be held in trust for the purpose of making new settlements of the Scheduled Castes.

(4) The Commission shall be empowered to purchase new land under the Land Acquisition Act from private owners to complete the scheme of settlements of the Scheduled Castes.

(5) The Constitution shall provide that the Central Government shall grant to the Settlement Commission a minimum sum of rupees five crores per annum to enable it to carry out their duty in this behalf.

RESOLUTION NO. 12

"The Working Committee of the A.I.S.C. Federation unanimously resolves that it places its complete confidence in Dr. B. R. Ambedkar and authorises him to negotiate on its behalf and on behalf of Scheduled Castes with other political parties or their leaders as and when necessity arises."

APPENDIX XII

Communal Distribution of Population by Minorities in the Provinces of British India.

Province	Total Population	Muslims Population	Muslims Percentage	Scheduled Castes Population	Scheduled Castes Percentage	Indian Christians Population	Indian Christians Percentage	Sikhs Population	Sikhs Percentage
Ajmere-Merwara	583,693	89,899	15.4	*Nil(?)*	—	3,895	.7	867	.15
Andaman Nicobar	33,768	8,005	23.7	*Nil*	—	779	2.3	744	2.2
Assam	10,204,733	3,442,479	33.7	676,291	6.6	37,750	.4	3,464	.03
British Baluchistan	501,631	438,930	87.5	5,102	1.0	2,633	.5	11,918	2.3
Bengal	60,306,525	33,005,434	54.7	7,878,970	13.0	110,923	.2	16,281	.03
Bihar*	36,340,151	4,716,314	12.9	4,840,379	13.3	24,693	.07	13,213	.04
Bombay	20,849,840	1,920,368	9.2	1,855,148	8.9	338,812	1.6	8,011	.04
Central Province & Berar ...	16,813,584	783,697	4.7	3,051,413	18.1	48,260	.3	14,996	.09
Coorg	168,726	14,780	8.8	25,740	15.3	3,309	2.0	*Nil*	—
Delhi	917,939	304,971	33.2	121,693	13.3	10,494	1.1	16,157	1.8
Madras	49,341,810	3,896,452	7.9	8,068,492	16.4	2,001,082	4.06	418	.001
N.W.F.P.	3,038,067	2,788,797	91.8	*Nil*	—	5,426	.2	57,989	1.9
Orissa	8,728,544	146,301	1.7	1,238,171	14.2	26,584	.3	232	.003
Punjab	28,418,819	16,217,242	57.0	1,248,635	4.4	486,038	1.7	3,757,401	13.2
Pant Piploda	5,267	251	4.8	918	17.4	216	4.1	*Nil*	—
Sind	4,229,221	3,054,635	72.2	191,634	4.5	13,232	.3	31,011	.7
United Provinces‡	55,020,617	8,416,308	15.3	11,717,158	21.3	131,327	.2	232,445	.4
Total	295,502,935	79,244,863	26.9	40,919,744	13.9	3,245,453	1	4,165,147	1
*Bihar	28,823,802	4,168,470	14.4	3,919,619	13.6	12,651	.04	3,204	.01
Chota Nagpur	7,516,349	547,844	7.3	420,760	5.6	12,042	.2	10,009	.1
†C.P.	13,208,718	448,528	3.4	2,359,836	17.9	42,135	.3	12,766	.1
Berar	3,604,366	335,169	9.3	691,577	19.2	6,125	.2	2,230	.06
Agra	40,906,[illegible]47	6,231,062	15.2	8,018,803	19.6	120,549	.3	226,096	.5
Oudh	14,114,470	2,185,246	15.5	3,698,355	26.2	10,778	.08	6,349	.05

APPENDIX XIII

Communal Distribution of Population by Minorities in Indian States.

States and Agencies	Total Population	Muslims		Scheduled Castes		Indian Christians		Sikhs	
		Population	Per-cent-age	Population	Per-cent-age	Population	Per-cent-age	Population	Per-cent-age
Assam	725,655	31,662	4.4	265	.04	25,913	3.6	381	.05
Baluchistan	356,204	346,251	97.2	65	.02	40	.01	126	.04
Baroda	2,855,010	223,610	7.8	230,794	8.1	9,182	.3	566	.02
Bengal	2,144,829	372,113	17.3	269,729	12.6	564	.03	28	.001
Central India	7,506,427	439,850	5.9	1,027,009	13.7	7,582	.1	2,731	.04
Chattisgarh	4,050,000	28,773	0.7	483,132	11.9	11,820	.3	507	.01
Cochin	1,422,875	109,188	7.7	141,154	9.9	399,394	28.1	9	—
Deccan (and Kolhapur) ...	2,785,428	182,036	6.5	306,898	11.0	17,236	.6	22	.001
Gujarat	1,458,702	58,000	3.9	55,204	3.8	4,215	.3	182	.01
Gwalior	4,006,159	240,903	6.0	—	—	1,352	.03	2,342	.06
Hyderabad	16,338,534	2,097,475	12.8	2,928,048	17.9	215,989	1.3	5,330	.03
Kashmere and Feudatories ...	4,021,616	3,073,540	76.4	113,464	2.8	3,079	.08	65,903	1.6
Madras	498,754	30,263	6.0	83,734	16.8	20,806	4.2	5	—
Mysore	7,329,140	485,230	6.6	1,405,067	19.2	98,580	1.3	269	.004
N.W.F.P.	46,267	22,068	47.7	*Nil*	—	571	1.2	4,472	9.1
Orissa	3,023,731	14,355	0.47	352,088	11.6	2,249	.07	151	.005
Punjab	5,503,554	2,251,459	40.9	349,962	6.4	6,952	.1	1,342,685	24.4
Punjab Hill	1,090,644	46,678	4.3	238,774	21.9	188	.02	17,739	1.6
Rajputana	13,670,208	1,297,841	9.5	—	—	4,349	.03	81,896	.6
Sikkim	121,520	83	0.07	76	.06	34	.03	1	—
Travancore	6,070,018	434,150	7.2	395,952	6.5	1,958,491	32.3	31	—
U. P.	928,470	273,625	29.5	152,927	16.5	1,281	.1	731	.08
Western India...	4,904,156	600,440	12.2	358,038	7.3	3,105	0.6	239	.005
Total	90,857,901	12,659,593	13.9	8,892,380	9.7	2,792,972	3.1	1,526,346	1.7

Appendix XIV

Particulars of Scheduled Castes Constituencies in regard to seats and voting strength Province by Province :—

Appendix XIV : (1) Madras

" " (2) Bombay

" " (3) Bengal

" " (4) U. P.

" " (5) Punjab

" " (6) Bihar

" " (7) C. P. & Berar.

" " (8) Assam

" " (9) Orissa

APPENDIX XIV (1) MADRAS

Name of Constituency	Total Number of Seats in the Constituency		Total Number of Candidates		Total Number of Voters in the Constituency		
	For General	For Scheduled Castes	For General Seat	For Scheduled Caste Seat	General	Scheduled Castes	Percentage of Scheduled Caste Voters to General
(1)	(2)	(3)	(4)	(5)	(6)	(7)	(8)
Madras City, South Central	1	1	4	1	13,318	2,909	22
Chicacole	1	1	4	4	54,012	7,461	14
Amalapuram	1	1	2	3	46,163	23,110	50
Cocanada	1	1	3	1	50,384	12,066	24
Ellore	1	1	3	3	45,452	11,463	25
Bandar	1	1	2	3	77,627	13,314	17
Ongole	1	1	2	2	67,851	10,885	16
Gudur	1	1	2	4	35,094	7,436	21
Cuddapah	1	1	2	3	74,497	10,630	14
Penukonda	1	1	2	2	54,864	11,396	21
Bellary		1	3	2	63,092	9,232	15
Kurnool	1	1	2	4	53,687	13,433	25
Tiruttani	1	1	2	2	52,875	6,350	12
Chingleput	1	1	2	2	46,237	19,366	42
Tiruvallur	1	1	2	3	57,029	21,033	37
Ranipet	1	1	3	4	53,632	10,370	19
Tiruvannamalai	1	1	3	4	67,861	16,705	25
Tindivanam	1	1	3	4	63,485	19,500	31
Chidambaram	1	1	3	1	68,713	19,947	29
Tirukkoyilur	1	1	2	2	75,874	22,986	30
Tanjore	1	1	1	1	78,874	14,718	19
Mannargudi	1	1	3	4	45,283	11,767	26
Ariyalur	1	1	2	3	85,125	16,076	19
Palni	1	1	1	2	60,453	11,400	19
Sattur	1	1	2	2	58,648	6,843	12
Koilpatti	1	1	2	3	59,101	12,526	21
Pollachi	1	1	2	4	39,239	12,919	32
Namakal	1	1	2	2	43,437	14,561	34
Coondapur	1	1	2	3	35,679	8,843	25
Malappuram	1	1	2	3	47,299	10,355	22

APPENDIX XIV (2) BOMBAY

Name of Constituency	Total Number of Seats in the Constituency		Total Number of Candidates		Total Number of Voters in the Constituency		
	For General	For Scheduled Castes	For General Seat	For Scheduled Caste Seat	General	Scheduled Castes	Percentage of Scheduled Caste Voters to General
(1)	(2)	(3)	(4)	(5)	(6)	(7)	(8)
Bombay City North and Bombay Suburban District ...	2	1	6	4	61,831	9,880	16
Bombay City (Byculla and Parel) ...	2	1	4	3	71,100	10,486	15
Kaira District ...	3	1	4	1	92,388	6,231	7
Surat District ...	3	1	6	4	51,711	3,929	8
Thana, South ...	2	1	3	3	42,003	2,263	5
Ahmednagar South ...	2	1	4	3	36,065	4,814	13
East Khandesh, East ...	3	1	7	4	56,733	4,842	9
Nasik, West ...	3	1	7	2	44,517	8,881	20
Poona, West ...	2	1	4	2	43,147	7,206	17
Satara, North ...	3	1	5	4	57,839	6,692	12
Sholapur, North East ...	2	1	6	4	36,210	6,741	19
Belgaum, North ...	3	1	6	4	49,507	12,493	25
Bijapur, North ...	2	1	4	4	42,301	7,525	18
Kolaba District ...	3	1	7	3	59,490	4,804	8
Ratnagiri, North ...	3	1	8	3	21,908	3,961	18

Appendix XIV (3) Bengal

Name of Constituency	Total Number of Seats in the Constituency		Total Number of Candidates		Total Number of Voters in the Constituency		
	For General	For Scheduled Castes	For General Seat	For Scheduled Caste Seat	General	Scheduled Castes	Percentage of Scheduled Caste Voters to General
(1)	(2)	(3)	(4)	(5)	(6)	(7)	(8)
Burdwan, Central	1	1	2	3	35,294	14,450	41
Burdwan, North West	1	1	2	3	41,817	8,693	21
Birbhum	1	1	3	3	52,569	18,506	35
Bankura, West	1	1	1	4	44,115	19,272	44
Midnapur, Central	1	1	2	2	75,903	19,664	26
Jhargram-cum-Ghatal	1	1	2	4	40,598	9,917	24
Hooghly, North East	1	1	3	3	35,500	12,254	35
Howrah	1	1	2	3	68,526	22,470	33
24-Parganas, South East	1	1	3	3	29,342	37,556	128
24-Parganas, North West	1	1	2	4	42,214	24,404	58
Nadia	1	1	2	4	53,247	20,957	39
Murshidabad	1	1	2	3	46,122	11,692	25
Jessore	1	1	4	2	50,966	43,425	85
Khulna	1	2	3	6	41,639	54,530	131
Malda	1	1	2	4	30,916	22.728	74
Dinajpur	1	2	1	2	25,985	89,880	346
Jalpaiguri-cum-Siliguri	1	2	3	8	9,074	54,657	602
Rangpur	1	2	2	5	21,497	68,759	320
Bogra-cum-Pabna	1	1	3	4	41,539	31,459	76
Dacca, East	1	1	2	4	38,810	36,749	95
Mymensingh, West	1	1	2	4	47,974	30,036	63
Mymensingh, East	1	1	2	4	42,237	29,745	70
Faridpur	1	2	2	8	63,532	73,946	116
Bakarganj, South West	1	1	1	4	23,477	37,895	161
Tippera	1	1	3	4	65,898	27.475	41

APPENDIX XIV (4) U. P.

Name of Constituency	Total Number of Seats in the Constituency		Total Number of Candidates		Total Number of Voters in the Constituency		
	For General	For Scheduled Castes	For General Seat	For Scheduled Caste Seat	General	Scheduled Castes	Percentage of Scheduled Caste Voters to General
(1)	(2)	(3)	(4)	(5)	(6)	(7)	(8)
Lucknow City	1	1	3	4	29,133	6,821	23
Cawnpore City	1	1	2	4	49,485	14,462	29
Agra City	1	1	2	4	27,805	6,103	22
Allahabad City	1	1	1	4	27,313	6,503	24
Saharanpur District	1	1	2	2	27,053	3,720	14
Bulandshahr District	1	1	4	3	32,434	4,648	14
Agra District	1	1	3	4	33,230	4,476	13
Mainpuri District	1	1	3	4	41,044	5,356	13
Budaun District	1	1	4	4	32,763	7,558	23
Jalaun District	1	1	2	4	40,862	10,356	25
Mirzapur District	1	1	2	1	26,803	2,969	11
Gorakhpur District	1	1	2	4	25,113	3,697	15
Basti District	1	1	2	1	27,193	4,143	15
Azamgarh District	1	1	3	2	36,541	7,231	20
Almora District	1	1	3	1	93,380	17,809	19
Rae Bareili District	1	1	2	1	38,320	10,829	28
Sitapur District	1	1	3	3	45,130	18,868	42
Fyzabad District	1	1	4	2	46,337	10,035	22
Gonda District	1	1	2	1	47,666	7,428	16
Barabanki District	1	1	2	4	41,957	14,649	35

APPENDIX XIV (5) PUNJAB

Name of Constituency	Total Number of Seats in the Constituency		Total Number of Candidates		Total Number of Voters in the Constituency		
	For General	For Scheduled Castes	For General Seat	For Scheduled Caste Seat	General	Scheduled Castes	Percentage of Scheduled Caste Voters to General
(1)	(2)	(3)	(4)	(5)	(6)	(7)	(8)
South East Gurgaon	1	1	4	1	27,177	2,842	10
Karnal, North	1	1	4	3	23,224	2,698	12
Ambala and Simla	1	1	5	3	26,918	7,611	28
Hoshiarpur, West	1	1	2	4	27,589	11,701	42
Jullundur	1	1	2	4	12,967	14,744	114
Ludhiana and Ferozepur	1	1	4	4	20,334	12,299	60
Amritsar and Sialkot	1	1	2	1	21,610	5,374	25
Lyallpur and Jhang	1	1	2	3	13,909	3,805	27

APPENDIX XIV (6) BIHAR

Name of Constituency	Total Number of Seats in the Constituency		Total Number of Candidates		Total Number of Voters in the Constituency		
	For General	For Scheduled Castes	For General Seat	For Scheduled Caste Seat	General	Scheduled Castes	Percentage of Scheduled Caste Voters to General
(1)	(2)	(3)	(4)	(5)	(6)	(7)	(8)
East Bihar	1	1	2	2	23,966	3,944	16
South Gaya	1	1	2	1	35,104	9,675	28
Nawada	1	1	3	2	28,149	7,060	25
East Central Shahabad	1	1	4	1	34,138	6,491	19
West Gopalganj	1	1	3	1	25,419	3,361	13
North Bettiah	1	1	2	1	22,596	2,985	13
East Muzaffarpur Sadr	1	1	2	1	23,007	3,382	15
Darbhanga Sadr	1	1	3	1	22,189	2,018	9
South East Samastipur	1	1	2	1	29,595	2,642	9
South Sadr Monghyr	1	1	3	1	38,772	5,739	15
Madhipura	1	1	2	2	21,251	1,383	6
South West Purnea	1	1	2	2	33,071	2,440	7
Giridih-cum-Chatra	1	1	2	1	39,670	4,528	11
North East Palamau	1	1	2	2	13,853	4,174	30
Central Manbhum	1	1	2	2	22,930	5,075	22

Appendix XIV (7) C. P. & Berar

Name of Constituency	Total Number of Seats in the Constituency: For General	Total Number of Seats in the Constituency: For Scheduled Castes	Total Number of Candidates: For General Seat	Total Number of Candidates: For Scheduled Caste Seat	Total Number of Voters in the Constituency: General	Total Number of Voters in the Constituency: Scheduled Castes	Total Number of Voters in the Constituency: Percentage of Scheduled Caste Voters to General
(1)	(2)	(3)	(4)	(5)	(6)	(7)	(8)
Nagpur City	1	1	2	4	34,816	8,574	24
Nagpur-Umrer	1	1	3	4	20,795	5,451	25
Hinganghat-Wardha	1	1	3	4	25,275	3,088	12
Chanda-Brahmapuri	1	1	3	4	21,747	4,582	21
Chhindwara-Sausar	1	1	3	4	32,040	3,929	12
Jubbulpore Patan	1	1	3	4	23,667	1,519	6
Saugor-Khurai	1	1	3	2	23,487	4,679	20
Damoh-Hatta	1	1	3	2	29,069	3,461	12
Narsinghpur-Gadarwara	1	1	4	2	31,873	1,927	6
Raipur	1	1	2	2	20,209	10,885	54
Baloda Bazar	1	1	2	3	27,045	14,386	53
Bilaspur	1	1	2	3	22,343	10,963	49
Mungeli	1	1	2	3	17,412	10,032	58
Jangir	1	1	2	3	28,303	13,641	48
Drug	1	1	3	1	23,493	8,663	37
Bhandara-Sakoli	1	1	2	4	68,889	8,591	13
Ellichpur-Daryapur-Melghat	1	1	3	4	21,862	2,183	10
Akola-Balapur	1	1	3	4	20,529	2,761	13
Yeotmal-Darwha	1	1	3	3	31,052	1,954	6
Chikhli-Mehkar	1	1	5	3	28,971	2,792	10

APPENDIX XIV (8) ASSAM

Name of Constituency	Total Number of Seats in the Constituency		Total Number of Candidates		Total Number of Voters in the Constituency		
	For General	For Scheduled Castes	For General Seat	For Scheduled Caste Seat	General	Scheduled Castes	Percentage of Scheduled Caste Voters to General
(1)	(2)	(3)	(4)	(5)	(6)	(7)	(8)
Kamrup Sadr (South), General	2	1	2	4	17,501	1,203	7
Nowgong (North East), General	1	1	3	4	13,173	1,825	14
Jorhat (North), General	1	1	6	2	12,785	657	5
Sunamganj, General	1	1	2	1	15,907	6,502	41
Habiganj (North), General	1	1	3	3	12,628	7,615	60
Karimganj (East), General	1	1	4	2	9,611	7,323	76
Silohar, General	1	1	2	3	15,459	1,587	10

Appendix XIV (9) Orissa

Name of Constituency	*Total Number of Seats in the Constituency*		*Total Number of Candidates*		*Total Number of Voters in the Constituency*		
	For General	*For Scheduled Castes*	*For General Seat*	*For Scheduled Caste Seat*	*General*	*Scheduled Castes*	*Percentage of Scheduled Caste Voters to General*
(1)	(2)	(3)	(4)	(5)	(6)	(7)	(8)
North Cuttack Sadr	1	1	2	1	17,288	4,159	24
East Jajpur	1	1	3	2	15,338	4,808	31
North Puri Sadr	1	1	4	2	13,803	3,182	23
East Bargarh	1	1	3	1	22,849	1,237	5
West Bhadrak	1	1	2	3	16,187	5,152	32
Aska-Surada	1	1	2	4	24,914	1,475	6

APPENDIX XV

Particulars regarding Election to seats reserved for Scheduled Castes Province by Province :

Appendix XV : (1) Madras
„ „ (2) Bombay
„ „ (3) Bengal
„ „ (4) U. P.
„ „ (5) Punjab
„ „ (6) Bihar
„ „ (7) C. P. & Berar
„ „ (8) Assam
„ „ (9) Orissa

N.B.—All figures except those in column 8 are actuals. Those in column 8 are calculated as actuals are not obtainable. They are calculated on the assumption that the percentage of Scheduled Caste Voters and of Hindu Voters who went to the polls was the same. How far the assumption is justified, it is not possible to say.

Name of Constituency	Contested or Uncontested	Party Ticket of Successful Candidate	Distribution of Votes Polled by Successful Candidate			Votes Polled by Unsuccessful Candidates	Total Scheduled-Caste Votes Polled
			Scheduled-Caste Votes	Hindu Votes	Total		
(1)	(2)	(3)	(4)	(5)	(6)	(7)	(8)
Madras City (South Central) ...	Unopposed	Non-Congress	—	—	—	—	—
Chicacole	Contested	Congress	2,380	5,259	7,639	4,036	6,416
Amalapuram	Contested	Congress	9,742	*Nil*	9,742	5,523	29,119
Cocanada	Unopposed	Congress	—	—	—	—	—
Ellore	Contested	Congress	7,532	6,796	14,328	4,848	12,380
Bandar	Contested	Congress	9,935	*Nil*	9,935	2,004	18,393
Ongole	Contested	Congress	6,513	*Nil*	6,513	3,807	11,973
Gudur	Contested	Congress	4,293	344	4,637	4,778	9,072
Cuddappah	Contested	Congress	8,284	344	8,628	4,047	12,331
Penukonda	Contested	Congress	4,731	*Nil*	4,731	1,749	9,801
Bellary	Contested	Congress	4,019	*Nil*	4,019	910	8,124
Kurnool	Contested	Congress	5,362	*Nil*	5,362	5,929	13,164
Tiruttani	Contested	Congress	4,966	*Nil*	4,966	741	8,128
Chingleput	Contested	Non-Congress	12,360	*Nil*	12,360	6,110	22,852
Tiruvallur	Contested	Congress	3,107	6,216	9,323	14,140	17,247
Ranipet	Contested	Non-Congress	2,969	*Nil*	2,969	4,000	8,296
Tiruvannamalai	Contested	Congress	3,342	*Nil*	3,342	4,938	12,696
Tindivanam	Contested	Congress	6,396	*Nil*	6,396	2,541	12,480
Chidambaram	Unopposed	Non-Congress	—	—	—	—	—
Tirukkoyilur	Contested	Congress	9,957	4,436	14,393	6,133	16,090
Tanjore	Unopposed	Congress	—	—	—	—	—
Mannargudi	Contested	Congress	2,294	20,494	22,788	8,296	10,590
Ariyalur...	Contested	Congress	1,208	10,084	11,292	8,759	9,967
Palni	Contested	Congress	1,469	29,436	30,905	10,615	12,084
Sattur	Contested	Congress	*Nil*	18,514	18,514	11,894	6,980
Koilpatti	Contested	Congress	4,199	6,284	10,483	811	5,010
Pollachi	Contested	Congress	9,703	*Nil*	9,703	2,217	15,244
Namakal	Contested	Congress	8,141	8,153	16,294	3,217	11,358
Coondapur	Contested	Congress	1,425	*Nil*	1,425	1,798	11,673
Malappuram	Contested	Congress	7,154	*Nil*	7,154	2,606	10,148
Total of Scheduled-Caste Votes secured by Congress Candidates			126,152			Total ...	321,616

Total of Scheduled-Caste Votes 321,616
Total of Scheduled-Caste Votes secured by Congress Candidates 126,152

Scheduled Caste Votes secured by Non-Congress Candidates 195,464

Appendix XV (2) Bombay

Name of Constituency	Contested or Uncontested	Party Ticket of Successful Candidate	Distribution of Votes Polled by Successful Candidate			Votes Polled by Unsuccessful Candidates	Total Scheduled-Caste Votes
			Scheduled-Caste Votes	Hindu Votes	Total		
(1)	(2)	(3)	(4)	(5)	(6)	(7)	(8)
Bombay City North & Bombay Suburban District	Contested	Congress	2,414	15,004	17,418	9,738	12,152
Bombay City (Byculla & Parel)	Contested	Non-Congress	8,494	4,751	13,245	11,662	8,494
Kaira District	Unopposed	Congress	—	—	—	—	—
Surat District	Contested	Congress	7,913	*Nil*	7,913	7,245	12,101
Thana South	Contested	Non-Congress	4,006	227	4,223	2,733	4,006
Ahmednagar, South	Contested	Non-Congress	6,499	296	6,795	1,976	6,499
East Khandesh, East	Contested	Non-Congress	9,519	*Nil*	9,519	4,689	10,846
Nasik, West	Contested	Non-Congress	16,605	*Nil*	16,605	5,679	18,472
Poona, West	Contested	Non-Congress	9,512	2,599	12,111	532	9,512
Satara, North	Contested	Non-Congress	6,736	*Nil*	6,736	10,984	11,243
Sholapur, North East ...	Contested	Non-Congress	7,622	*Nil*	7,622	2,891	9,303
Belgaum, North	Contested	Non-Congress	21,322	*Nil*	21,322	6,596	36,979
Bijapur, North	Contested	Non-Congress	4,566	*Nil*	4,566	4,423	11,965
Kolaba District	Contested	Congress	2,644	4,781	7,425	8,117	10,761
Ratnagiri, North	Contested	Non-Congress	5,523	*Nil*	5,523	not known	8,714
Total of Scheduled-Caste Votes secured by Congress Candidates			12,971			Total ...	171,047

Total of Scheduled-Caste Votes 171,047
Total of Scheduled-Caste Votes secured by Congress Candidates 12,971

Scheduled-Caste Votes secured by Non-Congress Candidates 158,076

Appendix XV (3) Bengal

Name of Constituency	Contested or Uncontested	Party Ticket of Successful Candidate	Distribution of Votes Polled by Successful Candidates: Scheduled-Caste Votes	Hindu Votes	Total	Votes Polled by Unsuccessful Candidates	Total Scheduled-Caste Votes Polled
(1)	(2)	(3)	(4)	(5)	(6)	(7)	(8)
Burdwan, Central	Contested	Non-Congress	2,383	*Nil*	2,383	2,728	17,918
Burdwan, North West ...	Contested	Non-Congress	2,332	*Nil*	2,332	2,506	9,388
Birbhum	Contested	Non-Congress	4,832	*Nil*	4,832	848	18,876
Bankura, West	Contested	Congress	5,100	4,501	9,601	1,838	6,938
Midnapur, Central	Contested	Non-Congress	1,851	*Nil*	1,851	1,733	16,124
Jhargram-cum-Ghatal... ...	Contested	Congress	1,171	*Nil*	1,171	869	11,305
Hoogly, North East	Contested	Congress	1,638	*Nil*	1,638	1,613	11,764
Howrah	Contested	Non-Congress	10,373	*Nil*	10,373	5,986	14,380
24-Parganas, South East ...	Contested	Non-Congress	7,289	*Nil*	7,289	745	27,791
24-Parganas, North West ...	Contested	Congress	14,964	*Nil*	14,964	2,361	20,987
Nadia	Contested	Non-Congress	5,219	*Nil*	5,219	8,967	20,957
Murshidabad	Contested	Non-Congress	2,529	*Nil*	2,529	2,129	10,522
Jessore	Contested	Congress	20,198	15	20,213	11,936	32,134
Khulna	Contested	Congress	16,575	*Nil*	16,575	20,307	76,887
		Non-Congress	32,662	*Nil*	32,662		
Malda	Contested	Non-Congress	2,229	*Nil*	2,229	1,413	21,364
Dinajpur	Unopposed	Non-Congress	—	—	—	—	—
		Non-Congress	—	—	—	—	—
Jalpaiguri-cum-Siliguri ...	Contested	Non-Congress	16,244	*Nil*	16,244	19,513	49,191
		Non-Congress	7,261	*Nil*	7,261		
Rangpur	Contested	Non-Congress	12,212	*Nil*	12,212	17,345	53,632
		Non-Congress	11,914	*Nil*	11,914		
Bogra-cum-Pabna	Contested	Non-Congress	10,502	*Nil*	10,502	9,920	27,054
Dacca, East	Contested	Non-Congress	17,413	*Nil*	17,413	12,062	30,869
Mymensingh, West	Contested	Non-Congress	11,822	*Nil*	11,822	8,987	21,025
Mymensingh, East	Contested	Non-Congress	10,720	*Nil*	10,720	16,509	31,530
Faridpur	Contested	Non-Congress	27,342	*Nil*	27,342	57,699	97,608
		Non-Congress	25,924	*Nil*	25,924		
Bakarganj, South West ...	Contested	Non-Congress	10,515	*Nil*	10,515	18,801	26,526
Tippera	Contested	Non-Congress	19,388	*Nil*	19,388	8,017	29,673
Total of Scheduled-Caste Votes secured by Congress Candidates			59,646			Total ...	684,443

Total of Scheduled-Caste Votes	684,443
Total of Scheduled-Caste Votes secured by Congress Candidates	59,646
Scheduled-Caste Votes secured by Non-Congress Candidates	624,797

APPENDIX XV (4) U. P.

Name of Constituency	Contested or Uncontested	Party Ticket of Successful Candidate	Distribution of Votes Polled by Successful Candidate			Votes Polled by Unsuccessful Candidates	Total Scheduled-Caste Votes Polled
			Scheduled-Caste Votes	Hindu Votes	Total		
(1)	(2)	(3)	(4)	(5)	(6)	(7)	(8)
Lucknow City	Contested	Congress	1,910	2,327	4,237	4,092	6,002
Cawnpore City	Contested	Congress	4,483	4,901	9,384	1,301	5,784
Agra City	Contested	Congress	1,018	4,389	5,407	3,132	4,150
Allahabad City	Contested	Congress	385	9,285	9,670	4,037	4,422
Saharanpur District	Contested	Congress	3,252	*Nil*	3,252	648	5,282
Bulandshahr District	Contested	Congress	3,853	547	4,400	2,365	6,228
Agra District	Contested	Non-Congress	1,851	*Nil*	1,851	2,513	5,550
Mainpuri District	Contested	Congress	2,317	932	3,249	4,431	6,748
Budaun District	Contested	Congress	1,557	*Nil*	1,557	2,676	9,070
Jalaun District	Contested	Congress	3,791	*Nil*	3,791	4,840	12,428
Mirzapur District	Unopposed	Congress	—	—	—	—	—
Gorakhpur District	Contested	Congress	2,762	*Nil*	2,762	819	4,954
Basti District	Unopposed	Congress	—	—	—	—	—
Azamgarh District	Contested	Congress	949	*Nil*	949	196	9,256
Almora District	Unopposed	Non-Congress	—	—	—	—	—
Rae Bareili District	Unopposed	Non-Congress	—	—	—	—	—
Sitapur District	Contested	Congress	12,535	*Nil*	12,535	955	20,000
Fyzabad District	Contested	Congress	5,771	*Nil*	5,771	22	13,848
Gonda District	Unopposed	Non-Congress	—	—	—	—	—
Barabanki District	Contested	Congress	8,026	*Nil*	8,026	7,283	18,458
Total of Scheduled-Caste Votes secured by Congress Candidates			52,609			Total ...	132,180

Total of Scheduled-Caste Votes 132,180
Scheduled-Caste Votes secured by Congress Candidates 52,609

Scheduled-Caste Votes secured by Non-Congress Candidates 79,571

APPENDIX XV (5) PUNJAB

Name of Constituency	Contested or Uncontested	Party Ticket of Successful Candidate	Distribution of Votes Polled by Successful Candidate: Scheduled-Caste Votes	Hindu Votes	Total	Votes Polled by Unsuccessful Candidates	Total Scheduled-Caste Votes Polled
(1)	(2)	(3)	(4)	(5)	(6)	(7)	(8)
South East Gurgaon	Unopposed	Non-Congress	—	—	—	—	—
Karnal, North	Contested	Non-Congress	3,318	*Nil*	3,318	1,299	3,777
Ambala and Simla	Contested	Non-Congress	5,237	*Nil*	5,237	4,911	10,960
Hoshiarpur, West	Contested	Non-Congress	8,599	*Nil*	8,599	14,640	11,701
Jullundur	Contested	Non-Congress	13,135	*Nil*	13,135	9,176	20,347
Ludhiana Ferozepur	Contested	Non-Congress	7,258	*Nil*	7,258	6,024	16,481
Amritsar and Sialkot	Unopposed	Non-Congress	—	—	—	—	—
Lyallpur and Jhang	Contested	Non-Congress	2,903	*Nil*	2,903	2,143	5,860
						Total ...	69,126

Total of Scheduled-Caste Votes 69,126
Total of Scheduled-Caste Votes secured by Congress Candidates ... ... *Nil*

Scheduled-Caste Votes secured by Non-Congress Candidates 69,126

APPENDIX XV (6) BIHAR

Name of Constituency	Contested or Uncontested	Party Ticket of Successful Candidate	Distribution of Votes Polled by Successful Candidate			Votes Polled by Unsuccessful Candidates	Total Scheduled-Caste Votes
			Scheduled-Caste Votes	Hindu Votes	Total		
(1)	(2)	(3)	(4)	(5)	(6)	(7)	(8)
East Bihar	Contested	Non-Congress	2,471	*Nil*	2,471	519	5,443
South Gaya	Unopposed	Congress	—	—	—	—	—
Nawada	Contested	Congress	3,079	*Nil*	3,079	1,629	10,449
East Central Shahabad ...	Unopposed	Non-Congress	—	—	—	—	—
West Gopalganj	Unopposed	Non-Congress	—	—	—	—	—
North Bettiah	Unopposed	Congress	—	—	—	—	—
East Muzaffarpur Sadr ...	Unopposed	Congress	—	—	—	—	—
Darbhanga Sadr	Unopposed	Congress	—	—	—	—	—
South East Samastipur ...	Unopposed	Congress	—	—	—	—	—
South Sadr Monghyr	Unopposed	Congress	—	—	—	—	—
Madhipura	Contested	Congress	70	1,688	1,75[illegible]	1,700	1,770
South West Purnea	Contested	Congress	2,040	2,878	4,918	1,669	3,709
Girdih-cum-Chatra	Unopposed	Congress	—	—	—	—	—
North East-Palamau	Contested	Congress	3,465	3,419	6,884	626	4,091
Central Manbhum	Contested	Non-Congress	2,539	*Nil*	2,539	1,973	5,379
Total of Scheduled-Caste Votes secured by Congress Candidates			8,654			Total ...	30,841

Total of Scheduled-Caste Votes	30,841
Total of Scheduled-Caste Votes secured by Congress Candidates	8,654
Scheduled-Caste Votes secured by Non-Congress Candidates	22,187

APPENDIX XV (7) C. P. & BERAR

Name of Constituency	Contested or Uncontested	Party Ticket of Successful Candidate	Distribution of Votes Polled by Successful Candidate			Votes Polled by Unsuccessful Candidates	Total Scheduled-Caste Votes
			Scheduled-Caste Votes	Hindu Votes	Total		
(1)	(2)	(3)	(4)	(5)	(6)	(7)	(8)
Nagpur City	Contested	Non-Congress	7,796	*Nil*	7,796	3,787	9,088
Nagpur-Umrer	Contested	Non-Congress	3,667	*Nil*	3,667	2,774	6,323
Hinganghat-Wardha	Contested	Non-Congress	2,964	262	3,226	3,093	2,964
Chanda Brahmapuri	Contested	Non-Congress	5,133	*Nil*	5,133	1,764	5,590
Chhindwara-Sausar	Contested	Non-Congress	1,477	*Nil*	1,477	4,035	4,400
Jubbulpur-Patan	Contested	Congress	473	2,017	2,490	1,198	1,671
Saugor-Khurai	Contested	Congress	2,986	*Nil*	2,986	1,417	5,147
Damoh-Hatta	Contested	Congress	3,056	259	3,315	958	4,014
Narsinghpur-Gadarwara ...	Contested	Congress	1,023	95	1,118	480	1,503
Raipur	Contested	Congress	3,856	*Nil*	3,856	1,332	9,361
Baloda Bazar	Contested	Congress	8,113	*Nil*	8,113	4,451	17,551
Bilaspur	Contested	Non-Congress	1,900	*Nil*	1,900	1,655	15,348
Mungeli	Contested	Non-Congress	5,357	*Nil*	5,357	4,730	14,045
Jangir	Contested	Non-Congress	2,411	*Nil*	2,411	3,299	17,188
Drug	Unopposed	Congress	—	—	—	—	—
Bhandara-Sakoli	Contested	Non-Congress	7,916	*Nil*	7,916	5,197	0,309
Ellichpur-Daryapur-Melghat ...	Contested	Non-Congress	1,697	*Nil*	1,697	3,086	2,532
Akola-Balapur	Contested	Non-Congress	1,823	*Nil*	1,823	1,726	3,203
Yeotmal Darwha	Contested	Non-Congress	1,150	*Nil*	1,150	864	1,329
Chikhli-Mehkar	Contested	Non-Congress	2,194	*Nil*	2,194	2,164	3,295
Total of Scheduled-Caste Votes secured by Congress Candidates			19,507			Total ...	134,861

Total of Scheduled Caste Votes 134,861
Total of Scheduled-Caste Votes secured by Congress Candidates 19,507

Scheduled-Caste Votes secured by Non-Congress Candidates 115,354

APPENDIX XV (8) ASSAM

Name of Constituency	Contested or Uncontested	Party Ticket of Successful Candidate	Distribution of Votes Polled by Successful Candidate			Votes Polled by Unsuccessful Candidates	Total Scheduled-Caste Votes Polled
			Scheduled-Caste Votes	Hindu Votes	Total		
(1)	(2)	(3)	(4)	(5)	(6)	(7)	(8)
Kamrup Sadr (South), General	Contested	Congress	*Nil*	4,832	4,832	3,665	1,841
Nowgong (North East), General	Contested	Non-Crongess	1,596	*Nil*	1,596	3,645	2,226
Jorhat (North), General ...	Contested	Congress	457	495	952	371	828
Sunamganj, General	Unopposed	Congress	—	—	—	—	—
Habiganj (North), General ...	Contested	Congress	4,863	*Nil*	4,863	4,397	10,356
Karimganj (East), General ...	Contested	Non-Congress	3,252	*Nil*	3,252	1,119	10,252
Silchar, General	Contested	Non-Congress	2,108	*Nil*	2,108	2,197	2,254
Total of Scheduled-Caste Votes secured by Congress Candidates			5,320			Total ...	27,757

Total of Scheduled Caste Votes	27,757
Total of Scheduled-Caste Votes secured by Congress Candidates	5,320
Scheduled-Casto Votes secured by Non-Congress Candidates	22,437

APPENDIX XV (9) ORISSA

Name of Constituency	Contested or Uncontested	Party Ticket of Successful Candidate	Distribution of Votes Polled by Successful Candidate			Votes Polled by Unsuccessful Candidates	Total Scheduled-Caste Votes Polled
			Scheduled-Caste Votes	Hindu Votes	Total		
(1)	(2)	(3)	(4)	(5)	(6)	(7)	(8)
North Cuttack Sadr	Unopposed	Non-Congress	—	—	—	—	—
East Jajpur	Contested	Congress	958	*Nil*	958	571	4,808
North Puri Sadr	Contested	Congress	3,416	602	4,018	339	3,755
East Bargarh	Unopposed	Non-Congress	—	—	—	—	—
West Bhadrak	Contested	Congress	1,504	*Nil*	1,504	734	5,049
Aska Surada	Contested	Congress	*Nil*	917	917	1,402	973
Total of Scheduled-Caste Votes secured by Congress Candidates			5,878			Total ...	14,585

Total of Scheduled-Caste Votes 14,585
Total of Scheduled-Caste Votes secured by Congress Candidates 5,878

Scheduled-Caste Votes secured by Non-Congress Candidates 8,707

Appendix XVI

THE WAVELL PLAN

(*i*) *White Paper presented to Parliament on 14th June 1945 by the Secretary of State for India, containing His Majesty's Government's Proposal relating to the Government of India.*

1. During the recent visit of Field-Marshal Viscount Wavell to this country His Majesty's Government reviewed with him a number of problems and discussed particularly the present political situation in India.

2. Members will be aware that since the offer by His Majesty's Government to India in March 1942 there has been no further progress towards the solution of the Indian constitutional problem.

3. As was then stated, the working out of India's new constitutional system is a task which can only be carried through by the Indian peoples themselves.

4. While His Majesty's Government are at all times most anxious to do their utmost to assist the Indians in the working out of a new constitutional settlement, it would be a contradiction in terms to speak of the imposition by this country of self-governing institutions upon an unwilling India. Such a thing is not possible, nor could we accept the responsibility for enforcing such institutions at the very time when we were, by its purpose, withdrawing from all control of British Indian affairs.

5. The main constitutional position remains therefore as it was. The offer of March 1942 stands in its entirety without change or qualification. His Majesty's Government still hope that the political leaders in India may be able to come to an agreement as to the procedure whereby India's permanent future form of government can be determined.

6. His Majesty's Government are, however, most anxious to make any contribution that is practicable to the breaking of the political deadlock in India. While that deadlock lasts not only political but social and economic progress is being hampered.

7. The Indian administration, over-burdened with the great tasks laid upon it by the war against Japan and by the planning for the post-war period, is further strained by the political tension that exists.

8. All that is so urgently required to be done for agricultural and industrial development and for the peasants and workers of

India cannot be carried through unless the whole-hearted co-operation of every community and section of the Indian people is forthcoming.

9. His Majesty's Government have therefore considered whether there is something which they could suggest in this interim period, under the existing constitution, pending the formulation by Indians of their future constitutional arrangements, which would enable the-main communities and parties to co-operate more closely together and with the British to the benefit of the people of India as a whole.

10. It is. not the intention of His Majesty's Government to introduce any change contrary to the wishes of the major Indian communities. But they are willing to make possible some step forward during the interim period if the leaders, of the principal Indian parties are prepared to agree to their suggestions and to co-operate in the successful conclusion of the war against Japan as well as in the reconstruction in India which must follow the final victory.

11. To this end they would be prepared to see an important change in the composition of the Viceroy's Executive. This is possible without making any change in the existing statute law except for one amendment to the Ninth Schedule to the Act of 1935. That Schedule contains a provision that not less than three members of the Executive must have had at least 10 years' service under the Crown in India. If the proposals I am about to lay before the House meet with acceptance in India, that clause would have to be amended to dispense with that requirement.

12. It is proposed that the Executive Council should be reconstituted and that the Viceroy should in future make his selection for nomination to the Crown for appointment to his Executive from amongst leaders of Indian political life at the Centre and in the Provinces, in proportions which would give a balanced representation of the main communities, including equal proportions of Moslems and Caste Hindus.

13. In order to pursue this object, the Viceroy will call into conference a number of leading Indian politicians who are the heads of the most important parties or who have had recent experience as Prime Ministers of Provinces, together with a few others of special experience and authority. The Viceroy intends to put before this conference the proposal that the Executive Council should be reconstituted as above stated and to invite from the members of the conference a list of names. Out of these he would hope to be able to choose the future members whom lie would recommend for appointment by His Majesty to the Viceroy's Council although the responsibility for the recommendations must of course continue to rest with him, and his freedom of choice therefore remains unrestricted.

14. The members of his Council who are chosen as a result of this arrangement would of course accept the position on the basis that they would whole-heartedly co-operate in supporting and carrying through the war against Japan to its victorious conclusion.

15. The members of the Executive would be Indians with the exception of the Viceroy and the Commander-in-Chief, who would retain his position as War Member. This is essential so long as the defence of India remains a British responsibility.

16. Nothing contained in any of these proposals will affect the relations of the Crown with the Indian States through the Viceroy as Crown Representative.

17. The Viceroy has been authorised by His Majesty's Government to place this proposal before the Indian Leaders. His Majesty's Government trust that the leaders of the Indian communities will respond. For the success of such a plan must depend upon its acceptance in India and the degree to which responsible Indian politicians are prepared to co-operate with the object of making it a workable interim arrangement. In the absence of such general acceptance existing arrangements must necessarily continue.

18. If such co-operation can be achieved at the Centre it will no doubt be reflected in the Provinces and so enable responsible Governments to be set up once again in those Provinces where, owing to the withdrawal of the majority party from participation, it became necessary to put into force the powers of the Governors under Section 93 of the Act of 1935. It is to be hoped that in all the Provinces these Governments would be based on the participation of the main parties, thus smoothing out communal differences and allowing Ministers to concentrate upon their very heavy administrative tasks.

19. There is one further change which, if these proposals are accepted, His Majesty's Government suggest should follow.

20. That is, that External Affairs (other than those tribal and frontier matters which fall to be dealt with as part of the defence of India) should be placed in the charge of an Indian Member of the Viceroy's Executive so far as British India is concerned, and that fully accredited representatives shall be appointed for the representation of India abroad.

21. By their acceptance of and co-operation in this scheme the Indian leaders will not only be able to make their immediate contribution to the direction of Indian affairs, but it is also to be hoped that their experience of co-operation in government will expedite agreement between them as to the method of working out the new constitutional arrangements.

22. His Majesty's Government consider, after the most careful study of the question, that the plan now suggested gives the utmost progress practicable within the present constitution. None of the changes suggested will in any way prejudice or prejudge the essential form of the future permanent constitution or constitutions for India.

23. His Majesty's Government feel certain that given goodwill and a genuine desire to co-operate on all sides, both British and Indian, these proposals can mark a genuine step forward in the collaboration of the British and Indian peoples towards Indian self-government and can assert the rightful position, and strengthen the influence, of India in the counsels of the nations.

(ii) Broadcast Speech by His Excellency the Viceroy at New Delhi on 14th June 1946.

I have been authorised by His Majesty's Government to place before Indian political leaders proposals designed to ease the present political situation and to advance India towards her goal of full self-government. These proposals' are at the present moment being explained to Parliament by the Secretary of State for India. My intention in this broadcast is to explain to you the proposals, the ideas underlying them, and the method by which I hope to put them into effect.

This is not an attempt to obtain or impose a constitutional settlement. His Majesty's Government had hoped that the leaders of the Indian parties would agree amongst themselves on a settlement of the communal issue, which is the main stumbling-block; but this hope has not been fulfilled.

In the meantime, India has great opportunities to be taken and great problems to be solved, which require a common effort by the leading men of all parties. I therefore propose, with the full support of His Majesty's Government, to invite Indian leaders both of Central and Provincial politics to take counsel with me with a view to the formation of a new Executive Council more representative of organised political opinion. The proposed new Council would represent the main communities and would include equal proportions of Caste Hindus and Moslems. It would work, if formed, under the existing Constitution. But it would be an entirely Indian Council, except for the Viceroy and the Commander-in-Chief, who would retain his position as War Member. It is also proposed that the portfolio of External Affairs, which has hitherto been held by the Viceroy, should be placed in charge of an Indian Member of Council, so far as the interests of British India are concerned.

A further step proposed by His Majesty's Government is the appointment of a British High Commissioner in India, as in the

Dominions, to represent Great Britain's Commercial and other such interests in India.

Such a new Executive Council will, you realise, represent a definite advance on the road to self-government. It will be almost entirely Indian, and the Finance and Home Members will for the first time be Indians, while an Indian will also be charged with the management of India's Foreign Affairs. Moreover Members will now be selected by the Governor-General after consultation with political leaders; though their appointment will of course be subject to the approval of His Majesty the King-Emperor.

The Council will work within the framework of the present constitution; and there can be no question of the Governor-General agreeing not to exercise his constitutional power of control; but it will of course not be exercised unreasonably.

I should make it clear that the formation of this interim Government will in no way prejudice the final constitutional settlement.

The main tasks for this New Executive Council would be:

First, to prosecute the war against Japan with the utmost energy till Japan is utterly defeated.

Secondly, to carry on the Government of British India, with all the manifold tasks of post-war development in front of it, until a new permanent constitution can be agreed upon and come into force.

Thirdly, to consider, when the Members of the Goverment think it possible, the means by which such agreement can be achieved. The third task is most important. I want to make it quite clear that neither I nor His Majesty's Government have lost sight of the need for a long-term solution, and that the present proposals are intended to make a long-term solution easier.

I have considered the best means of forming such a Council; and have decided to invite the following to Viceregal Lodge to advise me:

Those now holding office as Premier in a Provincial Government; or, for Provinces now under Section 93 Government, those who last held the office of Premier.

The Leader of the Congress Party and the Deputy Leader of the Muslim League in the Central Assembly; the leader of the Congress Party and the Muslim League in the Council of State; also the leaders of the Nationalist Party and the European Group in the Assembly.

Mr. Gandhi and Mr. Jinnah as the recognised leaders of the two main political parties.

Rao Bahadur N. Siva Raj to represent the Scheduled Classes.

Master Tara Singh to represent the Sikhs.

Invitations to these gentlemen are being handed to them today and it is proposed to assemble the Conference on 25th June at Simla where we shall be cooler than at Delhi.

I trust that all those invited will attend the Conference and give me their help. On me and on them will lie a heavy responsibility in this fresh attempt to make progress towards a final settlement of India's future.

If the meeting is successful, I hope that we shall be able to agree on the formation of the new Executive Council at the Centre. I also hope that it will be possible for Ministries to re-assume office and again undertake the tasks of government in the Provinces now administered under Section 93 of the Constitution Act and that these Ministries will be coalitions.

If the meeting should unfortunately fail, we must carry on as at present until the parties are ready to come together. The existing Executive Council, which has done such valuable work for India, will continue it if other arrangements cannot be agreed.

But I have every hope that the meeting will succeed, if the party leaders will approach the problem with the sincere intention of working with me and with each other. I can assure them that there is behind this proposal a most genuine desire on the part of all responsible leaders in the United Kingdom and of the British people as a whole to help India towards her goal. I believe that this is more than a step towards that goal, it is a considerable stride forward, and a stride on the right path.

I should make it clear that these proposals affect British India only and do not make any alteration in the relations of the Princes with the Crown Representative.

With the approval of His Majesty's Government, and after consultation with my Council, orders have been given for the immediate release of the members of the Working Committee of Congress who are still in detention. I propose to leave the final decision about the others still under detention as the result of the 1942 disturbances to the new Central Government, if formed, and to the Provincial Governments.

The appropriate time for fresh elections for the Central and Provincial Legislatures will be discussed at the Conference.

Finally, I would ask you all to help in creating the atmosphere of goodwill and mutual confidence that is essential if we are to make progress. The destiny of this great country and of the many millions who live in it depend on the wisdom and good understanding of the leaders, both of action and of thought, British and Indian, at this critical moment of India's history.

India's military reputation never stood higher in the world than it does at present ; thanks to the exploits of her sons drawn from all parts of the country. Her representatives at International conferences have won high regard for their statesmanlike attitude. Sympathy for India's aspirations and progress towards prosperity was never greater or more widespread. We have thus great assets if we can use them wisely. But it will not be easy, it will not be quick ; there is very much to do, there are many pitfalls and dangers. There is on all sides something to forgive and forget.

I believe in the future of India, and as far as in me lies will further her greatness. I ask you all for your co-operation and goodwill.

(iii) *Mr. Gandhi's Statement.*

As soon as I read the broadcast, I sent a wire to His Excellency the Viceroy drawing his attention to the fact that I have no *locus standi* as the "recognized representative of the Congress." That function belongs to the President of the Congress or whoever is appointed to represent the Congress on a particular occasion.

For several years, I have acted unofficially as an adviser to the Congress whenever required. The public will remember that I went with the same unrepresentative character for my talks with the Qaid-e-Azam Jinnah, and I can take up no other position with the British Government, in this instance represented by the Viceroy.

There is one aspect of the Viceregal broadcast which certainly offends my ear and, I hope, will offend that of every politically-minded Hindu. I refer to the expression "caste Hindus." I claim that there is no such person, speaking politically, as a "Caste Hindu," let alone the Congress which seeks to represent the whole of India which is yearning after political independence. Does Veer Savarkar or Dr. Syama Prasad Mookerjee of the Hindu Mahasabha represent caste Hindus? Do they not represent all Hindus without distinction of caste? Do they not include the so-called untouchables? Do they themselves claim to be caste Hindus? I hope not. Of all politically-minded Hindus, I know that even the revered Pandit Malaviyaji, though he observes caste distinction, will refuse to be called a caste Hindu, as distinguished from the other Hindus. Modern tendency in Hinduism is to abolish all caste distinctions and this I maintain in spite of my knowledge of reactionary elements in Hindu society. I can only hope, therefore, that the Viceroy has allowed himself to make use of the expression in utter ignorance. I want to acquit him of knowingly wounding the susceptibilities of the Hindu society or dividing it. I would not have dwelt on this matter but for the fact that it touches the political mind of Hindus in its sensitive spot and carries with it political repercussions.

The proposed conference can do much useful work if it is put in its proper political setting and is at the very outset rendered immune from any fissiparous tendency. Undoubtedly all invitees might appear as Indians conjointly bent on achieving India's natural goal and not as persons representing several sections of Indian society.

That is how I have viewed the Bhulabhai-Liaquat Ali understanding which I suppose laid the foundations for the forthcoming Viceregal conference. Sri Bhulabhai Desai's proposal has no such colouring as the Viceregal broadcast would seem to have. I am not ashamed of the part I have played in advising Sri Bhulabhai Desai when he consulted me about his proposal. Sri Bhulabhai Desai's proposal, as I understood it, attracted me as one interested in solving the communal tangle, and I assured him that I would use my influence with the members of the Working Committee and give reasons for acceptance of his proposal and I have no doubt that, if both parties to the proposal correctly represent their constituents and have independence of India as their common goal, things must shape well.

At this point, I must stop and the Working Committee has to take up the thread. It is for its members to declare the Congress mind on the impending questions.—*A.P.I.*

INDEX